The BRF Book
of 365 Bible Reflections

15 The Chambers, Vineyard
Abingdon OX14 3FE
brf.org.uk

Bible Reading Fellowship is a charity (233280)
and company limited by guarantee (301324),
registered in England and Wales

ISBN 978 1 80039 100 0
First published 2021
10 9 8 7 6 5 4 3 2 1 0
All rights reserved

Text by BRF authors and © external authors 2021
This edition © Bible Reading Fellowship 2021
Cover and inside background texture © stock.adobe.com/Kittiphan

The authors assert the moral right to be identified as the authors of this work

Acknowledgements
Every effort has been made to trace and contact copyright owners for material used
in this resource. We apologise for any inadvertent omissions or errors, and would
ask those concerned to contact us so that full acknowledgement can be made in
the future.

A catalogue record for this book is available from the British Library

Printed and bound by CPI Group (UK) Ltd, Croydon CR0 4YY

The BRF Book
of 365
Bible Reflections

with contributions from

BRF AUTHORS, SUPPORTERS
AND WELL-WISHERS

Contents

Together through the generations

How should we live?

Introduction

The BRF Book of 365 Bible Reflections is a celebration.

It celebrates BRF's long history of coming alongside people at all stages of faith, encouraging Bible reading and everyday faith ever since 1922. Even more than that, it's a celebration of the Bible itself and how it continues to speak into people's lives today. The overarching theme for BRF's centenary year, 'Sharing the Story', can be understood in a variety of different ways – referring to the Christian story in its broadest sense, to the story of the work of BRF and its ministries over the past century, and to the stories of God at work in the lives of countless individuals through the centuries before that.

This book contains a Bible reading and reflection for every day of the year. It's designed for people at all stages of faith; for those who already know something of BRF's work and those who don't. Our vision was to have each reflection written by a different contributor, and so we 'shared the story' between a large team of writers: those involved in BRF's ministries past and present, readers, supporters and well-wishers. We also included a section of reflections taken from the archives of our Bible reading notes. The result is a glorious range of different perspectives on God's word, and we are hugely grateful to everyone who has contributed to this celebration collection.

We have aimed to balance Old and New Testament content, seasonal material, favourite passages and thematic sections. As with any creative activity, storytelling isn't always neat and tidy, and we pondered how to achieve a coherent whole while allowing an element of free choice. Some writers were asked to focus on particular passages in order to ensure reasonable coverage of the Bible narrative. Others were allocated a theme and asked to select a passage which explored that theme. We hope that this mix of freedom and structure has worked – a controlled messiness to allow people's gifts and enthusiasms to shine through, rather than being too prescriptive. The writers also chose which Bible version they wished to use.

How to use this book

This is not a through-the-year devotional in the traditional sense. The reflections are not dated, and you will find yourself moving between sections rather than proceeding in a linear way from start to finish. The nature of the book, with its 365 readings, encourages daily Bible reading through the year, but don't worry if you miss a day here and there. The beginning is a good place to start, but there is nothing to stop you starting with one of the other sections instead.

The section 'Journeying through the Christian year' contains seasonal material to turn to at the appropriate point in the year. So, begin at the beginning, or anywhere else, but you can then turn to the section on Lent when that season arrives. There are precisely the correct number of reflections in that section to take you day by day from Ash Wednesday to Easter Day. However, we decided, perhaps controversially, to allow Advent only 24 days, assuming that the reader will read from 1 December to Christmas Eve, thus avoiding the issue of the variable length of Advent from year to year, depending on when Advent Sunday falls. Similarly, we opted for twelve days of Christmas, and a mere two weeks for Pentecost. So where there is a specific season to enjoy, do so. Otherwise, the book offers a selection of readings and reflections that progress through both Old and New Testaments, alongside other themed sections that can be read at any time. We hope that this is a resource you will find yourself coming back to time and again.

The final section is inspired by the five marks of mission adopted by the Anglican Communion: tell, teach, tend, transform and treasure. Through this framework, our writers explore how we should live and how the word of God can shape us and make a difference in our own lives and, through us, in the lives of others. Again, we can see the 'Sharing the Story' theme at work in relation to how faith is shared.

The Bible extract for each day is shown on the page, but we would encourage you to have a Bible to hand so that you can see the reading in the context of the whole chapter. Inevitably these passages only cover a tiny fraction of the Bible text, but you will find many of the key stories and most well-loved passages. We are delighted to have such a wide-ranging team of writers whose rich variety of tradition and Christian experience reflects BRF's ecumenical reach, and hope that you will enjoy the diversity of the contributions that this collection brings together. Within this diversity, you may not agree with every writer's approach, but we hope that there will be always something helpful to take away from your daily reading.

As a general rule, the readings and reflections stand by themselves and are not accompanied by a closing prayer. However, we would encourage you to pray through what you have read, to listen for what God may be saying, and to seek to apply it. For some suggestions of ways in which you can pray, please see **brf.org.uk/get-involved/pray**.

We hope that *The BRF Book of 365 Bible Reflections* becomes your daily companion for this stage of your journey.

OLIVIA WARBURTON AND KAREN LAISTER

The BRF Centenary Prayer

Gracious God,
We rejoice in this centenary year
that you have grown BRF
from a local network of Bible readers
into a worldwide family of ministries.
Thank you for your faithfulness
in nurturing small beginnings
into surprising blessings.
We rejoice that, from the youngest to the oldest,
so many have encountered your word
and grown as disciples of Christ.
Keep us humble in your service,
ambitious for your glory
and open to new opportunities.
For your name's sake
Amen

Seeing God in the Bible

TRY, FOR A MOMENT, to imagine what the Christian faith would be like if we had no Bible. No doubt something would exist, but it would have a very different shape to it. It is no accident that, down the centuries, followers of Christ have sought to dig deep into the Bible to allow it to shape their beliefs, their worship and the pattern of their lives.

But the Bible is not, of course, an end in itself. Like a signpost, its purpose is to point us to God – Father, Son and Holy Spirit. In the same way that a road sign points us to somewhere, but is not the place itself, so the Bible points us to the Trinity.

At the start of this year, as in every year, the Christian calendar leads us into the season of Epiphany – the time when we remember how Jesus was revealed to a wide variety of people: his family, the wise men, Simeon and Anna, as well as the shepherds earlier in the story. These were not the people many would have thought were the most obvious candidates for God to have chosen, but that is what he did, and from BRF's point of view it is interesting how they link so closely to many of the people touched by our key ministries.

Despite that revelation, that Epiphany, who Jesus really was remained a mystery to most, as is still the case today. But the Bible also speaks of another Epiphany – the end of time when all will be revealed and there will no longer be any doubt that Jesus is the Lord. Until then we are in 'in between' times, as we have been for the past 2,000 years. In these times the Bible remains that indispensable signpost, allowing us to discover more of the God we worship who revealed himself in Jesus and who actively discloses himself through the work of the Holy Spirit.

May you and many others discover more as you use this resource over the coming 365 days.

COLIN FLETCHER, BISHOP AND CHAIR OF TRUSTEES, BRF

The extra dimension

Jesus took with him Peter and James and John, and led them up a high mountain apart, by themselves. And he was transfigured before them, and his clothes became dazzling white, such as no one on earth could bleach them. And there appeared to them Elijah with Moses, who were talking with Jesus. Then Peter said to Jesus, 'Rabbi, it is good for us to be here; let us make three dwellings, one for you, one for Moses, and one for Elijah.' He did not know what to say, for they were terrified.

MARK 9:2–6 (NRSV)

Many cinemas offer the experience of 3D viewing. If you have previously watched two-dimensional films, suddenly, by wearing a set of special glasses, a third dimension is opened up before you on the screen, bringing a greater richness and depth to the whole experience.

In this passage, Jesus, who normally appeared just like another human being, another first-century rabbi, is suddenly transfigured before the eyes of his closest friends so that they can see an extra dimension of his being. It is still recognisably Jesus, but with this extra dimension of glory that they normally cannot see.

The Swiss theologian Karl Barth once wrote, 'Within the Bible, there is a strange new world: the world of God.' When we open the pages of the Bible, we see our usual, recognisable world. We see slavery, politics, hunger, birth and death, poverty and injustice – all the stuff of life. Yet at the same time we also see a new dimension. Slaves in Egypt are miraculously freed, kings confess their sins, a hungry crowd is fed out of meagre rations, a poor teenager becomes the mother of God, the dead are raised, widows get justice. Just as in the transfiguration, when the disciples are suddenly able to see the glory of Jesus, the Bible opens up to us this extra dimension of the presence and activity of God.

We read the Bible not just to see this extra dimension, but also to teach and train ourselves to see it more clearly in the world around us. When we lift our eyes from the pages of scripture to go about our daily business, it trains us to look more closely to see the signs of God's presence, his action and his glory. May we see glimpses of his glory today in the ordinary things of our lives.

GRAHAM TOMLIN, BISHOP OF KENSINGTON

You are what you eat

The voice which I had heard from heaven spoke to me again. It said, 'Take the opened scroll from the hand of the angel who is standing on the sea and on the land.' I went to the angel and asked him to give me the small scroll. He said to me, 'Take it and eat it. It will be bitter in your stomach, but it will be as sweet as honey in your mouth.'

REVELATION 10:8–9 (GW)

We're often told that 'we are what we eat'. This is the idea that, to be fit and healthy, we need to eat good food. What we take into ourselves has a bearing on our state of health and our well-being.

As with physical food, so with spiritual food.

'You are what you eat' connects with the striking metaphor used by the apostle John in the wonderful and enigmatic final book of the Bible (drawing from the prophet Ezekiel before him; compare Ezekiel 3:1–3). In response to the command from heaven, John approaches the angel, requests a book and then eats it. The book that he devours tells of the purposes of God worked out in human history. For us, this book is the Bible.

Note that John doesn't merely read scripture, or listen to it, or study it, important as all these things are. Instead, he ingests and digests it. Its writings enter the very fullness of his being. They get into his gut. They are absorbed into his bloodstream, such that he and they become inseparable.

We sometimes prefer to keep scripture at a safe distance from us. Deep down, we know that it can bring us discomfort and challenge, for it speaks of thoughts and ways which are not our own (compare Isaiah 55:8–9). Yet, we also know that we find unparalleled nourishment through these words. We cannot have the one without the other.

So, this day, what encouragement are we taking from scripture? Where are its words as sweet as honey in our mouth? And where is its challenge like a bitterness in our stomach? Most of all, how do we get its fullness of life in every sinew of our being – heart, mind, soul and strength?

'We are what we eat.'

MARK BRADFORD, VICAR, ST CUTHBERT'S FULWOOD (PRESTON), AND WRITER

A guide for life

But as for you, continue in what you have learned and have become convinced of, because you know those from whom you learned it, and how from infancy you have known the Holy Scriptures, which are able to make you wise for salvation through faith in Christ Jesus. All Scripture is God-breathed and is useful for teaching, rebuking, correcting and training in righteousness, so that the servant of God may be thoroughly equipped for every good work.

2 TIMOTHY 3:14–17 (NIV)

Have you been encouraged to believe and read the Bible from an early age, as Timothy was by his mother and grandmother? (A hint here for parents and grandparents!) Or have you come to it later in life? Whether we are old-timers or newcomers to scripture, these few verses give us a succinct but comprehensive answer to the big question, 'Why read the Bible?' Paul writes of its origin (God-breathed) and its purpose (to help us to understand God's plan of salvation through Jesus). He tells us that it is all inspired by the Spirit – though that doesn't mean we are going to get equal nourishment from all parts of it; a chapter of Old Testament genealogy may feed us less than, say, the sermon on the mount or one of Paul's epistles.

But I want to focus on verses 16 and 17. Four strands of usefulness in our lives, Paul says: 'teaching, rebuking, correcting and training'. I notice that just one of those strands is for our minds, while three strands are for our lifestyle. Scripture is not just to help us understand what God is like and what he has done. It is meant to make a difference to the way we live.

God wants us to walk along his path. The Bible rebukes us when we stray off the path, puts us back on the straight and narrow (notice the reference to Matthew 7:14, one of countless biblical phrases that have been absorbed in regular English usage) and leads us along that path. Let us pray that we are increasingly sensitive and obedient to the nudges he gives us as we continue to read, meditate and act on his word, so that we may gladly fulfil his purpose for us as his loving servants.

ROSEMARY GREEN, AUTHOR, SPEAKER AND ORDINARY CHRISTIAN

Never alone in God's word

All the people came together as one in the square before the Water Gate. They told Ezra the teacher of the Law to bring out the Book of the Law of Moses, which the Lord had commanded for Israel. So on the first day of the seventh month Ezra the priest brought the Law before the assembly, which was made up of men and women and all who were able to understand... All the people listened attentively to the Book of the Law.

NEHEMIAH 8:1–3 (NIV, abridged)

In Nehemiah 8 two giants of the faith, Ezra and Nehemiah, join together in guiding and leading God's people. The people had been living in exile; Jerusalem and her walls were destroyed. Now they return to the towns they had been exiled from (Nehemiah 7): a journey reminding them of God's grace in the face of exile. A few months pass and the people gather with intent ('came together as one'), asking Ezra to bring out the Book of the Law. As Ezra reads, 'the people listened attentively'.

This short passage poses big questions: what are you intentional about? What are you listening attentively to? To read scripture with others, you don't have to be with them physically. Even if you are sitting on your own right now, it is impossible to read scripture alone.

As you hold this book in your hands, others will be doing exactly the same. Perhaps in your street, village or town. Maybe in the same country or on the other side of the world. Scripture is engaged with in every single minute of the day. There has never been a moment in your life when you have read the Bible and someone else was not also doing the same.

Scripture shows that God is with you as you read; it is God-breathed (2 Timothy 3:16). God will open your eyes (Psalm 119:18) to the wonders of his word. Jesus opens our minds to hear (Luke 24:45) and the Spirit helps us remember (John 14:26). You are never alone.

Ezra shared with God's people the word that brings life. It is what they wanted, what their hearts longed for. What does your heart long for today? Nehemiah 8 reminds us that we are never alone in God's word.

RUSSELL WINFIELD, DEAN, ST MELLITUS COLLEGE

The flip

And the scripture, foreseeing that God would justify the Gentiles by faith, declared the gospel beforehand to Abraham, saying, 'All the Gentiles shall be blessed in you.' For this reason, those who believe are blessed with Abraham who believed... Christ redeemed us from the curse of the law by becoming a curse for us – for it is written, 'Cursed is everyone who hangs on a tree' – in order that in Christ Jesus the blessing of Abraham might come to the Gentiles, so that we might receive the promise of the Spirit through faith.

GALATIANS 3:8–9, 13–14 (NRSV)

We tend to think of Paul as communicating theological 'facts' – fully formed and final teachings. But in his letters, which would have been dictated to a secretary, he is generally thinking aloud, going through a process. We have the privilege of seeing his working (even when it is messy!). This working is often marked by epiphanies, eureka moments when his experience of Jesus illuminates the scriptures that, as a Pharisee, he knew so well.

For Paul, as for all faithful Jews, the big stumbling block in recognising Jesus as the Messiah had been his death by crucifixion, hanging on a tree. Deuteronomy 21:22–23 says that this is a mark of God's curse and that the executed criminal defiles the land. Interestingly the preceding verses pronounce on a rebellious son who is 'a glutton and a drunkard', words also applied to Jesus (Matthew 11:19; Luke 7:34). Jesus carries stigma, shame, pollution and curse.

Some scholars have suggested that Paul was meditating on Deuteronomy 21 on the Damascus road, deeply troubled and with the martyrdom of Stephen fresh in his mind. What is certain is that his perspective on these verses flipped when he met Jesus. To put it better, it was *in* the flip that Paul met Jesus. We know this because afterwards Paul would never preach the Messiah without his cross (1 Corinthians 1:23). In Jesus' death stigma is turned to glory, shame to boasting, pollution to healing, and a curse on the land to a blessing for the whole world.

In today's passage, Paul returns to the scriptures and places his insight within the bigger story of God's saving plan in Abraham, also drawing on the prophet Habakkuk. The 'law and the prophets' are brought alive by Jesus, and Jesus is seen to be the fulfilment of all that they promised.

JOANNA COLLICUTT, SUPERNUMERARY FELLOW (PSYCHOLOGY OF RELIGION), HARRIS MANCHESTER COLLEGE

It's all about Jesus

'I have testimony weightier than that of John. For the works that the Father has given me to finish – the very works that I am doing – testify that the Father has sent me. And the Father who sent me has himself testified concerning me. You have never heard his voice nor seen his form, nor does his word dwell in you, for you do not believe the one he sent. You study the Scriptures diligently because you think that in them you have eternal life. These are the very Scriptures that testify about me, yet you refuse to come to me to have life.'

JOHN 5:36–40 (NIV)

I remember growing up with a lot of teaching around the Bible, what it is and how to navigate it. The analogy that was always presented to me was that the Bible was the 'instruction manual for life'. I was happy with this explanation, and it made sense for quite a while.

The problem was that as I grew older, I realised that I hardly ever open instruction manuals for things – do you? If I do, it would only be because something wasn't working properly. So I had inadvertently believed the same about the Bible: when things go wrong I need to open the manual, but what about the rest of the time?

John 5:39–40 completely changed my understanding of what the Bible is really for and how I was to interact with it. *Every* word of scripture exists for one primary purpose – to reveal Jesus. The written word reveals the living Word Jesus. I kind of understood that from the gospels, but what about other books and the Old Testament?

In Luke 24, Jesus puts John 5 into practice as he leads the disciples on the road to Emmaus in a Bible study through the whole of the Old Testament (as that's all there was) and uses that to show all that had to happen to the Messiah – to reveal the truth about himself.

So as you engage with the Bible, there are many ways the Bible can give wisdom, comfort, knowledge, encouragement and context for our lives. But let us not miss the primary reason it exists – to reveal Jesus to us. No matter what you read, New Testament or Old, think about how this is seen, shaped and fulfilled through Christ. That way, we won't fall into the trap of diligent study that yields no life.

JAMIE HILL, FORMER EXECUTIVE DIRECTOR, KINGSWAY CLC TRUST

My strength and song

Then Moses and the children of Israel sang this song to the Lord, and spoke, saying: 'I will sing to the Lord, For He has triumphed gloriously! The horse and its rider He has thrown into the sea! The Lord *is* my strength and song, And He has become my salvation; He *is* my God, and I will praise Him; My father's God, and I will exalt Him.'

EXODUS 15:1–2 (NKJV)

When I felt called to some form of ministry, in my case as a Reader (or licensed lay minister), I had to complete an application form. One section asked for a summary of my calling. A Bible phrase had recently leaped off the page at me: 'The Lord is my strength and song, And he has become my salvation.' A similar phrase appears in Isaiah 12:2 and Psalm 118:14.

I've found God speaks to me through the written word; sometimes it's a Bible passage, often some other book of prose or poetry. I believe God tailor-makes his approach to each one of us. We do have to sit still long enough and be sufficiently quiet to hear him, though! That is why it can take a reversal of fortune – an illness, a career setback, trouble in a relationship – for us to become sufficiently open to what he wishes to say. We may realise we've run out of our own resources. We turn to him for help and find his strength.

I was in my 40s when I started exploring my vocation. A wise person reminded me that I shouldn't wait until I was 'perfect' to respond to his call. What he wanted was me, as me; my personality, my voice, my 'song', if you like. I love the sense that our song wells up inside us, until we just *have* to sing… whether that be with joy, lament, exuberance or in the frailest of whispers. It depends on our story, particular to us. Once we've claimed God's strength for ourselves and have begun to sing out our lives in our own unique way, he comes to save us; to salve our wounds and heal us, giving us greater strength for our journey. Salvation means knowing the hope of eternal life set before us.

Now, that *is* worth singing about!

DEBBIE THROWER, ANNA CHAPLAINCY FOUNDER AND PIONEER, BRF

Journeying
through the Bible

The story of the Old Testament

'**E**VERY SCRIBE who has been trained for the kingdom of heaven,' said Jesus, 'is like the master of a household who brings out of his treasure what is new and what is old' (Matthew 13:52, NRSV). It is widely thought that Matthew, who brings us this saying of Jesus, is thinking of himself. Certainly, alongside 'new' treasures – the stories of Jesus – Matthew brings us many 'old' ones, showing us how Jesus connects to the Old Testament promises. 'As it is written' is one of Matthew's favourite sayings (see also 2:5 or 11:10, for example).

All of this means that if we are to understand the New Testament properly, it is essential that we have a decent grasp of the Old. And what a book it is! Spanning thousands of years, it tells of kings and paupers, the wise and the foolish, the good and the wicked. Its settings vary from mountaintops to deserts, from kings' bedrooms to the belly of a fish. It lays bare human wickedness and folly, and shows God's enduring love and patience towards humanity.

Above all, it is a great story – a story of God patiently working with, through and sometimes despite humanity, towards his great goal of redeeming not just individual souls but the whole, broken cosmos. From the rich, hospitable garden of Eden (Genesis 2:8–17) to Isaiah's vision of a future kingdom of peace and human contentment (11:6–9; 65:17–25), the whole thrust of the story is about God's good plan for the world.

As you read this glorious book, seek the 'old' treasures as well as the 'new'. Discover that God's love for humanity is as old as the earth. And look for the golden threads that point towards Jesus.

HELEN PAYNTER, BAPTIST MINISTER AND BIBLICAL STUDIES TUTOR,
BRISTOL BAPTIST COLLEGE

The creative creation

And God said, 'Let the waters bring forth swarms of living creatures, and let birds fly above the earth across the dome of the sky.' So God created the great sea monsters and every living creature that moves, of every kind, with which the waters swarm, and every winged bird of every kind. And God saw that it was good. God blessed them, saying, 'Be fruitful and multiply and fill the waters in the seas, and let birds multiply on the earth'... And God said, 'Let the earth bring forth living creatures of every kind...' And it was so.

GENESIS 1:20–24 (NRSV, abridged)

This passage describes the participation of creation itself in the bringing into being of more life. God commands the waters to bring forth the fish, and this is followed by the earth being called upon to bring forth living creatures of every kind. In other words, he does not just bring creation into being but also empowers the earth and waters to bring forth more living things. Nor is the earth and waters' role limited: the waters bring forth every conceivable aquatic creature, from the biggest sea monsters to the smallest swarming things. The earth likewise brings forth every living creature of every kind in all their marvellous diversity.

But the cycle of creation does not stop there, for the newly created animals are themselves blessed by God and invited to participate in his gift of bringing new life into being. The call to humanity to be fruitful and multiply and fill the earth is much quoted, but it is preceded by the same blessing bestowed on the fish and the birds. In between the two blessings we have the creation of the living creatures of the earth and finally humans. Are we to imagine that the land animals are not blessed and invited to fill the earth? This seems inconceivable. All creation is invited to flourish together and the cycle of procreation must continue until the earth and waters are teeming with life.

These verses encourage us to participate in God's continuing work of creation by enabling all creatures to flourish. Though the waters and soil might not spontaneously generate new life in a strictly literal sense, all living things are dependent on them. We must protect them from pollution and ensure space for God's 'good', vibrant and diverse creation to be fruitful and multiply as he intended.

REBECCA S. WATSON, LECTURER AND DIRECTOR OF STUDIES,
EASTERN REGION MINISTRY COURSE, CAMBRIDGE

Beware: sea monsters!

Now the serpent was more crafty than any other wild animal that the Lord God had made. He said to the woman, 'Did God say, "You shall not eat from any tree in the garden"?' The woman said to the serpent, 'We may eat of the fruit of the trees in the garden; but God said, "You shall not eat of the fruit of the tree that is in the middle of the garden, nor shall you touch it, or you shall die."' But the serpent said to the woman, 'You will not die… you will be like God.'

GENESIS 3:1–5 (NRSV, abridged)

In the languages of the Bible, there are several words which are translated into English as 'sin'. For example, one has its origins in a word meaning 'to miss the mark'; another implies the notion of falling when one should have remained upright. In terms of our relationship with God, we all miss the mark or fall at some stage; sometimes the fault is entirely ours, yet on other occasions we get caught up in circumstances. I will come back to this.

I don't really like snakes! It is a little unfair, because they are just another of God's creatures, but in truth, the writer of Genesis does not help by using the word 'serpent', a word with a slightly sinister feel to it. The same Hebrew word means 'sea monster'.

I mention this because there is a bit of a conundrum in Genesis 3. On the one hand, the idea of the serpent being just one animal among many in the garden reminds us that we must not put the blame for our sin on to something else. We are responsible for our own actions.

On the other hand, as we have noted, the writer portrays the serpent negatively and so introduces the notion of evil coming from elsewhere. Yes, we have to be responsible for our own actions, but there are forces of evil abroad in the world which are sometimes difficult to avoid. Every time we buy something from a country which oppresses its people; when we ignore obvious corporate sin; when we overlook injustice – then we become part of that falling away from what God would wish.

Not only do we have to make difficult choices about these things, but we should go further and speak against them. We really need God's help in all of this.

GEOFF LOWSON, RETIRED PRIEST, COUNTY DURHAM

Flood warning

And God saw that the earth was corrupt; for all flesh had corrupted its ways upon the earth. And God said to Noah, 'I have determined to make an end of all flesh, for the earth is filled with violence because of them; now I am going to destroy them along with the earth. Make yourself an ark... I will establish my covenant with you.'

GENESIS 6:12–14A, 18A (NRSV)

I'm not sure how encouraging it is to know that 'pandemics' have been a fact of life since the days of Noah: a series of perplexing instructions, isolation, shielding, being cooped up for months, not even able to leave 'home' for exercise... but reassuring, perhaps, to remember that God has given a rainbow promise never again to destroy all of mankind!

As I write, we are still in the throes of the Covid nightmare, wondering just how long it will be before we can resume some kind of more normal life. Noah knew that it would rain for 40 days; but he too must have experienced frustration, desperation even, as he waited... and waited... for the floodwater to abate. Was he tempted to ask, 'Where is God in all of this? What is he saying to us? Has he brought us this far only to abandon us?' Or did his history of faithfulness and trust in God enable him to hold on to the fact that God's plan must surely include his family's well-being?

And how is it for us? Hopefully by the time you read this, Covid's worst will be over; but there will always be times of suffering, times of perplexity, times of deep frustration and questioning. Where is God in all of this? What is he saying to us? How long, O Lord? The Genesis story is one of cause and effect; it is the wickedness of the majority of people on earth that prompts God so dramatically to wash the slate clean. In so many ways, in so many places, we too have turned our backs on God, ignored his commands and dishonoured his name. It is therefore always relevant to ask if there is a need for repentance before there can be healing and restoration.

SHEILA WALKER, ASSOCIATE PRIEST, OXFORDSHIRE

Abram's choice

Abram said to Lot, 'Let's not have any quarrelling between you and me, or between your herdsmen and mine, for we are close relatives. Is not the whole land before you? Let's part company. If you go to the left, I'll go to the right; if you go to the right, I'll go to the left.' Lot looked around and… chose for himself the whole plain of the Jordan and [they] parted company: Abram lived in the land of Canaan, while Lot lived among the cities of the plain.

GENESIS 13:8–12 (NIV, abridged)

Abram had travelled to Egypt during a famine in Canaan, and his nephew Lot went with him and was blessed similarly to Abram. But this sudden prosperity brought new difficulties upon their return to Canaan. Their shepherds quarrelled over access to the limited resources, and so Abram had to make a choice.

Abram had been told by God that the land would be his. As the more senior family member, it would have been completely understandable for him to press his rights. But he didn't. He knew that he had a promise of a glorious future from God, and he trusted that God would fulfil his promises. With such powerful divine blessings working for his good, he knew that there was no need to selfishly seek his own gain. So Abram treated Lot with great humility, told him to choose where he wanted to go and promised to stay out of his way. Abram placed the good of Lot ahead of his own. They separated, on good terms, with a healthy relationship, and with a commitment to remain family. For Abram, this commitment was so strong that when Lot was captured in battle (Genesis 14), Abram pursued the victorious army for hundreds of kilometres and rescued his nephew.

As we consider the privilege and blessings that God has given us, whether material or spiritual or positional, let us ask ourselves if we have the humility of Abram. As citizens of God's kingdom, we must be committed to servant leadership, to surrender our rights rather than grasp for them, to leverage what we have to do good for others. In so doing, we will follow the example of Abram, the father of all the faithful, and even more the example of Jesus, our servant king.

ASHLEY HIBBARD, RESEARCH ASSOCIATE, CENTRE FOR THE STUDY OF THE BIBLE AND VIOLENCE

Faith in God's future

Abram said, 'O Lord God, what will you give me, for I continue childless, and the heir of my house is Eliezer of Damascus?' And Abram said, 'You have given me no offspring, and so a slave born in my house is to be my heir.' But the word of the Lord came to him, 'This man shall not be your heir; no one but your very own issue shall be your heir.' He brought him outside and said, 'Look towards heaven and count the stars, if you are able to count them.' Then he said to him, 'So shall your descendants be.' And he believed the Lord; and the Lord reckoned it to him as righteousness.

GENESIS 15:2–6 (NRSV)

Abram represents all of us when we lose faith in God's future. The future is, of course, always unknown; the issue for us, as for Abram, is whether it is in God's hands. We are all inclined to worry about our personal tomorrows and also the bigger issues such as the health of our planet. For Abram, the issue is highly specific. God has promised land and prosperity to his descendants, but the promise appears blocked because of his childlessness. Abram is torn by his loyalty to God and the actual reality of being without an heir who is his son. He must have wondered whether God was mocking him, whether he had done something to invalidate the promise or whether he had misunderstood it in the first place, and his slave was always going to be his only heir.

God needs Abram to detach himself from his fantasies of frustration and trust him in naked faith. So he takes him to contemplate the night sky, full of stars, the constellations wheeling above. Abram cannot count the stars. They are a sign of God's creative abundance and Abram's limited knowledge. Shining against the dark backdrop of night, they point to a God whose purposes can be neither thwarted nor fully understood. Abram is simply to trust that he will have generations of descendants. Abram, whose name means 'father of a people', will later be known as Abraham, 'father of many people'. Among those many people are Christians including ourselves, descendants of Abraham, as the apostle Paul would put it, through the virtuous faith we inherit from him, and try, each day, to practise with courage.

ANGELA TILBY, CANON EMERITUS, CHRIST CHURCH CATHEDRAL, OXFORD

God tests Abraham

Some time later God tested Abraham. He said to him, 'Abraham!' 'Here I am,' he replied. Then God said, 'Take your son, your only son, whom you love – Isaac – and go to the region of Moriah. Sacrifice him there as a burnt offering on a mountain that I will show you.' Early the next morning Abraham got up and loaded his donkey. He took with him two of his servants and his son Isaac. When he had cut enough wood for the burnt offering, he set out for the place God had told him about.

GENESIS 22:1–3 (NIV)

This deeply moving story has captured the imagination of readers over the years, though many have also found it troubling. Why would God demand such an act? We are certainly left wanting to know more, but the author drops enough breadcrumbs for us – like Abraham and Isaac – to come out the other side.

One big clue is in the command to 'go' (v. 2), which echoes God's first call to Abraham to 'go from your country… to the land I will show you' (Genesis 12:1). This story is the climax of his long, up-and-down journey of faith. Through it all, God has stayed faithful and has provided Isaac, the one through whom God will bless all nations.

How, then, will Abraham respond to this test?

He responds with ready obedience, and seems sure that 'God himself will provide the lamb for the burnt offering' (v. 8). His confidence in God's promise is noted by the angel of the Lord towards the end of the story – 'Now I know that you fear God' (v. 12) – demonstrating the trust and reverence to which all God's people are called. No wonder that James cites Abraham as an example of faith lived out (James 2:20–24), and the writer to the Hebrews sees him as exercising a resurrection-shaped trust in God (Hebrews 11:17–19).

Our own journey of faith may take us into the unknown, perhaps for long stretches of time, but we can walk on with the assurance that God will provide. As Paul affirms in Romans 8:32, 'He who did not spare his own Son, but gave him up for us all – how will he not also, along with him, graciously give us all things?'

The God who makes promises stays faithful to them.

ANTONY BILLINGTON, SENIOR PASTOR, BEACON CHURCH, ASHTON-IN-MAKERFIELD, AND THEOLOGY ADVISOR, THE LONDON INSTITUTE FOR CONTEMPORARY CHRISTIANITY

Only one blessing

When Esau heard his father's words, he burst out with a loud and bitter cry and said to his father, 'Bless me – me too, my father!' But he said, 'Your brother came deceitfully and took your blessing… I have made him lord over you and have made all his relatives his servants… So what can I possibly do for you, my son?' Esau said to his father, 'Do you have only one blessing, my father? Bless me too, my father!' Then Esau wept aloud… Esau held a grudge against Jacob because of the blessing his father had given him.

GENESIS 27:34–41 (NIV, abridged)

It's impossible not to feel sympathy for Esau's distress on realising that he has been cruelly cheated by his younger brother Jacob (in conspiracy with their own mother). An already dysfunctional family is now ripped apart by betrayal and a thirst for revenge.

If we're looking for an immediate lesson to take away from this Bible story, the obvious one is this: don't deceive and plot against your family members. It will end in bitter tears and estrangement.

It's also striking, though, that Isaac has 'only one blessing' to give – unique and irrevocable. The loss of it is a catastrophic event in Esau's life, or so it seems to him in this moment of horror. But in fact, God is not as stingy as these characters believe. When Esau and Jacob meet again (Genesis 33), both are wealthy and blessed with children and livestock. More importantly, they are able to forgive and be reconciled. This is the grace of God working in both men's hearts over the 20 years or more that they are apart.

As servants of the same God, but with the added benefit of knowing Jesus and living under the new covenant, we can be assured today that God has a lot more than 'one blessing' to give. As Paul writes, God has 'blessed us in the heavenly realms with every spiritual blessing in Christ' (Ephesians 1:3). His blessings on each of us are unlimited, and there is blessing for all in the kingdom of his son, Jesus.

LISA CHERRETT, EDITORIAL PROJECT MANAGER, BIBLE SOCIETY, AND FORMER
BRF STAFF MEMBER

Struggling with identity

The same night [Jacob] got up... and crossed the ford of the Jabbok... Jacob was left alone; and a man wrestled with him until daybreak... He struck him on the hip socket; and Jacob's hip was put out of joint... He said to him, 'What is your name?' And he said, 'Jacob.' Then the man said, 'You shall no longer be called Jacob, but Israel, for you have striven with God and with humans, and have prevailed'... And there he blessed him. So Jacob called the place Peniel, saying, 'For I have seen God face to face, and yet my life is preserved.'

GENESIS 32:22–30 (NRSV, abridged)

Who am I? How can I be sure that God loves me? Jacob faces these questions in this archetypal tale of the struggle of humans with God. Jacob found it hard to accept that God loved him and that God wanted him for himself. Today, we too need to rediscover our true worth in God's eyes.

Passing through the waters – The splashing and scrambling amidst the swirling currents evokes the liberating waters of exodus and baptism.

Alone with God – 'Jacob was left alone.' Space in our prayers for solitude enables deeper encounter with God. Solitude is a place where we can be real with God, in vulnerability and utter openness.

Entering the darkness – Jacob's struggle with the divine stranger takes place in the darkness. It is night. The 'dark night of the soul' means allowing God to lead us into greater surrender. The experience of darkness in our spiritual life can at once be bewildering and transformative.

The wounding – 'Jacob's hip was put out of joint.' He is brought to a point of brokenness. He had often been on the run – from Esau, from Laban, from God – but now he can run no longer. His running symbolised his desire to stay in control: he went where he wished. Now he can only limp. God disables him: his wounding represents the melting of his stubbornness, wilfulness and self-centredness.

A new identity – Jacob's pride is brought low, his ego surrendered to God. He receives blessing and a new name – profound affirmation by God. The new name denotes the singular vocation God has in store for each person. Formerly, Jacob's name meant 'grasper'. The new name that will come to denote a nation and represent the people of God means 'one who struggles with God'. It is okay to struggle!

ANDREW D. MAYES, BORDERLANDS RETREATS

Joseph: an unpromising beginning

Jacob lived in the land where his father had stayed, the land of Canaan... Joseph... was tending the flocks with his brothers, the sons of Bilhah and the sons of Zilpah, his father's wives, and he brought their father a bad report about them. Now Israel loved Joseph more than any of his other sons, because he had been born to him in his old age; and he made an ornate robe for him. When his brothers saw that their father loved him more than any of them, they hated him and could not speak a kind word to him.

GENESIS 37:1–4 (NIV, abridged)

The beginning of Joseph's story in Genesis 37 reads like a soap opera. Everyone behaved badly. Jacob favoured Joseph, born to his beloved wife Rachel. (The ornate coat he gave him was a symbol of higher status as well as just favour: not the best move a father ever made.) The brothers were more than a bit jealous: their hatred of Joseph is mentioned several times as the chapter goes on. Joseph, meanwhile, was not remotely tactful, wearing his special coat out into the fields and, worse, proclaiming his dreams which foresaw a day when he would rise above them.

On the one hand, we can understand why each person felt as they did, if we put ourselves into their shoes. Jacob only ever wanted to marry Rachel; the brothers were rightly annoyed; Joseph was a teenager and didn't yet know any better. On the other hand, none of this justifies their behaviour, which was variously uncaring, thoughtless, hateful and arrogant. However, from this unpromising beginning, the story of Joseph unfolds through the rest of Genesis, with all its twists and turns, as Joseph is sold by his brothers to the Ishmaelites, ends up in Egypt, in slavery, then prison, and finally, extraordinarily, works as second-in-command to Pharaoh ruling over the land.

For us this story carries warnings, and hope. The warnings: there is usually a cause behind someone's actions, so let us try to understand. Even so, selfish, thoughtless and ultimately violent behaviour is not excusable; we should challenge it in others and beware of it ourselves, *especially* if we feel we have a 'right' to it. But there is also this great hope: God eventually brought healing to that family and used Joseph in an amazing way to fulfil his plans.

ROSIE BUTTON, LECTURER, ALL NATIONS CHRISTIAN COLLEGE

Dreaming with meaning

Pharaoh dreamed that he was standing by the Nile, and there came up out of the Nile seven sleek and fat cows, and they grazed in the reed grass. Then seven other cows, ugly and thin, came up out of the Nile after them, and stood by the other cows on the bank of the Nile. The ugly and thin cows ate up the seven sleek and fat cows. And Pharaoh awoke.

GENESIS 41:1–4 (NRSV)

Pharaoh must have been relieved to wake up. No doubt we can quote similar experiences of relief after waking up from an alarming dream. Pharaoh couldn't get it out of his mind. His dream is the beginning of a vital episode leading from the intimate life of an Egyptian leader to the ultimate activity of God's salvation plan.

In its historical context, the story is a powerful one, which saved a nation from economic catastrophe by the careful storing and distribution of food and, significantly, providing relief for neighbouring nations. The pivotal figure is Joseph – a Hebrew, sold into slavery in Egypt by his jealous brothers, who became a trusted servant noted for his insight and personal faith. His capacity for interpreting dreams became well known and, as the story unfolds, he became a powerful figure in the plan to save the nation from potential starvation.

From our perspective, we can see the long-term outcomes of this story. It led to Joseph being reunited with his father, Jacob, and eleven brothers, as they came to Egypt to buy the food which had been so wisely stored. The twelve sons of Jacob were the founders of the twelve tribes of Israel. It was these tribes who eventually left Egypt and founded the nation through which God sent Jesus. Jesus himself is both intimate, because he is human, and ultimate, because he is divine.

The smallest of incidents can have significance beyond our dreams, not only for us but for everyone with whom we have to do. 'Sow a thought, reap an action. Sow an action, reap a habit. Sow a habit, reap a character. Sow a character, reap a destiny' (Stephen R. Covey).

My Lord and my God, let me see your purposes in the intimacies of my life.

MICHAEL TURNBULL, BISHOP AND VICE-PRESIDENT, BRF

Strength in weakness

Now a new king arose over Egypt, who did not know Joseph... The king of Egypt said to the Hebrew midwives, one of whom was named Shiphrah and the other Puah, 'When you act as midwives to the Hebrew women, and see them on the birthstool, if it is a boy, kill him; but if it is a girl, she shall live.' But the midwives feared God; they did not do as the king of Egypt commanded them, but they let the boys live.

EXODUS 1:8, 15–17 (NRSV)

If the Bible was a TV serial, Exodus 1 would be the start of season two. The book of Genesis ends with victory and hope, with the sons of Jacob reunited through Joseph, who looks forward to the fulfilment of God's promise to give the Israelites their own land. The book of Exodus begins in the same vein, with Jacob's descendants growing in numbers and strength. This happy bubble is burst by the arrival of a king who does not appreciate the historical connection between Egypt and the Israelites. He is terrified of them and brings them into slavery to keep them down.

Exodus 1 already hints how the Israelites will get out of this mess. The seeds of salvation are sown through two midwives who 'feared God'. They, unlike the king, are given names, remembered and celebrated for their faithfulness and courage. This is a story of the weak confounding the strong. The midwives trick the king into believing that they cannot get to the Hebrew women quick enough to take their children. Perhaps the king should be afraid, after all.

Throughout the scriptures, God takes the side of the weak against the strong. It may be easier to identify with the underdog, but what if we are actually on the side of strength, the side of the king? Who do we fear? Competitors, strangers, people who challenge our sense of who we are? Or do we 'fear' – are we faithful to – God? The midwives were not afraid, though they had good reason to be. Instead, they feared God and were blessed for it. Exodus 1 promises that despite power, despite the ways of the world, those who fear God and do what is right will be blessed. In what areas of our lives might that be true for us today?

BETH DODD, LECTURER, SARUM COLLEGE, SALISBURY

I have seen

'Do not come any closer,' God said. 'Take off your sandals, for the place where you are standing is holy ground.' Then he said, 'I am the God of your father, the God of Abraham, the God of Isaac and the God of Jacob.' At this, Moses hid his face, because he was afraid to look at God. The Lord said, 'I have indeed seen the misery of my people in Egypt. I have heard them crying out because of their slave drivers, and I am concerned about their suffering.'

EXODUS 3:5–7 (NIV)

There are some episodes in the Bible which command a 'wow', episodes so dripping in drama and intrigue that you want to step into the story. In this story, we find Moses living in the desert, a fugitive from Egypt, his homeland, where he left behind a murder scene, a crime committed by his hand. Here we see Moses' first, but certainly not only, encounter with the living God, 'YAHWEH, I AM', who grabs Moses' attention in the form of a burning bush.

We might have expected God to point out the crime Moses committed. We might expect him to challenge Moses over the fleeing of his homeland. We may expect him to command a contrite heart and an expression of unworthiness, but he does not. In these few verses at the start of their encounter, God does two things. He reveals who he is – 'the God of your father' – and he lets Moses know that he has seen the suffering of his people.

When we go through hard times, we too can be certain of two things: God is who he has always been – the almighty God who has revealed his power, his authority, his mercy and his love over countless generations. And he sees. He sees our pain, he sees our struggles, he sees our doubts and our insecurities. Of course, the story didn't end there for Moses and it doesn't need to for us. Our faithful God will be involved in our liberation, just as he was for the people of Israel. These two ideas can be held together in a simple line I once heard taught about Moses: 'I am not, but I know I AM.'

BECKY MAY, MINISTRY CONSULTANT AND FREELANCE WRITER
AT THE RESOURCES CUPBOARD / THE TREASURE BOX PEOPLE

Heading to the promised land

'When you enter the land that the Lord will give you as he promised, observe this ceremony. And when your children ask you, "What does this ceremony mean to you?" then tell them, "It is the Passover sacrifice to the Lord, who passed over the houses of the Israelites in Egypt and spared our homes when he struck down the Egyptians."' Then the people bowed down and worshipped. The Israelites did just what the Lord commanded Moses and Aaron.

EXODUS 12:25–28 (NIV)

The people of Israel are on the cusp of a new life. It is time to leave their years of slavery in Egypt behind and to journey towards a new land which God has promised will be theirs. But before they depart, they have marked this change in their lives with the Passover meal, precisely instructed in how to cook and eat it. The taste of the lamb, the unleavened bread and the bitter herbs is still in their mouths as they wait in the dark hour before dawn.

Escape from Egypt and from the cruelty of Pharaoh is something they must have thought would never happen. Maybe they thought God had forgotten about them and had abandoned them to their fate. Yet soon they – with their children, their aged parents, their animals and their cooking pots – are streaming out of the city. They are a people on the move.

Was there fear in their hearts, mingled with the joy? If they had known the unimaginable danger and hardships that awaited them, would they have hesitated? Perhaps. But none of them will forget this night; the Passover is a part of them now: 'This is a day you are to commemorate; for the generations to come you shall celebrate it as a festival to the Lord' (Exodus 12:14). This day marks the moment they have become a nation for the first time. Many years will pass before they reach the promised land, but they are the children of Israel, guided by the same God who guided their ancestors, Abraham, Jacob and, special to them, Joseph, the first of them to come to Egypt.

Like those before them, they can put their trust in God, a trust that will be renewed each time they celebrate the Passover meal which he has given them.

SUSAN HIBBINS, WRITER, EDITOR AND FORMER UK EDITOR, *THE UPPER ROOM*

Trusting God amidst fear and panic

Moses answered the people, 'Do not be afraid. Stand firm and you will see the deliverance the Lord will bring you today. The Egyptians you see today you will never see again. The Lord will fight for you; you need only to be still.' Then the Lord said to Moses, 'Why are you crying out to me? Tell the Israelites to move on. Raise your staff and stretch out your hand over the sea to divide the water so that the Israelites can go through the sea on dry ground.'

EXODUS 14:13–16 (NIV)

Exodus 14 is the climax of the story of the Israelites fleeing Egypt. After Pharaoh toing and froing about letting them go, he has at last agreed to it. And we join the story today just when the Israelites think they are finally free. But then Pharaoh has yet another change of heart and pursues them into the desert!

The Israelites see the Egyptians approaching and are terrified and cry out to God, but their cries quickly turn into blaming Moses for putting them in this situation. They appear to have completely forgotten about how tough life was in Egypt and tell Moses they would prefer to return to Egypt.

But rather than get angry or join in with their panic, Moses' response is to tell them, 'Do not be afraid' (v. 13). He has seen God work in seemingly impossible situations before and trusts that God will rescue them again here. He trusts in God, even amidst the panic and fear all around him. Even when God tells him to raise his staff and divide the sea, he doesn't seem fazed by it. Perhaps because Moses had previously seen God use his staff to do supernatural things, he trusts that God can work through him to bring about salvation.

Do we remember how God has worked in our lives and the lives of those around us, and allow that to encourage us in our faith when we are faced with fear and panic? Do you have a Moses-like figure who helps you remember the goodness and power of God? Is God calling you to be a Moses figure to someone else today?

MIRIAM THURLOW, CURATE, YORKSHIRE

Testing God

The Lord said to Moses, 'Go on ahead of the people, and take some of the elders of Israel with you; take in your hand the staff with which you struck the Nile, and go. I will be standing there in front of you on the rock at Horeb. Strike the rock, and water will come out of it, so that the people may drink.' Moses did so, in the sight of the elders of Israel. He called the place Massah and Meribah, because the Israelites quarrelled and tested the Lord, saying, 'Is the Lord among us or not?'

EXODUS 17:5–7 (NRSV)

God leads his people to the wilderness, but he doesn't always lead them to oases. Due to the lack of water, the Israelites complain to Moses and even question whether he intends to kill them, their children and livestock. Moses rebukes them for testing the Lord. Thereafter the names of Massah ('test') and Meribah ('strife/contention') have become a paradigm for testing God; as Deuteronomy 6:16 puts it: 'Do not put the Lord your God to the test, as you tested him at Massah.'

What is 'testing God'? It means putting God to the proof. When the Israelites question, 'Is the Lord among us or not?', they try to manipulate God to make water materialise in order to prove his presence. That's exactly what the devil tries to do when he tempts Jesus to jump down from the top of the temple. But Jesus rebukes him by alluding to the Massah event: 'Do not put the Lord your God to the test' (Matthew 4:7).

It seems unthinkable that the Israelites could test God shortly after experiencing the greatest miracle ever in their history, crossing the Red Sea, and the timely provision of quails and manna as food. Have they not witnessed enough of the divine presence? Human tendency to turn faith into sight by manipulating God for proof of his existence hasn't changed much over time. Some Christians may test God by wearing a beautiful garment of piety outside. Claiming to act in faith, some look for God's protection from life-threatening disease, while completely ignoring medical care and self-care. Some try to manipulate God to act by frequent, long prayers, believing that more prayers can change God's will. They are simply 'testing God' in disguise. We all need to be mindful not to make this mistake.

ALISON LO, ASSOCIATE PROFESSOR OF OLD TESTAMENT, BETHEL SEMINARY, MINNESOTA

God's commandments – still relevant?

**I am the Lord thy God, which have brought thee out of the land of Egypt...
Thou shalt have no other gods before me. Thou shalt not make unto thee any
graven image... Thou shalt not bow down thyself to them, nor serve them...
Thou shalt not take the name of the Lord thy God in vain... Remember the
sabbath day, to keep it holy... Honour thy father and thy mother... Thou shalt
not kill. Thou shalt not commit adultery. Thou shalt not steal. Thou shalt not
bear false witness against thy neighbour. Thou shalt not covet.**

EXODUS 20:2–17 (KJV, abridged)

In any compilation of significant Bible passages, the ten commandments surely
rank among the top ten. Along with the apostles' creed and Lord's Prayer, they
have been a feature of Christian liturgy and teaching from earliest times.

Yet we might struggle to recall them all – or even some! But the issue isn't
how many we remember; it is whether we live by them.

These commandments, first mediated at Sinai (and found again in Deuteronomy 5), form a core part of God's covenant with his people. And they have
been of prime importance to Jews and Christians since.

An objection is that they are framed negatively, as restrictive prohibitions:
the sharp 'thou shalt not's of the KJV make us feel as if God's finger is pointing
straight at us. But instructing our children as to what is off-limits – not running
into the road, for example – is the best way both to ensure their safety and
to maximise their liberty. The commandments are like a fence set along a
cliff edge, guarding us from harm while freeing us to enjoy the grassy hilltop
and open air.

These commands are summarised by two entirely positive 'thou shalt'
imperatives: to love God fully (Deuteronomy 6:5) and to love our neighbour
as ourselves (Leviticus 19:18). These overarching directives are endorsed by
Jesus in Matthew 22:37–40, as, by implication, are all of the ten (see Matthew 5:17).

The human-ward commands that form the last six cannot be separated
from the God-ward commands comprising the first four. Christian love and
respect of others is distinctive because it flows from our love for God – and
his for us. 'We love because he first loved us' (1 John 4:19, NIV).

DAVID DEWEY, BAPTIST MINISTER, YORKSHIRE

Is God good, or not?

'But the people who live there are powerful, and the cities are fortified and very large'… Then Caleb silenced the people before Moses and said, 'We should go up and take possession of the land, for we can certainly do it.' But the men who had gone up with him said, 'We can't attack those people; they are stronger than we are.' And they spread among the Israelites a bad report about the land they had explored.

NUMBERS 13:28A, 30–32A (NIV)

This story comes at a key moment in Israel's journey. After wandering in the wilderness, heading for the promised land of milk and honey, they stand on the cusp, about to put God's claims to the test. Their entry strategy was a sound one: send a chief from every tribe on an exploratory mission to find out what kind of people live there and in what sort of dwellings; and bring back some of what the land produces for everyone to see.

The 'spies' covered a vast geographical area in their 40-day search. They returned with a variety of fruits, including a single cluster of grapes that took two men to carry it – proof, surely, of the land's abundance. But they also delivered a verbal report that cut through the truth of this evidence. 'Never mind the size of the grapes, you should have seen the people! And their walled cities are impossible to breach!' Whatever leaving Egypt had been about, it wasn't to live here.

It was Caleb who reacted entirely differently. The inhabitants could easily be overcome, he declared, and no time should be lost in taking possession of the land. This was either madness or faith, but it boils down to one simple question (the same one Eve faced in the garden of Eden): is God good, or not?

You see, when the way ahead looks dark and difficult, we have a choice. We can focus on the darkness and shrink back, or reach for the light and step forward in faith. Following Caleb's example, let's not allow the evidence of our eyes to undermine what God has promised.

Lord, help me see things from your perspective. I choose to trust you today, whatever I have to face. Amen

JANE WALTERS, AUTHOR AND BROADCASTER

God is with you

'Be strong and courageous; for you shall put this people in possession of the land that I swore to their ancestors to give them. This book of the law shall not depart out of your mouth; you shall meditate on it day and night, so that you may be careful to act in accordance with all that is written in it... Be strong and courageous; do not be frightened or dismayed, for the Lord your God is with you wherever you go.'

JOSHUA 1:6–9 (NRSV, abridged)

The great hymn of William Williams Pantycelyn, 'Arglwydd arwain trwy'r anialwch', gives us the English version 'Guide me, O thou great Jehovah', and we may have sung it many times with gusto. The hymn wields powerful imagery from the arrival at Canaan where Jordan represents the boundary between this life and the next. This journey is anticipated in our reading today and is a vital part of Israel's history. We will feel a mismatch between the wider story of God establishing a people for himself and the promises to dispossess another people. In the period of its writing, there would have been no contradiction in the minds of writers or hearers, even though it creates discomfort now.

The task of leading the journey into Canaan is given to Joshua. He is instructed not to depart from God's command and to be courageous and strong. And these are linked. In the context of what must have been threatening territory, the invitation is to hold to what is firm and true, to what God has said. This kind of security speaks into the command not to fear nor be afraid. When the odds might have seemed stacked against him, Joshua could well have done exactly that.

We will experience times no less challenging than Joshua's, even if different in type. And when the odds seem stacked against us, God speaks the same word to us too: do not fear. When there is the threat of fear-inducing paralysis, God reminds us we are not isolated and alone. It's this which allows us to go forward and face the future, however great the threat.

Lord God, speak into my heart your assuring word so that I do not face the next step without you. With you, I know I can meet each hurdle and get to the other side. Amen

ANDY JOHN, BISHOP OF BANGOR

Rahab: edging in

Then Joshua son of Nun sent two men secretly from Shittim as spies, saying, 'Go, view the land, especially Jericho.' So they went, and entered the house of a prostitute whose name was Rahab, and spent the night there. The king of Jericho was told, 'Some Israelites have come here tonight to search out the land.' Then the king of Jericho sent orders to Rahab, 'Bring out the men who have come to you, who entered your house, for they have come only to search out the whole land.' But the woman took the two men and hid them.

JOSHUA 2:1–4A (NRSV)

Dave is a homeless man who spends his days on a bench on the edge of Christ Church meadow in Oxford. He encourages runners as they pass by, is always ready for a cheery chat and on occasion he tells me about students he's worried about. Dave lives on the fringes of society and yet he reveals God's love to those who encounter him.

Rahab the prostitute literally lived on the edge of her community – in a house in the walls surrounding Jericho. And yet, she is named in the genealogy of Christ (Matthew 1:5) and is described as a hero of faith (Hebrews 11:31) and as an example of faith in action (James 2:25). Rahab's story is one of courage. She is approached by Israelite spies who are on a reconnaissance mission for Joshua, gives them shelter overnight and helps them escape by misdirecting the king's soldiers as they hunt for them. In return, she and her family are spared when Joshua's forces sack Jericho, and her whole family become Israelites. The method of their deliverance echoes the first Passover – they mark their houses with red cords at the windows, and the destructive forces pass them by.

Jesus was criticised by the religious leaders for spending time with those they considered to be 'sinners': the prostitutes, lepers and others considered 'unclean'. Yet they were so often the first to recognise that he was the Saviour and to have the courage to announce this to others. Rahab's story reminds us that God's story of salvation has always incorporated those on the edges and margins, and God's love continues to be revealed through those we often overlook.

CLARE HAYNS, COLLEGE CHAPLAIN, CHRIST CHURCH, OXFORD

The commander of the Lord's army

Now when Joshua was near Jericho, he looked up and saw a man standing in front of him with a drawn sword in his hand. Joshua went up to him and asked, 'Are you for us or for our enemies?' 'Neither,' he replied, 'but as commander of the army of the Lord I have now come.' Then Joshua fell face down to the ground in reverence, and asked him, 'What message does my Lord have for his servant?' The commander of the Lord's army replied, 'Take off your sandals, for the place where you are standing is holy.' And Joshua did so.

JOSHUA 5:13–15 (NIV)

'Are you for us or for our enemies?' That is all Joshua needed to know on the eve of the battle of Jericho. Yet he is told that the commander of the Lord's army is on neither side. He might have been surprised, even disappointed, to hear this. Was he himself not doing the Lord's work, entrusted with a leadership assignment of the utmost importance? Joshua does not challenge the answer – hardly surprising when the commander of the Lord's army stands before you, battle ready, with sword drawn!

The task before Joshua is part of the unfolding story of God's plan to redeem the whole world through another 'Joshua' (Jesus). But he cannot assume that once he has accepted God's commission and public affirmation, he can proceed thinking he has God at his personal disposal. Too many Christian leaders have set out with good and godly intentions and yet caused untold damage as, over time, God has become someone to do their bidding and enhance their standing. We can all be prone to this temptation, even over the seemingly small things in our lives. How do we overcome it?

Joshua asked for a message from God, perhaps hoping for some final word of encouragement for the battle ahead. Once more the answer is not what he might have expected, but perhaps it would become the most important leadership lesson of his life. Not simply the reassurance that 'your God is with you' but that 'your God is holy'.

This is not a message *from* God but a moment *with* God. Joshua's biggest fears and darkest temptations are addressed not by increasing his confidence in himself but through battle-proofing his confidence in God. This is the decisive moment in the battle of Jericho: face down in the holy presence of God. This is how we fight our battles and address our deepest fears. Whatever today may hold, face down in worship is the best place to begin.

PAUL WILLIAMS, BISHOP OF SOUTHWELL AND NOTTINGHAM

God keeps his promises

Now the gates of Jericho were securely barred because of the Israelites. No one went out and no one came in. Then the Lord said to Joshua, 'See, I have delivered Jericho into your hands, along with its king and its fighting men. March round the city once with all the armed men. Do this for six days. Make seven priests carry trumpets of rams' horns in front of the ark. On the seventh day, march round the city seven times, with the priests blowing the trumpets. When you hear them sound a long blast on the trumpets, make the whole army give a loud shout; then the wall of the city will collapse and the army will go up, everyone straight in.'

JOSHUA 6:1–5 (NIV)

When you think about a wall, what do you see? An obstacle? A border to your house and garden? The walls surrounding the city of Jericho were massive! Not your average garden wall that you can hop over, but tall, strong walls built to keep people in and keep people out of the city. When God told Joshua that the walls would fall as a result of the army marching around the city with a few priests blowing trumpets, I wonder what Joshua's first thought was. Did he trust in the promise God had made immediately? Or did it take time?

Although it must have seemed foolish, Joshua followed God's instructions to the letter, and on the seventh day, as promised, when the people shouted, the walls collapsed and fell to the ground instantly, giving the city to them. Obedience even when God's commands seem foolish brings victory. When we are faced with our own 'Jericho', with situations that seem insurmountable, we can learn from this story that our faithful obedience to God will bring the walls down and make a way.

The grace of God and our obedience to him go hand in hand. If we believe and trust in God and his promises, our faith is in action. This story also reminds us that God keeps his promises. The walls of Jericho fell because God said they would, and God's promises to us today are just as real. We may not see a wall collapse in front of us, but we will have had times when we know we have trusted and obeyed God, and his promise to us, in all its beauty, has wonderfully changed our lives.

SHARON PRITCHARD, CHILDREN'S MINISTRY ADVISER, DIOCESE OF DURHAM

God's grace at work

Whenever the Lord raised up judges for them, the Lord was with the judge, and he delivered them from the hand of their enemies all the days of the judge; for the Lord would be moved to pity by their groaning because of those who persecuted and oppressed them. But whenever the judge died, they would relapse and behave worse than their ancestors, following other gods, worshipping them and bowing down to them. They would not drop any of their practices or their stubborn ways.

JUDGES 2:18–19 (NRSV)

Israel in the book of Judges is pretty typical of humanity. They would much rather live by their own rules and choices than God's and his covenant of justice. When they move away from God, God moves away from them. He does not force his presence. But when Israel tries to go it alone, they find that they are no more than what they are – a small, disparate people in a land already occupied by much more powerful nations. They forget that it is God who led them out of Egypt and think that their achievements are their own. Reduced to their own means, they lose on the battlefield and are put to forced labour or oppressed and harassed by surrounding nations, as if they were back in Egypt. Yet God intervenes.

Even though the people do not repent (they only 'groan'), God is moved to compassion by their pain. This is no mechanical relationship based on actions and consequence. It is pure grace, based on the overwhelming love of God, who cannot bear to see his people suffer – even if that suffering is of their own making, even when they repeat the cycle again and again, seemingly incapable of learning from history.

Isn't that often what we are as human beings? Repeating the mistakes of past generations, thinking that we are powerful, following our own ways? I cannot think of greater comfort than to see the story of God and his people – the love, the care, the overwhelming grace that, again and again, rescues both nation and individuals. It seems that nothing can place us beyond the grace of God: not what we do, not what others do to us. Take time today to consider God's immense grace and love for you, a love that nothing can separate you from.

ISABELLE HAMLEY, SECRETARY FOR THEOLOGY AND ECUMENICAL RELATIONS
AND THEOLOGICAL ADVISER TO THE HOUSE OF BISHOPS

My story vs. God's story

Early in the morning, Jerub-Baal (that is, Gideon) and all his men camped at the spring of Harod. The camp of Midian was north of them in the valley near the hill of Moreh. The Lord said to Gideon, 'You have too many men. I cannot deliver Midian into their hands, or Israel would boast against me, "My own strength has saved me." Now announce to the army, "Anyone who trembles with fear may turn back and leave Mount Gilead."' So twenty-two thousand men left, while ten thousand remained. But the Lord said to Gideon, 'There are still too many men.'

JUDGES 7:1–4a (NIV)

Gideon must have been puzzled. 'Lord, I've created a substantial army to drive out the invaders oppressing your people, and *now you want me to send most of them home*?'

One of the most frustrating things I know about God is his inability to see things my way. I can make all sorts of clever plans for myself and others, but he keeps working instead to his own targets and timescales. It's almost as if he knows better than me.

Daily, I have to remember that my own story is only a small part of God's much bigger story, a complex tapestry of events and personalities working its way out in complicated patterns too vast for me to understand, because I am too close to it. As God once said to the prophet Isaiah, 'My thoughts are not your thoughts' (55:8).

It took courage for Gideon to send those soldiers home before a battle, after realising it wasn't his story anymore, but God's – and that made all the difference. Afterwards, his decisive victory against the Midianites made an impact outlasting all his failures in the bigger scheme of things, because Gideon made space for God to speak and then show his mighty power.

Today, as part of the Lord's Prayer, you and I can choose to pray, 'Your kingdom come, your will be done, on earth as it is in heaven,' dedicating the day's work to the one who is ultimately in control. This deliberately passes on the final responsibility to him, and makes us part of God's bigger story. Having done that, we may well find our day starts looking rather different – and our choices then become much more significant.

CHRIS HUDSON, AUTHOR, SPEAKER, SCHOOLS WORKER AND FORMER BRF STAFF MEMBER

Ruth: the outsider's outsider

[Naomi] said, 'See, your sister-in-law has gone back to her people and to her gods; return after your sister-in-law.' But Ruth said, 'Do not press me to leave you or to turn back from following you! Where you go, I will go; where you lodge, I will lodge; your people shall be my people, and your God my God. Where you die, I will die – there will I be buried. May the Lord do thus and so to me, and more as well, if even death parts me from you!'

RUTH 1:15–17 (NRSV)

The book of Judges ends with the comment that at that time everyone did what was right in their own eyes. Ruth begins by setting itself in the time of the Judges. It is a story of fearing and loving God and one another in a time of anarchy, defeat and dismay.

It can rightly be read as a tale of morality and loyalty, yet it goes far beyond that to uncover in a minimum of words of surpassing beauty the key human issues of identity and covenant, of law and grace.

Ruth is the outsider's outsider. Everything in the first chapter provokes a sense of shock to the reader. She should never have been married to a good Jewish lad – she was from Moab, the enemy. And quite rightly everything goes wrong. Your self-righteous reader feels that the trauma is well deserved. But hang on a moment, like the sailors in Jonah – more faithful than the prophet – Ruth is surpassingly loyal and obeys the law. She honours Naomi. And she meets another person who in a time of anarchy is loyal to Yahweh. From Boaz' opening greeting to his workers and their cheerful reply (2:4), we see a man who has God at the centre. He obeys the command to leave the edges of the field for gleaners, the outdoor relief and social security of his day, and even goes beyond.

The end result is not only social justice – the poor are fed – but inclusion into the people of God, and not just any people but the forerunner of David and thus of Jesus. What a story! Romance, comedy (Boaz waking up to find a beautiful woman at his feet), integrity, dignity. The Lord is everywhere, yet never speaks.

This story is one for all time and all people. It reveals God in a fresh way, challenges our prejudices, demands our response. Read it and rejoice!

JUSTIN WELBY, ARCHBISHOP OF CANTERBURY

Glimmers of hope

'The Lord bless him!' Naomi said to her daughter-in-law. 'He has not stopped showing his kindness to the living and the dead.' She added, 'That man is our close relative; he is one of our guardian-redeemers.' Then Ruth the Moabite said, 'He even said to me, "Stay with my workers until they finish harvesting all my grain."'

RUTH 2:20–21 (NIV)

In front of me is an icon. Ruth stands in the middle. She holds a sheaf of grain and gestures towards another woman, Naomi, who holds a baby. Behind Ruth a man stands protectively: Boaz. (Find this image at the artist's website, **silviadimitrova.co.uk**.)

This is an image inspired by Ruth's final chapter. A story begun in grief and continuing through difficulty ends well – even to the extent that Ruth's story is woven into Jesus' story (4:13–22).

But today we're reading Ruth 2: we're not there yet. Ruth and Naomi are in dire straits: they are women alone, one of whom is a foreigner. They have little to no means of supporting themselves.

Ruth voices one option: 'Let me go to the fields.' She gleans grain behind the workers – a dangerous occupation, as women working alone in fields were at risk of abuse by men also working there. It was a bleak situation, perhaps hopeless. Bring to mind a moment when you've felt hopeless. In the memory of that moment, you can relate to how Ruth and Naomi would have felt.

Into this hopelessness comes a glimmer of possibility. Boaz arrives and shows Ruth kindness, allowing her to stay in his field and telling his workers to leave her extra grain. He blesses Ruth, voicing a new hope: that she would find refuge under God's wings.

Through Boaz's actions, hope is revived. Kindness sows hopeful seeds for what will come to fruition at the end of the story. Naomi's faith even begins to be restored: 'The Lord bless him… he has not stopped showing his kindness to the living and the dead.'

Where can you look for hope being revived? In hopeless times, how can you see what seeds are being sown that will grow into a better, brighter future?

HANNAH FYTCHE, AUTHOR AND PASTORAL ASSISTANT

An ear-tingling prophecy

Now the Lord came and stood there, calling as before, 'Samuel! Samuel!' And Samuel said, 'Speak, for your servant is listening.' Then the Lord said to Samuel, 'See, I am about to do something in Israel that will make both ears of anyone who hears of it tingle. On that day I will fulfil against Eli all that I have spoken...' Eli said, 'What was it that he told you?'... So Samuel told him everything and hid nothing from him... And all Israel from Dan to Beer-sheba knew that Samuel was a trustworthy prophet of the Lord.

1 SAMUEL 3:10–20 (NRSV, abridged)

Ear-tingling experiences aren't the same as spine-tingling or heart-warming ones. Here it is more similar to an 'ear-burning' experience. Eli learns that God had spoken about him to Samuel, with a terrible message of judgement on Eli and his family. They had consistently withheld the respect, honour and sacrifices due to God by indulging their own desires with what should have been offered to God instead. Often the pattern of Old Testament prophecy is that the specific (which here applies to Eli) implies the general (which embraces Israel) and can also point to the universal message (which might include us in our own time and place).

Samuel's ear-tingling prophecy marks the beginning of an amazing prophetic ministry, often speaking truth to power, during a very significant period in Israel's history: from the era of the Judges until King David's reign. A friend, a doctor, explains that ear-tingling is not a disease in itself, but could be a warning of an infection that will need treating to prevent total deafness. In our generation it might be better to describe this infection, once known as sin or idolatry, as following and worshipping the world's values, rather than God. It is the same infection and still requires treatment, as it increasingly makes us deaf to God's word.

The God who spoke to Samuel still seeks out those required to speak ear-tingling messages in a world becoming deaf to God's word and God's values. Like Samuel, there will be those hearing a persistent voice that keeps them awake at night. Through prayer, Bible study, worship and by discussing with other people, some will conclude that they are, in fact, hearing the voice of God, calling them to give an ear-tingling message, here and now, to those in danger of becoming totally deaf to God's word.

STUART BUCHANAN, FORMER MISSION PROGRAMMES MANAGER, CHURCH MISSION SOCIETY, AND PROJECT OFFICER, ANGLICAN COMMUNION OFFICE

Succession planning

All the elders of Israel gathered together and came to Samuel at Ramah. They said to him, 'You are old, and your sons do not follow your ways; now appoint a king to lead us, such as all the other nations have.' But when they said, 'Give us a king to lead us,' this displeased Samuel; so he prayed to the Lord. And the Lord told him: 'Listen to all that the people are saying to you; it is not you they have rejected, but they have rejected me as their king.'

1 SAMUEL 8:4–7 (NIV)

At first glance, the request for a king seems very reasonable – after all, good succession planning is important! The elders have seen that Samuel's sons are not up to the job of replacing him and they show foresight by proposing a system of governance that's been tried and tested by others. Of course, Samuel is upset as he is forced to face his own personal failure (much like Eli before him), but he does the one thing that matters: he turns to God in prayer. And this is the turning point, because God sees things very differently. This is not about Samuel's leadership, but God's.

From God's point of view, the nation already has a king! When God freed them from slavery in Egypt, he became their true king. Human leadership is delegated by God and to be exercised under his authority. By seeking a king 'such as all the other nations have' (v. 5), the elders have forgotten this. They have taken God out of the equation.

Amazingly, God does not refuse their request. Nor, though, will he abandon his people. God will use the monarchy to raise up a king unlike any other who will turn the people back to him. It begins with King David, but ultimately it is Jesus who through service and sacrifice will uniquely reveal God's reign, his radical love for his people and his world.

This is a great lesson in leadership. But it's also a lesson for life. When good things take God's place, we fall short of our calling. But praise God that his perspective is greater! As we offer ourselves to Jesus today, turning away from worldly patterns and being transformed by the renewing of our minds (Romans 12:1–2), so we become ambassadors of the King wherever we go.

ANDY BUCKLER, VICAR, ST BARNABAS KENSINGTON

No fancy weapons needed

David said to the Philistine, 'You come against me with sword and spear and javelin, but I come against you in the name of the Lord Almighty, the God of the armies of Israel, whom you have defied. This day the Lord will deliver you into my hands, and I'll strike you down and cut off your head. This very day I will give the carcasses of the Philistine army to the birds and the wild animals, and the whole world will know that there is a God in Israel.'

1 SAMUEL 17:45–46 (NIV)

The story of David and Goliath is one of the best known in the Bible and one of my all-time favourite stories. My Sunday school teacher in Kenya, where I grew up, told this story in an astonishing way. She compared David and Goliath to a mouse and an elephant, which made it tangible for me. There's an African myth about the elephant fearing the mouse – funny, right? It is the unpredictability of the mouse's movement that keeps the elephant on edge. I can imagine Goliath thinking, 'What's that little guy up to?', when he saw David approaching him.

We are bound to encounter all sorts of challenges in life, but the size of these challenges doesn't really matter. We can rely on God. Faith in God was all the armour David needed. He boldly declared to Goliath, 'The battle is the Lord's.'

Scripture says, 'For God has not given us a spirit of fear and timidity, but of power, love, and self-discipline' (2 Timothy 1:7, NLT).

We have to trust with our whole being, believing that God has got us covered and that he will help us and take care of us. He knows what is best, but to truly grasp what he has planned for us, we have to trust him completely.

Consider whether you have confidence that God can help you in even the most impossible and incomprehensible situations. How do you find courage to face the difficult things in your life?

CAROLYNE KADDU RASMUSSEN, REGISTERED NURSE

David and Saul

Saul thereupon went in search of David and his men opposite the Rocks of the Mountain Goats. He came to a cave, and went in to cover his feet. Now David and his men were sitting in the recesses of the cave... David got up and, unobserved, cut off the edge of Saul's cloak... Saul then left the cave and went on his way. After this, David called after Saul, 'My lord king!' Saul looked behind him and David did reverence. Then David said to Saul, 'Why do you listen to people who say, 'David is seeking to harm you'?

1 SAMUEL 24:3–10 (RNJB, abridged)

Young David was ambitious. He wanted to be king in place of Saul, who had failed as king, been rejected by the Lord and become almost bipolar – or was he only defending himself against an unscrupulous young rival? So Saul expelled David from court. David replied by setting up his own army of malcontents. So Saul pursued David down to this gully beside the Dead Sea. In this scene, while David and his men are hiding, deep in one of the caves, Saul slips in to relieve himself. While Saul 'has his trousers down', David stealthily snips off the edge of his discarded outer garment. As soon as Saul is at a safe distance, David taunts him but declares his own loyalty. The story is told from David's point of view: David cannot put a foot wrong, but Saul is a manic depressive. Did David still love and revere Saul, or was he only feathering his own nest for the future, when he himself would be king? No one should raise a hand against the Lord's anointed!

David is a complex, passionate character, capable of great sin. He committed adultery and, in an attempt to hide his own crime, had the cuckolded husband, one of his own serving officers, killed. Yet he was capable, too, when resolutely rebuked by Nathan, his personal prophet, of heartfelt repentance. When the product of the illicit union falls ill and dies, David's officials fear he will kill himself, yet he obediently accepts God's will. Why was David chosen to be ancestor of the Messiah? Why was the promise of an eternal line of kings given to him? Not for a blameless life! Jesus' words in Luke 15:7 – 'There will be more rejoicing in heaven over one sinner repenting than over ninety-nine upright people who have no need of repentance' – can be an encouragement to us all.

HENRY WANSBROUGH, MONK OF AMPLEFORTH

A promise fulfilled through kindness

David asked, 'Is anyone still left in Saul's family? I want to show kindness to that person for Jonathan's sake!' Now there was a servant named Ziba from Saul's family. So David's servants called Ziba to him... The king asked, 'Is anyone left in Saul's family?...' Ziba answered, 'Jonathan has a son still living who is crippled in both feet'... King David had servants bring Jonathan's son from the house of Makir son of Ammiel in Lo Debar. Mephibosheth, Jonathan's son, came before David and bowed facedown on the floor.

2 SAMUEL 9:1–6 (NCV, abridged)

Not many kings of this time would have shown mercy and forgiveness in this situation. It was safer to eliminate your rivals and close relatives, leaving no direct challengers to claim the throne, and the crippled Mephibosheth would have been an easy target. But David wasn't just a king; he was a man who, despite all his failings, had a heart for God, and he showed great kindness to Mephibosheth, thus honouring his promise to Jonathan. Jonathan had helped his friend David at his own personal risk when David was removed from Saul's court, and David responded in love and grace when the opportunity arose.

Are we willing to show kindness to others? At the height of the turbulent times of pandemic, we saw numerous stories in the media of strangers helping each other, loving each other and being a shining beacon of goodness among unkind words, divisive actions and poor behaviour recorded for posterity on social media platforms. With so many things vying for our attention, it can be easy to ignore the needs of those around us, those who are our family, our friends and our neighbours. Are we too complacent, too comfortable with temporary pleasures and material possessions?

It is important to speak words of kindness into the lives of those around us; and these words will reveal what our heart is really like. Are we willing to allow the Holy Spirit to work in us and renew us, heart and mind, body and soul, to give each of us new and life-giving words to enable us to speak healing and restoration into the lives of others?

TRISH HAHN, MESSY CHURCH SEND UK COORDINATOR

Fallible king, redeeming God

It happened, late one afternoon, when David rose from his couch and was walking about on the roof of the king's house, that he saw from the roof a woman bathing; the woman was very beautiful. David sent someone to inquire about the woman. It was reported, 'This is Bathsheba daughter of Eliam, the wife of Uriah the Hittite.' So David sent messengers to fetch her, and she came to him, and he lay with her... Then she returned to her house. The woman conceived; and she sent and told David, 'I am pregnant.'

2 SAMUEL 11:2–5 (NRSV, abridged)

This chapter relates the most notorious of David's crimes. David has no business being on the roof of his palace – his army and officers are at war, and a king's place is with his army. Instead, David is lounging about at home, taking long siestas in the middle of the day and ogling the local women. We should be under no illusions about what happens next. Bathsheba has sometimes been vilified, cast as the seductress, the woman who causes the virtuous king to fall. But we're not even told that she is naked. Bathing in the open air, and very specifically purifying herself after her period, probably meant that she was discreetly washing beneath her garments. Either way, the balance of power is enormously in David's favour. How could Bathsheba possibly refuse a royal summons like this? The modern notion of consent does not even come into the equation.

As many readers will know, Bathsheba's pregnancy marks the beginning of David's downward spiral, as he desperately tries to conceal his guilt, arranging for her husband to be murdered. And in the next generation, we see that his son Amnon has learned his father's ways: *You see a woman you want, you take her.* In Amnon's case, it was his sister Tamar whom he desired, raped, and ruined (2 Samuel 13).

As you read, spare a thought for Nathan, charged by God in the following chapter to deliver divine judgement upon the king. It takes courage to be a prophet.

But, above all, notice that after judgement and repentance comes divine mercy; and, more than that, restoration. For it is through David and Bathsheba's line that Jesus Christ is born (Matthew 1:6). We worship the God who works all things into good.

HELEN PAYNTER, BAPTIST MINISTER AND BIBLICAL STUDIES TUTOR,
BRISTOL BAPTIST COLLEGE, AND FORMER EDITOR, *GUIDELINES*

49

The path of wisdom

That night the Lord appeared to Solomon in a dream, and God said, 'What do you want? Ask, and I will give it to you!'... [Solomon replied,] 'Give me an understanding heart so that I can govern your people well and know the difference between right and wrong. For who by himself is able to govern this great people of yours?' The Lord was pleased that Solomon had asked for wisdom.

1 KINGS 3:5, 9–10 (NLT)

'God gave Solomon very great wisdom and understanding, and knowledge as vast as the sands of the seashore' (1 Kings 4:29). Solomon rebuilt the temple so the Israelites could worship God. He worked on the book of Proverbs so people could live out God's teaching in their lives. Paraphrased proverbs, such as 'pride comes before a fall' (see Proverbs 16:18), have become embedded in modern-day culture.

Solomon's wisdom was shown in several ways. First, he took his responsibilities seriously: he wanted only wisdom from God for the challenges he would face as king. Second, he was willing to review his choices in the light of his faith in God: 'Seek his will in all you do, and he will show you which path to take' (Proverbs 3:6).

Third, he handled pressure intelligently. Two women came to him, one whose baby had died; the other claiming the grieving mother had stolen her baby. His plan – pretending he would have the baby cut in two – drew out the truth. 'When all Israel heard the verdict the king had given, they held the king in awe, because they saw that he had wisdom from God to administer justice' (1 Kings 3:28, NIV).

Fourth, he worshipped God. The book of Proverbs shows how Solomon understood that the 'fear of the Lord is the foundation of wisdom' (9:10).

Sadly, Solomon's wisdom would ultimately give way to a temptation for power, fame and wealth (1 Kings 11:1–13). We should note that Solomon's gradual mixing of his own self-interest with his faith in God happened over a period of time. Character formation is a slow process. No one becomes instantly wise or immediately foolish. If we pray for wisdom, God will not answer us with wisdom fully formed; he will give us opportunities to be wise and to grow into the person God would have us be.

BOB MAYO, CHAPLAIN, HMP ROCHESTER

Simply the rest

'But now the Lord my God has given me rest on every side, and there is no adversary or disaster. I intend, therefore, to build a temple for the Name of the Lord my God, as the Lord told my father David, when he said, "Your son whom I will put on the throne in your place will build the temple for my Name."'

1 KINGS 5:4–5 (NIV)

Rest is a key idea throughout the Bible. It's the entire purpose of 'day seven' of creation. Rest is Jesus' promised gift to the weary and heavy-laden. Rest has a day entirely given over to it. Rest is the description of a believer's eternal resting place. There at the start, there at the end.

Rest will not happen by accident; Solomon's rest only came after battle and work. It has to be fought for. Has 'rest' ever been the first entry on to a page in your diary? True rest is not found in the gaps between everything else. Do you crash at the end of the day, or do you work with joy from a place of rest? Rest is God's gift. The first encouragement today is to turn to the next empty page in your diary and begin writing in 'rest' each day.

But what to do with this rest? Solomon determined to use the rest God had given him to build a place of encounter with God. The temple was to be a place where people could approach God, hear his voice, grow community, know forgiveness, appreciate beauty, pray, worship, rediscover their identity, be creative and go somewhere special. How could your rest be inspired by this?

It would be wrong to ignore the painful reality in 1 Kings 5:13, that Solomon's temple robbed rest from others. Our challenge is to be wiser than Solomon. If our rest is built on the hunger or forced labour of others, it cannot be considered godly rest. Why not use your next period of rest to undertake a lifestyle eco-audit? There are plenty online (including on the A Rocha website) which can help you bless others with rest.

May you build a temple to God today, full of creative, beautiful and generous rest.

PADDY HARRIS, CHURCH LEADER

Pause, listen widely, choose wisely

King Rehoboam took counsel with the older men who had attended his father Solomon while he was still alive… They answered him, 'If you will be a servant to this people and speak good words to them, they will be your servants forever.' But he disregarded the advice the older men gave him, and consulted with the young men who had grown up with him… [They] said to him… 'Thus you should say to them… "Whereas my father laid on you a heavy yoke, I will add to your yoke. My father disciplined you with whips, but I will discipline you with scorpions."'

1 KINGS 12:6–11 (NRSV, abridged)

The two books of Kings, and their prequels, 1 and 2 Samuel, form an epic saga with all the intrigue and intensity of the *Star Wars* series. The wild brother tribes of Israel banded together with ambitions of nationhood, asking God for a king to feel equal to the established nations around them. God warned them that no kings in the history of forever would fulfil their expectations.

In 1 Kings 12 the new king Rehoboam, Solomon's son, inherits a gloriously wealthy nation, though the people struggle under grinding taxes. Rehoboam pauses to consider his options. What kind of king will he be? Will he use the wealth of the country to bring relief to the ordinary person on the street? On the edge of our seats, we wonder, 'Is this a moment of justice?' It isn't.

Rehoboam and his peers narrow-mindedly shut out the perspective of other generations. Israel and Judah are plunged into a downwards spiral of disunity. Conflict, hardship and violence impoverish the country.

Where is God in this? Rehoboam sees his kingship through the eyes and approval of his friends. God doesn't appear on Rehoboam's radar.

This episode offers us some personal challenges. Do we find moments – as an individual or community – to pause and ask if there is a way we can shift direction to lighten the load? To speak to God honestly about our strengths and stockpiles of resources, our needs and burdens? Who do we listen to and allow to influence us? Rehoboam listened to the echo chamber of his contemporaries. Every generation – young and old – can fall into this trap.

Yet faith communities are wonderful places to intentionally listen to those who have lived in different times and places, to help us find the ways of God – the ways of justice, freedom and mercy for those who carry heavy loads.

ELIZABETH WALDRON BARNETT, INTERGENERATIONAL PRACTITIONER AND THEOLOGIAN

Why is this happening?

After this the son of the woman… became ill; his illness was so severe that there was no breath left in him. She then said to Elijah, 'What have you against me, O man of God? You have come to me to bring my sin to remembrance, and to cause the death of my son!' But he said to her, 'Give me your son'… The Lord listened to the voice of Elijah; the life of the child came into him again, and he revived. Elijah took the child… and gave him to his mother; then Elijah said, 'See, your son is alive.'

1 KINGS 17:17–23 (NRSV, abridged)

The story of Elijah being fed by ravens, and then by the widow (a story reminiscent of the magic porridge pot!), is recounted in children's Bibles. But as often happens in biblical teaching, the difficult parts are left out. The drought may not be explained as God's punishment for the people worshipping the fertility and rain god Baal. The reality of death is quickly forgotten as we rush to the 'happily-ever-after' and the woman's realisation that 'the word of the Lord… is truth' (v. 24).

Why does God inflict drought on a whole nation? Many had deserted God for Baal, but surely Elijah wasn't the only loyal believer! What about those who had never heard about God? Why punish them? The widow had already lost her husband. Why take her son too? Does God use suffering to prove a point?

For me, the difficult questions arising from this story of human suffering are the main reason to study it with fellow disciples, whatever their age or stage of faith. As I write, we are back in lockdown and the coronavirus is more virulent than ever. People of all faiths and none have questions. Why is this happening? How long will it last? How many more people will suffer or die before the virus is contained?

As I talk with those asking questions, as I ask them myself, I tell stories of people like the widow who blamed God for their suffering. I recall psalms where people rant and rave at God. But I also recollect that God is Immanuel, God-with-us in the challenge and despair of life. God is big enough to cope with our questions; and we must give ourselves permission to wrestle with them if we are to remain faithful to ourselves and grow in our relationship with God.

DEBORAH HUMPHRIES, METHODIST PRESBYTER

Test of faith

The prophet Elijah came near and said, 'O Lord, God of Abraham, Isaac, and Israel, let it be known this day that you are God in Israel, that I am your servant, and that I have done all these things at your bidding. Answer me, O Lord, answer me, so that this people may know that you, O Lord, are God, and that you have turned their hearts back.' Then the fire of the Lord fell and consumed the burnt-offering, the wood, the stones, and the dust, and even licked up the water that was in the trench. When all the people saw it, they fell on their faces and said, 'The Lord indeed is God; the Lord indeed is God.'

1 KINGS 18:36–39 (NRSV)

Four centuries of Israel's history are covered by the books of Kings, from the close of David's reign to the destruction of Jerusalem in 587BC. The contest with the prophets of Baal on Mount Carmel provided tangible evidence that God is God. It is interesting that Elijah made sure that the odds were stacked against him by soaking the sacrifice and the wood with water which flowed into a trench around the altar. Water would have been a rare commodity after three years of drought, so the emptying of the jars over the sacrifice was a double act of faith. Elijah was trusting God for rain as well as fire. His prayer shows his supreme faith at this crucial moment in Israel's history.

But how can we put our trust in a God that we cannot see? The author of Hebrews 11:1 writes, 'Faith is the assurance of things hoped for, the conviction of things not seen', and the Christian faith provides us with ways to understand both ourselves and our world. The words of the Bible and the Holy Spirit reveal hidden forces at work, and this is why Christians meet to read the Bible, to pray and to discuss what God might be saying to them.

Faith means casting oneself unreservedly on the mercy of God, laying hold of the promises of God in Christ, relying entirely on the finished work of Christ for salvation and the power of the Holy Spirit for daily strength.

On Mount Carmel Elijah demonstrated that we should have complete reliance on, and be fully obedient to, the one true God.

DAVID MASON, MESSY CHURCH SUPPORT TEAM LEADER

Keep calm and carry on

[Elijah] went a day's journey into the wilderness, and came and sat down under a solitary broom tree. He asked that he might die: 'It is enough; now, O Lord, take away my life, for I am no better than my ancestors.' Then he lay down under the broom tree and fell asleep. Suddenly an angel touched him and said to him, 'Get up and eat.' He looked, and there at his head was a cake baked on hot stones, and a jar of water.

1 KINGS 19:4–6a (NRSV)

The words 'Keep calm and carry on' have become a mantra for when times get really tough. They first appeared on a British government poster in 1939, intended to raise the nation's morale as it braced itself for bombing raids at the beginning of World War II. But it barely left the stock room, deemed too patronising and divisive for such a time of war. Only now, for a future generation, as it speaks of the stoicism, perseverance and fortitude which was shown during that great time of crisis, does it fulfil the task it was meant to perform then and bring to many the hope and courage to go on.

Elijah is in crisis. Jezebel, the wife of Ahab, has put a death mark on his head for proving to the people of God that Baal is false and killing all his prophets. Escaping from the scene of his triumph, he flees into the wilderness. Elijah has reached the end of his road. In utter terror and despair, he turns to the Lord and begs that he may be allowed to make the ultimate escape and not have to follow the dangerous path the Lord calls him to walk. Into this whirlwind of crisis comes a moment of peace, as Elijah falls asleep. The angel comes with few words, just the bare necessities of life: a loaf of bread and a jar of water which restore Elijah so he may hear God once again in the silence following wind, earthquake and fire.

So at our moments of crisis we are reminded to return to the basics of life, the small acts which make up the everyday and root us back into the sustaining presence of God in the ordinary, thereby enabling us to stay calm and carry on.

EMMA PENNINGTON, CANON MISSIONER, CANTERBURY CATHEDRAL

How do we respond?

Naboth replied, 'The Lord forbid that I should give you the inheritance of my ancestors.' So Ahab went home, sullen and angry... His wife Jezebel came in and asked him, 'Why are you so sullen? Why won't you eat?' He answered her, 'Because I said to Naboth the Jezreelite, "Sell me your vineyard; or if you prefer, I will give you another vineyard in its place." But he said, "I will not give you my vineyard."' Jezebel his wife said, 'Is this how you act as king over Israel? Get up and eat! Cheer up. I'll get you the vineyard of Naboth the Jezreelite.'

1 KINGS 21:3–7 (NIV, abridged)

Sometimes, the way life works means we don't always get what we want, and we hear the word 'no', just as Ahab did in this passage. This can feel unfair, and make us angry and sullen, like Ahab. Jezebel's solution ultimately meant that he murdered Naboth and took the land he wanted forcibly – not a loving and just way to rule a country! Ahab, however, was challenged by the prophet Elijah, who spoke the truth in love to him and helped him to see the error of his ways. This led to Ahab feeling remorse for what he had done, and to a time of fasting and prayer.

Have you ever been told 'no'? How did you respond? Sometimes, we don't react in the way we should to bad news, or when we don't get our own way. It is important at these times to find someone to talk things through with, someone who will speak the truth in love to you. This can help to provide a different perspective, or a healthier way forward.

Are there times when you have allowed yourself to be stirred up, or wound up by another person, as Jezebel stirred up Ahab, or when you have done this yourself? What did that do to the situation? To you? It is important when we get things wrong to apologise and to try and make it right. Is there someone you need to apologise to? How could you make the situation better? Let's ask God for help next time we are under pressure – to react well, and not to stir things up.

LYDIA HARRISON, MESSY CHURCH SUPPORT TEAM MEMBER

I don't want to miss a thing

When the Lord was about to take Elijah up to heaven in a whirlwind, Elijah and Elisha were on their way from Gilgal. Elijah said to Elisha, 'Stay here; the Lord has sent me to Bethel.' But Elisha said, 'As surely as the Lord lives and as you live, I will not leave you.' So they went down to Bethel. The company of the prophets at Bethel came out to Elisha and asked, 'Do you know that the Lord is going to take your master from you today?' 'Yes, I know,' Elisha replied, 'so be quiet.'

2 KINGS 2:1–3 (NIV)

I'm embarrassed to say that the first film I ever cried during was *Armageddon* – the rather melodramatic tale of miners being sent to save humanity from a hurtling earth-bound asteroid. The climactic scene, and the cause of my awkward 13-year-old tears, involves Bruce Willis' character sacrificing himself to save his daughter's fiancé as Aerosmith's 'I don't want to miss a thing' blares out. It is not exactly a classic, but there was an intensity that moved me as Bruce said goodbye to his daughter, knowing that he had saved a future life for her that he would now miss.

Our scene today between Elijah and Elisha made me think of *Armageddon*. The basic structure above repeats three times. Elijah tries to save himself a painful goodbye by telling Elisha to stay. Elisha says, 'Where you go, I go.' Three times prophets will attempt to tell Elisha that Elijah is leaving. And Elisha will say, 'Shh, I know.'

Elisha knows that their journey is coming towards its end and he's not ready for it. He won't give up a moment of time together. He won't be distracted. He doesn't want to miss a thing. Elijah will finally ask how he can bless Elisha, and Elisha asks for a double portion of Elijah's spirit. He wants more of this. He wants more of Elijah. And then he will say goodbye.

Who have been the important companions on your journey? What was it about them that meant so much to you? Thank God for them and don't miss what they taught you.

Who are the important companions on your journey today? You won't always have them, so how can you silence the noise and pay attention to your time together? They are a gift, so make sure you don't miss a thing.

JONATHAN FILLIS, MINISTER, HADDENHAM CUM DINTON BAPTIST CHURCH
AND FORMER BRF STAFF MEMBER

So much more

Elisha said, 'Go round and ask all your neighbours for empty jars. Don't ask for just a few. Then go inside and shut the door behind you and your sons. Pour oil into all the jars, and as each is filled, put it to one side.' She left him and shut the door behind her and her sons. They brought the jars to her and she kept pouring. When all the jars were full, she said to her son, 'Bring me another one.' But he replied, 'There is not a jar left.' Then the oil stopped flowing.

2 KINGS 4:3–6 (NIV)

'All you have to do, Madam, is answer this simple survey,' said the lady on the end of the phone, 'and you'll win a free holiday to Spain.' Well, I was young and impressionable, so I believed her. A few questions, a convoluted booking process and quite a lot of money later, we did indeed have a holiday in Spain… and it rained all week!

Some things really are too good to be true, and Elijah's plan must have sounded ridiculously naive to a woman who knew full well how far one little jar of olive oil would go. Everything in her must have wanted to hold on to it, to keep it safe and use it sparingly, yet there he was telling her to pour it out. Everyone knows the quickest way to waste oil is to pour it from one container to another, because it sticks to the sides and you end up with less than you started with. She must have been tempted to smile politely and go home.

But this was no dodgy holiday scam. This was God longing to teach his beloved daughter something about the extravagant mathematics of heaven.

Whenever people ask me how prayer works, I point them to this story. Prayer is a pouring out; sometimes we pray with words, sometimes with our hands, our bodies and our silence; sometimes we pray with joy, sometimes with tears. When we pray, we pour out the little we have in ourselves. It can feel costly, even pointless, but we choose to do it anyway, and when we do, God pours out the limitless resources of heaven in response.

Try pouring yourself out in a prayer today, bringing God your needs, then notice the unexpected droplets of goodness landing on you throughout the day.

LYNDALL BYWATER, FREELANCE WRITER, SPEAKER AND BROADCASTER

Healing in humility

Naaman went with his horses and chariots and stopped at the door of Elisha's house. Elisha sent a messenger to say to him, 'Go, wash yourself seven times in the Jordan, and your flesh will be restored and you will be cleansed.' But Naaman went away angry... Naaman's servants went to him and said, 'My father, if the prophet had told you to do some great thing, would you not have done it? How much more, then, when he tells you, "Wash and be cleansed"!'

2 KINGS 5:9–11a, 13 (NIV)

Naaman was a man of great position, highly regarded in the sight of others. Yet he needed healing from leprosy – a physical affliction that denoted spiritual uncleanliness. On the advice of an Israelite servant, he seeks the prophet Elisha.

To this encounter he brings pride, self-assurance in worldly status, expectation of acknowledgement and how this encounter should look for such a man as him. Met by a messenger and sent away with a menial instruction, he is furious: 'My time has been wasted – I have not been acknowledged.' But with humility and obedience comes the healing he seeks.

I became a Christian in my 30s; I was outwardly successful, accomplished and well-regarded, often asked to speak if testimony was needed. Full of enthusiasm for what I might bring to my new faith, I signed up to help on a local Alpha course and rearranged my bulging schedule to ensure I was available.

At the pre-course briefing, I was not allocated a role. Amongst the 'left over', I was asked to supervise car parking – in snowy January! I was livid: 'My time has been wasted – I have not been acknowledged.'

Then, not a servant, but a song came to me ('It's all about you, Jesus' – consistently first on my shuffle list the following week), and God tangibly showed me the extent of my pride and spoke to me of humility and obedience.

Whoever the world tells us we are, we all have equal need of Jesus. In his outrageous grace, he gives everything, and we need bring nothing. With his help, we can strike the balance between using our gifts to bless others and always being ready to dip ourselves in the Jordan or spend joyful, cold and healing hours waving cars into parking spots, when that is what we are asked to do.

SALLY HOBSON, DOCTOR PASSIONATE ABOUT WORK WITH VULNERABLE CHILDREN

Who are you encouraging today?

In the seventh year of Jehu, Joash became king, and he reigned in Jerusalem for forty years. His mother's name was Zibiah; she was from Beersheba. Joash did what was right in the eyes of the Lord all the years Jehoiada the priest instructed him… Joash said to the priests, 'Collect all the money that is brought as sacred offerings to the temple of the Lord… Let every priest receive the money from one of the treasurers, then use it to repair whatever damage is found in the temple.'

2 KINGS 12:1–5 (NIV, abridged)

The other day, I was pinning up notices on our church noticeboard when two ladies walked past. I smiled at them and wished them a good morning. When they were further along the path (presumably thinking I was out of earshot), one of the ladies turned to the other and said, 'So who was that man?', to which the other replied, 'That's no man, that's the rector!' It's always interesting to reflect on how others see us and what influence we are having on others.

In today's passage of 2 Kings 12, we find the fascinating account of King Joash, who reigned in Jerusalem for 40 years. Becoming king at a young age, he started his reign well, although he finished badly. And why was this? Well, we are told that in the early years of his reign he was helped by a wise, experienced priest named Jehoiada, a man of faith who was prepared to take him under his wing. Thanks to his mentoring, Joash set about repairing the temple in Jerusalem, which had been built by Solomon but fallen into disrepair.

Can you think back over your life and give thanks for someone who has helped you? If so, why not get in touch with them, if you can, and let them know how thankful you are? We all need help from time to time, especially those young in years or faith. Another thing to consider is this: who are you helping at the moment? Is there a young person you know who could do with some help, or someone who is young in their faith and could do with your prayers and guidance? God guides and provides, but he also uses us to encourage and inspire, so who can you be helping today?

DAVID WILLIAMS, AREA DEAN, AYLESBURY, AND TEAM RECTOR, RISBOROUGH, BUCKINGHAMSHIRE

Hezekiah's sickness

In those days Hezekiah became sick and was at the point of death. The prophet Isaiah son of Amoz came to him, and said to him, 'Thus says the Lord: Set your house in order, for you shall die; you shall not recover.' Then Hezekiah turned his face to the wall and prayed to the Lord: 'Remember now, O Lord, I implore you, how I have walked before you in faithfulness with a whole heart, and have done what is good in your sight.' Hezekiah wept bitterly.

2 KINGS 20:1–3 (NRSV)

Hezekiah is dying. The tone is abrupt. Illness is not sentimental. Nor is God. But that a prophet, not a doctor, announces this is a clue this will not be the end of the story. And so it proves. Hezekiah cries out to God, and before Isaiah has left the palace the diagnosis is reversed. Hezekiah will live long after all. He seeks, and is granted, supernatural confirmation, but the cure is a simple local remedy – a poultice of figs. Why this prescription had not been suggested before we are not told.

In the Bible, history is not simple factual record. We are 'shown' rather than 'told' things. Events happen – not always in order. People, and God, speak and act – but often without explanation. It is more like open theatre. We, the watchers, are invited to notice, question and discern, joining our faith and voices to theirs as we sift for meaning and gift for our time and context.

This story is one example.

Hezekiah was a king who cleansed land, temple and people from the terminal sickness of idolatry. He is named as 'prince of my people', in the direct line of King David. His deliverance from death also parallels the promise of the nation's deliverance from Assyria. This is no small matter, for the tiny kingdom of Judah lived under the constant threat of competing superpowers on its borders. But as the unfolding story will make clear, practising wise and trusting faith in such complex contexts is never straightforward.

Throughout this narrative, one conviction is never lost. The destiny of this nation, along with the empires that encircle it, is to be found in the story that God is telling – and only there.

DAVID RUNCORN, WRITER, SPEAKER AND SPIRITUAL DIRECTOR

A deeply spiritual material discovery

King Josiah… sent Shaphan… the secretary, to the house of the Lord, saying, 'Go up to the high priest Hilkiah, and have him count the entire sum of the money that has been brought into the house of the Lord… let them give it to the workers… and let them use it to buy timber and quarried stone to repair the house…' The high priest Hilkiah said to Shaphan the secretary, 'I have found the book of the law in the house of the Lord'… Shaphan then read it aloud to the king. When the king heard the words of the book of the law, he tore his clothes.

2 KINGS 22:3–11 (NRSV, abridged)

A good king tries to do the right thing by God and for the community. Josiah employs a huge workforce in the rebuilding of the Jerusalem temple. It seems that he is getting his priorities right. The money-offerings brought by worshippers are going to be used in its reconstruction. There's a feel-good element to it – we might read the first part of the story in 2 Kings 22 as a piece of 'good news journalism' to lift the spirits in hard times.

But when Josiah's emissary turns up to deliver the money, the High Priest doesn't even acknowledge it. He has already found something else, as solid as cash in its materiality, but priceless in its significance. Powerful mortals may use minions and go-betweens, but God's law speaks for itself and cuts to the heart. Realising that it shows up the spiritual cracks which need a different sort of restoring than the structure and decoration of the temple, Josiah first laments before God in the traditional way, and then, as the story continues, sends his messengers to find someone to draw out further, or 'exegete', what it means for them all.

He is promised that he will die peacefully before the disaster from long years of neglecting the word of God comes upon the people; but this double-edged news doesn't stop him from trying to put things right in the present. The prophetic word may not always be entirely accurate in its detail: Josiah will die in battle, but he won't have to witness the temple's destruction and the kingdom's fall. 'Thank God they didn't have to experience this' can sometimes be a genuine prayer of gratitude in dark times.

HAZEL SHERMAN, MINISTER, WEST WORTHING BAPTIST CHURCH,
AND CHAPLAIN, WESTERN SUSSEX HOSPITALS NHS FOUNDATION TRUST

Outside help

The king said unto me, Why is thy countenance sad, seeing thou art not sick? this is nothing else but sorrow of heart. Then I was very sore afraid, And said unto the king, Let the king live forever: why should not my countenance be sad, when the city, the place of my fathers' sepulchres, lieth waste, and the gates thereof are consumed with fire? Then the king said unto me, For what dost thou make request? So I prayed to the God of heaven... And the king granted me, according to the good hand of my God upon me.

NEHEMIAH 2:2–5A, 8b (KJV)

The fierce isolationism of the Hebrews is a constant theme throughout the Old Testament. It was sometimes interpreted as racial purity, although at other times mixed marriages were permitted – but all the way through, the Jews were to rely on God and God alone. And yet here is the vital work that Nehemiah has been given – rebuilding the walls of Jerusalem – made possible only by the grace of Artaxerxes, ruler of the Achaemenid Empire, a Zoroastrian.

He had probably secured his throne by violence. Nehemiah, serving as the king's cupbearer, was 'sore afraid' to be discovered not displaying the cheerfulness that the court clearly required. Artaxerxes quizzes him, hears of his anxiety about the ruined state of Jerusalem and, instead of a reprimand, gives Nehemiah leave to sort it out, supplying timber and an armed escort. This last proved necessary, given the attitude of the local magnates, Sanballat the Horonite and 'Tobias, the servant, the Ammonite' who, despite the poetry of their names, turn out to be hostile and obstructive.

So, although the rebuilding is a DIY job, it would not have happened without outside help. But of course, there is no 'outside' where God is concerned. The author is careful to ascribe the king's generosity to the 'good hand' of God; but he doesn't disguise the involvement of someone of another race and creed. It's a lesson that some Christians might want to remember. God loves it when believers muck in and solve problems themselves. But there must be times when God wonders: 'Why don't they just call in the professionals? After all, they work for me, too.'

PAUL HANDLEY, EDITOR, *CHURCH TIMES*

Wise response to opposition

When Sanballat, Tobiah, the Arabs, the Ammonites and the people of Ashdod heard that the repairs to Jerusalem's walls had gone ahead and that the gaps were being closed, they were very angry. They all plotted together to come and fight against Jerusalem and stir up trouble against it. But we prayed to our God and posted a guard day and night to meet this threat.

NEHEMIAH 4:7–9 (NIV)

Nehemiah's experience of rebuilding the walls of Jerusalem after the return from exile shows us that, even when we are faithfully doing the work of God and following his call, we can face opposition. As with Nehemiah, this can come in the form of hostility, ridicule or at times even direct physical attack. How are we to respond in a way that is both wise and godly?

I am struck that Nehemiah's first and instant response was to pray. Even before finishing his description of the opposition they faced, Nehemiah cries out to God for deliverance, protection and vindication. And whatever form the opposition we face may take, our first and wisest response must be to mirror Nehemiah's example and to turn to God in prayer.

But it is also striking that Nehemiah had a wonderfully practical spirituality. Alongside prayer, he posted a guard so that they would be ready to meet the threat against them. The chapter goes on to describe how, throughout the work of rebuilding the wall, half of the men did the building, while the other half stood alert, armed with spears and shields, ready to defend the workers from attack when it came.

I hear in this advance echoes of Jesus' instructions to Peter, James and John in the garden of Gethsemane, that they should both watch and pray, and also his instruction to all of his disciples – us included – that we should adopt this same wonderfully earthy double attitude, that in our response to opposition, we should be 'shrewd as snakes and as innocent as doves' (Matthew 10:16, NRSV).

So, whatever form opposition may take, let us learn from and follow the example of Nehemiah: look to God in prayer, and look to the resources he has given us – including the people he's given to stand alongside us. And as we do so, may we also mirror Nehemiah's experience and find that where God calls us to a task, he is faithful to bring us through all opposition to a fruitful conclusion.

GAVIN COLLINS, BISHOP OF DORCHESTER

Purpose in adversity

But when the attendants delivered the king's command, Queen Vashti refused to come. Then the king became furious and burned with anger… 'Therefore, if it pleases the king, let him issue a royal decree and let it be written in the laws of Persia and Media, which cannot be repealed, that Vashti is never again to enter the presence of King Xerxes. Also let the king give her royal position to someone else who is better than she.'

ESTHER 1:12, 19 (NIV)

When we face difficult decisions, hurt or rejection, we may find it hard to see beyond the present moment. Yet unexpected challenges, pain or disappointment can be a catalyst for change and have a purpose far greater than we understand at the time.

Today's passage tells the story of the deposing of Queen Vashti after she refused to appear before King Xerxes. There is no detail given of the exact nature of the king's request or the reasons for her refusal to comply, but her defiance made a way for the queen who replaced her. She sets the scene for Esther to take her place in history and play her part in God's plan to rescue her people from destruction. The story of Esther has become one of the most powerful examples of God's plans at work through the bravery of unlikely people.

Reflecting back on some of the hardest times in our life, we often realise that the challenges we encountered or an unexpected change in our circumstances paved the way for something better. It can be so hard to see any positives in pain, hurt or humiliation, but when we are under duress we can find new strength, and often some of the most significant growth happens. The Bible reminds us that every season has a purpose and God works for our good in every difficulty we face (Romans 8:28). What feels like a disaster at the time is often the very thing God will use for good in our lives.

Know that you are exactly where you are meant to be. The struggles you face today are preparing you for something significant. Remember that God can rebuild you or reveal a new beginning out of the adversity you're going through.

CLAIRE DANIEL, AUTHOR AND SPEAKER

A text for our times

Look, O Lord, and see how worthless I have become. Is it nothing to you, all you who pass by? Look and see if there is any sorrow like my sorrow, which was brought upon me, which the Lord inflicted on the day of his fierce anger.

LAMENTATIONS 1:11b–12 (NRSV)

In Lamentations 1 we hear the situation of Jerusalem, lonely and comfortless after the destruction brought by the Babylonians in 586BC. We hear the city personified as a widow crying out in agonised lament to God at the catastrophe she faces.

It's a text for our times. The first line is painfully relevant as we recall lockdowns: 'How lonely sits the city that once was full of people!' (v. 1). Lamentations offers a roadmap through the valley of the shadow of death. This is not the way of avoidance, or denial, but the pathway of honesty. Hear the direct expression of pain and despair, the cry of profound loneliness: 'My eyes flow with tears; for a comforter is far from me' (v. 16). It is the cry of faith from one squeezed in the vice of suffering: 'My heart is wrung within me, because I have been very rebellious' (v. 20). She refuses to duck her responsibility for her situation, but still calls out to the Lord. There is tremendous courage here.

The book of Lamentations is a gift. To cry out to God from the place of despair is a confession of faith. To rage at the absence of light is to declare that you know the light. Lamentations is a poem painted in grey and muted tones: loneliness, grief, betrayal, sorrow; a world away from frothy worship songs and easy grace. The glory days are gone, replaced by darkness, accompanied by the soundtrack of suffering and mockery. It's a text to accompany images of NHS workers, faces bruised by masks; coffins stacked up; empty streets; soaring infection figures; raging twitterstorms; political maelstrom; businesses gone bust. It's a bleak read. But...

Lamentations is a statement of confession and a declaration of faith. The voice of lament screams into the night and in so doing she declares her faith in the light. Whatever lies behind and whatever we face, Lamentations urges us to radical trust in God, expressed with courageous and penitent honesty. It's a text for our times.

KATE BRUCE, RAF CHAPLAIN

Resurrection hope

I saw a great many bones on the floor of the valley, bones that were very dry. [The Spirit of the Lord] asked me, 'Son of man, can these bones live?' I said, 'Sovereign Lord, you alone know.' Then he said to me, 'Prophesy to these bones and say to them, "Dry bones, hear the word of the Lord! This is what the Sovereign Lord says to these bones: I will make breath enter you, and you will come to life… Then you will know that I am the Lord."'

EZEKIEL 37:2–6 (NIV, abridged)

In 597 BC the Israelites were taken into exile in Babylon. There could have been no greater crisis. God's people were distraught. Prophets such as Jeremiah, Isaiah and Ezekiel tried to remind them that, even in the desert of exile, they could still rely on God, who had brought them through the wilderness. But the people Ezekiel sees in the valley are dead. Surely there is no hope for them?

God, however, has a resurrection plan. He calls Ezekiel to speak to the bones. Ezekiel speaks God's creative, restorative word, and the bones come together; muscles and flesh grow back over them. He speaks again, and God's Spirit comes and brings life to the inanimate bodies.

Note the two stages of resurrection here. The Spirit is needed for complete transformation: God's word and Spirit working together to do what no other power, politician, product or programme could do. The lifeless people of Israel are resurrected. A secure future, a homecoming, is promised.

If we are looking to bring transformation to the world around us, a resurrection mindset is what will make the difference. We need to know God's word and proclaim it in the power of his Holy Spirit; read the Bible regularly and try to understand it better; speak God's truth in love and trust that it will be effective; pray with prophetic faith; remind ourselves of God's promises whenever we are struggling.

The bones couldn't help themselves; they were too far gone. Are there people we know who are in despair, so far from the fullness of life God longs to give? How can we be Ezekiel to them? How can we 'prophesy to the breath' so that it fills them, offering words of light and life to dispel shadows and death? And if we feel that we ourselves are the dry bones, well, then, God help us. And that's not an exclamation of despair, but a statement of confidence, because he can!

OLIVIA WARBURTON, HEAD OF CONTENT CREATION AND LIVING FAITH LEAD, BRF, AND JOINT EDITOR, *GUIDELINES*

Where is God at work?

But Daniel resolved not to defile himself with the royal food and wine, and he asked the chief official for permission not to defile himself in this way. Now God had caused the official to show favour and compassion to Daniel, but the official told Daniel, 'I am afraid of my lord the king, who has assigned your food and drink. Why should he see you looking worse than the other young men of your age? The king would then have my head because of you.'

DANIEL 1:8–10 (NIV)

Pause for a moment. Where do you think God might be at work in your life?

Daniel and his friends find themselves in exile in a foreign land under a foreign king with foreign ways. It would have been easy for them to hunker down and hope for a time when they might return to their land and how things had been in the past. But they didn't.

Daniel 1 is a beautiful reminder of God at work wherever we find ourselves. Three times in the chapter we hear of his hand influencing things in unexpected ways (vv. 2, 9, 17). Perhaps it is because of this confidence that God is with them that Daniel dares not to 'defile himself with the royal food and wine'. So he engages wisely with the chief official, not making a demand but asking for permission to act differently to others, and then giving a sensible way for the official to protect his own life (vv. 11–16).

God grants Daniel and his friends 'favour' and gives them 'knowledge and understanding' (v. 17) so that they outshine all the others in the kingdom (v. 19). He has things he wants them to do in the unfolding story of this foreign land.

Many of us will have our 'foreign land', a place where we wonder if God is present – our workplace, place of education, community, street, even home. Yet the book of Daniel reminds us that God is with us, working in unexpected ways to enable us to live as ambassadors of the King, wisely engaging with those around us as we seek to faithfully represent his kingdom.

Ponder: what might that look like for you today, this week? Pray for the ability to see what he is doing and for the courage to join in.

JAMES LAWRENCE, LEADERSHIP PRINCIPAL, CPAS

Faith under fire

Nebuchadnezzar said to them, 'Is it true, Shadrach, Meshach and Abednego, that you do not serve my gods or worship the image of gold I have set up?...' Shadrach, Meshach and Abednego replied to him, 'King Nebuchadnezzar, we do not need to defend ourselves before you in this matter. If we are thrown into the blazing furnace, the God we serve is able to deliver us from it, and he will deliver us from Your Majesty's hand. But even if he does not, we want you to know, Your Majesty, that we will not serve your gods or worship the image of gold you have set up.'

DANIEL 3:14, 16–18 (NIV)

The story of Shadrach, Meshach and Abednego being thrown into a furnace is one of the best-known passages in the Bible. Christians seem mostly interested in the mysterious fourth figure who is seen in the furnace with them (v. 25). Was this man an angel or an appearance of Jesus before the incarnation? He was certainly evidence that God is with his people in desperate situations.

But we should also reflect on the amazing faith of the three men. King Nebuchadnezzar erected a golden image and demanded that people worship it, showing his supreme rule (v. 1), but these men refused, as this would mean breaking the first two commandments (Exodus 20:3–5a). When threatened with death, they tell Nebuchadnezzar that they believe God's power can save them, and they continue to refuse.

This is already inspiring enough, but even more remarkable is what they say next. They declare their faith in God, their complete devotion to him, and their willingness to be killed rather than betray him. Their faith was strong enough whatever the cost, and whether or not God spared them. Their faith and devotion did not depend on a miraculous deliverance from persecution and death. We don't know if they even saw the fourth figure that Nebuchadnezzar saw when they were thrown into the furnace; nothing is said about that.

God does deliver them, and that miracle becomes a powerful testimony to Nebuchadnezzar and his officials. However, as Christians, we should pray for that same gift of faith, being prepared to suffer for the Lord – if it ever comes to that – rather than expect miraculous deliverance. In the words of Jesus, 'Blessed are those who are persecuted because of righteousness, for theirs is the kingdom of heaven' (Matthew 5:10).

WALTER RIGGANS, LEARNING AND DEVELOPMENT MANAGER, CONGREGATIONAL FEDERATION

Facing your pride

At the first light of dawn, the king got up and hurried to the lions' den. When he came near the den, he called to Daniel in an anguished voice, 'Daniel, servant of the living God, has your God, whom you serve continually, been able to rescue you from the lions?' Daniel answered, 'May the king live forever! My God sent his angel, and he shut the mouths of the lions. They have not hurt me, because I was found innocent in his sight. Nor have I ever done any wrong before you, Your Majesty.'

DANIEL 6:19–22 (NIV)

As one of the most exciting Old Testament stories, Daniel and the lions' den has been dramatically told in many a Sunday school. Quite rightly, the retelling usually focuses on Daniel's faithfulness and God's powerful intervention to save him; however, does the role of King Darius also have anything to teach us?

Having witnessed Daniel's exceptional qualities, Darius had it in mind to promote him, but, duped by the jealousy of other servants, the king's pride causes him to issue an edict that they know will be impossible for Daniel to comply with. Having fallen into their trap, Darius allows his most trusted servant to be thrown into the lions' den rather than repeal the decree and look weak in the eyes of others.

In his distress, however, even as Darius throws Daniel into the lions' den, he says, 'May your God, whom you serve continually, rescue you!' (v. 16) and is then unable to sleep or eat. At dawn, he heads straight back to the den and, overjoyed on discovering that God had indeed protected Daniel, he issues a new decree commanding his people to fear and reverence God, 'For he is the living God and he endures forever' (v. 26).

How many times in our own lives do we let pride get in the way and end up trapped by what others may think, rather than doing what we know is right? Proverbs 16:18 (MSG) says, 'First pride, then the crash – the bigger the ego, the harder the fall.' Yet however great our fall, God in his love always seeks to rescue us and give us the opportunity to turn from our pride and choose what God requires of us: 'To act justly and to love mercy and to walk humbly with your God' (Micah 6:8).

RACHEL GOTOBED, CAKE BAKER AND SCRIPT WRITER

Turning points

'Throw me into the sea,' Jonah said, 'and it will become calm again. I know that this terrible storm is all my fault.' Instead, the sailors rowed even harder to get the ship to the land. But the stormy sea was too violent for them, and they couldn't make it… Then the sailors picked Jonah up and threw him into the raging sea, and the storm stopped at once! The sailors were awestruck by the Lord's great power, and they offered him a sacrifice and vowed to serve him.

JONAH 1:12–13, 15–16 (NLT)

The book of Jonah tells how the God of love forgives and restores each person in this narrative and each one of us, despite initial rebellion. Notice the contrasts. Jonah refuses to take the word of God to a foreign land and to foreign people, and yet he finds himself revealing God to the sailors on board this ship. He does not want to save the people of Nineveh, but the sailors do all they possibly can to save him even at peril of their own lives. Jonah has turned away *from* God in verse 3, but the sailors who shouted to their own gods in verse 5 turn *to* God in verse 16.

So often we think that we can only contribute to God's plans through perfect service, but the book of Jonah reminds us that God can use us even when we mess up, even when we don't understand his plan or are reluctant to join in. Verse 12 is the turning point, the point at which Jonah admits that he has failed God and that therefore the storm is all his fault. The situation is not transformed immediately from that point forwards, but that is the pivot point of the account: when Jonah decides to work with God rather than against him. Amazing things happen as a result. When we are reluctant to join in God's plans, it is worth remembering that it is never too late for us to admit that we are going our own way and need to turn around. When we align ourselves with God, amazing things will happen.

Pause and reflect on where God is leading you. Maybe you are struggling. If so, ask God for strength and resolve to follow his leading.

ANDREW DIXON, AUTHOR AND PREACHER

Your will be done

But to Jonah this seemed very wrong, and he became angry. He prayed to the Lord, 'Isn't this what I said, Lord, when I was still at home? That is what I tried to forestall by fleeing to Tarshish. I knew that you are a gracious and compassionate God, slow to anger and abounding in love, a God who relents from sending calamity. Now, Lord, take away my life, for it is better for me to die than to live.' But the Lord replied, 'Is it right for you to be angry?'

JONAH 4:1–4 (NIV)

In the 2019 film of Louisa May Alcott's *Little Women*, Beth is gravely ill with scarlet fever. Her sister, Jo, wiping her forehead in the hope of reducing her temperature, reassures her that all will be well. Beth answers, 'We can't stop God's will.' Jo's reply echoes what so many of us feel as we struggle to control our lives. 'Well,' she says, 'God hasn't met my will yet; what Jo wills shall be done!'

Today's passage from the book of Jonah can release us from being hampered by our own desires and expectations. Jonah had already decided how he wanted his situation to play out and how God should be acting. His disappointment has turned to anger. God had not destroyed Nineveh as he had hoped and, like a petulant teenager, he stamps his foot and sulks. As my daughter used to exclaim when I read this story to her: 'Oh, grow up, Jonah the Groaner!'

But the reality is that all of us sometimes want to dictate terms with the almighty. At these times, our need for control can become a great burden. It can lead to despair, frustration or even anger. In facing those moments, it can be hugely liberating to remind ourselves that, ultimately, everything is in God's hands. As the 18th-century monastic Jean Pierre de Caussade put it, we need to 'abandon ourselves to divine providence'.

Surrendering to God does not mean giving in or giving up. And it certainly doesn't relinquish us from making stands for justice and righteousness and doing our part to usher in God's kingdom of compassion, hope, peace, equality and love. It does, though, liberate us from the burden of control, as we recognise God's ultimate sovereignty in whatever situation we face and as we affirm: 'not *my* will be done, but *thy* will be done'.

TRYSTAN OWAIN HUGHES, AUTHOR AND THEOLOGIAN

Rebuild the Lord's house

This is what the Lord Almighty says: 'These people say, "The time has not yet come to rebuild the Lord's house."' Then the word of the Lord came through the prophet Haggai: 'Is it a time for you yourselves to be living in your panelled houses, while this house remains a ruin?' Now this is what the Lord Almighty says: 'Give careful thought to your ways.'

HAGGAI 1:2–5 (NIV)

When the people of Israel returned from their exile in Babylon, they understandably wanted to rebuild what they had lost. However, when they started with their own homes rather than the temple (the Lord's home), they received this sharp rebuke. Through the prophet Haggai, they were told to 'give careful thought to your ways'.

I've never been a refugee or exile, but I have moved house more times than I would have liked. Every time I do so, I look at my new bedroom as a new prayer space. I think about where I could put a candle, where I could sit to read my Bible and how I could make the room feel contemplative and spiritual.

But that isn't building the Lord's house; that is me decorating my own 'panelled house'. God no longer resides in the Jewish temple, or in any of my bedrooms, but in the hearts of those who believe in him. If we really want to rebuild the Lord's house, we too must 'give careful thought' to our ways and work on our hearts. It's easy to look Christian on the outside while the state of our hearts remains 'a ruin'.

Luckily, we have the Holy Spirit to help us, just as the people of Israel had divine help when they faced the near-impossible task of rebuilding the temple after the exile (see the book of Ezra). For us, we rebuild the Lord's house every time we obey Jesus' commands: to love one another, to love the Lord and to do good.

After hearing this message from Haggai, the people of Israel 'obeyed the voice of the Lord their God' (v. 12). But before they even lifted one finger to start rebuilding the temple, God said, 'I am with you' (v. 13). It's an amazing truth that, no matter how much of a ruin we feel our spiritual lives are, God is still with us.

RACHEL TRANTER, EDITORIAL MANAGER, BRF, AND JOINT EDITOR, *GUIDELINES*

The refiner

'Then suddenly the Lord you are seeking will come to his temple; the messenger of the covenant, whom you desire, will come,' says the Lord Almighty. But who can endure the day of his coming? Who can stand when he appears? For he will be like a refiner's fire or a launderer's soap. He will sit as a refiner and purifier of silver; he will purify the Levites and refine them like gold and silver. Then the Lord will have men who will bring offerings in righteousness.

MALACHI 3:1b–3 (NIV)

Under Ezra's leadership the Jews had rebuilt the temple in 516BC. There had been many prophecies that the Lord would come and inhabit the temple. But in Malachi's day, some 80 years after the temple had been rebuilt, God's people were still waiting for them to come true. Malachi prophesised that the Lord would return to his temple suddenly. Simeon saw that promise fulfilled many years later in Luke 2, when, moved by the Spirit, he went into the temple courts as Mary and Joseph brought in the baby Jesus. Jesus was the Lord who had come to his temple.

While we imagine Jesus in many roles, I suspect 'refiner' is not one of the first that comes to mind. But three times Malachi emphasises this: Jesus is 'like a refiner's fire', 'he will sit as a refiner', 'he will… refine them'. Refining is the process by which unwanted elements are removed from a substance; for silver, that required melting it in a crucible over a hot furnace. Jesus' desire as the refiner is to remove the impurities of our character from us. He's looking for our growth in holiness.

What needs refining in your life? Verse 5 suggests a range of areas that the refiner might tackle in people's lives: misdirected faith, unfaithfulness in marriage, giving false testimony, oppressing the disadvantaged, depriving foreigners of justice and mistreating employees and contractors. As I was writing this, the Lord reminded me to pay our window cleaner on time!

The process of refining has finished and all the dross has been burned away when the refiner can look into the crucible and see their image plainly reflected in the molten silver. Ask the Holy Spirit to show you one way in which you might more fully reflect the character of Jesus today.

KEITH DUNNETT, VICAR, CHRIST CHURCH, ABINGDON

The story of the New Testament

For God so loved the world that he gave his only Son, so that everyone who believes in him may not perish but may have eternal life.

JOHN 3:16 (NRSV)

W E ARE not a people of a book, however interesting, challenging or thought-provoking that book is. We are the children of God, and have been made his heirs through the life, death and resurrection of his Son, Jesus Christ. We follow a person, not a page; the Word, not words.

That said, in the New Testament we are shown who Jesus is. We are offered stories of his life, his teachings and his love. The objects and actions of everyday life become infused with glory as the lilies of the field, wine for a wedding and the death of a friend help us understand how God's love inhabits every atom of creation, made perfect in Christ. We learn that we must act generously, love with abandonment, forgive freely. We learn from the examples of those first followers, and allow their journey to inform ours, as we follow The Way, by walking in his way, conscious always that Jesus is the path beneath our feet, the guide alongside us and the one who comes to meet us at our journey's end.

As you read and reflect, I join my prayer with that of the apostle Paul:

That with the eyes of your heart enlightened, you may know what is the hope to which he has called you, what are the riches of his glorious inheritance among the saints, and what is the immeasurable greatness of his power for us who believe, according to the working of his great power.
EPHESIANS 1:17–19

SALLY WELCH, VICAR, WRITER AND FORMER EDITOR, *NEW DAYLIGHT*

Surprised and scared, silent and speaking

Then an angel of the Lord appeared to him, standing at the right side of the altar of incense. When Zechariah saw him, he was startled and was gripped with fear. But the angel said to him: 'Do not be afraid, Zechariah; your prayer has been heard. Your wife Elizabeth will bear you a son, and you are to call him John.'

LUKE 1:11–13 (NIV)

What stops you in your tracks? An arresting image on a screen, a shock medical diagnosis, sudden job loss or, perhaps, an unexpected relationship change? In such circumstances, we often ask, 'Where is God?' Sometimes the event that disrupts the normal flow of our lives and stuns us into silence is a joyous one – an overwhelming gift, a surprise visit from a loved one, a remarkable act of grace beyond our imagining. In these situations, we may more easily recognise the presence of God and be prompted towards praise. Or sometimes, as in the experience of Zechariah, it can be hard in the moment to work out what is really going on.

The event that stopped Zechariah in his tracks, disrupting his priestly duty and leading to his imposed silence, was the appearance of an angel. Not unreasonably, Zechariah was surprised, scared and – like the shepherds later in the story – in need of reassuring words from the angel ('Do not be afraid'). However, unlike the shepherds, who responded with enthusiasm to what they had heard, Zechariah, in his bewilderment and confusion, responded with doubt. The consequence was Zechariah being made 'silent and not able to speak' (Luke 1:20) until the naming of the newborn son as John. As soon as this happened, though, Zechariah's 'mouth was opened and his tongue set free, and he began to speak, praising God' (Luke 1:64).

When we are stopped in our tracks – whether on account of great stress or great joy – the reassuring answer to the question 'Where is God?' can be 'God is with us'. In the ebb and flow of our lives, there will be times when we need to heed the words, spoken aloud by companions or whispered to our hearts by the Holy Spirit, 'Do not be afraid'. Our mix of doubt and trust is not a barrier to God's purposes being fulfilled in and through us. Through amazing grace our silence, as well as our speaking, can point to God's faithfulness and power.

CHRIS BARNETT, INTERGENERATIONAL MINISTRY (CHILDREN AND FAMILIES), UNITING CHURCH SYNOD OF VICTORIA AND TASMANIA

Embracing God in the unexpected

[The angel] came to her and said, 'Greetings, favoured one! The Lord is with you' But she was much perplexed by his words... 'Do not be afraid, Mary, for you have found favour with God. And now, you will conceive in your womb and bear a son, and you will name him Jesus'... Mary said to the angel, 'How can this be, since I am a virgin?' The angel said to her, 'The Holy Spirit will come upon you, and the power of the Most High will overshadow you'... Then Mary said, 'Here am I... let it be with me according to your word.'

LUKE 1:28–38 (NRSV, abridged)

Unexpected news can hit us like a hand grenade, exploding in happy surprise or dreadful shock. When the news is shocking, and devastates all our hopes and plans, fear, confusion, doubt and questioning may surface in our hearts, just as they did in Mary's.

When Gabriel appeared unexpectedly in her home that day, his announcement threatened everything in Mary's settled life: her plans, her reputation – life as she knew it. Her reaction is not a million miles from ours when unsettling news arrives – 'she was thoroughly shaken' (MSG), 'confused and disturbed' (TLB) – and her bewildered 'How can this be?' is echoed in our own lives as we try to make sense of what we are experiencing.

But what do we make of Mary's response – 'Here am I, the servant of the Lord; let it be with me according to your word'? What could inspire such wholehearted surrender to God?

'The Lord is with you.' It seems that Mary *trusted* Gabriel's words to her. Those words brought strength and comfort, displacing fear with faith and with the courage to embrace whatever the future held. As we face our own unexpected, disruptive, life-changing circumstances, Gabriel's words might address us too – inviting us to trust that the Lord is with us. Here. Now. Always. However unforeseen the circumstances, however great the upheaval, however impossible a good outcome may seem, the promise of God's presence with us is our steadying, redemptive hope.

One morning, a young girl said her 'Yes' to God and to the possibilities wrapped in the unexpected, and it made all the difference in the world. Literally. May we who know her Son breathe our own 'Yes' to that same God, come what may.

MAGS DUGGAN, AUTHOR, SPIRITUAL DIRECTOR AND RETREAT LEADER

Receiving encouragement from one another

At that time Mary got ready and hurried to a town in the hill country of Judea, where she entered Zechariah's home and greeted Elizabeth. When Elizabeth heard Mary's greeting, the baby leaped in her womb, and Elizabeth was filled with the Holy Spirit. In a loud voice she exclaimed: 'Blessed are you among women, and blessed is the child you will bear! But why am I so favoured, that the mother of my Lord should come to me? As soon as the sound of your greeting reached my ears, the baby in my womb leaped for joy. Blessed is she who has believed that the Lord would fulfil his promises to her!'

LUKE 1:39–45 (NIV)

Soon after Mary's visit from the angel, she travelled to visit Elizabeth. God had set in motion the most important event in history, and yet he still cared enough for Mary to let her know that her relative was enjoying an unexpected pregnancy too (v. 36).

Even though she was finally having her own longed-for baby, Elizabeth gladly celebrated the fact that Mary's had a far greater destiny. Her greeting must have flooded Mary with fresh faith. It is wonderful to see how even John, while still in the womb, recognised who Jesus was.

Mary stayed with Elizabeth for three months. I imagine she would have learned much from her older relative that she would have stored up to help her when others shunned her for being pregnant out of wedlock. It is this sense of receiving encouragement that I want to focus on. We have been made by God for community. That is why there are so many verses in the Bible about loving one another and encouraging each other. It is also challenging to think about whether we celebrate as well as Elizabeth when we can see God at work in greater measure in someone else's life. It is far too easy to fall into the trap of comparison; we are called, instead, to champion and cheer one another on.

We need those around us who recognise the giftings God has placed in us and encourage us to go deeper in our faith, and we need to do the same for others. God may bring someone into our lives for a season who has experienced a similar situation to our own and can share wisdom with us. Are we open and humble enough to notice that gift?

CLAIRE MUSTERS, AUTHOR, SPEAKER AND EDITOR

The birth of Christ

[Mary] gave birth to her firstborn, a son... And there were shepherds living out in the fields near by... An angel of the Lord appeared to them... The angel said to them, '... I bring you good news that will cause great joy for all the people... A Saviour has been born to you; he is the Messiah, the Lord. This will be a sign to you: you will find a baby... lying in a manger.' Suddenly a great company of the heavenly host appeared with the angel, praising God and saying, 'Glory to God... and on earth peace.'

LUKE 2:7–14 (NIV, abridged)

You probably know this story! The familiar words, sung in carols, performed in nativity plays – even sometimes included in Christmas cards. I love hearing them read in an ancient candlelit church or sung in a glorious rendering of Handel's *Messiah*.

Meet again the nativity-set characters: Mary and Joseph, forced far from home by a distant emperor's diktat; the baby, conceived in faith-stretchingly dubious circumstances and born in unwelcoming and unhealthy surroundings; the shepherds, widely regarded as desperately unreliable and yet the first to be told of this earth-shattering event – in their case, sky-shattering, as the angels sing.

The coming of Jesus was good news, of great joy. How vital that at Christmas, indeed all year round, Christians communicate that Jesus is still good news and full of joy! Jesus is the Saviour, the longed-for Messiah, the Lord.

And what is the 'sign' that this is true? It's a baby, lying in a manger. Almighty God has entered human history as a human being... as a tiny, helpless, totally dependent scrap of humanity. The word 'sign' can be translated 'miracle'; it often links with the word 'wonder'. At the heart of the Bible story is the God who shows his glory and brings peace on earth by being born as a baby. It's a sign of who God is, of what he's like. It's definitely a miracle, and a wonder.

Give yourself a few minutes alone to read these verses again; then close your eyes and imagine that your Father God has placed a tiny baby in your arms and whispered to you, 'This is my Son.' And you can reply, 'Thank you... for the glory, for the peace, for the miracle, for the sign.'

STEPHEN RAND, COMMUNICATOR AND CAMPAIGNER

Tightrope walkers

Now there was a man in Jerusalem whose name was Simeon... It had been revealed to him by the Holy Spirit that he would not see death before he had seen the Lord's Messiah. Guided by the Spirit, Simeon came into the temple; and when the parents brought in the child Jesus... Simeon took him in his arms and praised God, saying, 'Master, now you are dismissing your servant in peace, according to your word; for my eyes have seen your salvation, which you have prepared in the presence of all peoples.'

LUKE 2:25–31 (NRSV, abridged)

Simeon, and his female counterpart Anna (see vv. 36–38), despite their age, are tightrope walkers. They walk steadily along between their passionate commitment to the faith which has sustained their lives and an openness to something new, to what God is doing now.

They have been loyal to the law, the covenant of the Old Testament, for their entire lives, but this hasn't made them content to settle down where they are. Instead, it has set them on fire with hope for something more.

This is a tricky place to be. It's far easier to be either satisfied with the faith I have and how it shapes my life or dissatisfied, perhaps even disillusioned, with it and keen to move on, to try something new. To live firmly rooted in present faith, while being at the same time not just open to the new but eager for it, and full of faith that it will come in my time, is indeed a tightrope walk.

We're told of Simeon that 'the Holy Spirit rested on him' (v. 25). That living flame seems to have shaped his life and led him to the temple on this day. How did he know that this baby, out of all the babies being brought to the temple, was the one he'd been waiting for? His prayerful, expectant life had made him sensitive to what God was revealing, even though it was just a glimpse of the promised Messiah – not a conquering hero, but the tiny child of poor parents.

How ready are we to let go of our familiar faith and its expressions and to acknowledge God at work in the unfamiliar? We need the help of the Holy Spirit to lead us to the right place and to open our eyes.

HELEN JULIAN CSF, FORMERLY FRANCISCAN SISTER AND AUTHOR

King against king

After Jesus was born in Bethlehem in Judea, during the time of King Herod, Magi from the east came to Jerusalem and asked, 'Where is the one who has been born king of the Jews?'... When Herod realised that he had been outwitted by the Magi, he was furious, and he gave orders to kill all the boys in Bethlehem and its vicinity who were two years old and under, in accordance with the time he had learned from the Magi.

MATTHEW 2:1–2, 16 (NIV, abridged)

Herod the Great was in many ways a successful king – winning battles, riding the waves of political change and leaving a host of fine building projects. He was also an utter brute. His long reign was littered with the executions of anyone he suspected to be an opponent or rival. As he slowed down in old age, and sons jostled for succession, insecurity took over. Herod had his three eldest sons killed, and the slaughter in Bethlehem is horribly typical of that stage of his life.

The opening verses of Matthew 2 pit king against king: old versus new; fading tyrant and child Messiah; fear facing threat. Bethlehem had been King David's town, centuries earlier. So Jesus would bring a pedigree and promise that Herod could never match. God was stirring, and Herod's time was almost done. His reaction was ugly and terrible.

So what are this awful man and his evil massacre doing in the Christmas story? Pointing to Jesus' cross is one answer. Jesus is born into a rough world, and from the start he journeys in the shadow of violence towards his own degrading and savage death. Speaking of new power is a second answer. The torturers and troublers of the world bitterly resent the kingdom of God and of his Christ. Good news of hope and mercy always upsets and disturbs those who would grasp and destroy.

Christmas is not just a comfort zone. It is a challenging place, soured and shaken by Herod and his bloody schemes and darkened by the prospect of the cross. Yet in such a world Christians are called to be tough and tender, siding with the victims, speaking against the tyrants, serving without fear in the name of Jesus. The Herods always perish. Jesus lives.

JOHN PROCTOR, RETIRED MINISTER, UNITED REFORMED CHURCH

Doing what is needed

After [the wise men] had left, an angel of the Lord appeared to Joseph in a dream and said, 'Get up, take the child and his mother, and flee to Egypt, and remain there until I tell you; for Herod is about to search for the child, to destroy him.' Then Joseph got up, took the child and his mother by night, and went to Egypt, and remained there until the death of Herod. This was to fulfil what had been spoken by the Lord through the prophet, 'Out of Egypt I have called my son.'

MATTHEW 2:13–15 (NRSV)

No one wants to be told their child is threatened. This must have been doubly terrifying for Joseph, as the child in his care was the son of God! He therefore did what many parents have had to do and left under cover of darkness, travelling to the relative safety of an unknown land, presumably relying on the kindness of strangers as he tried to find accommodation and a means to buy food.

This Bible passage focuses on the fulfilment of the prophecy of Hosea, a reminder that God had kept his promises of a Saviour made hundreds of years before. Mary and Joseph's knowledge of the reality of God's promise alive in their arms, and his presence with them, must have kept them going through their long and treacherous journey as refugees, particularly as news spread of what was happening in Bethlehem, but that does not mean it wasn't challenging and frightening.

Fear can sometimes be crippling, but for many refugees it is the impetus to finding themselves on the move. It can also be our motive for not doing all we can to welcome those in need. Jesus said that when we provide nourishment and comfort for those in need, it is as if we are caring for him (Matthew 25:35–40). I wonder if, as he said these words, he was remembering the worried whispered conversations of his parents, and the relief of generous and welcoming smiles and provision as they settled into their new community.

Either way, this terrifying and brutal, and therefore often overlooked, part of the Christmas story reminds us that Jesus knows what it is to be a refugee and what he would like us to do in response.

CAROLYN EDWARDS, CHILDREN AND YOUTH ADVISER, DIOCESE OF YORK

From fear to faith

After three days they found him in the temple courts… When his parents saw him, they were astonished. His mother said to him, 'Son, why have you treated us like this? Your father and I have been anxiously searching for you.' 'Why were you searching for me?' he asked. 'Didn't you know I had to be in my Father's house?' But they did not understand what he was saying to them. Then he went down to Nazareth with them and was obedient to them. But his mother treasured all these things in her heart.

LUKE 2:46, 48–51 (NIV)

Jesus is twelve years old when his parents fear they've lost him on a trip to Jerusalem. As observant Jews, they travelled 80 miles from Nazareth to celebrate Passover. A day into their journey home, Mary and Joseph realise Jesus isn't with them. They imagine he must be with friends and relatives they'd travelled with – he isn't. Where is he?

We sense their hearts racing as they look for him. Three long days later, they find Jesus in conversation with experienced rabbis in the temple. Here we get a glimpse of Jesus, the man. His unique knowledge and insight, for a boy his age, amaze everyone around him. His parents are astonished too. Yet, with this growth and independence comes conflict.

Jesus affirms what the angel told Mary at his conception: he is God's son. But in that moment, he is also her child, and she thought she'd lost him. By staying in the temple, Jesus has driven his earthly parents wild with worry, and they don't understand what he is saying.

Mary is anxious because she is human. Her faithfulness comes from how she manages this fear. Although she doesn't understand Jesus, Mary listens and lets his words take root in her heart. Here any sense to be made will come from a loving rather than a fearful space.

If only we stopped worrying about children at age twelve! How often do we feel, 'Why have you treated us like this?' when our loved one's actions have nothing to do with us? Sometimes we worry because we aren't seeing others as they truly are, and then we are surprised by their strength and capability.

For times when we struggle to understand, ask Jesus to help us listen and manage our anxieties, to move our hearts from fear to faith.

CARMEL THOMASON, AUTHOR, JOURNALIST AND SPEAKER

Natural temptations

The crowds asked [John], 'What then should we do?' In reply he said to them, 'Whoever has two coats must share with anyone who has none; and whoever has food must do likewise.' Even tax-collectors came to be baptised, and they asked him, 'Teacher, what should we do?' He said to them, 'Collect no more than the amount prescribed for you.' Soldiers also asked him, 'And we, what should we do?' He said to them, 'Do not extort money from anyone by threats or false accusation, and be satisfied with your wages.'

LUKE 3:10–14 (NRSV)

These verses, among the least-quoted from the biblical account of the ministry of John the Baptist, are crucial. The Dead Sea Scrolls, discovered less than a hundred years ago, demonstrated that there was no shortage of religious ascetics heading off to find a purer life in the deserts of first-century Palestine. But John's appeal goes well beyond the pious. Soldiers, when they appear in the gospels, are Gentile enforcers of hated Roman rule. Tax collectors may be Jewish by faith, but they were widely discounted as collaborators. 'The crowds' is a term most commonly used to refer to the easily swayed, uneducated poor. John is calling to God's kingdom the very dregs of society.

As Jesus himself will do later (Matthew 28:19–20), John forges a firm link between baptism and behaviour. Moreover, what he offers are no mere general platitudes; his commands are specific to the conditions of his questioners. The poor are urged to resist the temptation to cling tightly to the little they have. Tax collectors are to eschew the chance to levy that bit extra to fill their own coffers. Soldiers are to forgo the opportunities to extort money by brute force. John's call to repentance directs each of us to pay attention to the particular ways our station in life, and our work, open us up to sin.

Such repentance may begin in the heart, but it doesn't confine itself to establishing a new inner disposition. It seeks to break and renew us, forming us into the likeness of Christ. Too hard to achieve in our own strength, it becomes a prayer that the Holy Spirit come to our aid; calling us back to the assurance of that self-same Spirit which lies at the heart of Christian baptism.

DAVID WALKER, BISHOP OF MANCHESTER

The baptism of Jesus

Then Jesus came from Galilee to John at the Jordan, to be baptised by him. John would have prevented him, saying, 'I need to be baptised by you, and do you come to me?' But Jesus answered him, 'Let it be so now; for it is proper for us in this way to fulfil all righteousness.' Then he consented. And when Jesus had been baptised, just as he came up from the water, suddenly the heavens were opened to him and he saw the Spirit of God descending like a dove and alighting on him. And a voice from heaven said, 'This is my Son, the Beloved, with whom I am well pleased.'

MATTHEW 3:13–17 (NRSV)

Picture a classroom and a new child being presented to the class. The teacher starts by saying, 'This is…', and goes on to tell the class a little about the new child standing there, perhaps a little nervously, before all her new classmates. But the teacher gets the other pupils' attention and eases the way for the new child to be welcomed among them. Imagine what they are thinking.

I feel that Matthew portrays Jesus' baptism as God's presentation of Jesus to John and to the crowd. He changes Mark's personal declaration 'You are' (Mark 1:11) to the more public and objective statement 'This is' (Matthew 3:17). Jesus' obedience in undergoing baptism brings the response from God not simply for his own assurance but for all who are willing to hear.

Here for the first time, in words from Isaiah 42:1 and Psalm 2:7, Jesus is proclaimed as 'Son of God', a declaration repeated on the mountaintop (Matthew 17:5), with the disciples told to listen to him. His baptism in the river Jordan, identifying with suffering and sinful humanity, is a foretaste of his baptism of the cross. The Son of God, who trusts in God with his very self and is loved by and pleasing to God, will undergo a greater and more far-reaching baptism for the sake of all. He will again be proclaimed as Son of God, this time by a hardened Roman centurion watching him die (Matthew 27:54). Will we welcome this Son of God in our midst today?

TERRY HINKS, UNITED REFORMED CHURCH MINISTER AND AUTHOR

Lead us not into temptation

The tempter... said to him, 'If you are the Son of God, command these stones to become loaves of bread.' But [Jesus] answered, 'It is written, "One does not live by bread alone, but by every word that comes from the mouth of God."' Then the devil took him to the holy city and placed him on the pinnacle of the temple, saying to him, 'If you are the Son of God, throw yourself down...' Jesus said to him, 'Again it is written, "Do not put the Lord your God to the test."' Again, the devil... showed him all the kingdoms of the world and their splendour; and he said to him, 'All these I will give you, if you will fall down and worship me.' Jesus said to him, 'Away with you, Satan! for it is written, "Worship the Lord your God, and serve only him."'

MATTHEW 4:3–10 (NRSV, abridged)

We know it is part of God's plan for Satan to tempt Jesus, because the Holy Spirit leads him to where it must take place. Three times Satan offers Jesus something in the hope it will do the trick. The first temptation is about food, not to persuade Jesus to eat (he has fasted for 40 days, and there is nothing sinful in eating bread) but as a means to an end – to tempt Jesus to check that his calling from God is real. 'If you're the Son of God, do a little miracle,' he wheedles. The plan fails.

Next, he goes up a gear: nothing so trivial as food. Again, he offers Jesus a chance to prove his true identity, but this time with a miraculous rescue from death. We already know from the other end of the gospel that this won't work; Jesus is not afraid enough of death to commit sin as a way of avoiding it. On his third go, Satan gives up targeting Jesus' doubts about his identity as Son of God. That is not going to work. Now he offers the whole world in exchange for rejecting God.

Jesus comes through the temptations, but we are left in no doubt how powerful and cunning they were. It's a reminder of how insidious the temptations which beset us can be. We need to remember that he tells Satan, 'Get out of my way!' These can be our words, too, whenever temptation besets us.

CALLY HAMMOND, DEAN AND DIRECTOR OF STUDIES IN THEOLOGY,
GONVILLE AND CAIUS COLLEGE, CAMBRIDGE

Stop, look and listen

When they had done so, they caught such a large number of fish that their nets began to break… When Simon Peter saw this, he fell at Jesus' knees and said, 'Go away from me, Lord; I am a sinful man!' For he and all his companions were astonished at the catch of fish they had taken, and so were James and John, the sons of Zebedee, Simon's partners. Then Jesus said to Simon, 'Don't be afraid; from now on you will fish for people.' So they pulled their boats up on shore, left everything and followed him.

LUKE 5:6, 8–11 (NIV)

How many of you remember the Green Cross Code? Stop – Look – Listen. It was to help us get safely across the road as children. Today's Bible passage can help us get safely through life and we can learn a lot from it, as the disciples had to stop, look and listen.

Stop: It is interesting to note that Jesus called the disciples to follow him in their everyday lives. When they had set out the night before, they probably did not know it was going to be a special day; it seemed like any other day to them. Then something astonishing happened which caused them to stop in their tracks. They had not caught many fish up until that point. Then Jesus came along, they witnessed a miracle and they stopped in amazement. When did God last stop you in your tracks?

Look: Can you imagine what it must have been like for the disciples to see the boats teeming with fish, so many that they could not count them? They didn't understand what was happening, and Jesus had to tell them not to be afraid. How many miracles of God do we miss in our everyday lives because we do not take the time to look around us at what he is doing? When did you last see one of God's miracles in your life?

Listen: The purpose of the miracle was not just for the disciples to be amazed – there was a greater purpose. Jesus used it to call the disciples to something much greater; to have an impact in his kingdom, by 'fishing for people'. We are told that they listened and followed him. Are you ready to listen to what God is calling you to today?

SHARON PRIOR, SENIOR TUTOR, MOORLANDS COLLEGE

Mother knows best?

On the third day there was a wedding in Cana of Galilee, and the mother of Jesus was there. Jesus and his disciples had also been invited to the wedding. When the wine gave out, the mother of Jesus said to him, 'They have no wine.' And Jesus said to her, 'Woman, what concern is that to you and to me? My hour has not yet come.' His mother said to the servants, 'Do whatever he tells you.' Now standing there were six stone water-jars for the Jewish rites of purification... Jesus said to them, 'Fill the jars with water.'

JOHN 2:1–7 (NRSV, abridged)

Thinking about it, this, Jesus' first miracle, is quite domestic and seems almost trivial compared to the majority of the other life-changing miracles in the gospels. These include physical healing and even being raised from death, yet here we are at a wedding where the guests had already finished off the wine provided, and Jesus creates even more!

It's interesting to note that it's Mary, Jesus' mother, who points out the need – and gives him a nudge towards this first miracle. Jesus' response seems quite abrupt: 'Woman, what concern is that to you and me? My hour has not yet come' (v. 4). It seems that Mary has received a prompt. There are references to Mary in Luke's gospel which describe her as thoughtful and 'pondering' on what she is learning – from the shepherds' visit to the stable and when Jesus gets lost in the temple as a boy. Mary tells Jesus off for worrying them, but also treasures this event in her heart. Perhaps Jesus the man needed her sensitive encouragement, her openness to God's guidance, as he began his ministry.

We also know from reading the whole passage that there is powerful symbolism: the water came from the jars used in Jewish purification – a sign that Jesus had come to bring purification to the world in a new way, through his death. His first miracle occurred at a wedding, and this points to the heavenly banquet prepared for all God's people. It also 'revealed his glory' (v. 11), inspiring faith in his disciples.

But I'm also encouraged that Jesus, encouraged by his mother, met human need in a very practical yet awesome way. I pray that you are able to experience Jesus in this way too – and point others to signs of Jesus in their lives.

DEBBIE ORRISS, PIONEER EVANGELIST, CHURCH ARMY

Topsy-turvy values

Blessed are the poor in spirit, for theirs is the kingdom of heaven. Blessed are those who mourn, for they will be comforted. Blessed are the meek, for they will inherit the earth. Blessed are those who hunger and thirst for righteousness, for they will be filled. Blessed are the merciful, for they will be shown mercy. Blessed are the pure in heart, for they will see God. Blessed are the peacemakers, for they will be called children of God. Blessed are those who are persecuted because of righteousness, for theirs is the kingdom of heaven.

MATTHEW 5:3–10 (NIV)

There has been a vogue in recent years to focus on 'happiness' as an indicator of well-being, as opposed to income or wealth. But what does it mean to be happy? For Jesus, as he teaches about the kingdom of heaven, more important than the subjective sense of happiness is the objective reality of being blessed by God. To be blessed is to be made happy by God.

Jesus sets out qualities that should define Christian character: the means of blessing, with a down payment now and fulfilment in heaven. They may surprise or even shock us, because they are the inverse of the world's values. The world lauds material wealth acquired through power and strength. Jesus, by contrast, commends spiritual qualities characterised by poverty and weakness. Christians are to acknowledge their spiritual poverty, grieve over their sinfulness, show a humble and gentle attitude to others and hunger for righteousness. Such attitudes before God will be reflected in their behaviour to others: showing mercy, being sincere and seeking reconciliation.

Even more surprisingly, perhaps, these topsy-turvy values lead to persecution – hardly something most people associate with happiness. Yet, this mark of Christian authenticity is well attested by saints past and present; it was the experience of Christ's first followers and continues today. No wonder Jesus says persecution should be a source of rejoicing (Matthew 5:12).

The world's values are all around us. They are unavoidable, but we can escape their influence if we immerse ourselves in God's word, meditating on it day and night (Joshua 1:8). Let us pray for God's Holy Spirit to open our eyes to perceive spiritual realities, which will develop the qualities that Jesus specifies. Therein God's blessing is to be found.

KEITH CIVVAL, FORMER CHAIR, SCRIPTURE UNION, AND FORMER TRUSTEE, WYCLIFFE BIBLE TRANSLATORS

Seeing their faith

**Some people came, bringing to him a paralysed man, carried by four of them...
When Jesus saw their faith, he said to the paralytic, 'Son, your sins are forgiven.'
Now some of the scribes were sitting there, questioning in their hearts, 'Why
does this fellow speak in this way? It is blasphemy! Who can forgive sins but
God alone?'... [Jesus] said to them, 'Why do you raise such questions in your
hearts? Which is easier, to say to the paralytic, 'Your sins are forgiven', or to
say, 'Stand up and take your mat and walk?'**

MARK 2:3, 5–9 (NRSV)

It's good to have friends. They can be our support and encouragement and a
reminder that we're not alone and that we are loved. In times of joy, friends
celebrate with us, and in times of sorrow or need, they offer us strength.

In this story, it's the paralysed man that is the focus of our attention, his
vulnerability and helplessness put centre stage. It's he to whom Jesus reaches
out with gentleness and generosity, offering the opportunity for a new beginning, freed from the disability that has made him dependent upon the charity
of others. Yet it is the man's friends who make this healing possible. They
carry him to the house where Jesus is speaking, they lift him up to the roof
when crowds block their way, they dig through the roof covering and lower
him down upon his mat at the Saviour's feet. Without their efforts, the man
would have remained unseen.

Jesus offers mental and physical healing, gently forgiving the man his sins
and then commanding him to stand up and walk. But he does this seeing the
faith of the man's friends. The implication is that they are the ones who believe
that Jesus can bring about a miraculous transformation; they who have made
the effort to place their comrade in front of the teacher who heals, despite
the difficulties they face in entering into his presence. Their trust in Christ is
rewarded as their friend takes up his mat and walks.

It's a reminder that surrounding ourselves with good friends can be a
blessing that can help us to sustain our own faith at times when it is under
strain. It's a reminder too that Jesus' love reaches out to all in need. All we
have to do is ask.

AMANDA BLOOR, ARCHDEACON OF CLEVELAND

Diversity and inclusion

Now during those days he went out to the mountain to pray; and he spent the night in prayer to God. And when day came, he called his disciples and chose twelve of them, whom he also named apostles: Simon, whom he named Peter, and his brother Andrew, and James, and John, and Philip, and Bartholomew, and Matthew, and Thomas, and James son of Alphaeus, and Simon, who was called the Zealot, and Judas son of James, and Judas Iscariot, who became a traitor.

LUKE 6:12–16 (NRSV)

What it is to be included and to be chosen! From those who had responded to his call to follow and be disciples, Jesus chooses twelve to have a particular role. This is clearly an important and careful decision, because Jesus goes up a mountain, a sign of meeting with God, and prays all night. And Luke thinks it important to name them for us (and does so again in Acts 1). So, we might ponder two particular things.

First, the fact that Jesus calls twelve apostles seems to be a deliberate echo of the twelve tribes of Israel in the Old Testament and an indication that in Jesus God is restoring and making new his people. They will have a role to play in Jesus' mission, but more than that they have a representative role; they are the beginning of a whole new people of God.

Second, there seem to be some hints about the diversity of the group. Matthew, we learn from Matthew's gospel, was a tax collector; Philip was a Jew but has a Greek name; there was a second Simon, called the Zealot, maybe to distinguish him from Simon Peter, but Zealots were those who often adopted violent opposition to the Romans; and there was also a traitor called Judas. Yes, they were all male and Jewish, but they demonstrated a wide range of backgrounds and personalities.

After Jesus has called his apostles, he begins teaching: not just the apostles but a whole crowd of disciples with even greater diversity. Jesus calls twelve not to exclude others, but to point to a new people where, down on level ground, all are called to listen, learn and belong. It means that we can be included, but we can also include those who may be quite different from us.

ANTHONY CLARKE, SENIOR TUTOR, REGENT'S PARK COLLEGE, OXFORD

Faith at a distance

Jesus went with them, but when he was not far from the house, the centurion sent friends to say to him, 'Lord, do not trouble yourself, for I am not worthy to have you come under my roof; therefore I did not presume to come to you. But only speak the word, and let my servant be healed'… When Jesus heard this he was amazed at him, and turning to the crowd that followed him, he said, 'I tell you, not even in Israel have I found such faith.'

LUKE 7:6–7, 9 (NRSV)

'I don't get what this Jesus guy has to do with my life today.' The man said these words to me in a tone of slightly bemused curiosity. He wasn't averse to talking about Jesus (we were in a pub where I had just held a 'grill the bishop' event), but he couldn't make the connection. He was voicing the concern of many people today, who wonder why we continue to talk about and worship a person who lived so long ago, in a place so far away.

It seems that Luke had two particular reasons for including this story in his gospel.

The remarkable healing of the centurion's servant is a clear sign that Jesus is the 'coming one', the Messiah (see Jesus' response to the messengers from John the Baptist in Luke 7:18–23). As such, Jesus is inaugurating the kingdom of God with signs of the healing and blessing that God intends for all creation.

Yet the story is also remarkable for the faith of the centurion, who dares to believe that Jesus can cure his servant with a word and doesn't need to be physically present to do this. Luke is saying to his readers (or listeners) that this man, a Gentile and an officer in the Roman army, had faith in Jesus, so you too, even though you have never met Jesus in the flesh and live far away from Israel, can trust him for all your needs.

So my response to the man in the pub was a simple invitation: join with the centurion in saying 'only speak the word, and let me be healed' – and you'll start to see why some of us love talking about him so much.

MARTYN SNOW, BISHOP OF LEICESTER

The seed and the soils

While a large crowd was gathering and people were coming to Jesus from town after town, he told this parable: 'A farmer went out to sow his seed. As he was scattering the seed, some fell along the path; it was trampled on, and the birds ate it up. Some fell on rocky ground, and when it came up, the plants withered because they had no moisture. Other seed fell among thorns, which grew up with it and choked the plants. Still other seed fell on good soil. It came up and yielded a crop, a hundred times more than was sown.' When he said this, he called out, 'Whoever has ears to hear, let them hear.'

LUKE 8:4–8 (NIV)

Sowing seed is not something we immediately connect with in our hyper-technological world. Perhaps sharing posts, forwarding emails or retweeting would be a better cultural reference for today. Yet the story of the sower is a well-known, well-loved parable, and, despite its fame, there remain things to learn, to seek and to hear.

The usual title, 'the parable of the sower', is unfair to the seed and the soils – both are more prominent in the story and more central to its understanding. The common missional response, to sow lots of seed, is also somewhat mis-placed. Perhaps as a result of this title, we seem to focus on ourselves as the sower rather than ourselves in the soil receiving the seed. How differently this story reads when we take ourselves out of the shoes of the sower and place ourselves instead in the sludge of the soil.

Jesus explains that within the soils in which the seed struggles, along the path, on the rocky ground and among thorns, lie the vulnerabilities of life. Life, even when one has received the seed, is not straightforward. Life is full of distractions, superficiality and rejection, which seek to draw us away from the word of God. The mark of good soil is not its freedom from these vulner-abilities but its resilience to take in the seed and to produce a harvest in spite of the world's distractions, superficiality and rejection.

Here again, as always with parables, is a message for those who have the desire to learn, the heart to seek and the ears to hear.

IMOGEN BALL, CURATE, ALL SAINTS, TRULL

The well is deep

The woman said to [Jesus], 'Sir, you have no bucket, and the well is deep. Where do you get that living water? Are you greater than our ancestor Jacob, who gave us the well, and with his sons and his flocks drank from it?' Jesus said to her, 'Everyone who drinks of this water will be thirsty again, but those who drink of the water that I will give them will never be thirsty. The water that I will give will become in them a spring of water gushing up to eternal life.'

JOHN 4:11–14 (NRSV)

Two people, meeting at a well, talking about water – it might seem common-place. But this encounter plumbed depths and released springs of life-giving water that gushed and spread. This conversation between Jesus and an unnamed Samaritan woman broke centuries of divides – race, gender, religion, purity laws, distrust. As they talked, life began to flow.

Let's sit by the well, feel the sun, feel their thirst and turn our attention to the woman who comes to draw water. She knows the well, its walls and depth, its history. I wonder if her heart felt like a well of sorrow and pain, separate and dark.

Listen as Jesus speaks of another water source – himself. How, in drinking the love and life he offers, we may know an echoing spring bubbling up within us, overflowing with endless life. Unlike a well, a spring needs no bucket to draw with. Its water flows and spreads to all around, greening and giving life where it flows. If we read more of the story, we'll see how this woman's joy spread throughout her community. Life, like water, must flow. This endless life Jesus offers first flows down, into her depths, and from these depths it bubbles up into new life.

How do our own depths respond to the depths of the love of God? Can we allow ourselves to be loved so deeply? Can we welcome those springs bubbling up within us, spreading across divides, bringing joy and life as the waters flow?

As a deer longs for flowing streams, so my soul longs for you, O God. Deep calls to deep at the thunder of your cataracts; all your waves and your billows have gone over me. By day the Lord commands his steadfast love, and at night his song is with me.
PSALM 42:1, 7–8

ANDREA SKEVINGTON, WRITER, SPEAKER AND BLOGGER

Breaking the cycle

Herod wanted to kill John, but he was afraid of a riot, because all the people believed John was a prophet. But at a birthday party for Herod, Herodias's daughter performed a dance that greatly pleased him, so he promised with a vow to give her anything she wanted. At her mother's urging, the girl said, 'I want the head of John the Baptist on a tray!' Then the king regretted what he had said; but because of the vow he had made in front of his guests, he issued the necessary orders. So John was beheaded in the prison.

MATTHEW 14:5–10 (NLT)

Herodias was King Herod's sister-in-law, but they got together anyway. John the Baptist (the people's prophet?), never known to mince his words, spoke out against their adultery and was imprisoned by Herod at Herodias' request. The resulting story of vengeance, lust, fear, impulse and regret would be unbelievable in most soap operas. It is hard to identify the most tragic figure: John loses his life for speaking truth to power. Herod, the weak-willed people-pleaser, discovers the consequences of not demonstrating personal integrity. Herodias is so absorbed with her desire to destroy John that she forgets her responsibility as a mother. But perhaps Herodias' daughter is the sorriest character in this unfortunate tale.

The account in Mark's gospel tells how, following the dance, the unnamed girl asks her mother's advice, having been promised up to half of Herod's kingdom. I imagine a teenager, giddy with choice: should she accept money, jewels, an amazing wardrobe, the equivalent of the most elaborate mobile phone or computer? I wonder how she felt as she took the tray with the head of John the Baptist to the woman who advised her so selfishly. I wonder how she treated her own daughter.

Only the might of God can destroy the cycle of hatred, fear, guilt and all the other experiences that blight the lives of countless families across the generations. The power that raised Jesus from death will bring forgiveness and healing in the worst circumstances. Amid his grief at John's death, Jesus healed the sick. Perhaps you can pray about those seemingly impossible, destructive relationships you face or know about. As you cry out to God, the Holy Spirit can transform the desire for immediate personal satisfaction and show you the next step towards love, joy and peace.

LAKSHMI JEFFREYS, VICAR, NORTHAMPTONSHIRE

Believe the impossible

Then a man named Jairus, a leader of the local synagogue, came and fell at Jesus' feet, pleading with him to come home with him. His only daughter, who was about twelve years old, was dying... While [Jesus] was still speaking... a messenger arrived from the home of Jairus, the leader of the synagogue. He told him, 'Your daughter is dead. There's no use troubling the Teacher now.' But when Jesus heard what had happened, he said to Jairus, 'Don't be afraid. Just have faith, and she will be healed.'

LUKE 8:41–42, 49–50 (NLT)

Jairus was at his wits' end. As an influential Jewish official, he had no doubt consulted the most skilled doctors, but nothing had worked. He could see his beloved daughter was dying. In desperation he sought out this new teacher and healer that many of his peers had serious misgivings about, and he humbled himself to beg Jesus to come and heal her.

As Jesus and Jairus walked along the road together, the distraught father's hopes must have been raised. Then a messenger brought the dreaded news: 'Your daughter is dead. There's no use troubling the Teacher now' (v. 49). Into this hopelessness Jesus spoke: 'Don't be afraid. Just have faith, and she will be healed' (v. 50).

Against all rational thought Jairus persevered and led Jesus to his home of mourning. The weepers and wailers laughed when Jesus told them: 'Stop the weeping! She isn't dead; she's only asleep' (v. 52). They knew she was dead. It was final. There were no grounds at all for hope, until Jesus did what only God can do. The young girl heard his voice of authority pierce the shroud of death and command her to come back to the realm of the living. 'Her life returned and she immediately stood up!' (v. 55).

Apart from Jesus' promise, Jairus had no tangible evidence on which to base his faith. The crowd had given up hope, and I would probably have done the same. The vital ingredient that made the difference was that Jesus, Almighty God, was actively present and had given his promise.

No situation is too dire for God. Let's not fall into the trap of giving up and thinking, 'There's no use troubling the Teacher now.' With God, there is always hope.

CHRISTINE PLATT, WRITER

A late-night takeaway?

When it was evening, the disciples came to him and said, 'This is a deserted place, and the hour is now late; send the crowds away so that they may go into the villages and buy food for themselves.' Jesus said to them, 'They need not go away; you give them something to eat.' They replied, 'We have nothing here but five loaves and two fish.' And he said, 'Bring them here to me.' Then he ordered the crowds to sit down on the grass. Taking the five loaves and the two fish, he looked up to heaven, and blessed and broke the loaves, and gave them to the disciples, and the disciples gave them to the crowds. And all ate and were filled; and they took up what was left over of the broken pieces, twelve baskets full.

MATTHEW 14:15–20 (NRSV)

In the picture by Eularia Clarke entitled *The Five Thousand*, held in the Methodist Modern Art Collection, the scene from this passage is wonderfully depicted and updated with bicycles and babies, a brew-up, a pulpit and half – just the bottom half – of a priest. The meal being enjoyed by the masses is fish and chips (out of newspaper). It reminds me of church outings to Littlehampton! People are dozing, toddlers toddling and the crowd includes babes in arms and the elderly. Celebrating all that the church should be, it is a great image of intergenerational engagement, hospitality, community and faith. For most eyes are directed towards the open and the spoken word at the pulpit.

With well in excess of 5,000 in the biblical crowd (gratifyingly Matthew's headcount expressly includes women and children) such focus must have been lacking, at least for those furthest from the action. But we read that the humble meal of fish and bread (the potato was still a long way off, literally) was distributed efficiently, and all ate their fill with twelve baskets left over.

Among the many aspects of the story which Clarke's picture mirrors and develops from Matthew's account is the focus on the word – being spoken and passed on from one to another, just as was the food.

When we eat a meal today or grab a snack, let us fix our eyes on Jesus, thanking him not only for the food that curbs our physical hunger but recognising our spiritual hunger, which only his word can feed.

HELEN HANCOCK, TEAM RECTOR, TOLWORTH HOOK AND SURBITON TEAM MINISTRY

How to do the impossible

Jesus immediately said to them: 'Take courage! It is I. Don't be afraid.' 'Lord, if it's you,' Peter replied, 'tell me to come to you on the water.' 'Come,' he said. Then Peter got down out of the boat, walked on the water and came towards Jesus. But when he saw the wind, he was afraid and, beginning to sink, cried out, 'Lord, save me!' Immediately Jesus reached out his hand and caught him. 'You of little faith,' he said, 'why did you doubt?'

MATTHEW 14:27–31 (NIV)

Our gospel writer, Matthew, wants to share important lessons about the focus of our thoughts. This account comes within a series of experiences through which Jesus tries to teach the disciples how to overcome challenges using God's solutions. He needs them to learn that faithful focus on God is key to performing the miraculous deeds they have been watching. Here he gives them a vivid lesson on the powerful effects of where they choose to focus their thoughts. We can focus on the size of the challenge, or on God and his encouragements.

Peter aligns himself with Jesus from the outset in asking for a command to walk on water. We read that he did the 'impossible', and only took fright when he saw the wind. Jesus' question indicates that the sinking was caused by doubt.

Matthew notes that Peter was walking on water even while the wind raged, but it was only when he took his attention off Jesus and considered the wind that he began to sink. His focus had changed. Peter did not lose his faith in God; he just turned his focus to the strength of the wind. The fear of the storm and the invitation to the miraculous were both constantly at work, but Peter's focus on faith or doubt affected the outcome. Having faith doesn't mean that the challenge goes away. We feed our faith or fear by choosing what to focus on.

Thankfully, Jesus knows how easily we sink, and Matthew shows Jesus' willingness to rescue us. How firmly Jesus' feet are planted on the water, that he can save us when we sink!

When you fix your eyes on Jesus, how might he be encouraging you today?

VICTORIA BYRNE, SENIORS PASTOR AND WRITER

Transfigured Christ: transformed disciples

Jesus took with him Peter, James and John the brother of James, and led them up a high mountain by themselves. There he was transfigured before them. His face shone like the sun, and his clothes became as white as the light. Just then there appeared before them Moses and Elijah, talking with Jesus... While [Peter] was still speaking, a bright cloud covered them, and a voice from the cloud said, 'This is my Son, whom I love; with him I am well pleased. Listen to him!'

MATTHEW 17:1–5 (NIV, abridged)

This amazing mountaintop encounter happens just six days after Peter declares Jesus to be the Messiah and Jesus predicts his own death, challenging the disciples about what kind of Messiah he would be. That Jesus would suffer and die conflicted with the disciples' ideas of a saviour. They wrestled with the tension between what Jesus said and who they thought he was.

In the Bible, mountains are often places of encounter with God: Abraham discovers God's provision, Moses receives the ten commandments and Elijah defeats the prophets of Baal. The transfiguration is another such encounter. Peter, James and John watch as Jesus is joined by Moses the lawgiver and Elijah the honoured prophet. As Jesus shines with the glory of God, his superiority over Moses and Elijah is revealed and his status as Messiah is confirmed. The voice from the cloud echoes the words spoken at his baptism, adding the command 'Listen to him!' (v. 5).

Four key things are communicated in those words. *Identity* – 'This is my Son' confirms that Jesus truly is the Messiah and that Peter's declaration (Matthew 16:16) was correct. *Affection* – 'whom I love' conveys the deep love of the Father for the Son, which will sustain Jesus through the painful journey to the cross. *Affirmation* – 'with whom I am well pleased' assures the disciples that Jesus is neither mistaken nor confused; his life is pleasing to God. *Command* – 'Listen to him!' is both an admonishment to Peter who rebuked Jesus (Matthew 16:22) and an encouragement to the disciples to heed Jesus now.

We may not experience the three disciples' mountaintop revelation, but God's word still confronts us about responding to Jesus. As God's beloved Son do we honour him in our lives? Are we really willing to listen to him?

LIZ KENT, METHODIST MINISTER AND DIRECTOR, WESLEY STUDY CENTRE, DURHAM

The clever trap

**The teachers of the Law and Pharisees brought a woman caught in adultery...
and said to Jesus, 'Teacher, this woman was caught in the act of adultery. In
the Law Moses commanded us to stone such women. Now what do you say?'...
When they kept on questioning him, he... said to them, 'Let any one of you who
is without sin be the first to throw a stone at her'... At this, those who heard
began to go away one at a time... until only Jesus was left, with the woman...
Jesus [said to her,] 'Go now and leave your life of sin.'**

JOHN 8:3–11 (NIV, abridged)

Like a television news report, these verses capture a moment in time when
the spotlight rested on a compromised woman and the rabbi's response,
before moving swiftly to the next item. Magnetic viewing, but the backstory
is more interesting.

The woman caught 'in the act' was obviously not alone. Where was the
man? Because the Law states both the man and the woman must die (Deuteronomy 22:22). Duplicitous Pharisees and teachers of the law, driven by corro-
sive emotions of jealousy, fear and ambition, had hatched a deliberate plot
to undermine Jesus' authority and reputation. Here we have a gospel golden
nugget, a blueprint for behaviour that is transformational for all relationships,
personal, community and international. Today, we still encounter moral
superiority devoid of self-awareness and compassion.

These brief verses highlight the clash when rigid law meets the forgiving
mercy of God. Let us feel the silence as Jesus' finger scratched on the ground
before delivering his verdict. Clearly, Jesus did not condone adultery. Her sin
was acknowledged, but his incisive reply forced the teachers of the law and
Pharisees to admit their own sin. This is an uncompromising, uncomfortable
cameo, for it directs us to confront our own motives, judgements and prejudices. What are our attitudes and actions towards other people? Sadly, we
discover we are not perfect. But our priceless advantage in this life is that we
have Jesus, the perfect example to follow.

What we have done cannot be undone, but Jesus offers us a new beginning with forgiveness, mercy and hope. These are blessings to embrace –
and pass on.

ELIZABETH RUNDLE, METHODIST MINISTER AND WRITER

Go and do likewise

But he… said to Jesus, 'And who is my neighbour?' Jesus replied, 'A man was going down from Jerusalem to Jericho, and he fell among robbers, who stripped him and beat him and departed, leaving him half dead. Now by chance a priest was going down that road, and when he saw him he passed by on the other side. So likewise, a Levite, when he came to the place and saw him, passed by on the other side. But a Samaritan, as he journeyed, came to where he was, and when he saw him, he had compassion.

LUKE 10:29–33 (ESV, abridged)

Cities can be these amazing places filled with the bustle and energy of life. Busy cars, busy people and little time to meet your neighbours in the flat upstairs. It's a good thing, then, that this passage doesn't just refer to those people whom we live alongside. When the lawyer questions Jesus, he doesn't use the word neighbour as those living nearby; instead, he means the community we live within. It's a much larger reference for the people we are in society with and come across in all aspects of daily living.

This passage ends with a command to 'go, and do likewise' (v. 37). How? I think the key word here is 'compassion', as in entering into the other person's place. If I was the broken person on the roadside, how would I want people to respond to me? There is no doubt that showing compassion means placing the other person's needs above yours, otherwise we would all walk by just like the priest and the Levite.

Showing compassion is how we love our neighbours, how we love the strangers that live in our communities. Practising compassion is how we cross the bridges that divide us. Compassion costs. It cost the Samaritan time and money. However, not practising compassion, I believe, has a greater cost. Choosing not to stop means hardening our hearts to what we see and hear.

Whether we live in a big city or a tiny village, showing compassion to strangers is how we love God and how we love our neighbours. It is how we practise 'going to do likewise'. If you know that God loves you, know that he loves your neighbour just as well, even when they are completely different from you. Let's take a breath and show this love to a broken, suffering and estranged world.

BOLA ADAMOLEKUN, CHAPLAIN

Choose wisely

[Jesus] came to a village where a woman named Martha opened her home to him. She had a sister called Mary, who sat at the Lord's feet listening to what he said. But Martha was distracted by all the preparations that had to be made. She came to him and asked, 'Lord, don't you care that my sister has left me to do the work by myself? Tell her to help me!' 'Martha, Martha,' the Lord answered, 'you are worried and upset about many things, but few things are needed – or indeed only one. Mary has chosen what is better, and it will not be taken away from her.'

LUKE 10:38–42 (NIV)

Martha was distracted. Well, that is certainly a word I could use to describe myself: distracted by emails, laundry, social media, cleaning, phone calls, cooking, the news, notifications, this, that and the other! We live in a world that seems to prize the false sense of purpose that busyness gives us, even when it drives us to worry and fret. And those distractions pull hard on our time, energy and attention.

Of course, many of the things that keep us busy are also important – like feeding our family or connecting with friends – and Martha was right that there were preparations to be made. But she was wrong to make those things the centre of her attention when she had the presence of God in the room with her in the person of Jesus. I wonder too whether she was seeking a sense of importance and purpose from that anxious busyness? You might say she was too busy laying the table to remember to sit down and enjoy the feast in front of her.

It wasn't that her sister Mary was choosing laziness; in fact, Mary may have wrestled with her conscience nagging her to keep up with the endless tasks of the day. But the presence of Jesus had called to her to stop and listen and, in the middle of it all, she chooses 'what is better' (v. 42). She chooses his presence and words of life.

The very best thing we can do today is to stop and recognise the loving presence of Jesus. Just as Mary and Martha had Jesus with them, we too can be reminded of our true purpose, refreshed and reassured that, whatever today holds, he promises to be with us.

ALI HERBERT, CURATE, ST LUKE'S GAS STREET, BIRMINGHAM,
AND FORMER EDITOR, *DAY BY DAY WITH GOD*

The parable of the lost sheep

[Jesus] told them this parable: 'Which one of you, having a hundred sheep and losing one of them, does not leave the ninety-nine in the wilderness and go after the one that is lost until he finds it? When he has found it, he lays it on his shoulders and rejoices. And when he comes home, he calls together his friends and neighbours, saying to them, "Rejoice with me, for I have found my sheep that was lost." Just so, I tell you, there will be more joy in heaven over one sinner who repents than over ninety-nine righteous persons who need no repentance.'

LUKE 15:3–7 (NRSV)

At the centre of Shek Pik Prison in Hong Kong is the chapel, a place of sanctuary where the prisoners come to catch a glimpse of what freedom might feel like. It seemed my vocation as prison chaplain was especially to search out those in solitary. My visit to Lam Po was my first and thankfully not the last. I had been told by the governor that he was particularly depressed. When I arrived, I found him curled up in a ball on his bed. He refused to talk with me. I promised to pray for him and left a Chinese Bible on his table.

Little did I know he was contemplating taking his own life when I interrupted him. He told me later that, after I had left, he caught sight of the Bible, which had fallen open at Psalm 23. He thought, 'Could there be someone like that?' He knew I held a service in the prison chapel and asked to attend.

After a couple of years sitting at the back, he approached me and said that he wanted to join this community. When I asked why, he said, 'They care for one another, they share their troubles and they trust each other. As I have listened to the stories of Jesus, I have experienced the Good Shepherd who cares even for us black sheep.'

So he was baptised! He also took up calligraphy and designed wonderful cards with passages from the Bible which he gave to the guards and inmates. He changed so much that after 23 years of a life sentence, he was pardoned and set free.

Let us not underestimate the power of the stories of Jesus.

ROB GILLION, BISHOP FOR THE ARTS, DIOCESE OF SOUTHWARK, AND FORMER TRUSTEE, BRF

The parable of the lost son

A man had two sons. One took his inheritance early, moved away and wasted it until he was so broke the only work he could find was feeding pigs. He said, I'll go home and say, 'I'm truly, deeply sorry,' and I'll ask to be a servant. But his father was delighted to see him, saying, 'Let's celebrate, for my son was lost and is found.' The other brother was angry and said, 'You throw a party for him, when I have been so loyal!' 'My son,' the father said, 'everything I have is yours, but your brother was dead and is alive again; was lost and is found.'

LUKE 15:11–32 (paraphrased and abridged)

On the face of it, Jesus told this story to illustrate the enormity of God's capacity for forgiveness. It seems simple: the son hurts his father – really hurts him – and brings shame on the family (that is how the crowds who were listening would have interpreted it – feeding pigs was the lowest of the low). Then at his most miserable he makes his way home and apologises. His father is delighted, forgives him and welcomes him back.

It seems straightforward. The father represents God, the spendthrift son represents all of us – the whole of humankind. It's a much longed-for message: no matter what we've done, when we are truly sorry and prepared to change, God forgives.

However, there's another brother and another message, too. This older brother knows his brother to be a wastrel; he cannot see why his father is thrilled to take him back. He is jealous about the party and, in a fit of self-righteous grumpiness, he refuses to be drawn into the fun.

As Jesus was speaking, his audience would have recognised him as depicting people who could only see wrong in the way Jesus himself behaved. People who could not see the healing or the lives transformed and the joy that Jesus brought, but chose to focus on his choice of company – tax collectors and sinners – or illegal miracles on the sabbath. Today, perhaps, this brother would be one who harks back to 'the good ol' days', forgetting that those days were cold and dark, as he takes a dramatic stand against change and belittles 'progress'.

It's a challenging story with many messages, and we don't know what happens next, but it begs huge and humbling questions. Can I see myself in here? Which character might be me?

LINDA RAYNER, FRESH EXPRESSIONS COORDINATOR, UNITED REFORMED CHURCH

How (not) to pray

Two men went up to the temple to pray, one a Pharisee and the other a tax-collector. The Pharisee, standing by himself, was praying thus, 'God, I thank you that I am not like other people: thieves, rogues, adulterers, or even like this tax-collector. I fast twice a week; I give a tenth of all my income.' But the tax-collector, standing far off, would not even look up to heaven, but was beating his breast and saying, 'God, be merciful to me, a sinner!' I tell you, this man went down to his home justified rather than the other; for all who exalt themselves will be humbled, but all who humble themselves will be exalted.

LUKE 18:10–14 (NRSV)

This parable contrasts two pray-ers in the Jerusalem temple. Jesus' Jewish audience knew which one Jesus would commend: the Pharisee, of course! The Pharisees were godly, and took God's law incredibly seriously. As students of scripture, they applied the law to every part of life – even their herb gardens (11:42). Like all prayer in the ancient world, the Pharisee prayed aloud, which meant others would hear. Jesus' hearers would assume the Pharisee was sincere and correct in describing his own godliness, and contrasting himself with other, less godly Jews.

Jesus' audience would also expect the tax collector to get it in the neck. Tax collectors were the lowest of the low: they collaborated with the hated Roman occupiers to collect Roman taxes and tolls. Indeed, tax collectors were notorious for lining their own pockets by collecting more than the Romans required (see Luke 19:8).

And yet! Jesus reverses human expectations – it's not what they've done, but their attitudes that are crucial. How do they see God? The Pharisee assumes God welcomes people who are self-congratulatory about their relationship with God and who show that off in public. The tax collector recognises that he deserves nothing at all from God. It's not that he has (as we might say) low self-esteem: he knows he is a sinner and absolutely needs God's mercy. God's radical generosity, expressed as the tax collector being 'justified' (language more familiar from Paul), means that the key thing to grasp in prayer is that God loves and welcomes genuinely humble people (rather than 'humble braggers') who recognise their need of God. And ultimately, that's all of us.

STEVE WALTON, PROFESSOR OF NEW TESTAMENT, TRINITY COLLEGE, BRISTOL

Does God care?

Now a certain man was ill, Lazarus of Bethany, the village of Mary and her sister Martha… When Jesus saw [Mary] weeping, and the Jews who came with her also weeping, he was greatly disturbed in spirit and deeply moved. He said, 'Where have you laid him?' They said to him, 'Lord, come and see.' Jesus began to weep… [Jesus] cried with a loud voice, 'Lazarus, come out!' The dead man came out, his hands and feet bound with strips of cloth, and his face wrapped in a cloth. Jesus said to them, 'Unbind him, and let him go.'

JOHN 11:1, 33–44 (NRSV, abridged)

'Where is God?' Where is God when the earth quakes, when mudslides engulf, when cancer strikes, when disease incapacitates, when prayers seem unanswered? Does he care?

The sisters sent a message to Jesus that Lazarus was ill, but Jesus didn't come immediately. Why not? This story reminds us that our timing is not God's timing. We want things *now*, but God may keep us waiting, trusting. By the time Jesus reached the home of his friends, Lazarus had been dead for four days, long past any hope of revival or resuscitation.

We may be surprised to see Jesus in emotional turmoil, and shedding tears. It's not just evidence that Jesus was a real human being; they are the tears of a God who weeps with us in our pain and grief. God cares. He weeps with us. And he wants us in turn to be channels of his grace in a hurting world. Jesus' tears are also tears of anger – at death itself, at all the sin, sickness and suffering of a fallen world. Bethany is near Jerusalem, and just a few weeks later Jesus would face his own death, and in doing so would deal with death once and for all. That's how much he loves us. Jesus is with us in our deepest darkness. He is also the gateway to eternal life.

'Take away the stone,' says Jesus (v. 39), before he summons Lazarus out of the tomb. Just a few weeks later Jesus would be standing by another stone, another tomb. He would have a resurrection body, one that will never die, a trailer for the resurrection and life of us all. Jesus told Martha, 'I am the resurrection and the life' (v. 25). Where Jesus is, resurrection and life must be.

ROSIE WARD, RETIRED VICAR AND AUTHOR

Deal or no deal?

Someone came to [Jesus] and said, 'Teacher, what good deed must I do to have eternal life?' And he said to him, '... Keep the commandments.' He said to him, 'Which ones?' And Jesus said, 'You shall not murder... You shall not steal... also, You shall love your neighbour as yourself.' The young man said to him, 'I have kept all these...' Jesus said to him, 'If you wish to be perfect, go, sell your possessions, and give the money to the poor, and you will have treasure in heaven; then come, follow me.' When the young man heard this word, he went away grieving, for he had many possessions.

MATTHEW 19:16–22 (NRSV, abridged)

Right before our story, Matthew tells us about the children who were brought to Jesus. They have no possessions of their own, live in utter dependence on the goodwill of others and know nothing of the law and its demands. Jesus says that the kingdom of heaven belongs to those who are like them. The children stand in stark contrast to the person in our story.

A man asks Jesus a question that gives the game away. He sees his relationship with God as being like a business deal. God has something he wants, and he's interested in knowing what God wants in return. Jesus reminds him that God is good and tells him to keep the commandments, highlighting the ones that focus on care for other people, including the one, love your neighbour, that explains the motive behind keeping the rest.

The man says he's kept them all. Perhaps he has obeyed the first few. But he has not obeyed the vital one. His claim to have done so reveals a lack of self-awareness, blindness to the poor and failure to understand what it means to love. When Jesus explains what love for your neighbour really means, he walks away. The demand is too great. This is not a deal he can make.

We cannot bargain with God. We have nothing he needs, and he will not work with us on a business basis. Some can only think in such terms and wonder if anyone can be saved. Jesus explains that God works differently. If we approach with trust, recognising we have nothing to trade with, then out of his goodness, his utter generosity, God will offer us eternal life. There can be no negotiation, no chance to strike a deal. We either receive it as a gift or we go without.

STEPHEN FINAMORE, PRINCIPAL, BRISTOL BAPTIST COLLEGE

Jesus heals the blind man

As Jesus and his disciples, together with a large crowd, were leaving the city, a blind man, Bartimaeus (which means 'son of Timaeus'), was sitting by the roadside begging. When he heard that it was Jesus of Nazareth, he began to shout, 'Jesus, Son of David, have mercy on me!' Many rebuked him and told him to be quiet, but he shouted all the more, 'Son of David, have mercy on me!' Jesus stopped and said, 'Call him.' So they called to the blind man, 'Cheer up! On your feet! He's calling you.' Throwing his cloak aside, he jumped to his feet and came to Jesus. 'What do you want me to do for you?' Jesus asked him. The blind man said, 'Rabbi, I want to see.' 'Go,' said Jesus, 'your faith has healed you.' Immediately he received his sight and followed Jesus along the road.

MARK 10:46–52 (NIV)

Bartimaeus calls out, 'Jesus, Son of David, have mercy on me!' (v. 47). This shows remarkable insight, as 'Son of David' suggests that Bartimaeus understands and accepts Jesus' messianic identity, an identity that Jesus has not yet proclaimed (Mark 8:27). No wonder his faith heals him, with such insight and understanding!

Many people tried to stop him. It is clear, though, that there was no way Bartimaeus was going to be silenced by the crowd. He kept shouting until he had Jesus' attention. From being determined and forthright so that he could be heard amid and against the crowd, we read how Bartimaeus is also humble: 'Son of David, have mercy on me!' Bartimaeus knew he didn't deserve to be healed, but placed his hope in the grace of Jesus Christ.

There are a few lessons that we can learn from Bartimaeus. Do we accept Jesus as true Lord of our lives, with total sovereignty? Are we humble before him? And in a culture where it isn't always popular to worship, serve and pray to God, do we let the crowds stop us? The more we worship, pray and read the Bible, the greater understanding we will have of who Jesus is and can be in our lives. Maybe we can attain similar levels of faith and understanding to Bartimaeus.

HELEN LAIRD, MISSION ENABLER

Tree tops, taxes and teatime

Jesus was going through the city of Jericho... Zacchaeus... a wealthy, very important tax collector... was too short to see above the people. So he... climbed a sycamore tree so he could see him... Jesus said, 'Zacchaeus, hurry! Come down! I must stay at your house today'... Everyone saw this. They began to complain, 'Look at the kind of man Jesus is staying with. Zacchaeus is a sinner!' Zacchaeus said to the Lord, 'I want to do good...' Jesus said... 'Even this tax collector is one of God's chosen people. The Son of Man came to find lost people and save them.'

LUKE 19:1–10 (ERV, abridged)

Can you imagine the hustle and bustle of Jericho city and people clambering to get a glimpse of Jesus? Zacchaeus must have been frustrated, not being able to see above the crowd. Have you ever climbed a tree? It's not an easy task, especially when you are trying to climb as quickly and as high as you can. Zacchaeus climbs the tree, enduring the taunts of a crowd that hated him. Zacchaeus was a tax collector, someone who cheated and oppressed his own people. He was looked down on and shunned, an outcast because of his job.

Can you imagine Jesus choosing to speak to Zacchaeus? Zacchaeus, of all people! Not only that, but Jesus wanted to stay at *his* house. Zacchaeus received an invitation from Jesus and was reminded of who he was in God. Before meeting Jesus, Zacchaeus had been seeking so many of the wrong things, but now his identity was restored in Jesus. Jesus called Zacchaeus by name, and his life was changed. He promised to follow Jesus and do good, to give half of his money to the poor and pay back those he had cheated. Zacchaeus had everything he needed in Jesus and began to show love and compassion to those he had hurt.

Take some time today and think about what you are seeking and why you are seeking it. Does it bring you the satisfaction you're looking for? Jesus is passing by and calling *you* by name. Challenge yourself to pursue Jesus as Zacchaeus did. No matter what we've done or what people say, we can change and be fulfilled in our relationship with Jesus.

HANNAH TARRING, CHILDREN AND FAMILIES COORDINATOR, MELKSHAM

Waiting and working

The crowd was listening to everything Jesus said. And because he was nearing Jerusalem, he told a story to correct the impression that the Kingdom of God would begin right away. He said, 'A nobleman was called away to a distant empire to be crowned king and then return. Before he left, he called together ten of his servants and divided among them ten pounds of silver, saying, "Invest this for me while I am gone"... After he was crowned king, he returned and called in the servants to whom he had given the money. He wanted to find out what their profits were... "To those who use well what they are given, even more will be given."'

LUKE 19:11–15, 26 (NLT, abridged)

The 'I want it now' feeling is in every child and never leaves us. When Jesus talked about the kingdom of God, many people wanted him to be that king – which he was – but to be a 'power figure' king – which he was not! And they wanted it *now*.

Parables throw out clues to deeper meanings, but you have to look for them. The man who was about to be king left his business in the hands of his servants and told them to carry on in his cause. They must trade with the money he handed over to them, and they did not know how long he would be away.

Waiting is part of the Christian experience (1 Thessalonians 1:10). We believe there will be better times to come when God will rule. Until then he shares his wealth with us – we all have God-given gifts in us – and he wants us to carry on his 'business' even now in our world. When we pray 'Your kingdom come', part of the answer to that lies with us, to use the gifts God has given us. We are not only called to *wait* but also to *work*.

His story continued, however, and the man returned and found that two of his servants had traded with his wealth successfully, but one had buried it so that it might not be lost. The story ended with judgement for those who were faithful and for the one who was not.

We all have gifts, and God looks to us to use them while we wait for better times.

GAVIN REID, HONORARY ASSISTANT BISHOP, SPEAKER AND WRITER

Love song for a vineyard

There was a landowner who planted a vineyard... Then he leased it to tenants and went to another country. When the harvest time had come, he sent his slaves to the tenants to collect his produce. But the tenants seized his slaves and beat one, killed another, and stoned another. Again he sent other slaves, more than the first; and they treated them in the same way. Finally he sent his son to them, saying, 'They will respect my son.' But when the tenants saw the son, they said to themselves, 'This is the heir; come, let us kill him and get his inheritance.'

MATTHEW 21:33–38 (NRSV, abridged)

If you want to eat, plant wheat and pray for your daily bread. If you want a stake in a place, in a community, plant a vineyard. They take a long time to grow to maturity but will provide fruit for years.

The vineyard is a sign of hope in the Bible, a sign of permanence, of long-term commitment, of a willingness to get dug right in. This vineyard has been built by God, it is a love song (see Isaiah 5), but it has been despoiled by the tenants. They have disregarded all that is just and righteous, they have taken without care and are prepared to kill all who oppose them. What should be done about the perpetrators of violence and injustice, asks Jesus. 'Why,' respond the Pharisees, to whom this parable is addressed, 'they should be put to death and the vineyard given to those who will value it and cherish it, who will give the owner his due so all can thrive.' Thus the Pharisees, masters of hypocrisy and greed, condemn themselves with their own words.

And what about us? We are the tenants in the vineyard of the world – more particularly the vineyard which is our community, our workplace, our family, our soul. God has given us everything we need to grow and cultivate our vineyards, and we must work in them lovingly and responsibly. We must be in it for the long run; we must not be afraid to begin projects which will outlive us; we must nurture the new stock as well as the mature and take care to prune carefully all aspects of our lives which produce the dead wood of hatred and greed. And then, by the grace of God, we will be able to rejoice in our vineyards as they produce good fruit.

SALLY WELCH, VICAR, WRITER AND FORMER EDITOR, *NEW DAYLIGHT*

Uncomfortable words

When the Son of Man comes in his glory, and all the angels with him, he will sit on his glorious throne. All the nations will be gathered before him, and he will separate the people one from another as a shepherd separates the sheep from the goats. He will put the sheep on his right and the goats on his left. Then the King will say to those on his right, 'Come, you who are blessed by my Father; take your inheritance, the kingdom prepared for you since the creation of the world.'

MATTHEW 25:31–34 (NIV)

With this passage Jesus concludes his teaching in Matthew's gospel about the final things. We need to get our imaginations in gear, for the setting is stupendous. Jesus, the Son of Man, has taken his rightful place as the king of glory. The king of kings is seated on his throne, attended by the whole angelic host, and all nations are gathered before him.

But what then happens can make many of us feel very uncomfortable. It's so non-PC in our politically correct, secular and pluralistic world. For Jesus is depicted separating people, just as a shepherd separates sheep from goats. It is a separation that Jesus' original listeners would have found easy to relate to, for Middle Eastern sheep and goats were often pastured together. The animals were similar in colour and size and yet needed separating at the end of each day to keep the less hardy goats warm at night.

What stuns me most, though, is the complete surprise that accompanies that separation. There is the wonder of those whose natural daily attitude was one of compassion, care and love for those in need around them. Jesus says to these people that as they fed the hungry, provided hospitality and visited the sick and incarcerated, they were doing it for him. And then there is the disbelief of those who had neglected to help others, who are now presented with the reality that they had overlooked Jesus in those in need.

We see in this passage Jesus' close identification with the poor, the outcast and the suffering. His identification with those who have fallen through the cracks in our society. And we see faith, real faith, in action. The faith that loves sacrificially, just as Jesus loves us and gave himself for us.

SARAH HAYES, TRUSTEE, BRF

Majestic man

As he approached Bethphage and Bethany at the hill called the Mount of Olives, he sent two of his disciples, saying to them, 'Go to the village ahead of you, and as you enter it, you will find a colt tied there, which no one has ever ridden. Untie it and bring it here. If anyone asks you, "Why are you untying it?" say, "The Lord needs it."' Those who were sent ahead went and found it just as he had told them… They brought it to Jesus, threw their cloaks on the colt and put Jesus on it.

LUKE 19:29–32, 35 (NIV)

Jesus is preparing to enter the city of Jerusalem at the busy time of Passover. He is publicly declaring that he is the king of the Jews and coming to save them. Having heard about his miracles, crowds line the streets anxious to see him. So, of course, for this pivotal moment, he makes his entrance… trotting on a baby donkey!

Why did he choose such an odd mode of transport? It is partly, and importantly, to fulfil prophecies made in the Old Testament that said the Messiah would arrive in this way (Zechariah 9:9). However, sadly, many still did not recognise him (Luke 19:44). Later, the disciples did work this out (John 12:16), giving them more confidence in their faith. In our present day, this also gives us the same confirmation as we read the Bible and compare the two sections written so many years apart. It astounds me, and I love to look and see anywhere the Old Testament relates to Jesus' life in the New Testament. To me, this detailed book intricately weaves together an ironclad case for belief in him.

The donkey is also an unassuming working animal, and in eastern tradition is symbolic of peace. Here, it shows its regal rider is coming to draw alongside his people, not to wield his power over them in tyranny. Jesus entered the earth just as modestly by being born in a manger, and he exited as a convict nailed to a cross.

Again, this all speaks powerfully to us today as we work out who Jesus is and what he means to us personally. The almighty Son of God understands and loves us just as we are. We can welcome this king into our lives confident that he comes both in godly majesty and humble humanity.

KARIN LING, WRITER, SPEAKER AND MOTHER OF FOUR

The zeal of Jesus

The Passover of the Jews was near, and Jesus went up to Jerusalem. In the temple he found people selling cattle, sheep, and doves, and the money-changers seated at their tables. Making a whip of cords, he drove all of them out of the temple, both the sheep and the cattle. He also poured out the coins of the money-changers and overturned their tables. He told those who were selling the doves, 'Take these things out of here! Stop making my Father's house a market-place!' His disciples remembered that it was written, 'Zeal for your house will consume me.'

JOHN 2:13–17 (NRSV)

In about 1600, El Greco created a painting called *The Purification of the Temple*. Christ is the central figure. His right hand holds a whip at head height, his arm is traversing across his body as he is about to let the full force of a back swing catch the people cowering away from him in terror. Jesus' body, by contrast, is a calm and beautiful arc, the musculature tense and strong.

On his left-hand side, figures draped in togas are quietly discussing what is happening. So, on one side of the painting there are people about to be whipped; on the other side, people calmly looking on, and in the middle, Jesus himself, his body poised to let the potency of his anger fall upon the hapless merchants. It's powerful, disturbing stuff.

Art historians sometimes suggest that the painting represents a message about the power of the Counter-Reformation being let loose. Be that as it may, what strikes the 21st-century viewer is Jesus' implacable will being enforced. This is a fierce and wrathful Christ.

For those of us inclined to regard Jesus as a person committed to peace and reconciliation, his wrath and fury are frequently ignored. It's too difficult an idea for us to handle; it threatens and destabilises our thought patterns.

When John placed this episode in Jesus' life at the beginning of his gospel, perhaps it was his intention to shake us from our preconceptions – to remind us that Jesus is not containable by our normal ways of thinking, that he always breaks free. After all, in this same story John continues to talk about the destruction of the temple, a cataclysmic event, though the story points forward to the vast energy to be let loose by Christ in his resurrection. From zeal emerges hope.

CHRISTOPHER HERBERT, BISHOP AND VISITING PROFESSOR OF CHRISTIAN ETHICS, UNIVERSITY OF SURREY

Love has eternal significance

While [Jesus] was in Bethany, reclining at the table… a woman came with an alabaster jar of very expensive perfume… She broke the jar and poured the perfume on his head. Some of those present were saying indignantly… 'Why this waste of perfume? It could have been sold for more than a year's wages and the money given to the poor'… 'Leave her alone,' said Jesus… 'The poor you will always have with you, and you can help them any time you want. But you will not always have me… Wherever the gospel is preached… what she has done will also be told.'

MARK 14:3–9 (NIV, abridged)

Perhaps, like me, you have wondered whether the indignant onlookers had a point – after all, Jesus had told the rich young man to sell all he had and give the proceeds to the poor. Yet Jesus defends the woman. He reminds them (and us) that, on the one hand, we are always to be generous to those in need. On the other hand, we should remember that, in our fallen world, there is no utopian dream of eradicating poverty. No political system will ever achieve this, because of the state of the human heart. However, this human heart is also capable of admirable acts of extravagant and sacrificial love, and Jesus recognises this moment as one of them.

The woman's deep love for Jesus gave her the courage to become vulnerable, cause a stir, forgo her reputation and relinquish her security for the future. Such a love-inspired action was a challenge to those around her and remains so for us. Once again, the Lord was commending heart attitudes over rule-keeping. We do not even know the woman's name, yet ever since, as Jesus foresaw, generations have learned from her example of costly, devoted worship.

It is not clear whether the woman had learned of the scheme to arrest Jesus and put him to death. Perhaps she did not realise the significance of her act until she heard Jesus saying that she had anointed his head for burial. She definitely would not have imagined that, 20 centuries later, her action would still be bearing fruit. We can take great encouragement from this. Our loving words and actions, seemingly temporal, can have far-reaching and life-changing consequences. They, like the perfume, are never wasted, but have eternal value. Jesus saw the greater significance of her act and he sees ours.

FIONA STRATTA, TUTOR AND SPEECH AND DRAMA TEACHER

Remembering the future

[Jesus] said to them, 'I have wanted so much to eat this Passover meal with you before I suffer! For I tell you, I will never eat it until it is given its full meaning in the Kingdom of God.' Then Jesus took a cup, gave thanks to God, and said, 'Take this and share it among yourselves. I tell you that from now on I will not drink this wine until the Kingdom of God comes.'

LUKE 22:15–18 (GNT)

This story is so familiar to most Christians – it brings to mind famous paintings, scenes in films and the practices of church services. But how often do we think of this only as a memorial or remembrance that points to an event in the past? After all, Jesus himself says it is to be done in memory of him (Luke 22:19). For Christians, these verses recall Jesus' last meal with his disciples before his crucifixion.

And yet, there is an incredible and inspiring future aspect to this story. Somewhat like a birthday party that marks an important milestone in a person's life, we celebrate the years past but also offer best wishes for the years ahead. Jesus' words to his friends at this last supper are like that. The Passover remembers God's miraculous liberation of Israel from slavery in Egypt (Exodus 12—14), but it also anticipates a future time when God's kingdom of justice and peace will be available to all.

Imagine yourself as one of the disciples. Your country is overrun by a foreign power and there is little hope of change. Into this situation Jesus says: give thanks to God, share your food and wine, because I will share this with you again in God's reign! What an amazing promise and what hope!

For many months many of us have only enjoyed celebrating these words on a screen, but even into the bleak situation of a global pandemic, Jesus calls us to remember the future – we know how the story ends and that Christ himself will wipe away every tear. Hope is not a feeling, it is a practice that we learn through following Jesus. As disciples we have the privilege of sharing this hope and this future with all, because Christ is with us even now.

ROSALEE VELLOSO EWELL, DIRECTOR OF CHURCH RELATIONS, UNITED BIBLE SOCIETIES

Lord, who is it?

Jesus was troubled in spirit and testified, 'Very truly I tell you, one of you is going to betray me.' His disciples stared at one another, at a loss to know which of them he meant. One of them, the disciple whom Jesus loved, was reclining next to him. Simon Peter motioned to this disciple and said, 'Ask him which one he means.' Leaning back against Jesus, he asked him, 'Lord, who is it?' Jesus answered, 'It is the one to whom I will give this piece of bread when I have dipped it in the dish.' Then, dipping the piece of bread, he gave it to Judas, the son of Simon Iscariot. As soon as Judas took the bread, Satan entered into him.

JOHN 13:21–27 (NIV)

I live close to the city of Derry/Londonderry in Ireland/Northern Ireland – take your pick, and there are many more alternatives. A crucial moment in its history as part of the British plantation and settlement of Ireland is 1688–89. The city was besieged and the governor, Colonel Robert Lundy, thought the best course was to surrender. History and myth get somewhat entangled, but a small group of apprentices considered this to be betrayal. They closed the gates of the walled city, which then held out until ships were able to breach the boom across Lough Foyle months later and the siege was lifted. This episode is still commemorated every year with events that include the burning of an effigy of Colonel Lundy.

History gives us numerous examples of what is considered to be betrayal. Perpetuated in story and myth, they go to the heart of conflicts and are very hard to move on from. Jesus was betrayed. Judas sold Jesus out to the Romans for a decent sum of money, and then couldn't live with himself afterwards. Jesus knew all about it, and the events unfolded as a crucial and integral part of the journey to the cross and our salvation history.

The incident is about betrayal, but that is only a part. Perhaps it is more about the depth to which we are known by God and the loving response of Christ to us, even when we fail him and make a total mess of our lives. No matter how badly we fall and fail, God knows us and offers forgiveness. Our betrayal would be to reject this forgiveness. We are known, and, amazingly, loved completely.

STEPHEN SKUCE, DISTRICT SUPERINTENDENT,
NORTH WESTERN DISTRICT OF THE METHODIST CHURCH IN IRELAND

The cost of the cup

Then Jesus went with his disciples to a place called Gethsemane, and he said to them, 'Sit here while I go over there and pray.' He took Peter and the two sons of Zebedee along with him, and he began to be sorrowful and troubled. Then he said to them, 'My soul is overwhelmed with sorrow to the point of death. Stay here and keep watch with me.' Going a little farther, he fell with his face to the ground and prayed, 'My Father, if it is possible, may this cup be taken from me. Yet not as I will, but as you will.'

MATTHEW 26:36–39 (NIV)

The Passover meal was over, but a long night lay ahead. In a lonely olive grove, Jesus writhed in a vice-like grip of mental and spiritual anguish, crushed by sorrow as he faced humiliation, prolonged torture and one of the most painful deaths devised by man.

But was this what filled the cup Jesus so dreaded drinking? I don't think that accounts for its full contents. No doubt the ordeal he faced was terrible, and he was fully man as well as fully God. But he had told his followers to 'rejoice and be glad' in the face of persecution. It is more likely his suffering was of an order different from being unable to practise what he preached. Later, following a merciless beating, 'the apostles left the Sanhedrin, rejoicing because they had been counted worthy of suffering disgrace for the Name' (Acts 5:41). Martyrs through the ages have gone hymn-singing to their deaths. No one would argue that they were drawing on superior reserves of holy joy than Jesus had available. So what could have been in the cup?

Here is one suggestion. We know Jesus was soaked in scripture. In the Old Testament, over and over again from Job to the Psalms to Ezekiel, Isaiah and Jeremiah, 'the cup of God's wrath' is mentioned. It may be at odds with the 'anything goes, love means never getting mad, what right does anyone have to judge anyone else' approach of the current climate, but the Bible is clear: God does indeed get angry about sin. And Jesus was about to bear the sins of the whole world and the consequent divine judgement.

He wanted nothing more than to be spared this cup of sin and judgement, but he drank it anyway. And in so doing, he gained us an invitation to eternal life in God's presence.

JO SWINNEY, HEAD OF COMMUNICATIONS, A ROCHA INTERNATIONAL,
AUTHOR AND SPEAKER

Betrayed with a kiss

[Judas] went away and conferred with the chief priests and officers of the temple police about how he might betray [Jesus] to them. They were greatly pleased and agreed to give him money. So he consented and began to look for an opportunity to betray him to them when no crowd was present... While [Jesus] was still speaking, suddenly a crowd came, and the one called Judas, one of the twelve, was leading them. He approached Jesus to kiss him; but Jesus said to him, 'Judas, is it with a kiss that you are betraying the Son of Man?'

LUKE 22:4–6, 47–48 (NRSV)

Do you recall your last kiss? Perhaps you have recently kissed a friend in greeting, a parent in parting or a partner in passion. Try for a moment to bring the occasion to mind. Usually when we kiss, we first smile and often we close our eyes. There is a vulnerability and an intimacy in the act of kissing as we enter another's space, feel their breath and touch their skin. It is an intimacy we can imagine Judas having with Jesus. Judas was one of the twelve. He had been a close companion for years. He was so trusted that he had responsibility for their common purse (John 12:6). He managed their money. Jesus, and the disciples, placed their trust in him.

Nonetheless, Judas comes leading a crowd. I suspect it is easier to betray someone or something if you are part of a crowd. It is possible to be whipped up into a delusional frenzy when you are part of a crowd, especially these days online. Jesus speaks into this madness: 'Judas, is it with a kiss that you are betraying the Son of Man?' He calls his name: 'Judas'. He reaches out to the man being carried along by the crowd. He reminds him of their intimacy as he highlights the betrayal.

In the story of Judas and throughout history we encounter trusted and responsible disciples of Jesus who make a mess of things, not least when caught up in a crowd. And yet, Jesus continues to call us by name. He continues to invite each one of us into that place of intimacy and vulnerability, despite our actions. Step away from the crowd, be still and hear his voice.

TIM LING, DIRECTOR OF LEARNING AND DEVELOPMENT, CHURCH ARMY

You need a rooster

Peter… said to Jesus, 'I will never leave you, even though all the rest do!' Jesus said to Peter, '… Before the rooster crows tonight, you will say three times that you do not know me'… The men standing there came to Peter. 'Of course you are one of them,' they said. 'After all, the way you speak gives you away!' Then Peter said, 'I swear that I am telling the truth! May God punish me if I am not! I do not know that man!' Just then a rooster crowed, and Peter remembered what Jesus had told him… He went out and wept bitterly.

MATTHEW 26:33–34, 73–75 (GNT, abridged)

A rooster's cry – not just a bird noise, but a reminder to Peter that Jesus' words always come true. Not just a bird noise, but a reminder to Peter that his competitive, macho bravado ('I will never leave you; I will out-faithful the rest of them') will always crumble when faced with reality. It was an unpleasant sound at the time, but Jesus clearly felt it was necessary. The rooster made Peter cry, and Peter's tears stung, but ultimately, they were part of his healing.

Luther thought it was so necessary for God's people to be reminded of this story that he used his influence to have a metal rooster fixed on top of every Lutheran church. So maybe every time I lift my eyes to a weathercock, I can remember that I can trust in Jesus rather than in my swagger or bluster. And if I don't look at the roosters on church spires frequently, maybe I can put a drawing of a cockerel on my wall. Or have a rooster as an icon on my desktop to click on. Or a cockcrow ringtone. Or I could keep chickens and let them preach.

Of course, today may be one of those days when we feel like we don't need a rooster. Today, we may be entirely confident that we are somehow superior to our compromised fellow-believers, sure that we will never be too cowardly to admit what Jesus means to us, that we will never find ourselves weeping in shame. My sister or brother, excuse me for saying it, but at such times we, above all, need a rooster.

ANDY GRIFFITHS, ADULT EDUCATOR, DIOCESE OF CHELMSFORD

Power in weakness

When morning came, all the chief priests and the elders of the people conferred together against Jesus in order to bring about his death. They bound him, led him away, and handed him over to Pilate the governor... Now Jesus stood before the governor; and the governor asked him, 'Are you the King of the Jews?' Jesus said, 'You say so.' But when he was accused by the chief priests and elders, he did not answer. Then Pilate said to him, 'Do you not hear how many accusations they make against you?' But he gave him no answer, not even to a single charge, so that the governor was greatly amazed.

MATTHEW 27:1–2, 11–14 (NRSV)

Power is a dangerous thing and so often misused, even with good intentions. It looks as though all the wrong people hold the power at Jesus' sham trial, wielding their might in the trumped-up and unjust charges made against him.

Pilate thought he had power; he held the title of governor after all. According to the account of these events in John's gospel, Pilate reminded Jesus that he had the power to release him if he chose, though Jesus disabused him of this illusion, saying, 'You would have no power over me unless it had been given you from above' (John 19:11).

The elders and chief priests thought they had power, too, but they had to resort to twisting the truth to get their way.

At first sight, Jesus has no power whatsoever. He allows himself to be handed over to worldly authorities in a way that seems to concede that evil has won. Jesus knew that he could call down a mighty army of angelic forces that would have vindicated him once and for all (Matthew 26:53). He also knew that this was not God's way. Jesus chose, of his own free will, the paradox of power in weakness. This was the power that would be revealed on the cross.

It is power that looks foolish in the eyes of the world. This kind of power, however, sets us free from the burden of trying to do things our own way by sheer force, whether of muscle or will. What a relief it is to hand over our struggles to the one who is humble and meek, yet all-powerful.

LIZ HOARE, TUTOR IN SPIRITUAL FORMATION, WYCLIFFE HALL, OXFORD

Caught in the crowd

As they led him away, they seized a man, Simon of Cyrene, who was coming from the country, and they laid the cross on him, and made him carry it behind Jesus. A great number of the people followed him, and among them were women who were beating their breasts and wailing for him. But Jesus turned to them and said, 'Daughters of Jerusalem, do not weep for me, but weep for yourselves and for your children.'

LUKE 23:26–28 (NRSV)

Coming home from school at the weekends, I used to walk from Charing Cross Station to our flat in Westminster. This took me past the protest route, so more often than not I would find myself squeezing through angry, chanting demonstrations for at least one stretch of my journey. I seldom had any idea what they were protesting about, but for the length of a street I would be caught up and counted among the number of some unknown cause.

That's how I imagine the characters in this passage. Simon of Cyrene probably had no idea who Jesus was when a Roman soldier forced him to shoulder the cross. As for the women of Jerusalem, they were crying for Jesus, but is that because they knew him or simply because of the pitiful sight that he must have been by that stage: beaten, near collapse and on his way to execution?

Jesus turns to the women and, addressing them tenderly as 'daughters of Jerusalem', he somehow musters the energy to communicate an urgent message. Don't weep for me, he says. Weep for yourselves. Bad times are coming, the fulfilment of prophecies is on the way (he is quoting from Hosea 10:8). There is a bigger picture here, he implies, that you don't yet understand.

Did they listen? I think the mere fact that we know about this exchange suggests that these women took their questions, eventually, to the followers of Jesus. Similarly, the fact that we know Simon of Cyrene's name (and, from Mark's gospel, those of his sons) suggests that he did not remain an outsider after his experience.

It's easy to get caught up in despair, but the suffering that we experience and see daily in the world exists in the wider context of a salvation story. When we believe that, it can do more than shift our perspective – it can change the course of our lives.

AMY SCOTT ROBINSON, AUTHOR AND STORYTELLER

Responding to the cross

Jesus called out with a loud voice, 'Father, into your hands I commit my spirit.' When he had said this, he breathed his last. The centurion, seeing what had happened, praised God and said, 'Surely this was a righteous man.' When all the people who had gathered to witness this sight saw what took place, they beat their breasts and went away. But all those who knew him, including the women who had followed him from Galilee, stood at a distance, watching these things.

LUKE 23:46–49 (NIV)

Throughout his gospel, Luke has been intent on bringing us a full picture of the many different kinds of people who encounter Jesus. Luke is a Gentile and understandably fascinated by Jesus as the Jewish Messiah who has come for the salvation of all humanity. And so it is that here, at the most poignant moment of his gospel, when Jesus breathes his last breath and surrenders his spirit to his heavenly Father, Luke registers the response of those who are looking on.

Immediately Luke brings us unexpected words of praise from the lips of a non-Jewish onlooker – the Roman centurion – a man charged with ensuring an orderly execution. The centurion's words of praise to God are jarring in this moment of death, but burst from his lips as he beholds the evident innocence of Jesus.

The crowd of Jerusalem residents would have come perhaps seeking to be entertained by the day's gory events. Instead they find themselves grieved as they watch the way in which Jesus gives himself up to death. Unknown to them at this moment, their witness at the cross is preparation for their own conversion to Christ on the day of Pentecost, when thousands in the city respond to the Spirit-empowered preaching of Peter.

The male and female disciples watching from a distance must have been deeply perplexed. The death of Jesus left them with searing questions. How could his life have ended in this way? How can the kingdom of God come if the Messiah is crucified?

Luke invites us to participate in this moment. At the cross there are swirling emotions and no easy answers. As we draw near, we ask our own searing questions. We wrestle, we watch, we grieve – and we praise.

RUTH BUSHYAGER, BISHOP OF HORSHAM

123

You too have seen the Lord

[Mary] saw Jesus standing there, but she did not know that it was Jesus. Jesus said to her, 'Woman, why are you weeping? For whom are you looking?' Supposing him to be the gardener, she said to him, 'Sir, if you have carried him away, tell me where you have laid him...' Jesus said to her, 'Mary!'... 'Do not hold on to me, because I have not yet ascended to the Father. But go to my brothers...' Mary Magdalene went and announced to the disciples, 'I have seen the Lord.'

JOHN 20:14–18 (NRSV, abridged)

It's not hard to imagine how Mary Magdalene must have been feeling as she gazed helplessly into the empty tomb. The man who had transformed her life, and whom she believed would transform the world, had been brutally executed, and now she was unable even to find and anoint his body. Grief, tears and bewilderment have blinded her. When the risen Jesus comes alongside her, she doesn't recognise him, until, crucially, he speaks her name.

This is not just an encounter from long ago, but a wake-up call to moments in our own lives too. The risen Lord is all around us, approaching us in a thousand different guises, but we so often fail to recognise him. A stranger smiles at us and breaks through our loneliness. A friend offers help when we feel we can't go a step further. A child's laughter bubbles up through the tedium of a hard day. Notice, today, where you catch a glimpse of the risen Christ, inviting you, as he once invited Mary, to tell his story and reveal his love in the world. Such moments are the very presence of the resurrected Christ, speaking our name.

This process of recognition and empowerment begins as Jesus addresses his grieving friend simply as 'Woman' (v. 15). Then, when she is ready to hear it, he calls her by name, 'Mary!' (v. 16), breaking through the wall of her grief. Finally, in her full name and authorised by his Holy Spirit, he sends her to his brothers, as the first apostle, Mary Magdalene.

But this comes with a warning. 'Don't hold on to what has been and all you think you have lost,' we might hear him say, 'but walk forward, with me, to everything that is still to be, for you too, like Mary, have seen me and known me.'

MARGARET SILF, AUTHOR AND SPEAKER

But we had hoped...

**Now on that same day two of them were going to a village called Emmaus...
While they were talking and discussing, Jesus himself came near and went
with them, but their eyes were kept from recognising him. And he said to them,
'What are you discussing with each other as you walk along?'... They replied,
'The things about Jesus of Nazareth... and how our chief priests and leaders
handed him over to be condemned to death and crucified him. But we had
hoped that he was the one to redeem Israel.'**

LUKE 24:13, 15–17, 19–21 (NRSV)

The account of the two disciples' meeting with the risen Christ on the road
to Emmaus is perhaps one of the most familiar of the post-resurrection nar-
ratives, but we shouldn't let its familiarity blind us to its strangeness. Why
do these two disciples not recognise their travelling companion as Jesus?
Even as we ask the question, we may remember that other accounts of post-
resurrection meetings contain similar puzzling examples of lack of recognition
among Jesus' followers: Mary at the tomb thought Jesus was the gardener
(John 20:15); similarly, when Jesus met his disciples on the beach, 'they did
not know that it was Jesus' (John 21:4).

One reason for this strange bewilderment among those who knew Jesus
best lies in the sheer *mystery* of what had taken place; the gospel writers were
struggling to record divine events for which there was no precedent and which
were impossible to adequately describe in human terms. But there is another
reason, closer to our own experience, and it is perhaps here that our greatest
challenge lies: to come to Christ freely, openly, trustingly, without any attempt
to impose our pre-arranged agendas upon him ('Just as I am, without one
plea'). The travellers to Emmaus thought they knew Jesus and understood
his mission, but the limited nature of their expectations ('We had hoped that
he was the one to redeem *Israel*', v. 21) proved otherwise.

Like the disciples, we too may not recognise the Christ who is present with
us, if our expectations of him are confined to the limited field of our own
vision. Can we trust his love enough to allow him to escape the limits we place
upon him, so we may see and recognise him *as he truly is*?

BARBARA MOSSE, RETIRED PRIEST AND WRITER

Honest to God

Thomas was not with the others when Jesus came. They told him, 'We've seen the Lord!' But he replied, 'I won't believe it unless I see the nail wounds in his hands… and place my hand into the wound in his side.' Eight days later the disciples were together again… suddenly Jesus was standing among them. He said, 'Peace be with you.' Then he said to Thomas, 'Put your finger here and see my hands… Don't be faithless any longer. Believe!' 'My Lord and my God!' Thomas exclaimed. Jesus told him, 'You believe because you've seen me. Blessed are those who haven't seen me and believe anyway.'

JOHN 20:24–29 (paraphrased)

Thomas wasn't with the others when they saw Jesus alive; he was out while his friends were in hiding. You can imagine the scene when he returned and the others were bombarding him with the news. 'You should have been here! You missed it!' So Thomas reacts and tells them he won't believe just because they say he should. He can't believe in the resurrected Jesus unless he has his own encounter. He can't piggyback on the faith of others.

A week later Jesus appears again, this time specifically to help Thomas. And having declared he'd need to examine the scars of Jesus, Thomas doesn't. He's immediately convinced, and he worships.

Jesus understood Thomas, then spoke for the rest of us: 'Blessed are those who'll believe without seeing.' Even as Thomas falls on his knees, Jesus begins to think about you and me. Those of us who won't get the same encounter. Blessed are you and I who have had different encounters. I have most often met Jesus in others, in the kind, courageous, honest things they have said and done.

He's gone down in history as 'doubting Thomas', but *honest* Tom would be more accurate. Doubts and questions are not the enemies of faith; they are part of it. Jesus encouraged his friends to keep asking, to keep searching. As he was dying, he cried, 'Why have you forsaken me?' – a question which many would identify with down the years. Jesus knew what it was to long for God's presence, to long for his assurance.

Let's not be afraid to be honest with God. He understands us; he knows how we tick. Let's keep asking those questions, so that our faith in Jesus may be rooted in reality.

DAVE HOPWOOD, AUTHOR AND SPEAKER

Follow me!

Jesus said to Simon Peter, 'Simon, son of John, do you love me more than these?' 'Yes, Lord,' he said, 'you know that I love you.' Jesus said, 'Feed my lambs.' Again Jesus said, 'Simon, son of John, do you love me?' He answered, 'Yes, Lord, you know that I love you.' Jesus said, 'Take care of my sheep.' The third time he said to him, 'Simon, son of John, do you love me?' Peter was hurt because Jesus asked him the third time, 'Do you love me?' He said, 'Lord, you know all things; you know that I love you.'

JOHN 21:15–17 (NIV, abridged)

We find ourselves today in a fishing boat on Lake Galilee. The inky-black sky starts to brighten along the horizon as the great red sun begins to rise. Our seven companions are cold, exhausted and demoralised – despite fishing all night, they've caught nothing. Admittedly, it's been a few years since they fished, but how could they have caught absolutely nothing? The smell of charcoal and cooking fish wafts over the water, and suddenly a voice is heard shouting curious advice.

You know the story. On the other side of the boat is an enormous shoal of fish. John suddenly senses, perhaps it's a spiritual thing, that the man on the shore is Jesus. But it's Peter who impetuously jumps into the water and swims the 90 metres to greet him.

After breakfast, Jesus takes Peter for a walk, asking him three painful questions about his love for him. As Peter professes his love for Jesus, he's given the opportunity for a new start, putting his three devastating denials behind him. He is to become a shepherd like the Good Shepherd himself – one who feeds, protects and cares for his sheep. It will cost him everything.

Peter asks about John's calling but is quickly rebuffed. 'Follow me!' (v. 19) is all Jesus wants of him – it is his own, very personal commission. How extraordinary that Jesus chooses the one who has utterly failed him to build his church! He doesn't ask for perfection, knowledge or strategy, just love.

As we listen today for the voice of the risen Jesus calling over the deep waters of our lives, we may need to admit failure, maybe even change direction. Certainly we need to follow his instructions, put on the mantle made just for us, and set about loving him. From this everything else will flow.

HELEN WILLIAMS, MUSICIAN AND WRITER

Looking up at the sky

'After saying this, he was taken up to heaven as they watched him, and a cloud hid him from their sight. They still had their eyes fixed on the sky as he went away, when two men dressed in white suddenly stood beside them and said, 'Galileans, why are you standing there looking up at the sky? This Jesus, who was taken from you into heaven, will come back in the same way that you saw him go to heaven.'

ACTS 1:9–11 (GNT)

When the disciples responded to Jesus' call to follow him, they did not know that their lives would be turned upside down – transformed – by doing so. Constantly on the move, Jesus taught them in parables and they witnessed many miracles and wonders. They experienced a see-saw of emotions, none more so than when they saw Jesus crucified, and then saw him again after the resurrection. It was hard to take it all in; some doubted, yet they trusted him.

And then, the ascension. We are told that they gazed up, transfixed, as if time stood still. Perhaps they realised he had really gone and tried to hold on to those last precious moments with him. Perhaps they were afraid or hoped he would come back down.

It took the arrival of the two men dressed in white to bring them back down to earth. These messengers questioned why the disciples were looking up into the sky, saying that Jesus had returned to heaven; and, more, that he would return from there one day. Then the disciples remembered what Jesus had said to them. They returned to Jerusalem to pray together, and await the Holy Spirit's empowering, as they prepared for the next step on their journey to witness to others.

I wonder how many of us have found our own lives transformed by following Jesus? I know I have. Like the disciples, sometimes we might find our path is not an easy one, but God has a plan for us. We can be sure that we will be empowered by God's Holy Spirit to witness to Christ and for tasks of service. We can trust him.

FAITH FORD, POET AND WRITER

Fire and wind... and trolls

When the day of Pentecost arrived, they were all together in one place. And suddenly there came from heaven a sound like a mighty rushing wind, and it filled the entire house where they were sitting. And divided tongues as of fire appeared to them and rested on each one of them. And they were all filled with the Holy Spirit and began to speak in other tongues as the Spirit gave them utterance... And all were amazed and perplexed, saying to one another, 'What does this mean?' But others mocking said, 'They are filled with new wine.'

ACTS 2:1–4, 12–13 (ESV)

Everybody's a critic. Go on, try posting something on social media without at least one person objecting to what you have to say! All right, hamster piano memes don't count, but you know what I mean. And so do these followers of Jesus.

They do what he has told them to do. They go to Jerusalem and wait for the gift he has promised. And with a whoosh of wind and fire, the gift arrives and the Holy Spirit blesses them with the ability to pass the good news of Jesus on to a world full of nations watching outside.

'Amazed and astonished' (v. 7) – that is the first reaction, as the crowd recognises them as Galileans who can somehow speak each of their languages. 'Perplexed' gets added to the list (v. 12), as they try to puzzle out what this mystery means. But then the trolls kick in. 'Nah, they're drunk,' they shout.

And maybe that's just the way of things. We'd like to think that 'amazed and astonished' would always be the response when we act in obedience to God's will. We'd like to hope that even 'perplexed' would give us the opportunity to teach and to enlighten. But nobody likes to be criticised.

So what do we do? Explain, for a start. That's what Peter does. And then don't let the criticism – or the possibility of criticism – put you off doing what is right. As the book of Acts reveals, time and time again, these early followers of Jesus do just that. They follow God's will. They meet resistance. They explain what they are doing. And then they carry on doing it.

And the result? The church just keeps on growing, in spite of the trolls. Or maybe, in a strange way, because of them – and the way the church reacts!

BOB HARTMAN, STORYTELLER

Truly thankful

Now a man who was lame from birth was being carried to the temple gate called Beautiful, where he was put every day to beg from those going into the temple courts. When he saw Peter and John about to enter, he asked them for money… Then Peter said, 'Silver or gold I do not have, but what I do have I give you. In the name of Jesus Christ of Nazareth, walk.' Taking him by the right hand, he helped him up, and instantly the man's feet and ankles became strong. He jumped to his feet and began to walk. Then he went with them into the temple courts, walking and jumping, and praising God.

ACTS 3:2–3, 6–8 (NIV)

When was the last time you were truly thankful to God for something to the point that, like the lame man, you let go and praised and worshipped him with your whole being? What stops us from truly worshipping God with abandonment? Perhaps we don't feel worthy enough for God to answer our prayers, feeling ashamed that we had to ask God to help because we were not strong enough to deal with the problems ourselves.

The lame man got the first thing right by strategically sitting at the most favoured entrance to the temple and at exactly the right time, when people were arriving to pray. Similarly, we might go to a church service with the intention of praying or being prayed for by others; seeking out God to help us sort out our problems and answer our prayer requests.

Although we are in the right place with the right intention, we might end up surprised at the answer we receive from God: what he gives us might not be what we wanted, but rather exactly what we need. The lame man asked for money but he ended up with something far more valuable – he got back the use of his legs. How often do we go to God in prayer asking for the same things over and over again, and are surprised when he does not give us the answer we were expecting? And yet he might have something better for us than we could ever have hoped for.

Next time God does immeasurably more in our lives than we ever expected, let's show our thankfulness by praising and worshipping him with abandonment, just like the lame man did.

IAIN NASH, CHILDREN'S PASTOR

Character and gifting

What they said pleased the whole community, and they chose Stephen, a man full of faith and the Holy Spirit, together with Philip, Prochorus, Nicanor, Timon, Parmenas, and Nicolaus, a proselyte of Antioch. They had these men stand before the apostles, who prayed and laid their hands on them... Stephen, full of grace and power, did great wonders and signs among the people. Then some of those who belonged to the synagogue of the Freedmen (as it was called), Cyrenians, Alexandrians, and others of those from Cilicia and Asia, stood up and argued with Stephen. But they could not withstand the wisdom and the Spirit with which he spoke.

ACTS 6:5–6, 8–10 (NRSV)

When food distribution caused friction in the Jerusalem church, Stephen was top of their list of problem-solvers (v. 5). He was evidently practical, therefore, but maybe also something of a miracle worker (v. 8), a defender of the faith (v. 10), and, as we know from chapter 7, an effective and courageous preacher. A gifted man, for sure!

But wait a moment, I've seen a lot of gifted people who don't impress me. They come with a reputation and, sure enough, they make an impact. They speak well, but there's something missing. They come over as arrogant – untouchable, unteachable, unaccountable. They can't – they won't – take criticism. They've nothing to learn, it seems, least of all from those who are supposedly less gifted.

We don't see this in Stephen, because, as gifted as he surely was, the major emphasis is on his character. He is described as a man 'full of the Spirit and of wisdom' (v. 3); also 'full of faith and the Holy Spirit' (v. 5) and 'full of grace and power' (v. 8). Even when he is arrested, his face 'was like the face of an angel' (v. 15), which suggests that something about his countenance spoke of the presence of God with him.

Gifting in God's service is good, but that gifting, if it is to honour God and make a lasting impact, needs to reside in a person whose character exhibits the fruit of the Spirit. We often major on gifting when considering others – 'she could do that' or 'he'll get the job done'. But always evaluate character, too – no matter how strong someone's gifts. We are not chosen for performance. We are chosen to reflect Christ.

DAVID KERRIGAN, FORMER GENERAL DIRECTOR, BMS WORLD MISSION

Open to the Spirit

Now there was an Ethiopian eunuch, a court official of the Candace, queen of the Ethiopians, in charge of her entire treasury. He had come to Jerusalem to worship and was returning home; seated in his chariot, he was reading the prophet Isaiah. Then the Spirit said to Philip, 'Go over to this chariot and join it.' So Philip ran up to it and heard him reading the prophet Isaiah. He asked, 'Do you understand what you are reading?' He replied, 'How can I, unless someone guides me?' And he invited Philip to get in and sit beside him.

ACTS 8:27b–31 (NRSV)

I love 'God-incidences' – those occasions when you are aware that God has brought you to somewhere or to meet someone at just the right moment. That's how it was for Philip in our reading. A high-ranking Ethiopian official had been in Jerusalem to worship God. He was reading the Jewish scriptures out of a longing to know God. He was a seeker. God engineered a meeting between him and someone able to help him forward on his spiritual journey. He was on his way home; in a very short while he would be well clear of Jerusalem. Not much time to lose. Philip comes on the scene. He is open to one of those nudges by the Holy Spirit: 'See that chariot in the distance? I want you to meet up with it and have a conversation with the man sitting in it.'

Philip might have been tempted to argue that he couldn't go up and start a conversation with a complete stranger. But he is willing to listen to that inner prompting. Once seated beside the Ethiopian, he discovers he's reading a passage of Isaiah that finds its deepest fulfilment in the person of Jesus and his death on the cross. What a God-given opportunity. He shares with him the good news of Jesus. The Ethiopian believes, is baptised and goes on his way rejoicing.

If we are prepared to be open to an inner prompting of the Holy Spirit, maybe God could use one of us to be a Philip to someone who, even in our very secular society, is searching, open to being introduced to Jesus, or to give a word of comfort and hope to someone going through a difficult time. God is able to use us in unexpected ways if we are prayerfully open to him and those inner promptings by his Spirit.

JOHN WENT, BISHOP AND FORMER TRUSTEE, BRF

Transforming grace

Meanwhile Saul, still breathing threats and murder against the disciples of the Lord, went to the high priest and asked him for letters to the synagogues at Damascus, so that if he found any who belonged to the Way, men or women, he might bring them bound to Jerusalem. Now as he was going along and approaching Damascus, suddenly a light from heaven flashed around him. He fell to the ground and heard a voice saying to him, 'Saul, Saul, why do you persecute me?' He asked, 'Who are you, Lord?' The reply came, 'I am Jesus, whom you are persecuting.'

ACTS 9:1–5 (NRSV)

In Acts 9, we read one of the most famous stories of conversion, the transformation of Saul the persecutor to Paul the apostle. The conversion is so significant in Acts that it appears three times (9:1–19; 22:6–16; 26:12–18), and this first account prepares the way for Paul's leading role in Acts as missionary to the Gentiles.

The chapter begins with Saul (the Jewish name of Paul) breathing 'threats and murder' against the disciples of Jesus. Seeking to stamp out 'the Way' (an early description of Christian faith), Saul seeks authorisation from the high priest to arrest followers of Jesus in the synagogues in Damascus, a city 135 miles from Jerusalem.

On the road, Saul encounters the risen Christ. Jesus appears as a blinding light and a voice that speaks and reveals that Saul's persecution of the church is a persecution of Jesus himself. The encounter leads to Saul's baptism, inclusion into the church and first efforts at evangelism.

While few can claim such a dramatic conversion as Saul's, the grace that transformed Saul is the same that changes all who come to Jesus. Saul's conversion is not a template for how God meets us but an illustration that God can transform hostile enemies into faithful servants (1 Timothy 1:15). This is good news for us all. It means that no one is beyond the reach of God's love, and it reminds us that the God of grace who calls us is the God of grace who continues to transform us. And today we can continue to pray to know that grace more deeply, or, as Paul puts it in Ephesians, 'to know the love of Christ that surpasses knowledge, so that you may be filled with all the fullness of God' (Ephesians 3:19).

ED MACKENZIE, LECTURER IN BIBLICAL THEOLOGY AND MISSION, CLIFF COLLEGE

A healing community

Now in Joppa there was a disciple whose name was Tabitha, which in Greek is Dorcas. She was devoted to good works and acts of charity. At that time, she became ill and died... When [Peter] arrived, they took him to the room upstairs. All the widows stood beside him, weeping and showing tunics and other clothing that Dorcas had made while she was with them. Peter put all of them outside, and then he knelt down and prayed. He turned to the body and said, 'Tabitha, get up.' Then she opened her eyes, and seeing Peter, she sat up.

ACTS 9:36–37a, 39b–40 (NRSV)

The widows who surrounded Tabitha's death bed were present as she passed. I imagine that they showed up at her home when she first became ill. In my two life professions, nurse and pastor, I have sat with family and friends as they encircled their loved one with prayer. Sharing stories, scripture and much-loved hymns or just sitting in sacred silence is a 'thin place' experience. In the Celtic tradition, a thin place is where the veil between this world and the eternal world is 'thin'. At the bedside of one close to death, God's love and presence is palpable.

Tabitha is introduced at the beginning of this story as a disciple, suggesting that she was a leader in the early church of Joppa. The widowed women who encircled her were members of the church community. They came to be with their friend and with one another. Perhaps they brought food as well as the tunics Tabitha had made that they cherished. In their communal tears of grief, they remembered and gave thanks for their friend who had shared her gifts with them. Just as today when we grieve, the shared customs of mourning provide healing for our body, mind and soul.

Summoned from another town, Peter arrives in Joppa. After his prayer, Tabitha miraculously opens her eyes and 'gets up' as instructed. In biblical stories, we often focus on the miracle worker rather than reflecting on those who have been present from the story's beginning. In this narrative, the women provide a circle of healing in their everyday acts of kindness.

Today, give thanks for those in your life who show up when you experience difficulties. Say a prayer of gratitude for the moments you have experienced God's healing presence through your community.

ROBERTA J. EGLI, EXECUTIVE DIRECTOR, MESSY CHURCH USA

Dramatic deliverance

The very night before Herod was going to bring him out, Peter, bound with two chains, was sleeping between two soldiers, while guards in front of the door were keeping watch over the prison. Suddenly an angel of the Lord appeared and a light shone in the cell. He tapped Peter on the side and woke him, saying, 'Get up quickly.' And the chains fell off his wrists. The angel said to him, 'Fasten your belt and put on your sandals.' He did so. Then he said to him, 'Wrap your cloak around you and follow me.'

ACTS 12:6–8 (NRSV)

The story of Peter's dramatic deliverance from prison in Acts 12 ends with the observation that 'when morning came, there was no small commotion among the soldiers over what had become of Peter' (v. 18).

I should say so! Herod searches for Peter but can't find him. He examines the guards. After all, Peter was in prison, bound by two chains and sleeping between the soldiers while other guards kept watch at the door. We know it's not their fault that Peter's escaped. But it looks like negligence. Or, worse than that, they'd helped him get away.

Justice in those days was swift and brutal. They are put to death. The execution of the guards is, I suspect, a detail of the story that is rarely examined or preached about. But I can't help dwelling on it. God does this amazing thing. Peter is released from prison. His chains fall from his wrists. But the immediate consequence for those whose job it was to guard him is that they are killed.

Wouldn't it be easier if the Christian story was played out in a perfect world, in which all our motives were good, wicked people didn't do wicked things and when something good and beautiful happened there weren't terrible, unintended consequences for some? But if it was a perfect world, there would be no need for God to set us free and no need for the Christian story. Peter was released. But the soldiers died. Jesus is raised from the dead. But there is still wickedness and sorrow in our world. Innocent people still suffer.

Until all of us are released from the chains that bind us, we will continue to tell this story, like Peter, in a challenging, fallen and imprisoned world.

STEPHEN COTTRELL, ARCHBISHOP OF YORK

Meet the family

About midnight Paul and Silas were praying and singing hymns to God, and the prisoners were listening to them. Suddenly there was an earthquake... all the doors were opened and everyone's chains were unfastened. When the jailer... saw the prison doors wide open, he drew his sword and was about to kill himself... But Paul shouted in a loud voice, 'Do not harm yourself, for we are all here.' The jailer... fell down trembling before Paul and Silas... and said, 'Sirs, what must I do to be saved?'

ACTS 16:25–30 (NRSV)

Battered and bleeding, Paul and Silas were bundled into the city jail and handed over to the hard-bitten military veteran who was in charge. Did they have any idea in that moment that they were meeting the next member of their family of faith? There was no hint of sympathy, far less any soothing of their raw wounds as they were shoved into wooden stocks and doors slammed shut, leaving them and the other prisoners in darkness.

Cursing, pleading, complaining, cries of anguish punctuating the night, all of that was to be expected, but that night it was different. Amid the clamour, voices could be heard offering reverent prayer; songs of praise and faith rose up, stilling other noise. It was natural for people who found themselves in the Philippi jail to be preoccupied with their own injuries, resentments and fears. But these Jewish prisoners, who had got on the wrong side of exploitative slave-owners, been nearly lynched by a mob, denied the normal process of justice, beaten (illegally, as it turned out) by the police and summarily locked up, seemed to be not in a prison but in a temple. And there was a sense that the God they were worshipping was there as well.

Then came the earthquake. The whole building shook, bolts snapped, doors flew open. And there was the warden, ready to end his life in fear and shame, until the prisoner Paul shouted, 'No, we're all here!' A bizarre assembly of prisoners and guards watched and listened as the jailer fell on his face, pleading to know the way to salvation. Those who, in the midst of their own suffering, had looked upwards in trust and outwards in love had the privilege of introducing their tormentor to the Jesus whom they served. Meet the family!

GEORGE WIELAND, DIRECTOR OF MISSION RESEARCH AND TRAINING, CAREY BAPTIST COLLEGE, NEW ZEALAND

Minor details and major incident

On the first day of the week we came together to break bread. Paul spoke to the people and, because he intended to leave the next day, kept on talking until midnight. There were many lamps in the upstairs room where we were meeting. Seated in a window was a young man named Eutychus, who was sinking into a deep sleep as Paul talked on and on. When he was sound asleep, he fell to the ground from the third storey and was picked up dead. Paul went down, threw himself on the young man and put his arms round him. 'Don't be alarmed,' he said. 'He's alive!'

ACTS 20:7–10 (NIV)

I wonder who was most shocked when this tragedy happened, the gathered Christians or Paul? Those Christians had come together, many of them after a hard day's work as slaves. This is the first indication we have that the early church met on 'The Lord's Day' and not the Jewish sabbath. Although we can't be sure this was the norm, this minor detail links us directly to them, as Sunday has been our main day of worship.

Another aspect of this story that binds us together is that they listened to Paul, as we often do when we read and hear from his letters in our services. No doubt he taught them how to live as Christians as well as telling them about his mission activities.

But here our experiences part. Paul spoke for so long that one tired young man fell asleep, perhaps overcome by the stifling atmosphere of many people crowded together plus the fumes from all those lights. He fell three flights to the ground. Unsurprisingly people thought he was dead.

Rather than being fazed, this provided Paul with yet another way to proclaim the good news of Jesus. He 'threw himself on the young man' (v. 10), reminding us of Elijah's behaviour in a similar situation (1 Kings 17:17–24). It may sound like an elementary form of artificial resuscitation. But behind it was Paul's confidence that God could deal with even this.

Hopefully we won't have to cope with such long sermons! But we certainly will be faced with unexpected situations where we can either panic, freeze or exercise our faith in some appropriate way. Nourished by our times of worship, recollection of scripture and Holy Spirit inspired faith, we too can bring God's peace and victory into the lives of others.

DAVID SPRIGGS, BAPTIST MINISTER AND FORMER EDITOR, *GUIDELINES*

Journey through the storm

Keeping to the open sea, we passed along the coast of Cilicia and Pamphylia, landing at Myra, in the province of Lycia. There the commanding officer found an Egyptian ship from Alexandria that was bound for Italy, and he put us on board. We had several days of slow sailing, and after great difficulty we finally neared Cnidus. But the wind was against us, so we sailed across to Crete and along the sheltered coast of the island, past the cape of Salmone. We struggled along the coast with great difficulty and finally arrived at Fair Havens, near the town of Lasea. We had lost a lot of time.

ACTS 27:5–9 (NLT)

Paul had been in prison for two years, waiting to go to Rome for his trial. Finally the day had arrived and they boarded a boat. Halfway through the journey, Paul warned them not to sail. It was winter and storms were very likely. But they did not listen.

We read about how terrifying the storm was. After many days, Paul stood up and gave them a message of hope. He gently reminded them that they should have listened to his warnings about not sailing at this time. He told them that an angel had visited him during the night and told him that no men would die. Paul needed to keep reminding them of God's promise to protect them.

It might feel like you are in a season of waiting. You might spend time wondering, praying and planning for what is to come next. However, when the waiting is done, sometimes our hopes and plans are not what we expected.

Paul had to wait a long time to go to Rome. He spent that time encouraging others while keeping close to God. When he started his journey to Rome, God was very much with him. When God spoke to Paul, he listened and spoke God's truth, even when people didn't want to hear.

Psalms 37:7 says, 'Be still in the presence of the Lord, and wait patiently for him to act.' God and his word are true and something that we need to remember when the journey to the destination isn't what we had hoped for. If you are in a season of waiting, rest in God's presence. If you are in a season of journeying, lean into God. If you are in a season of arrival, rejoice that God got you there.

DAWN SAVIDGE, NATIONAL CHILDREN, FAMILIES AND YOUNG PEOPLE'S ADVISOR,
JESUS SHAPED PEOPLE

Despite everything, hold on!

And when I turned I saw seven golden lampstands, and among the lampstands was someone like a son of man, dressed in a robe reaching down to his feet and with a golden sash around his chest. The hair on his head was white like wool, as white as snow, and his eyes were like blazing fire. His feet were like bronze glowing in a furnace, and his voice was like the sound of rushing waters. In his right hand he held seven stars, and coming out of his mouth was a sharp, double-edged sword.

REVELATION 1:12b–16a (NIV)

Exiled for his testimony to Jesus, John needs to know that despite every appearance it is Jesus and not Caesar who rules as king. Who has final authority: the imperial official who had banished John to remote Patmos or Jesus, crucified by Roman nails? It's a difficult, dangerous time to be a follower of Jesus. Can his people, as represented by the seven churches in the province of Asia, hold on, even against powerful opposition?

Fittingly, it is on the Lord's Day, the day of resurrection, that God pulls back the curtain to reveal to John the full picture of what is happening. He sees the reality that is normally hidden from our eyes but which defines our lives.

Yes, there is a fierce battle – even one of cosmic dimensions – in which we all are caught up, but the cross of Jesus, his shed blood, has wonderfully won the victory over all that would harm us. So John exhorts these suffering saints that it is God who is controlling history, fighting for us.

And John is privileged to see Jesus in an altogether dazzlingly new light. Clearly he struggles to find the right words to describe his revelation, using a whole variety of stunning images drawn from the Hebrew scriptures, even those describing God himself. They tumble over each other to express this awesome majesty of Jesus as 'the ruler of the kings of the earth' (v. 5). His word, as shown by the double-edged sword, demonstrates total authority.

And this Jesus stands among the lampstands: he is with his people, speaking the message which runs through the entire Bible: 'Fear not!'

So we refuse to be taken in by appearances, to be menaced by those who would resist God's kingship. Hold on, persevere. Jesus is with us. Victory is assured.

ROSS MOUGHTIN, BLOGGER

The end of the story

'I, Jesus, have sent my angel to give you this message for the churches. I am both the source of David and the heir to his throne. I am the bright morning star.' The Spirit and the bride say, 'Come.' Let anyone who hears this say, 'Come.' Let anyone who is thirsty come. Let anyone who desires drink freely from the water of life… He who is the faithful witness to all these things says, 'Yes, I am coming soon!' Amen! Come, Lord Jesus! May the grace of the Lord Jesus be with God's holy people.

REVELATION 22:16–17, 20–21 (NLT)

Have you ever been tempted to read the last pages of the book you have just started? What is it that drives you in that moment to sneak a peek? Is it curiosity, impatience, a deadline for your book club?

If you did that with the final chapter of Revelation, you would probably only end up more confused, given the wildly fantastical writing and the apocalyptic nature of the text. It might, however, pique your curiosity to discover more, and that is never a bad thing, especially when it comes to reading the Bible.

We know the book to be a 'revelation' from Jesus Christ, partially in the form of seven letters (Revelation 1—3) and then as seven scenes or images (Revelation 4—22) for the whole church. To those of you who want to know the end of the story, it is summed up in these verses. Simply, Jesus is coming back, and all will be well for those who have remained in Christ Jesus. The things which we can see now, only partially, will be fulfilled. The kingdom which Jesus began to usher in during his earthly life over 2,000 years ago will be brought to fruition and fullness in a quite wonderful way.

So, don't spend your time now just waiting. Get involved! Spend your time, energy, creativity and imagination ushering in more of the kingdom. How do we do that? Love the Lord your God with all your heart, soul and mind; love your neighbour as you love yourself (Matthew 22:36–40); and make disciples of Jesus Christ (Matthew 28:19).

TIM LEA, CONSULTANT, COACH, NETWORKER AND FACILITATOR, FRESH EXPRESSIONS

Praying through the Psalms

WHO DOESN'T LOVE THE PSALMS? Over the centuries this ancient hymnbook from the Jewish temple has been a source of rich encouragement and inspiration to God's people throughout the world. Crossing cultures and bridging generations, these songs from of old speak to us all, because they address the human condition. Times may change, but the human heart stays the same, and so does our need of God.

There are many ways to classify individual psalms. Some are songs of joyful worship by which we too can exalt the Lord our God. Uninhibited praise is so liberating! Some are laments, sad songs, often with a note of complaint or questioning. They provide words to use in our times of distress and pain. Some are songs of testimony, telling of the Lord's deliverance, giving hope to us when we need help. They encourage us to tell our own story of God's faithfulness. Some are simply songs of thanksgiving, marvelling at the goodness of God in creation and daily life. They inform our understanding of God and form a template for our own thanksgiving.

When we read the Psalms, we are joining such heroes of faith as David and Moses, and lesser-known believers like Asaph, Ethan, Heman and the Sons of Korah. Each tells their own story with honesty and vulnerability, whether out of joy or sorrow.

In these daily readings you will read reflections from some contemporary people of faith who find solace and inspiration in the Psalms. Like others before them, they are responding to the text from their own lived experience, sharing something of their story with us.

> As you read, may you be inspired to turn the words into your response to God. As you reflect, may you be strengthened in your walk with him.

TONY HORSFALL, RETREAT LEADER, AUTHOR AND MENTOR

God reveals himself to us!

The heavens declare the glory of God; the skies proclaim the work of his hands. Day after day they pour forth speech; night after night they reveal knowledge. They have no speech, they use no words; no sound is heard from them. Yet their voice goes out into all the earth, their words to the ends of the world... The law of the Lord is perfect, refreshing the soul. The statutes of the Lord are trustworthy, making wise the simple... May these words of my mouth and this meditation of my heart be pleasing in your sight, Lord, my Rock and my Redeemer.

PSALM 19:1–4a, 7, 14 (NIV)

The first part of Psalm 19 says that God reveals himself through the created world. Notice the active words: 'declare', 'proclaim', 'pour forth', 'reveal' – indicating the revelatory activity of the skies and the heavens, though they are in reality devoid of words. They actively display something of the God who brought them into being and sustains them. They witness to God's being and purpose, his glory and continuing creative occupation, his governing and preserving. He is God. There is no other, they say!

How do they say that? The sky witnesses to the reality of God by simply being the sky. The fact that the sun rises each morning and sets at night speaks forcefully of God. The Lord sustains it in its daily course. The whole world sees this and knows its warmth, consistency, brightness, splendour and beauty.

In the second part, the words 'law', 'statutes', 'precepts', 'commands' and 'decrees' are synonyms, or close enough, signifying the word of God directed at faithful living, the imperatives of godliness. The psalmist delights in them for they are perfect, trustworthy, right and pure – as you would expect, as they originate with God himself.

This word is active (through the work of the Holy Spirit) in 'refreshing the soul', in giving wisdom and joy, light and (by implication) fear of or reverence for the Lord. If 'the heavens declare the glory of God', then the word of God shows us the divine will for our lives and daily existence.

It warns us against sinning and how to be godly, to walk blamelessly before the Lord. It teaches us that we need forgiveness for 'hidden faults' and the sanctifying activity of God – we cannot do it alone. The psalmist relies on the Lord, his Rock, his Redeemer to whom he offers this psalm of adoration.

MICHAEL PARSONS, MINISTER FOR DISCIPLESHIP, LECHLADE BAPTIST CHURCH, AND FORMER BRF STAFF MEMBER

Hold tight

The Lord is my shepherd, I shall not want. He makes me lie down in green pastures; he leads me beside still waters; he restores my soul. He leads me in right paths for his name's sake. Even though I walk through the darkest valley, I fear no evil; for you are with me; your rod and your staff – they comfort me. You prepare a table before me in the presence of my enemies; you anoint my head with oil; my cup overflows. Surely goodness and mercy shall follow me all the days of my life, and I shall dwell in the house of the Lord my whole life long.

PSALM 23 (NRSV)

Psalm 23 must be one of the best-known psalms in the Bible. Often sung as a hymn, the words have a comforting familiarity. It's a popular choice for funerals.

It's not hard to see why. In six short verses the psalm is a poignant cry of grief and loss, of pain and mourning. But also, and crucially, of comfort and compassion. Of hope, even in the face of death.

Poetic it may be, but it isn't sentimental. No chocolate hearts and fluffy cushions here. Think rather of being thrown overboard in the worst storm imaginable – and reaching out into the waves to grab hold of a life raft.

The author is David, the shepherd boy who became king. That metaphor is rich with resonance: the shepherd is someone who can track a route ('right paths'), however faint; who wants to steer us towards lush green grass and clear blue water, but knows the journey involves rocky, arid terrain along the way; who will be there to protect us when the wolves are on the prowl.

I like the psalmist's honesty. Life can be tough, he says. The valley of the shadow of death is a dark and chilly place. But take comfort: you're not on your own. Just cling on. God provides, says the psalmist. Rest in him, in those rich pastures.

Relax, says God. *I've got this.*

We don't need to be afraid. God will restore our soul.

Trust me, says God. *I'm here.*

His promise? Goodness and mercy. A seat at his table. A feast of good things. All we have to do is accept the invitation.

'You must sit down, says Love, and taste my meat,' writes the poet George Herbert. 'So I did sit and eat.'

SARAH MEYRICK, AUTHOR AND LAY CANON, CHRIST CHURCH CATHEDRAL, OXFORD

All we need

One thing I ask from the Lord, this only do I seek: that I may dwell in the house of the Lord all the days of my life, to gaze on the beauty of the Lord and to seek him in his temple. For in the day of trouble he will keep me safe in his dwelling; he will hide me in the shelter of his sacred tent and set me high upon a rock. Then my head will be exalted above the enemies who surround me; at his sacred tent I will sacrifice with shouts of joy; I will sing and make music to the Lord.

PSALM 27:4–6 (NIV)

A few years ago, I was in a horrific car accident. It was so bad I had to be airlifted to hospital. I was drifting in and out of consciousness and I remember wondering if I had died and gone to heaven. I realised that I couldn't have, as I was lying on my back and I knew that in heaven I would be on my knees or face down!

I was almost disappointed, because I knew my injuries were severe and recovery was going to be painful and slow. And it was. But, every moment of those weeks and months, I felt God so close and his Spirit filled me with a deep sense of peace. I did not worry or panic but simply rested in him. I truly felt 'safe in his dwelling'. Looking back now, I can see how the Lord comforted me and gave me extra strength to cope and people to support me. But best of all, I knew he was with me.

Before the accident my faith was strong, but during that time I became more aware of his constant presence and more certain of heaven. It is often when we are struggling and going through hard times that we become more aware of God's loving care. In times of sickness, for ourselves and those close to us, the sure and certain knowledge of heaven is a joy and comfort. When times are hard, call on him and trust him, for as John Wesley said, 'The best is yet to come!' It is enough to know he walks with you every day and is preparing a place for you in heaven. This is all we need.

PAM LEWIS, LOCAL PREACHER

Sing, play, pray and wait

Give thanks to the Lord with the lyre; make melody to him with the harp of ten strings! Sing to him a new song... By the word of the Lord the heavens were made... Let all the inhabitants of the world stand in awe of him... Our soul waits for the Lord; he is our help and our shield. For our heart is glad in him, because we trust in his holy name. Let your steadfast love, O Lord, be upon us, even as we hope in you.

PSALM 33:2–8, 20–22 (ESV, abridged)

As a child I loved singing, and that meant hymns. As I grew up it branched out to oratorio, and that is what I still enjoy most, though I sing all sorts of music. For me, music is primarily a way to worship God, so I love the start of this psalm.

We are not always full of joy, but we can offer a sacrifice of praise and 'make a joyful noise to the Lord' (Psalm 100:1). There are always things to thank God for, as the hymn 'Count your blessings' tells us. They may be simple things like the sunshine and the flowers, or much larger such as financial provision or health. Friends, too, are something to be thankful for, especially when we have no close family members. And what about the gift of prayer which means we can talk directly to God, who is our Father?

Verse 8 says that all the inhabitants of the earth should fear God – that is, not be frightened of him but stand in awe. In today's society, where there is much emphasis on evolution, it is worthwhile reminding ourselves that, in fact, God created us and our world.

The central section of the psalm deals with God's provision of wisdom for rulers and deliverance from difficulties for those who trust in him, and I'm sure we can all think of times in our lives when we have faced such problems.

The doxology of this psalm is so important: our soul waits for the Lord; we are glad in him, because we trust in him; our hope is in him alone. Whether or not you can sing or play an instrument, here is one thing everyone can do: talk to God, read his word, *wait* and listen for his voice.

HILARY HARTLEY, RETIRED RADIOGRAPHER

Peace like a river

God is our refuge and strength, a very present help in trouble. Therefore we will not fear, though the earth should change, though the mountains shake in the heart of the sea; though its waters roar and foam, though the mountains tremble with its tumult. There is a river whose streams make glad the city of God, the holy habitation of the Most High. God is in the midst of the city; it shall not be moved; God will help it when the morning dawns... 'Be still, and know that I am God!'

PSALM 46:1–5, 10a (NRSV)

Here is a vivid picture of a world in tumult, devastated by change and seemingly out of control. Sound familiar? But while this metaphorical water roars and foams in a maelstrom of horror and destruction, there is a very different body of water running through the eternal heavenly city. This is a river that 'makes glad' as its streams flow throughout, bringing the strength, joy and confidence of God's presence to all who dwell alongside it.

So often in life, we are caught up in a torrent of events and emotions that rush and roar at us so that we feel utterly overwhelmed. We fear that God is far from being a refuge and strength. Instead, we clutch at the flotsam and jetsam of what seem to be empty promises and seek peace that soon drifts away from us in a flood of hopelessness.

But Psalm 46, echoing Psalm 30:5 ('Weeping may linger for the night, but joy comes with the morning'), tells us that this maelstrom will be transformed with the dawn: that God *will* offer us refuge within the flow of himself amid us: a flow of peace and eternal reassurance.

So how do we respond to that offer of peace and reassurance from a place of uncertainty and fear?

Almost at the end of the psalm, we are asked to 'be still': to recognise God as God and allow a divine and saving grace to become the flow within us that sustains and refreshes until it becomes the place of refuge we seek. Only then will we be free from fear. We need not struggle in the storms of life but can let the promised river of life transform them: 'in quietness and in trust shall be [our] strength' (Isaiah 30:15).

WENDY BRAY, PRIEST AND WRITER

Open heart surgery

Create in me a pure heart, O God, and renew a steadfast spirit within me. Do not cast me from your presence or take your Holy Spirit from me. Restore to me the joy of your salvation and grant me a willing spirit, to sustain me… Open my lips, Lord, and my mouth will declare your praise. You do not delight in sacrifice, or I would bring it; you do not take pleasure in burnt offerings. My sacrifice, O God, is a broken spirit; a broken and contrite heart you, God, will not despise.

PSALM 51:10–12, 15–17 (NIV)

David sinned with Bathsheba and then arranged her husband's death on the battlefield.

David's faith in God was genuine, but at some point he had allowed his heart to wander away from his relationship with God. He thought he could get away with his sin. He had forgotten that God had chosen him to be king precisely because he could see what was in David's heart (1 Samuel 16:7). His neglect of God led to disastrous consequences. How easily we can fall foul of the 'sin that so easily entangles' (Hebrews 12:1)!

Having been exposed by the prophet Nathan, David now pours out his soul in this psalm. He chooses to turn to God and trust in his 'unfailing love' and 'great compassion' (v. 1). Crushed by the weight of his own sin, David pleads for God to give him a 'pure heart' and a 'steadfast spirit' (v. 10).

In the midst of David's unfaithfulness, God remained faithful. Failure isn't final where God is concerned. Indeed, our pride must be replaced with 'a broken spirit and contrite heart' (v. 17) so that we can enjoy a relationship with God.

In response to this psalm, what are we to do? The writer to the Hebrews advises us: 'Fixing our eyes on Jesus, the pioneer and perfecter of faith… so that you will not grow weary and lose heart' (Hebrews 12:2–3). Today, just as David poured out his heart to God, take some time to be honest with God. Confess your sins, allowing God, in his love, to remove any shame and guilt. Ask God to help you shift your focus on to Jesus.

PHIL MALTBY, PROJECTS OFFICER, METHODIST FORCES BOARD

Heart-cry

Hear my cry, O God; listen to my prayer. From the ends of the earth I call to you, I call as my heart grows faint; lead me to the rock that is higher than I. For you have been my refuge, a strong tower against the foe. I long to dwell in your tent forever and take refuge in the shelter of your wings. For you, God, have heard my vows; you have given me the heritage of those who fear your name. Increase the days of the king's life, his years for many generations. May he be enthroned in God's presence forever; appoint your love and faithfulness to protect him. Then I will ever sing in praise of your name and fulfil my vows day after day.

PSALM 61 (NIV)

Prayer is an instinctive human response, the cry of the heart towards God. No one tells us we must pray; we simply do. When we find ourselves in a crisis, our automatic response is to look for help from outside ourselves. In other words, we call out to God for divine assistance.

David was exiled from Jerusalem during the time of Absalom's rebellion (2 Samuel 15:1–14; Psalm 3). He feels far away from home physically ('the ends of the earth') and is emotionally drained ('my heart grows faint'). He is a long way from where he wants to be, feeling cut off and overwhelmed, alone in his despair.

One thing David knows, however, is that prayer can bridge any distance, whether geographical or emotional. So, he turns his heart towards God. Four images express his confidence that God will help him. God is a *rock*, immovable and utterly dependable. He is a strong *tower*, a refuge and place of safety. He is a *tent*, offering shelter and shade from the elements. Like a *bird*, his wings give comfort and protection.

Why not use these word pictures as a basis for your own prayers? He is your rock, your tower, your dwelling place, your comforting presence. No matter how you feel, or how difficult your circumstances, nothing can separate you from the love of God today. Wherever you find yourself, God will not only hear your cry, but will also listen to your plea for help. Like David, choose to find your refuge in him.

TONY HORSFALL, RETREAT LEADER, AUTHOR AND MENTOR

Where is your holy space?

How lovely is your dwelling place, O Lord of hosts! My soul longs, indeed it faints for the courts of the Lord; my heart and my flesh sing for joy to the living God. Even the sparrow finds a home, and the swallow a nest for herself, where she may lay her young, at your altars, O Lord of hosts, my King and my God. Happy are those who live in your house, ever singing your praise. Happy are those whose strength is in you, in whose heart are the highways to Zion.

PSALM 84:1–5 (NRSV)

This must be one of the most joyous of all the psalms; it's almost as if we get wrapped up in the longing and desire of the writer to be in the temple, the ultimate expression of the presence of God.

There is a tension in this passage, though, between home and pilgrimage. The psalmist longs to be at home in God's dwelling place like the sparrows and swallows who would have swooped and circused around the temple precincts and whose nests would have been found in its walls. Places do matter to us, because we are embodied beings in a physical world. It matters where we were born or grew up, where we experienced profound security (or not). It matters where we have experienced the 'peace of God which passes understanding' (or not) in church buildings or in moments in nature or with friends and fellowship. In Celtic spirituality these places of shared revelation are sometimes called 'thin places'.

Equally, however, the passage also reminds us that God can be found in all places at all times in all circumstances, because holy space is ultimately found in the human heart which seeks and finds the eternal God. We may long for physical spaces, but actually it is the spiritual connection that they allow which has the real power, and we also know that all landscapes, temples and homes will pass away one day. In this sense we are all pilgrims, making our way to our heavenly destination, and only there will our pilgrimage be complete. Our hearts are highways to the eternal God beyond time and space.

Call to mind and give thanks for your own holy spaces which have been physical places of deep spiritual connection. Then thank God that every place is a holy space if our hearts are 'highways to Zion'.

CHARLIE KERR, CHAPLAINCY ADVISER, OXFORD DIOCESAN BOARD OF EDUCATION

Finding joy

Make a joyful noise to the Lord, all the earth. Worship the Lord with gladness; come into his presence with singing. Know that the Lord is God. It is he that made us, and we are his; we are his people, and the sheep of his pasture. Enter his gates with thanksgiving, and his courts with praise. Give thanks to him, bless his name. For the Lord is good; his steadfast love endures forever, and his faithfulness to all generations.

PSALM 100 (NRSV)

What are your first thoughts when waking in the morning?

Psalm 100, known as the Jubilate Deo, regularly appears in Anglican Morning Prayer – for a good reason. It sets a course for the day, displacing our anxiety with joy and rooting us in God's continuing goodness, love and faithfulness.

The psalm asks us to make joy a practice, alongside lamentation (as expressed in many psalms), in whatever we are going through. It encourages us not to wait for joy to appear but to choose to find it, or, perhaps better, to choose to allow joy to find us.

It reveals that this is a joining in with 'all the earth' – a sharing in the joyful praise already being offered throughout creation and by many peoples. We are not alone!

How might we begin to shape a practice of joyful praise? The psalm suggests that joy is released by thanksgiving, by gratitude for our belonging in God and for God's blessing and provision for us in every area of our lives. Nurturing gratitude is at the heart of any practice of joy.

Here's an interesting thing. The psalm suggests that singing and music have particularly important roles to play in the practice of joy. This rings true! We know that to give ourselves to music works on us at many levels, freeing our spirit, releasing physical tension and – as the psalm suggests – opening us up to encounter, to God's presence.

What are your first thoughts when waking in the morning? Psalm 100 encourages us to allow those thoughts and words to become 'a joyful noise', released by thanksgiving for God's many blessings, whatever we are going through. So joy may become a practice for life, a day at a time.

IAN ADAMS, CHAPLAIN, RIDLEY HALL, CAMBRIDGE, AND SPIRITUALITY ADVISER, CHURCH MISSION SOCIETY

Wholehearted worship

Praise the Lord, my soul; all my inmost being, praise his holy name... As a father has compassion on his children, so the Lord has compassion on those who fear him; for he knows how we are formed, he remembers that we are dust. The life of mortals is like grass, they flourish like a flower of the field; the wind blows over it and it is gone, and its place remembers it no more. But from everlasting to everlasting the Lord's love is with those who fear him, and his righteousness with their children's children.

PSALM 103:1, 13–17 (NIV)

A faithful Christian once caught sight of a fellow worshipper who seemed lost in wonder, love and praise. Momentarily distracted, they pondered: why do I find it so hard to worship God with my whole being?

I've felt like that sometimes. Maybe you have too.

This great psalm of praise gives us so many reasons to worship: forgiveness, healing, redemption, love, compassion, generosity and more. Yet sometimes we still hold back from the *whole*hearted praise it describes. Here's one reason why this might be: perhaps we do not feel quite worthy of approaching God. So we hold back those parts of us which we are not sure are acceptable.

That is why the next part of the psalm is so helpful. It declares this truth: 'God knows of what we are made' (see v. 14). Our weakness and failures may surprise us sometimes, but God cannot be taken by surprise because he knows of what we are made. And yet he still has the same compassion on us as does a good father for his children.

That reassurance opens up my heart more to sing God's praise with my whole being. I need that especially because I know my weaknesses all too well.

Henry Francis Lyte wrote probably the best-known hymn version of Psalm 103. He knew ill health all his life and from this understanding of frailty was able to write these lines, which you could make your own prayer:

Fatherlike he tends and spares us;
well our feeble frame he knows.
In his hand he gently bears us,
rescues us from all our foes.
Alleluia, alleluia!
Widely as his mercy flows!
'Praise, my soul, the king of heaven' by Henry Francis Lyte (1793–1847)

PAUL SWANN, AUTHOR

My help comes

I lift up my eyes to the mountains – where does my help come from? My help comes from the Lord, the Maker of heaven and earth. He will not let your foot slip – he who watches over you will not slumber; indeed, he who watches over Israel will neither slumber nor sleep. The Lord watches over you – the Lord is your shade at your right hand; the sun will not harm you by day, nor the moon by night. The Lord will keep you from all harm – he will watch over your life; the Lord will watch over your coming and going both now and for evermore.

PSALM 121 (NIV)

Perhaps these verses are so familiar that the assurance of God's help and care fails to touch or to implant in our hearts and we miss the truths they contain. Have we found God to be present in difficult, lonely and uncertain times? David, the likely writer of the psalm, was certain of God's help. God would never let David down. David knew that as he looked to the hills; they were the reminder of God's past protection and provision, but also the scenes of a fugitive existence, fearing for his life, of being afraid; a place where pagan gods were honoured and worshipped. Yet David, in those hills, had seen God rescue him, provide for him and strengthen him. This gave him confidence that God was alongside to help in present times.

As you read and absorb the reality of God's diligent care and provision, perhaps you can recall God meeting you in the past, being your help. God will be our help now as we have seen him be before. David reminds us that God is constant in watching over us day and night. God watches over our going out and coming in. Those words became especially relevant to me when, as a GP, I went out alone on emergency visits all night. No one knew where I was going nor indeed of my return. With these words, I had the confidence that almighty God saw and he was with me.

God watches the detail of our lives, in the difficulties, the challenges and the anxious times as well as in the mundane routine. He knows everything about us; nothing is ignored. This psalm shouts out that God has not forgotten us. Today, hold on to God, because his help comes.

HILARY ALLEN, DOCTOR AND POET

The story we inherit

I was glad when they said to me, 'Let us go to the house of the Lord.' And now here we are, standing inside your gates, O Jerusalem... All the tribes of Israel – the Lord's people – make their pilgrimage here. They come to give thanks to the name of the Lord, as the law requires of Israel. Here stand the thrones where judgement is given, the thrones of the dynasty of David. Pray for peace in Jerusalem. May all who love this city prosper... For the sake of my family and friends, I will say, 'May you have peace.' For the sake of the house of the Lord our God, I will seek what is best for you, O Jerusalem.

PSALM 122 (NLT, abridged)

Let's imagine what an early singer of this psalm may have been thinking:

'I was so glad! This is my favourite time of year. We go all together. We tell the stories along the way – stories of how God saved us, of how God gave us a home, of great King David and all the good he did.

'It is a long way to Jerusalem. I always get hungry and tired. But I know it will be worth the journey. My feet get sore. I am hot and dusty. My throat is dry. But as we climb the final hill, all that melts away. It's a magical moment when we arrive. Everything seems so grand and magnificent.

'We are all so excited, but as we enter the temple court a hush falls. We know that the Lord is here. This is the actual place that so many stories are about. I am standing where King David stood in splendour, where Solomon sat in wisdom, where Jeremiah spoke in power. So many generations have passed through here. We make our offerings. We give thanks. My whole being is charged with God's presence in my people, my past, my story.

'I love Jerusalem. I love the Lord! I wonder what the future holds. How many more generations will pass through the gates here? I wonder how the Lord will bless and restore his people in the future. I wonder who will come after me, to keep telling that story. My story. As I pray for Jerusalem, I pray for all God's people – including those to come. May the Lord bless them on their pilgrimage, amid trials and tribulations, that they may journey on, rejoicing, delighting in God's story, and passing it on.'

What might you want to say to the singer now, if you could?

SIMON STOCKS, SENIOR TUTOR, ST AUGUSTINE'S COLLEGE OF THEOLOGY

Wings of the morning

If I take the wings of the morning, and dwell in the uttermost parts of the sea; Even there shall thy hand lead me, and thy right hand shall hold me.

PSALM 139:9–10 (KJV)

I have a ring which I never take off because it speaks to me of these verses. The fine gold band curves into waves – the heights and the depths – and between each wave a small diamond nestles, symbolising, for me, the constancy of God. I bought the ring in the jewellery shop in the Imperial Hotel in Delhi. This was many years after my first visit to the city, when I stayed for two nights before travelling on to the small mission hospital in Uttar Pradesh where I was going to work for three months as a volunteer.

At home in London, I was due to begin a theology course on my return. My excitement was marred by one thing: an intractable eating disorder. I secretly hoped that my time in India – somewhere so radically different from all that was familiar – would solve the problem.

Of course, it didn't – all it changed was the geography. I was exactly the same person, in a different place. No matter that I was 4,000 miles from home, there was no escape from myself.

And there's no escape from God. That's the promise of these verses. There's nowhere we can go to escape God's presence and, even more importantly, there's nothing we can do to put ourselves beyond God's love.

'If I take the wings of the morning… [If I] dwell in the uttermost parts of the sea.' Whatever we choose to do, whatever decisions we make – or are made for us – wherever we go, the psalmist promises God's presence with us. We fear making decisions, scared that if we get it wrong, God won't be there with us and for us. That's not true. Just as our deepest self – intricately wrought in our mother's womb – remains constant, so God remains constant.

God is always there, anywhere and everywhere, but God can also always be met in a new way in a new place. The insight I gained in India, hard though it was, was the first step on an even longer journey to health and well-being.

ELEY McAINSH, PRESS AND MEDIA OFFICER, BRF, AND EDITOR,
BIBLE REFLECTIONS FOR OLDER PEOPLE

What's in a name?

For it was you who formed my inward parts; you knit me together in my mother's womb. I praise you, for I am fearfully and wonderfully made. Wonderful are your works; that I know very well. My frame was not hidden from you, when I was being made in secret, intricately woven in the depths of the earth. Your eyes beheld my unformed substance. In your book were written all the days that were formed for me, when none of them as yet existed.

PSALM 139:13–16 (NRSV)

It is not generally the practice in the west to give a child a name because of its meaning, but that is still the case in many parts of the world. In some places, people choose to change their names when they become Christians. It was certainly so in biblical times. Moses means 'drawn out from the water'. Samuel means 'God has heard' and Peter means 'a rock'. When the angel announced the birth of God's Son to Mary, he told her to give him the name Jesus, which means 'the Lord saves'. It indicated the mission that God was to give his Son. When Moses asked God, 'What is your name?' the strange reply came back, 'I Am Who I Am... Say to the Israelites, "I AM has sent me to you"' (Exodus 3:14). The name of 'I AM' expresses God's character, his dependability, faithfulness and timelessness.

But did you realise that God has his own name for each of us? Isaiah 49:1 says: 'The Lord called me before I was born, while I was in my mother's womb he named me.' This suggests that it isn't the name my parents gave me or the nickname that I am known by. It is the name that is the very essence of myself – the true self that God created, and it will fit me perfectly. My husband was 6'5", but his name, Paul, actually means 'little one'! But God had a name for him and he has a name for me and a name for each of you, that is uniquely *you*. It is important that with God's help and revelation we grow in the understanding of who we really are and live life out of our truth and not out of other people's expectations of us.

I wonder what God's name is for you.

ANN PERSSON, FORMER TRUSTEE, BRF

Journeying through the Christian year

Advent

ADVENT means many things, from the deeply trivial to the profoundly spiritual. While it can be viewed simply as equivalent to the 'run-up to Christmas', characterised by calendars (with or without a daily treat), in the church it has always had a focus on the second coming (Parousia) of Christ in majesty and the imminent first coming manifested in the incarnation. Advent is about hope and light.

The biblical readings we encounter during Advent remind us of the promise of Emmanuel ('God with us'), and the 'Great Os' of the final days of Advent (see page 179) remind us of the 'long-expected Jesus', prophesied and predicted in scripture.

The church starts its year with Advent (derived from 'coming', or 'arrival' in Latin: *adventus*), which began as a six-week season (like Lent), preparing for the Christmas festival. Gregory of Tours knew it as a six-Sunday season in fifth-century Gaul, while in Spain and southern Italy it was five Sundays. In Rome, Advent came *after* Christmas. This reminds us of how Christmas can also be a preparation for the following Advent!

Christmas brings the light of Christ to dispel the darkness of this world, a light to bear us forward, to shine as Christmas recedes so swiftly, leaving the realities of sin, despair, gloom and doom. Yet God is not just for Christmas Day, but for the whole year, and it is Advent that helps us hold on to this. The Christmas light and hope that we bear through the year is both prepared by Advent and prepares us for the next Advent.

GORDON GILES, CANON CHANCELLOR, ROCHESTER CATHEDRAL,
AND EDITOR, *NEW DAYLIGHT*

Advent: glowing panes

The people who walk in darkness will see a great light. For those who live in a land of deep darkness, a light will shine... For a child is born to us, a son is given to us. The government will rest on his shoulders. And he will be called: Wonderful Counsellor, Mighty God, Everlasting Father, Prince of Peace. His government and its peace will never end. He will rule with fairness and justice from the throne of his ancestor David for all eternity. The passionate commitment of the Lord of Heaven's Armies will make this happen!

ISAIAH 9:2, 6–7 (NLT)

Christmas isn't Christmas without...?

... presents, according to Louisa May Alcott's *Little Women*. The *Radio Times*, according to, well, the *Radio Times*. What about you? Trees, turkeys, sprouts, Mariah Carey, *Love Actually*?

Sacred or secular, one custom comes back time and again: lights. From Yule logs to tree lights, candles to urban illuminations, whether we're lighting the flame ourselves or it's a button-pushing panto star on a rainy high street, we crave lights in winter.

In our own bleakest midwinters, sparks of hope light our way, anticipating better days. Perhaps treat bad times like an Advent calendar: count the days, read a little about Jesus each morning, try not to eat all the chocolate.

Advent is about expectation, whether today's Christmas-to-come or Isaiah's centuries-old promise of a Messiah. But it's also about better days ahead. In Christ, as the song goes, the best is yet to come (that should be a hymn).

The Advent candle is one of my family's favourite customs. We remember that Jesus said he is the light of the world, that if we follow him, we don't walk in darkness. I don't want to walk in darkness. I'll bring a torch, thanks – perhaps one that's Bible-shaped.

But like lights wrapped around a Christmas tree, we can all shine a little too, adding our own glow to a gloomy world at our windows. Our individual glimmers link together, a string of different colours and intensities, leading to the star on top. Centuries ago, it was the Christ-child we put on our trees, before angels and fairies. (One friend of mine puts a doughnut on top.)

Christmas isn't Christmas without Christ. Otherwise it's just 'mess'.

PAUL KERENSA, COMEDIAN, AUTHOR AND SITCOM WRITER

Immeasurably more than we can imagine

I pray that you, being rooted and established in love, may have power, together with all the Lord's holy people, to grasp how wide and long and high and deep is the love of Christ, and to know this love that surpasses knowledge – that you may be filled to the measure of all the fullness of God. Now to him who is able to do immeasurably more than all we ask or imagine… be glory in the church and in Christ Jesus throughout all generations, for ever and ever! Amen.

EPHESIANS 3:17–21 (NIV, abridged)

What does this passage have to say to us during this season of Advent?

We are given an initial insight in verse 20, where the apostle Paul describes God as being 'able to do immeasurably more then we can ask or imagine'.

In Advent we recall how the Old Testament prophets foretold the coming of the Messiah. But the Messiah that the Jews awaited so expectantly turned out to be way beyond their imagining. As we approach Christmas and prepare to celebrate the birth of Jesus, might we also need to be prepared to discover that the Saviour God has sent us is way beyond our imagining?

A good way to start our discovery would be to pray in the same way Paul prays in verse 18 – that we might have the power to grasp the extent of God's love for us revealed in Christ. The extent of this love has been described as being wide enough to embrace all humanity, long enough to last through the whole of history, high enough to bring us to the throne of God himself and deep enough to pick us up however low we fall. Grasping the extent of God's love for us should stretch our imagination, but Paul's prayer is that we might '*know* this love that surpasses knowledge'. That may be beyond our imagining – but let it not be beyond our asking, since in this way we 'may be filled to the measure of all the fullness of God' (v. 19).

And that makes this a supreme 'Emmanuel' Prayer – which is why this is an Advent passage. So why not pray verses 17–19 for yourself and any others who God is laying on your heart right now?

MARK SHEARD, MEMBER OF THE ARCHBISHOPS' COUNCIL OF THE CHURCH OF ENGLAND AND CEO, WORLD VISION

The one who brings abundant life

So again Jesus said to them, 'Very truly, I tell you, I am the gate for the sheep. All who came before me are thieves and bandits; but the sheep did not listen to them. I am the gate. Whoever enters by me will be saved, and will come in and go out and find pasture. The thief comes only to steal and kill and destroy. I came that they may have life, and have it abundantly.'

JOHN 10:7–10 (NRSV)

It's the time of year when Christmas cards start landing on door mats. So many show a neat and tidy stable, the ox and ass looking on in adoration, a heavenly glow emanating from Mary, Joseph and the baby Jesus in his crib. It's a sanitised picture. In reality, this was a messy, physical birth. Luke's gospel tells us that the Son of God was placed in a manger, a feeding trough for animals. And contrary to the words of that Christmas favourite 'Away in a manger', Jesus most likely did cry. He was a vulnerable human child who needed the protection and tender care of his earthly parents to enable him to grow stronger and flourish.

In this passage from John's gospel, Jesus reminds us why he came in flesh and blood to our broken world. In contrast to the 'thieves and bandits' who come only to 'steal and kill and destroy' (v. 10), Jesus comes to bring life – and life 'to the full', as some translations put it.

This life in all its fullness is what we should desire for every newborn child, every young person, as they grow to adulthood. Unfortunately, more than 2,000 years after the birth of Christ, there are still those in our society who seek to exploit already-vulnerable children and young people, who 'steal and kill and destroy' for their own gain.

What does it mean for a child or young person to flourish, or as the passage puts it in the pastoral language of Jesus' day, to 'go out and find pasture' (v. 9)? What are the barriers today that prevent children from living life to the full? Take a moment today to think about how you can help children and young people not just to survive, but to thrive.

MARK RUSSELL, CEO, THE CHILDREN'S SOCIETY

Searched and known

O Lord, you have searched me and known me. You know when I sit down and when I rise up; you discern my thoughts from far away. You search out my path and my lying down, and are acquainted with all my ways. Even before a word is on my tongue, O Lord, you know it completely. You hem me in, behind and before, and lay your hand upon me. Such knowledge is too wonderful for me; it is so high that I cannot attain it.

PSALM 139:1–6 (NRSV)

As Christmas cards start to arrive, Advent fills with images of the angel of the Annunciation appearing to Mary. Often the potential mother of God is caught alone, apparently at prayer in the normal surroundings of her everyday life. She appears to have entered an inner room (Matthew 6:6), a resting place in 'the shadow of the Almighty' (Psalm 91:1).

It can be challenging to sit alone with God, who searches us out and knows us; difficult to still the noises of the world and of our own inner thoughts; frightening to make ourselves available to him and to leave ourselves open to his demands, however gentle. But it is in this resting place that we truly come before God: no disguise, no bluster, no dishonesty. We find that, in the silence, we are searched, known and encompassed with love.

It is also in this place that, like Mary, we feel the hand laid upon us, our availability and willingness tested, the request made. But the one who asks also knows our sitting down and our rising up and what our response ('a word… on my tongue') will be, and his 'yoke is easy, and [his] burden is light' (Matthew 11:30). Mary's resting place, her stillness and receptiveness, led to the greatest human 'Yes' of all time: her word allows the Word to be realised and hope is born.

It is tricky in the bustle of everyday life with its to-do lists and commitments to find a time to listen rather than to speak, to receive rather than to ask or explain. The waiting time of Advent encourages us to find a resting place where we can sit quietly with our God, ready to say our own 'Yes', and to carry him into our busy world.

LYNN GOSLIN, RETIRED SPEECH AND LANGUAGE THERAPIST

Time to recalibrate

Love does no harm to a neighbour. Therefore love is the fulfilment of the law. And do this, understanding the present time: the hour has already come for you to wake up from your slumber, because our salvation is nearer now than when we first believed. The night is nearly over; the day is almost here. So let us put aside the deeds of darkness and put on the armour of light.

ROMANS 13:10–12 (NIV)

One day you will die. Although used by Mark Twain, the famous quote, 'The only two certainties in life are death and taxes,' was originally said by Benjamin Franklin in a letter to the French scientist Jean-Baptiste Leroy. And Franklin is pretty much right. From the moment we are born the clock starts ticking, and the older you get, the faster the birthdays seem to come around!

When Christ was born, he left the timeless dimension of eternity to dwell among us and live as a man among people with a limited earthly lifespan. I have at times wondered what it must have been like. It is a love beyond comprehension that he would leave heaven and face death on a cross to make a way for us.

As we journey through this time of waiting, every day that passes brings us closer to the moment we will meet Jesus. Every second that passes is a second closer to the moment when we will one day draw our last breath. The Bible is clear: don't think you've got forever to get right with God. You haven't. Live each day knowing that the night is almost over, and that the day is almost here. Let the light of Christ shine through your life and make the most of the opportunity each moment of our lives gives us.

One day we will die. And it will be like waking up from a dream, for we will truly be alive and be with Christ. What an amazing moment that will be as we look back and see that our earthly lives passed in the blink of an eye compared to the glory that awaits us.

CARL BEECH, CEO, EDGE MINISTRIES

O Lord, come down

O that you would tear open the heavens and come down... so that the nations might tremble at your presence!... From ages past no one has heard... no eye has seen any God besides you, who works for those who wait for him... We have all become like one who is unclean, and all our righteous deeds are like a filthy cloth... Yet, O Lord, you are our Father; we are the clay, and you are our potter; we are all the work of your hand. Do not be exceedingly angry, O Lord... Now consider, we are all your people.

ISAIAH 64:1–9 (NRSV, abridged)

The ancient people of God were desperate for God to reshape their lives. After years in exile from their country, knowing they had failed God hopelessly, Isaiah the prophet pleaded with God to act.

The dark days of Advent give us time to consider if we are ready to let God come close to us and our world.

As in the Psalms, the ideas in this prayer are often repeated in different words for emphasis. The people knew God had helped them in the past. They hadn't forgotten. They were honest about their failure to live God's way – even their best actions were like 'filthy rags' – and they accepted their consequences.

'Yet,' the prophet prayed, 'O Lord, you are our Father.' Despite the darkness which may be part of our lives too, whether we have caused it ourselves or whether we are affected by others, we know God remains our Father.

The prophet appeals again: 'We are the clay, and you are our potter; we are all the work of your hand. Do not be exceedingly angry... we are all your people.' Clay remains formless until held by the potter. God can reshape us.

Advent is a time of honest recognition of who we are, crying out from our darkness for God to act. It is a time of holding on to the promises we have been given, believing that God will act and looking forward to new signs of God at work. The prophet Isaiah shows us how to pray like this.

What do we long for God to do? Are we *ready* for God to act? Watch out for new signs of God's activity near you.

MARGARET DEAN, RETIRED TEACHER AND PRIEST, AND FORMER TRUSTEE, BRF

The advent of hope

The Lord is my light and my salvation – whom shall I fear? The Lord is the strong-hold of my life – of whom shall I be afraid?… Hear my voice when I call, Lord; be merciful to me and answer me. My heart says of you, 'Seek his face!' Your face, Lord, I will seek… I remain confident of this: I will see the goodness of the Lord in the land of the living. Wait for the Lord; be strong and take heart and wait for the Lord.

PSALM 27:1, 7–8, 13–14 (NIV)

As I write this, we are all dealing with the Covid-19 pandemic. Restrictions have been imposed and millions are facing the reality of not being able to be with loved ones for some time. Some are mourning the death of family or friends; others have themselves experienced symptoms of the virus. Even for those fortunate enough to have stayed healthy, the restrictions have had a significant impact on our routines, relationships, mental well-being and livelihoods. The prospect of vaccines has given us hope that life will soon get back to 'normal'. It's that hope that helps us to endure in anticipation of happier and healthier times.

At this time of Advent, the theme of hopeful waiting helps us to remember what Jesus' coming into this world was all about. Prophesied years before, many looked on his coming into the world, as a helpless baby, as the begin-ning of the end: an end to the restrictions of living under the authority of the occupying Roman army. Yet Jesus' mission was to be far more impactful. His coming was not to bring freedom from the Romans; rather, it was to bring salvation to all who would trust him.

His death dashed the hopes of those who had not fully understood his purpose. Yet his resurrection, return to heaven and promise to come again for those who love him give us an even greater hope – hope for a life filled with love, joy and peace; hope not just to survive, but to thrive in the situations in which we find ourselves; above all, hope that we will one day be in the eternal presence of the one who gave everything he had for us. We have nothing to give beyond grateful hearts and the gifts and talents he has given us.

PAUL COX, TRUSTEE, BRF

Keep me burning

'The kingdom of heaven will be like ten virgins who took their lamps and went out to meet the bridegroom. Five of them were foolish and five were wise. The foolish ones took their lamps but did not take any oil with them. The wise ones, however, took oil in jars along with their lamps. The bridegroom was a long time in coming, and they all became drowsy and fell asleep. At midnight the cry rang out: "Here's the bridegroom! Come out to meet him!"'

MATTHEW 25:1–6 (NIV)

During his public ministry, Jesus often told parables to explain about the kingdom of God. This is a story about some bridesmaids who were all ready and waiting for a wedding feast. It was their job to wait for the arrival of the bridegroom, and they were supposed to have their oil lamps lit and burning ready to welcome him. In this story, the bridegroom was delayed, and when he does eventually arrive five of the bridesmaids are ready for him and go into the wedding banquet and five are not ready and are left outside.

So what does this story mean?

The season of Advent is a time of waiting. Just as the bridesmaids were waiting for the arrival of the bridegroom and for the wedding feast, during Advent we are waiting for the feast of Christmas. In Advent we are thinking about the people of Israel waiting for the coming of their promised Messiah prophesied so long ago. We are preparing our own hearts to welcome him, to make room for him as Lord of our lives, and we are looking ahead to the time when he will come again. This story tells us that although it might seem that the second coming of Jesus is delayed, we must always be prepared and ready to welcome him with our lamps burning brightly.

So what does it mean to have our lamps burning? It means that we must constantly be replenished with the oil of the Holy Spirit so that we can keep going in our faith right to the end. We are replenished with this oil when we open ourselves to the action of the Spirit within us; when we make sure that we are right with God; when we pray and meditate on his word; when we keep meeting together to worship him; and when we live in the joyful hope that he is coming for us, to take us into the heavenly banquet when the time is right for us.

LINDSAY PELLOQUIN, LEAD CHAPLAIN, THE GIFT OF YEARS RUGBY

Faith in small things

When you reap the harvest of your land, you shall not reap to the very edges of your field, or gather the gleanings of your harvest... You shall leave them for the poor and the alien: I am the Lord your God... You shall not render an unjust judgement; you shall not be partial to the poor or defer to the great: with justice you shall judge your neighbour. You shall not go around as a slanderer among your people, and you shall not profit by the blood of your neighbour: I am the Lord.

LEVITICUS 19:9–16 (NRSV, abridged)

The laws of ancient Israel contain much wisdom. In comparison with other law codes from the ancient world, they mark something of an advance. Although some of the laws are no longer applicable in contemporary society, the church has always received and built upon their undergirding moral code. In these laws, the requirement to do justice and to care for the vulnerable is expressed in practical ways: leave the gleanings of the harvest, practise impartiality, do not slander your neighbour.

Among contemporary writers, the American novelist and essay-writer Marilynne Robinson has drawn our attention again to these biblical instructions and compared them with some of our current legal assumptions. Her essays and novels are living examples of this biblical wisdom. The Christian faith is authenticated in the way we live it out. If we do not love our neighbour or our family, we need to ask ourselves some difficult questions. If we do not show concern for those around us – whether friend or stranger – we have likely missed the point. As the apostle James wrote, 'Show me your faith without works, and I by my works will show you my faith' (James 2:18). Or, as John put it, 'Little children, let us love, not in word or speech, but in truth and action' (1 John 3:18).

We need at all times to hold the practical – the material, the very stuff of life – together with the spiritual. For Christ's incarnation, his perfect union of our humanity and God's divinity, shows that we cannot do otherwise. Today, set yourself the task of one practical good, one gentle act, for example, or one instance where you restrain yourself from speaking unkindly, and know that it is in these small things, rather than in spiritual heroics, that we live out the Christian faith.

CHRISTOPHER CHESSUN, BISHOP OF SOUTHWARK

Walking in the light

But if we walk in the light, as he is in the light, we have fellowship with one another, and the blood of Jesus, his Son, purifies us from all sin. If we claim to be without sin, we deceive ourselves and the truth is not in us. If we confess our sins, he is faithful and just and will forgive us our sins and purify us from all unrighteousness. If we claim we have not sinned, we make him out to be a liar and his word is not in us.

1 JOHN 1:7–10 (NIV)

A great delight of living just outside Oxford are the numerous areas where one can walk. On a beautiful, clear, sunny day the views are wonderful, whether that be towards the dreaming spires of the city, the Downs or along the Thames path. The latter has become one of our favourites, walking in the light and enjoying the beauty of God's creation.

This passage reminds us of our spiritual walk in the light, the light of God. As we prepare in Advent for the celebration of the birth of Jesus Christ and all that means, we also prepare for another Advent, the second coming of Jesus Christ. We are to 'walk in the light' (v. 7), a life characterised by holiness and truth. Our Christian character is transformed and developed through this walk with God, because we will have fellowship with him and one another through what Jesus did for us on the cross. When I am on one of my walks, whether it be with my wife or a friend, in the privacy of the walk it is great to chat, to be open, honest and truthful, which you can be with someone you love. Done correctly, it is liberating and the relationship is strengthened.

The latter part of this passage encourages us to have this stronger, closer relationship with God, a relationship that he so longs for, but we need to be open, honest and truthful with him and ourselves. Amanda Gorman, the US national youth poet laureate, said at the inauguration of President Biden that there is always light if only we're brave enough to see it… and to be it. Applied to our spiritual journey, Jesus is always there. The question is whether we are brave enough to have a relationship with him, to have our Christian character developed and to be his light to our family, friends, colleagues and neighbours.

ALISTAIR BOOTH, TRUSTEE, BRF

The hope we wait for

We have, then, my friends, complete freedom to go into the Most Holy Place by means of the death of Jesus. He opened for us a new way, a living way, through the curtain – that is, through his own body. We have a great priest in charge of the house of God. So let us come near to God with a sincere heart and a sure faith, with hearts that have been purified from a guilty conscience and with bodies washed with clean water. Let us hold on firmly to the hope we profess, because we can trust God to keep his promise. Let us be concerned for one another, to help one another to show love and to do good.

HEBREWS 10:19–24 (GNT)

In Advent a few years back, as well as looking towards Christmas I was waiting for an operation. The surgery was scheduled for just a few days before Christmas Day itself. When speaking to others in the run-up, people often said to me, 'What a shame you won't be able to celebrate Christmas this year.' I knew what they meant; it was not going to be a year with lots of people, food, drink and merriment. Instead I faced rest and recovery.

The planned celebrations may have been different, but Advent and Christmas were unchanged: the anticipation of Jesus, the great priest, our Saviour's arrival on earth; revisiting the scriptures, remembering when he came before and knowing he will come again.

In this Advent season, you may find yourself looking towards a Christmas you may spend alone, maybe due to bereavement or family members moving out. It could be that you find yourself in financial hardship or job insecurity. Perhaps you are struggling with your health or someone you love is unwell.

God's promise to us is unchanged, no matter the circumstances we find ourselves in. It is a promise we can trust in. As you wait for Christmas, be confident in the hope of Jesus, hold on to your faith and boldly draw closer to God.

'Let us hold on firmly to the hope we profess, because we can trust God to keep his promise.'

JAY ELLIOTT, HEAD OF FINANCE AND OPERATIONS, BRF

I choose to hope

A shoot will come up from the stump of Jesse; from his roots a Branch will bear fruit. The Spirit of the Lord will rest on him – the Spirit of wisdom and of understanding, the Spirit of counsel and of might, the Spirit of the knowledge and fear of the Lord – and he will delight in the fear of the Lord. He will not judge by what he sees with his eyes, or decide by what he hears with his ears; but with righteousness he will judge the needy, with justice he will give decisions for the poor of the earth.

ISAIAH 11:1–4a (NIV)

Take a moment and picture the stump of a once-great tree – it appears dead and decaying, now just a place where beetles, lichen and fungi can thrive. Not much of a legacy for something that once stood tall and grand.

It is from this inauspicious basis that Isaiah paints a picture in words of a new shoot of hope for all people – for every individual in every family in every clan in every nation. A shoot from that which was dead bearing fruit to feed and delight us all. A child of God who is steeped in the Father's Spirit; wise and authoritative. Verses 3–5 describe a leader who is able to see the big picture. He possesses a 'sixth sense' in order to lead and rule with righteousness and justice. He sees and he hears and is not deceived by fake news. Through and through, he is the sort of leader that I could follow.

Of course, we attribute these qualities to Jesus Christ, believing that Isaiah's words are prophetic. By studying them alongside other scripture, we get some sense of what God is like (just and faithful, to name two attributes); of how we would want to conduct ourselves (with love and tolerance towards all humankind); and of how we would want to be led by those with authority over us (with wisdom and humility).

Part of what makes us human is our ability to rise again, to hope when all hope seems lost. For me, this passage paints a multifaceted picture of that hope both in this life and in heaven. It may have been written over 2,700 years ago, but it can speak to us now, if we let it. And so I declare that 'I choose to hope.'

TONY SHARP, PROJECT MANAGER, WHO LET THE DADS OUT?

Overflowing with hope

'Praise the Lord, all you Gentiles; let all the peoples extol him.' And again, Isaiah says, 'The Root of Jesse will spring up, one who will arise to rule over the nations; in him the Gentiles will hope.' May the God of hope fill you with all joy and peace as you trust in him, so that you may overflow with hope by the power of the Holy Spirit.

ROMANS 15:11–13 (NIV)

Since living in Denmark a few years back, I have grown to really appreciate and love the season of Advent. In Scandinavia, Christmas and Advent are celebrated in quite distinctive ways. My previous UK experience had been that 'Christmas' seemed to start earlier and earlier (in November!) and that for most people, Christmas was over the day after Boxing Day. Advent, with its intentional space for preparation, waiting and expectation, was literally wiped out. Tragic, because Advent affords us times of reflection, especially around hope, joy, peace and love and their fulfilment in the arrival of a baby, a Saviour, the Messiah, Jesus Christ.

'Hope' is not about wishful thinking, saying, 'I hope something is going to happen or get better.' Hope is much stronger and definite. It is a recognition of something certain. In the Bible, hope is the confident expectation of what God has promised and our assurance is his faithfulness to us. 'A light came out of darkness, no light, no hope had we, till Jesus came from heaven, our light and hope to be' (William Hawley). Our hope is in Jesus, the Root of Jesse!

Paul, writing to the church in Rome, is desiring and effectively praying that as we put our trust in God we will be filled with all joy and peace and overflow with hope by the presence and power of the Holy Spirit within us (v. 13). That's an amazing Advent experience as we wait and prepare to truly celebrate Christmas. It is also an experience and blessing for every day of our lives. Filled with joy and peace, overflowing with hope, in Christ alone. As you meditate upon this verse, may it be a present reality for you today!

ANTHONY COTTERILL, COMMANDER, THE SALVATION ARMY IN THE UK AND IRELAND

Hallelujah anyway

When the builders laid the foundation of the temple of the Lord, the priests in their vestments and with trumpets, and the Levites (the sons of Asaph) with cymbals, took their places to praise the Lord, as prescribed by David king of Israel... And all the people gave a great shout of praise to the Lord, because the foundation of the house of the Lord was laid. But many of the older priests and Levites and family heads, who had seen the former temple, wept aloud when they saw the foundation of this temple being laid, while many others shouted for joy.

EZRA 3:10–12 (NIV, abridged)

It should have been such a joyful occasion, and yet... Yes, there was an out-pouring of praise, yet with the shouting and singing there was also weeping.

I needed to search my own heart. Where would I have stood in that great company? When you are old, it is easy to look back on the 'olden days' as good, when summer was always summer.

As a young Christian I was privileged to go to 'The Mount', as we used to call Penygroes, where a special annual gathering had started out of the Welsh revival, and God was still doing wonderful things.

Though there were those who would tell us that things were not as good as they used to be, for us they were days of heaven on earth. Working abroad as a missionary, 'Penygroes Week' was the time I felt homesick, longing to be there.

But years later, and now a staid pastor's wife, I found I was giving assent to the critics who looked back to the good old days. That was, until I met a couple who had come for the first time. For them it was days of heaven on earth, as it had been for us. I was convicted. Realising it was I who had changed, not God, I knew that if I would come seeking God, he would always be found by me. Faithful God, so unchanging!

I remember a missionary who had this banner in his office: 'HALLELUJAH ANYWAY'.

So in this time of Advent, are we going to join with the praisers, even though we may not yet see all things as we would wish? Like those who were seeking a Saviour so long ago, we too seek and we too will find him.

PAULINE LEWIS, PORTHCAWL READY WRITERS

In the waiting

But do not forget this one thing, dear friends: with the Lord a day is like a thousand years, and a thousand years are like a day. The Lord is not slow in keeping his promise, as some understand slowness. Instead he is patient with you, not wanting anyone to perish, but everyone to come to repentance. But the day of the Lord will come like a thief. The heavens will disappear with a roar; the elements will be destroyed by fire, and the earth and everything done in it will be laid bare.

2 PETER 3:8–10 (NIV)

During Advent, adults and children have wildly differing concepts of time. While young children beg for Christmas to come sooner, overstretched parents are all too aware of the day hurtling towards them faster than their ever-growing to-do lists can keep up with. They do look forward, but with the knowledge of all that still needs doing.

In this passage, Peter's contemporaries are looking forward to Christ's return, when he will wipe every tear and right every wrong. However, others are sowing doubts, and the believers risk being swayed. Like Advent children, perhaps some are getting a little fidgety. It feels too long. Surely there's been some mistake?

Peter, meanwhile, is like an Advent parent, looking forward but with a deep awareness of how much remains to be done. He reassures the believers that they are not forgotten: Jesus will come. God is simply waiting for everyone to catch up with the life-changing news of his love.

When you're going through a long, agonising wait, hanging on to a promise, every day really can feel like a thousand years. Waiting is painful. It feels like failure. We are powerless, conscious of our human limitations and frailties. There is an element of losing face. All our efforts cannot force this thing into being.

However, God wants to work in us and through us as we wait.

Within the pain of not knowing why or when or how long, God calls us to stop striving and rest in his love. Within our powerlessness, he calls us to be empowered differently, to live lives that help others catch up with the news of his great love.

Living hopefully within the waiting is a tough but life-giving choice, allowing God's goodness to infuse our lives with a love that draws others to him.

CLARE O'DRISCOLL, LANGUAGE TUTOR AND WRITER

Called to his eternal glory

With this in mind, we constantly pray for you, that our God may make you worthy of his calling, and that by his power he may bring to fruition your every desire for goodness and your every deed prompted by faith. We pray this so that the name of our Lord Jesus may be glorified in you, and you in him, according to the grace of our God and the Lord Jesus Christ.

2 THESSALONIANS 1:11–12 (NIV)

At this time of year, I imagine most of us have our hands and thoughts fully occupied with preparations for Christmas, that quiet first coming of Jesus to earth.

The believers in Thessalonica to whom Paul is writing this letter seem to be equally preoccupied, but for them it was Jesus' triumphant return in glory, his second coming, that was on their minds. Mired in persecution and 'suffering for the kingdom', they must have been longing for relief. In what to many of us might be a difficult passage on the last judgement (vv. 5–10), Paul reassures them that all will be well in the end. His main purpose in writing, though, seems to be to encourage them to concentrate on living well while they wait.

The time between the two comings in which we all live is a precious time. It is our opportunity, as Paul prays, to live grace-filled lives, empowered by God, and so display his glory. This glory is a mysterious thing; it radiates from God, and amazingly, by his grace, is in us his holy people (v. 10). We will probably never be conscious of it at all in ourselves, but it is growing in us as we spend time with Jesus and faithfully live our lives. It is there in our suffering. And it is what draws others to Christ and away from judgement.

Perhaps in the midst of the busyness of today, we could pause to marvel at the one who came so humbly to save us, who continues to sustain us and who one day we will see in all his grace and glory. And to remember those for whom persecution is a very real part of their life this day.

HELEN VINCENT, SURREY

To carry a miracle

An angel of the Lord appeared to him in a dream and said, 'Joseph, son of David, do not be afraid to take Mary as your wife, for the child conceived in her is from the Holy Spirit. She will bear a son, and you are to name him Jesus, for he will save his people from their sins.' All this took place to fulfil what had been spoken by the Lord through the prophet: 'Look, the virgin shall conceive and bear a son, and they shall name him Emmanuel', which means, 'God is with us.'

MATTHEW 1:20b–23 (NRSV)

This always takes my breath away: 'She was found to be with child from the Holy Spirit' (Matthew 1:18). The same beautiful, untamed Holy Spirit that was hovering over the waters at the very beginning is here, creating a miracle inside the womb of a young woman, barely more than a child herself.

Lesser miracles have been seen before: waters have parted to let the people pass, blind men have seen and bread has appeared in the desert. Even old women, barren for years, have held babies in their arms and kissed them, knowing that God has moved.

But this miracle is bigger, more extraordinary, even more beautiful. Quietly and without fanfare in an unknown village on the edge of nowhere, the Holy Spirit changes history forever – God and humanity become one in Jesus.

The child Mary carries is the one who will save his people; one who will offer himself as the bread of life, who will open the eyes of the blind and who, like Joshua his namesake, will lead his people home. But even more remarkable – even before his fingerprints are formed, he is completely man and completely God.

Today is a day to sit in awe of this story; of the girl who was willing to hold a miracle in her womb and then in her arms; of the unstoppable creative power of the Spirit; of the determination of the Father to restore his people to himself; and of the Son, fully able to understand what it means to be human, fully able to save us from our sins.

And as you ponder those things, I wonder what God has given you to carry, to hold in your hands while he weaves it together. Like Mary, may you find the courage and strength to carry it until it has grown.

ELLIE HART, AUTHOR, SPEAKER AND ARTIST

Mary's song of praise

'My soul glorifies the Lord and my spirit rejoices in God my Saviour, for he has been mindful of the humble state of his servant. From now on all generations will call me blessed, for the Mighty One has done great things for me – holy is his name. His mercy extends to those who fear him, from generation to generation. He has performed mighty deeds with his arm; he has scattered those who are proud in their inmost thoughts. He has brought down rulers from their thrones but has lifted up the humble. He has filled the hungry with good things but has sent the rich away empty. He has helped his servant Israel, remembering to be merciful to Abraham and his descendants forever, just as he promised our ancestors.'

LUKE 1:46–55 (NIV)

'Let all your thinks be thanks.' This variation of the poetic line by W.H. Auden states in a few words a revolutionary approach to life. When we practise gratitude – instead of grumbling about what we lack – our outlook shifts. We notice God's working in our lives, from the wonder of birdsong to the smile of a stranger to a welcome unexpected opportunity.

Mary pours out her thanks and praise to God in a well-loved song that people have prayed throughout the generations, known as the Magnificat (which is Latin for 'my soul magnifies the Lord'). As she visits her cousin Elizabeth, who calls her blessed in a prophetic realisation that Mary is the mother of Jesus, Mary immediately expresses her love for God. Her joyful words point to the mighty one who has bestowed this gift on her; she doesn't puff herself up but accepts God's invitation with humble gratitude.

Mary's song shows how steeped in scripture she is; it reflects several of the psalms and Hannah's song of praise when she dedicates her longed-for son, Samuel, to the Lord. Mary in her song echoes Hannah's statement of praise: 'My heart rejoices in the Lord... there is no one holy like [him]' (1 Samuel 2:1–2).

Advent can feel like a stressful season as we try to cram our preparations for Christmas into an already busy life. A simple shift in attitude as we embrace gratitude each day can help us to welcome the opportunities and tasks before us, instead of dreading them. Like Mary, we can rejoice in and be thankful to the God who saves us.

AMY BOUCHER PYE, AUTHOR, SPEAKER AND SPIRITUAL DIRECTOR

Pregnancy test(ing) and birth plans

'But you, Bethlehem Ephrathah, though you are small among the clans of Judah, out of you will come for me one who will be ruler over Israel, whose origins are from of old, from ancient times.'

MICAH 5:2 (NIV)

Discovering you are expecting a baby is one of those life-changing moments that is filled with a range of emotions: joy as you share your news with others, through to apprehension – how will we cope? Will we make good parents? The following months involve hospital appointments, decorating, purchasing clothes and baby equipment, NCT classes, perhaps a gender reveal party or a baby shower. The final phase, often known as 'nesting', includes the urge to clean and organise as the birth draws closer. I recall all of these activities as my wife and I prepared for the birth of our first child. No pregnancy is easy, but a bonus for us was living close enough to the hospital to make the uncomfortable journey between contractions!

Mary's preparations included angelic visitations and an awkward fallout with a confused Joseph. I wonder at what point Joseph broke the news that due to a census, they needed to travel to Bethlehem, 90 miles across rough terrain, vulnerable to attack and inclement weather – on a donkey! Apparently carrying the Son of God in your womb didn't ensure protection from stress and adversity. Even arriving exhausted in Bethlehem did not provide immediate relief – accommodation options were severely limited.

I wonder how Mary and Joseph coped; surely, like any first-time parents, they desired a smooth pregnancy and a straightforward birth plan. How did this make sense? Why a census and the upheaval of travelling to Bethlehem? Why was the only accommodation available a dirty stable for this precious baby? Mary and Joseph must have held on with unwavering trust. How often did this young couple have to take in yet another challenge, take a deep breath and just keep going?

Sometimes our faith only makes sense when we look back. Prophecies from ancient days, words recorded from the past suddenly reveal a divine plan. Despite our current trials and challenges, perhaps like Mary and Joseph we will one day look back on situations and circumstances in our lives and see that, though confusing at the time, it will make sense in the end.

ROB HARE, OPERATIONS LEAD, BIBLE ENGAGEMENT TEAM, BIBLE SOCIETY

Unlocking Christ's coming

[Jesus] stood up to read, and the scroll of the prophet Isaiah was given to him. He unrolled the scroll and found the place where it was written: 'The Spirit of the Lord is upon me, because he has anointed me to bring good news to the poor. He has sent me to proclaim release to the captives and recovery of sight to the blind, to let the oppressed go free, to proclaim the year of the Lord's favour.'

LUKE 4:16b–19 (NRSV)

When we sing the ancient Advent hymn, 'O Come, O Come, Emmanuel', we can be reminded of the ancient prophecies on which it is based.

Known as the 'Great Os', they flanked the singing of the Magnificat from 17 to 24 December. The texts, in reverse order, are: O Emmanuel, O Rex Gentium (King of the Nations), O Oriens (Dayspring), O Clavis David (Key of David), O Radix Jesse (Root of Jesse), O Adonai (Lord God) and O Sapientia (Wisdom). On Christmas Eve, the acrostic buried within is revealed. Taking the first letter of the keyword and reading backwards, it spells *ero cras*, which means 'I shall be present tomorrow', which is ultimately the meaning of the hymn and of the season.

20 December is 'O Clavis David': 'O Key of David and Sceptre of the house of Israel; that openest, and no one shutteth, and shuttest, and no one openeth: come and bring the prisoner out of the prisonhouse, and him that sitteth in darkness and the shadow of death.' Foretelling the coming of Christ, who in the synagogue associated himself with the prophecy of Isaiah (Isaiah 42:7), it also mentions the 'key of David' in Revelation 3:7.

These antiphons, rich in meaning and resonant with scripture, evolved into the hymn 'Veni, Veni, Emmanuel'. Just as Latin antiphons originally served as a refrain to the Magnificat, when the hymn was created, around the twelfth century, the hymn was given its own refrain: 'Gaude, gaude Emmanuel, nascitur pro te, Israel' ('Rejoice! Rejoice! Emmanuel shall come to thee, O Israel'). Thus we have a set of refrains, with a refrain.

This complex blend is like our modern Advent: the simple, penitential message of a promised Saviour, who came and will come again; combined with the richness and splendour of Christmas, beckoning us from every shop window and carol as we advance further into December.

GORDON GILES, CANON CHANCELLOR, ROCHESTER CATHEDRAL,
AND EDITOR, *NEW DAYLIGHT*

Longing fulfilled

**Hope deferred makes the heart sick, but a longing fulfilled is a tree of life...
A longing fulfilled is sweet to the soul, but fools detest turning from evil.**

PROVERBS 13:12, 19 (NIV)

It's much easier to be hopeful in a post-Jesus world. Gosh, what a sweeping statement. Is it really? Do we really, as a people, feel more hopeful? Perhaps some of us do, but that doesn't apply to everyone, surely. Or does it?

I often struggle to contextualise what life was like for Bible writers, especially for those pre-Jesus. Did they even know that the words they were writing at the time would become a Bible? What must the writer of this verse have been thinking? Maybe they were struggling with something specific, a prayer that hadn't been answered or a disappointment with God over something. I can relate to that – no matter how long ago these words were written.

However, even if I can relate to struggles and disappointment of a hope deferred, at least I live in a world where Jesus has already been born. That makes everything, even the dark days, hopeful.

As we travel through the Christmas season, I wonder how this might apply to Mary. She lived in a pre-Jesus world. She was pregnant, newly married, and she left her family with a man she hardly knew to travel miles away. What did hope look like for Mary? Was she full of expectation, or was she scared? I would venture she was feeling a lot of both. True, she was told by an angel that she was carrying 'the Saviour', but what might this have meant to a teenage girl? Perhaps she thought he might be a great leader or a king, but did she really believe that he would save the world? Indeed, that would have given her hope, but she didn't know then what I know now.

If only she had known that *my* hope, *your* hope, the world's hope was in the child she was carrying.

WENDY GRISHAM, GROUP PUBLISHING DIRECTOR, SPCK

Behold, he comes

Behold, he comes, leaping over the mountains, bounding over the hills. My beloved is like a gazelle or a young stag… My beloved speaks and says to me: 'Arise, my love, my beautiful one, and come away, for behold, the winter is past; the rain is over and gone. The flowers appear on the earth, the time of singing has come… Arise, my love, my beautiful one, and come away.'

SONG OF SONGS 2:8–13 (ESV, abridged)

Advent – a favourite season for many – remembers the first coming of Christ in such weakness, as well as looking for his glorious second appearing when, in the world of Narnia, 'wrong shall be right – when he comes in sight'.

The Song of Songs speaks of this destiny to any hearts which may be in need of healing balm – and to a groaning creation. The book can be read as a love poem about a prince and a shepherd girl. At the same time, it speaks as an allegory about the returning of the divine bridegroom. According to the beautiful description in verse 8, Christ leaps like a strong stag over huge mountains of difficulty and stands on the earth calling to his bride to 'come away'. And when he comes, 'flowers appear on the earth'. For the church fathers this had to do with Christ overcoming the heights of principalities and powers. His return will melt mountains of trouble that we may face in our personal situations: this is a comforting word.

In an allegorical reading of the Song, the meaning is at the same time that the end of winter on all the earth comes with the incarnation.

Christina Rossetti's 1872 hymn 'In the bleak midwinter' pictures the earth as 'hard as iron, long ago'. It is in the context of this frozen earth that 'in the bleak midwinter / a stable place sufficed / the Lord God Almighty / Jesus Christ'. The carol is sometimes criticised as being an 'anatopism' because it seldom snows in Bethlehem. But Rossetti's true achievement lies in describing the symbolism of this Song of Songs image as she imagines the earth where 'snow had fallen, snow on snow' now receiving the thawing love of Christ, whose love longs to warm up our world and return flowers to desert lands.

CHARLIE CLEVERLY, AUTHOR AND SPEAKER

God with us – past, present, future

The birth of Jesus Christ happened like this. When Mary was engaged to Joseph, just before their marriage, she was discovered to be pregnant – by the Holy Spirit… While [Joseph] was turning the matter over in his mind an angel of the Lord appeared to him in a dream and said, 'Joseph, son of David, do not be afraid to take Mary as your wife! What she has conceived is conceived through the Holy Spirit, and she will give birth to a son, whom you will call Jesus ('the Saviour') for it is he who will save his people from their sins.' All this happened to fulfil what the Lord had said through the prophet – 'Behold, a virgin shall be with child, and bear a son, and they shall call his name Immanuel. ('Immanuel' means 'God with us'.)

MATTHEW 1:18, 20–23 (JBP)

In the beginning, we were able to walk and talk with our maker, as God intended. But we have always wanted to strike out and do our own thing. Disastrously, that built an insuperable barrier to our relationship, which we could not remove. But God's first intention remained. God could wait.

Through the Old Testament prophets, God renewed the promise to be with not just leaders like Moses and David, but with all his people. Matthew records how this began to happen: how Jesus, God himself, came among us as our Saviour. What this cost is recorded in Philippians 2. Having stripped himself of all privilege, Jesus humbled himself by living a life of total obedience, even to the extent of dying for us. But he would rise again. So although he would no longer be present physically with his friends and followers, he could promise before he left them: 'I am with you always, even to the end of the world' (Matthew 28:20).

In Advent we celebrate God present with us now. And we look forward to a future presence, when wrongs are righted, when injustices are made good, when the barrier of our wilful wrongdoing will be totally removed. There will be new heavens, a new earth and a new city which 'has no need for the light of sun or moon, for the splendour of God fills it with light and its radiance is the Lamb' (Revelation 21:23).

Herein lies our firm and certain hope: praise be!

PAT ALEXANDER, EDITOR, *THE LION HANDBOOK TO THE BIBLE*

Making all things new

Then I saw 'a new heaven and a new earth,' for the first heaven and the first earth had passed away... And I heard a loud voice from the throne saying, 'Look! God's dwelling-place is now among the people, and he will dwell with them... "He will wipe every tear from their eyes. There will be no more death" or mourning or crying or pain, for the old order of things has passed away.' He who was seated on the throne said, 'I am making everything new!'

REVELATION 21:1–5 (NIV, abridged)

Our journey through Advent narrows down until our gaze is on one baby at one time in one place. Advent is also a time to expand our vision to all that will come from that single event around which all creation turns. The coming of Christ is the start of God making all things new through Christ, and this passage sets that great vision before us. We lift our hearts, souls and imaginations to look to that time when the babe of Bethlehem will come again, and we will see him as he is: King of kings and Lord of lords, and a new heaven and a new earth.

Over the Christmas season, we may well hear those words from John 1: 'Through him all things were made'. The Christ-child is the Lord of all creation. Here is our Advent vision: all creation renewed in Christ, through Christ and for Christ, the one through whom and for whom all things were created.

We regularly pray for 'your will to be done on earth, as it is in heaven'. If heaven is about a creation in harmony, the renewal of all things, if that is heaven's direction, what does it mean to pray, live and work with that vision before us now? Here are some answers from members of our local church family.

'I try to shop locally.' 'I've cut down on single-use plastics.' 'I've swapped to an electric car.' 'I've replanted my garden with more drought-tolerant plants.' 'I've let part of my lawn grow wild.' 'We've installed low-energy lighting in our church.'

All small things, but responses to this great vision of a new heaven and a new earth, when the babe of Bethlehem will come again as Lord of all, and all things will be made new in him. Your kingdom come. Your will be done. On earth. This earth. Our earth.

COLIN MATTHEWS, FORMER TRUSTEE, BRF

Christmas

'WILL GOD really dwell on earth with humans?' Solomon asked as he invited God's Spirit to fill the temple. God's answer was 'Yes' as fire came down from heaven and his glory filled the space. Years later his answer was a resounding 'Yes' when Mary gave birth to Jesus, he who was God but became man. And God keeps on saying 'Yes' through the Spirit of Jesus' continuing presence in his believers today.

How do we respond to this miracle of life and grace? The writers in the notes for this Christmas season welcome us to enter into the story instead of simply looking at the crib from a distance. Angela Ashwin invites us 'to be drawn ever more deeply into the creative, life-giving and transforming energy of love that came into the world when Jesus was born'. After all, as Alan Charter observes, 'in Jesus we find a life-changing, grace-filled invitation' – to know and enjoy God.

Pour yourself a mulled beverage and warm up a mince pie to enjoy while feasting on these reflections about the God who became a human baby to live among us and eventually to die that we might live. Wonder at this greatest gift as you savour the beauty of the Christmas season, a time set aside for praise, rejoicing and celebration.

AMY BOUCHER PYE, AUTHOR, SPEAKER AND SPIRITUAL DIRECTOR

Christmas Day: Will God really dwell on earth?

'But will God really dwell on earth with humans? The heavens, even the highest heavens, cannot contain you. How much less this temple that I have built! Yet, Lord my God, give attention to your servant's prayer and his plea for mercy. Hear the cry and the prayer that your servant is praying in your presence.'

2 CHRONICLES 6:18–19 (NIV)

It's a mind-boggling question for Christmas Day or any other, and originally posed by Solomon at the dedication of his magnificent temple centuries ago. In a world torn apart by war, seeking to combat Covid-19 and threatened by ecological disaster, is there anyone up and out there in our vast cosmos that cares?

For some, swimming in the sea of what is called the 'new atheism', time, chance and impersonal forces have combined to produce everything we know and observe. Here, the answer is straightforward – *impossible*! However, the downside is there's no ultimate right and wrong. And no hope, for death makes fools of us all.

For others, there must be something even non-believers can believe in, as the song *Alfie* has it. But given the immensity of the universe, wouldn't this planet be too small and insignificant for any God, however defined, to be bothered about it anyway? Effectively, we're on our own. Therefore, the answer is *improbable*!

For Christians, 'God is love' (1 John 4:8). There's something in us that almost intuitively recognises genuine love when we encounter it. It's the very opposite of self-promoting, 'me-first' selfishness that characterises much of our world, broken in so many places. Who or what can fix it? God's love! He didn't watch a world drowning and stay on the shore. He waded in personally. So the name 'Jesus' is so appropriate – God the Saviour/Rescuer. That's why John 3:16 wonderfully sums up the gospel: 'For God so loved the world that he gave his one and only Son, that whoever believes in him shall not perish but have eternal life.' Now the answer is – *inevitable*!

'Will God really dwell on earth?' *Impossible*? *Improbable*? *Inevitable*? My answer will determine how happy my Christmas, my life and my world really is!

STEVE BRADY, SENIOR PASTOR, FIRST BAPTIST CHURCH, GRAND CAYMAN, AND PRESIDENT, MOORLANDS COLLEGE

Picture language

Long ago God spoke to our ancestors in many and various ways by the prophets, but in these last days he has spoken to us by a Son... He is the reflection of God's glory and the exact imprint of God's very being, and he sustains all things by his powerful word.

HEBREWS 1:1–3 (NRSV, abridged)

Advent calendars reach the end of their story on 25 December, with the familiar scene of the baby in the manger, with Mary and Joseph. That's Christmas for many people, the end of the story and the end of the festivities. Lights are switched off, shops open again and life continues.

But the Book of Common Prayer has another few windows in its calendar, for the three days after Christmas. Christmas is about much stronger stuff than the little Lord Jesus safely asleep in the hay. We celebrate his birth because he grew up and challenged people to live in God's light. Some people chose, and choose, darkness.

26 December celebrates Stephen. He was stoned to death because he challenged the religious people of his day to let the light of Christ transform their lives. Their response was to reject the message and kill the messenger – but they didn't stop the light spreading.

27 December, St John's Day, reminds us that Jesus is the light of the world coming to live among us and transform our lives, the light that darkness cannot destroy.

Holy Innocents' Day on 28 December reminds us how King Herod, asked by the wise men where they might find the newborn king of the Jews and terrified of the challenge the new baby might represent, ordered all the children in the area under two years of age to be killed.

At the heart of that first Christmas there was pain: bleeding and crying, rejection and persecution. And that is still true of our world. But the darkness hasn't won, nor will it, as long as we choose to live in the light of Christ, 'the reflection of God's glory and the exact imprint of God's very being', who 'sustains all things by his powerful word'. The challenge of Christmas is to let the light of hope shine in and through us, transforming the communities in which we live. And that's not just for the Christmas season, it's for life.

ANN LEWIN, WRITER AND SPEAKER

We have seen his glory

In the beginning was the Word, and the Word was with God, and the Word was God. He was in the beginning with God. All things came into being through him, and without him not one thing came into being. What has come into being in him was life, and the life was the light of all people. The light shines in the darkness, and the darkness did not overcome it… And the Word became flesh and lived among us, and we have seen his glory, the glory as of a father's only son, full of grace and truth.

JOHN 1:1–5, 14 (NRSV)

These verses speak of an event and an experience. In the reckoning of Christians, the event is the most important thing that has ever happened. We call it the incarnation. In Jesus Christ God has come among us. God has done this in the person of one who is both Word of God and Son of God.

Words are used as a form of self-expression and as a medium of communication. In the Word the eternal God expresses God's own self. In a decisive form of cross-cultural communication, the eternal has now entered into time. This means that the ultimate mystery of the universe, the nature and reality of our final origin, can at last be understood. This is great news. The light shines in the darkness to illuminate everything. Jesus Christ, God's Word made flesh, is the key to unlocking who God is and consequently everything else. Christ can do this because he is God's own Son and so precisely resembles the Father. Because of the divinity of Christ, we can be sure of the Christlikeness of the divinity.

This glorious, objective truth is the bedrock of Christian faith and the turning point of human history. It has permanent and universal meaning. But it becomes personal and life-transforming when our eyes are opened and we 'see it': 'we have seen his glory'. This is the true enlightenment. The universal turning point thus becomes a personal turning point, a moment of conversion when everything is changed and becomes new. Yet this is more than just a 'moment'; rather, it is a process, something that goes on happening as we look to Christ and find him to be both Son and Word of the Father. To go on looking upon him is to be transformed into his image (2 Corinthians 3:18).

NIGEL G. WRIGHT, BAPTIST MINISTER AND PRINCIPAL EMERITUS, SPURGEON'S COLLEGE

God's plan from the beginning

When the woman saw that the tree was... to be desired to make one wise, she took of its fruit and ate, and she also gave some to her husband who was with her and he ate... Then the Lord God said to the woman, 'What is this that you have done?' The woman said, 'The serpent deceived me, and I ate.' The Lord God said to the serpent, 'Because you have done this... I will put enmity between you and the woman, and between your offspring and her offspring; he shall bruise your head, and you shall bruise his heel.'

GENESIS 3:6, 13–15 (ESV, abridged)

Reading these verses in a prayer meeting shortly before Christmas, the leader said that verse 15 had been regarded by many church fathers as the first proclamation of the gospel (the protoevangelium). At a time of year when we are so focused on the birth of Jesus and the start of his time on earth, it struck me afresh that God had planned for Jesus' redemptive work from the second that sin entered the garden of Eden. His plan didn't start 2,000 years ago with the virgin birth. Charles Simeon of Cambridge, the famous early 19th-century preacher, said that verse 15 was 'the sum and summary of the whole Bible'. That is quite a claim for one verse, so what did he mean?

Who are the offspring of the snake and of the woman? Although not explicit here, elsewhere in the Bible the snake is identified as Satan. The woman's offspring is from her only, not the man, and so this is the first announcement of the virgin birth of the Messiah. It is a prophecy that Christ will deal a fatal blow to the head of Satan. The Messiah will suffer bruises, but wounds to the heel are not fatal. Everything else in the Bible flows from these words.

Even if we are suffering (bruised) for our faith, we can be assured that God's kingdom has triumphed over Satan's, because we can look back to Christ's redemptive work on a cross outside a city wall which completed the work prophesied in Genesis.

MICHAEL WILKINSON, TRUSTEE, BRF

Born as one of us

We declare to you what was from the beginning, what we have heard, what we have seen with our eyes, what we have looked at and touched with our hands, concerning the word of life – this life was revealed, and we have seen it and testify to it, and declare to you the eternal life that was with the Father and was revealed to us – we declare to you what we have seen and heard so that you also may have fellowship with us; and truly our fellowship is with the Father and with his Son Jesus Christ. We are writing these things so that our joy may be complete.

1 JOHN 1:1–4 (NRSV)

We can almost feel the pulse of energy and enthusiasm in this opening passage of the first letter of John, as phrases tumble over each other in breathless exuberance. 'Yes!' insists the author, 'We saw him, we heard and touched him!' Jesus was born as a fully human being, not some hybrid demigod. Echoing the opening to John's gospel, often heard in Christmas services, we're reminded that the 'Word' of God, God's very life from the beginning, came to dwell among us in Jesus, sharing our flesh and blood. The first disciples had realised that, incredibly, when they were with Jesus they were also with God. Jesus was totally one with God, drawing everyone he encountered into a quality and depth of living here referred to as 'eternal life'.

Many scholars believe that the author is 'John the Elder', the revered leader of a Christian circle in Ephesus, cited in 2 John 1:1 and 3 John 1:1 and mentioned by the second-century bishop Irenaeus. He may well have known John 'the beloved disciple', and the sense of a first-hand experience, described so eagerly in these opening verses, does point to an immediate disciple of Jesus as the source here.

Crucially, the apostles' direct experience of Jesus is not just something to marvel at. We ourselves are invited into the love-relationship with God and with fellow believers that Jesus offers. John's sole desire and 'joy' is to share this gift of 'fellowship', a rich term conveying a communion of mutual friendship, trust and commitment. Thus, as we ponder the Christmas crib, will we simply look from a safe distance, or will we allow ourselves to be drawn ever more deeply into the creative, life-giving and transforming energy of love that came into the world when Jesus was born?

ANGELA ASHWIN, AUTHOR AND SPEAKER

Hail, the incarnate Deity!

Have this mind among yourselves, which is yours in Christ Jesus, who, though he was in the form of God, did not count equality with God a thing to be grasped, but emptied himself, taking the form of a servant, being born in the likeness of men. And being found in human form he humbled himself and became obedient unto death, even death on a cross. Therefore God has highly exalted him and bestowed on him the name which is above every name, that at the name of Jesus every knee should bow, in heaven and on earth and under the earth, and every tongue confess that Jesus Christ is Lord, to the glory of God the Father.

PHILIPPIANS 2:5–11 (RSV)

This passage is one of the most profound statements in all scripture of both the identity of Jesus Christ – the baby born in Bethlehem that first Christmas – and his work, what he came to do. Moreover, it is a very early statement; Paul's epistle predates the gospels and probably here quotes an early hymn which takes us back very close to the foundational events.

Jesus is not just a man, born at a particular place and time, but a person who has always existed. He was 'in the form of God' and entitled to equality with God. However, for the sake of us humans, Jesus chose not to take advantage of his position but to 'empty himself', taking the form of a servant and becoming one of us. We are familiar with those who have great positions and do take advantage of them. Jesus chose the opposite path: he humbled himself, became one of us and died on a cross for our sake.

Jesus' divinity is confirmed in what follows. The expression 'at the name of Jesus every knee should bow' mirrors Isaiah 45:23, when the Lord God says, 'To me every knee shall bow, every tongue shall swear.' The honour due to God is given to Jesus.

It is as we realise who Jesus is and what he has done for us that we are moved to action ourselves. We too are to be humble, not standing on any position we might occupy but looking to the interests of others rather than of ourselves. In short, we are to have the mind of Christ.

RODNEY HOLDER, EMERITUS COURSE DIRECTOR,
THE FARADAY INSTITUTE FOR SCIENCE AND RELIGION, CAMBRIDGE

Grace unrestrained

For the grace of God has appeared that offers salvation to all people. It teaches us to say 'No' to ungodliness and worldly passions, and to live self-controlled, upright and godly lives in this present age, while we wait for the blessed hope – the appearing of the glory of our great God and Saviour, Jesus Christ, who gave himself for us to redeem us from all wickedness and to purify for himself a people that are his very own, eager to do what is good.

TITUS 2:11–14 (NIV)

Have you ever received a gift that blew your socks off? Maybe not literally, or then again, maybe you've had some very special socks. Whatever may come to mind, it is rare to get a truly life-changing gift. As we take time to celebrate the coming of Christ in human form, it is good to remind ourselves that in Jesus we find a life-changing, grace-filled invitation. Jesus came, not just to teach us about the kingdom of God, but so that we might actually know God – personally.

What is truly outrageous here, though, is that the extent of God's grace means that this offer of salvation is available to all people. Everyone. There are people we might think of or read about who doubtless test the limits of that grace, and yet here it is, plain as day – an offer for all.

Hearing is good, seeing is better, but it is typically doing something that gives us a deeper understanding. So it is here. The receiving of this gift changes us as we seek to live it out. This outrageous grace, that extends to all people, works in us and we in turn can act in grace. It's a redemption journey, changing us from the inside out. God's work inside us becomes visible, tangible on the outside. This salvation story moves beyond words to actions. Our lives are woven in as part of the living testimony of that received grace. And if you think that is amazing, we're reminded here that it is only the faintest of glimmers of a day that is still to come when Jesus appears again. That will certainly do more than blow your socks off!

ALAN CHARTER, FACILITATOR, GLOBAL CHILDREN'S FORUM

Adopted by God

Praise be to the God and Father of our Lord Jesus Christ, who has blessed us in the heavenly realms with every spiritual blessing in Christ. For he chose us in him before the creation of the world to be holy and blameless in his sight. In love he predestined us for adoption to sonship through Jesus Christ, in accordance with his pleasure and will – to the praise of his glorious grace, which he has freely given us in the One he loves.

EPHESIANS 1:3–6 (NIV)

Whether or not adoption is part of our life experience, its truths and implications are at the heart of the Christmas narrative.

Joseph's likeness would never appear in Jesus' face; he couldn't even choose his name. But in obedience to God, Joseph adopted the role of father, choosing to lavish all he had on Mary's vulnerable child; to love, protect, provide, feed, care for and nurture. He raised the boy known as 'Joseph's son' in the ways and laws of Yahweh and taught him his carpentry trade – perhaps hoping Jesus might inherit his business one day.

Paul takes this glimpse of the gift of adoption much further, reminding us that *God* chose to adopt *us* as his children, a truth with immense implications and a fundamental spiritual legality. Adoption by God completely changes our outlook and prospects as we inherit every spiritual blessing in Christ: the fullness of God's love, peace, forgiveness, security, provision, wholeness, guidance and equipping. This inheritance releases us from past shame and failure, lavishing upon us the grace of worth, purpose and the gentle loving disciplines that mature us into the likeness of our holy Father. This inheritance grants us the authority of Christ's name. We can't earn or deserve this inheritance, but we can receive and embrace it more fully than any gift we may have hoped for this Christmas.

To live out our adoption, however, we may need to shake off indifference to these gifts from the heavenly realm, or undermining thoughts that we're not good enough to receive them. And we do that as we choose to believe every truth and promise in scripture, allowing them, one by one, to renew our minds, heal our emotions, nurture inward security and reset our priorities and perspective. Now surely that's a gift we can join Paul in praising God for.

ANNE LE TISSIER, AUTHOR AND SPEAKER

Gold seams

So then, if anyone is in Christ, that person is part of the new creation. The old things have gone away, and look, new things have arrived! All of these new things are from God, who reconciled us to himself through Christ and who gave us the ministry of reconciliation. In other words, God was reconciling the world to himself through Christ, by not counting people's sins against them. He has trusted us with this message of reconciliation. So we are ambassadors who represent Christ.

2 CORINTHIANS 5:17–20a (CEB)

I enjoy watching a TV show about repair work to antiques. Local artisans expertly repair damaged or age-worn items brought in by individuals. One artisan is a ceramics expert. She carefully glues and reassembles shards of broken heirlooms – like clocks, vases and figurines – to make them whole again. Then, with painstaking precision, she paints over the lines of glue to erase the visible signs of her repair work. When she is finished, you cannot tell that the pieces were ever broken.

This approach to repair work is in stark contrast with kintsugi, the Japanese art of repairing broken pottery using lacquer dusted or mixed with powdered metallic pigment – like gold or silver. The pigmented lacquer makes the repair work of kintsugi highly visible. The shards of broken pottery are accentuated by the gold seams of lacquer that make the piece whole again. Kintsugi as a philosophy is about acknowledging, not disguising, breakage and repair as part of an object's history or story. The beauty of kintsugi is not in the object appearing brand new; the beauty is in the gold seams, which bring together what was once broken.

The reconciling love that God offers us through Jesus Christ is like this. Today's quoted scripture describes how Jesus offers us a new way of being in relationship with God. We are loved and accepted by God – shards and all! We can trust that God is at work in our lives and in the world. At this season when we reflect on and celebrate Christ's birth, where do you see God's gold seams of repair in your life and in the lives of those around you?

TIA RUNION, DIRECTOR OF INTERNATIONAL RELATIONS, EUROPE,
AND GLOBAL CONTRACTS MANAGER, THE UPPER ROOM (USA)

Christian giving

Jesus said to him, 'If you wish to be perfect, go, sell your possessions, and give the money to the poor, and you will have treasure in heaven; then come, follow me.' When the young man heard this word, he went away grieving, for he had many possessions.

MATTHEW 19:21–22 (NRSV)

Christmas is a time which we celebrate by giving presents to our friends and family in memory of the amazing gift which God gave to the world, his son Jesus. It is also a time when we think of those who are less fortunate than ourselves and may give to charities which we wish to support. As an accountant who has spent his life advising others on financial matters, I long to understand the Christian teaching on wealth and giving.

The Bible has many warnings about the dangers of wealth. Jesus says of the rich young ruler, who 'went away grieving for he had many possessions', that 'it is easier for a camel to go through the eye of a needle than for someone who is rich to enter the kingdom of God' (Matthew 19:24). Relative to much of the world, in the west we are nearly all rich and have many possessions. What hope is there for us?

Jesus tells the parable of the wealthy landowner who has been blessed by an exceptional harvest which he stores away for his retirement, only to die that night (Luke 12:16–21). Yet we are encouraged to admire the wise man who made ten talents from the initial five (Matthew 25:20–21).

What should we learn from all of this? Like the monkey with a hand trapped in the peanut jar, the rich young man could not let go of what he already held. Think of what he might have achieved if he had become a disciple of Jesus, using his talents and resources to become an even better and more generous ruler.

The baby Jesus became the man who gave his life for our salvation. He gave us everything. God does want us to prosper and to use the talents he has blessed us with for his purposes. The apostle Paul taught that each 'should give what you have decided in your heart to give, not reluctantly or under compulsion, for God loves a cheerful giver' (2 Corinthians 9:7, NIV). To do this, we should recognise the needs of others and hold our wealth lightly in an open, outstretched hand.

PETER LLOYD, FORMER TRUSTEE, BRF

Someone's knocking...

'Here I am! I stand at the door and knock. If anyone hears my voice and opens the door, I will come in and eat with that person, and they with me. To the one who is victorious, I will give the right to sit with me on my throne, just as I was victorious and sat down with my Father on his throne. Whoever has ears, let them hear what the Spirit says to the churches.'

REVELATION 3:20–22 (NIV)

How do you respond to a knock at the door – especially when you're busy? How inconvenient! If only they'd told me they were coming… What a surprise, if we opened the door and found Jesus standing there!

How would I react if I knew it was Jesus standing at my door? Would I be excited? Or would I be worried?

As I reflected on Revelation 3:20, I was surprised to find myself having difficulty unlocking my 'door'. Lots of bolts to pull back, lots of locks.

In my imagination, I saw a fireplace, with two armchairs either side of a roaring fire. As Jesus settled himself in one of the chairs, it was as if he said, 'If you want the fire of the Holy Spirit in your life, you must keep me central in it.'

I saw a Christmas stocking hanging from the mantelpiece. It was pretty pathetic – so small. I thought, 'Wow, that wouldn't even hold a few marbles!' Then I thought, 'Is that what I expect from Jesus? Actually, very little?' Surely God is generous – and I'm not just talking about financially. So what are my expectations of God? Do I 'ask small' because I 'expect small'? What does this say about who I think God is?

In the Bible, we see God as a generous, lavish giver. I think we see this especially at Christmas, when he shared himself with humanity – at such great cost.

Getting to know God, spending time with him and keeping him central in our lives will expand not just our vision of him, but also our expectation.

How important it is, then, to invite Jesus in: to intentionally spend time with the one for whom there was 'no room' that first Christmas, keeping company with the one who loves us best.

SHEILA JACOBS, EDITOR, AUTHOR, DAY CHAPLAIN, SPEAKER AND RETREAT LEADER

Arise, shine!

'Arise, shine; for your light has come, and the glory of the Lord has risen upon you. For darkness shall cover the earth, and thick darkness the peoples; but the Lord will arise upon you, and his glory will appear over you. Nations shall come to your light, and kings to the brightness of your dawn... Then you shall see and be radiant; your heart shall thrill and rejoice, because the abundance of the sea shall be brought to you, the wealth of the nations shall come to you. A multitude of camels shall cover you, the young camels of Midian and Ephah; all those from Sheba shall come. They shall bring gold and frankincense, and shall proclaim the praise of the Lord.'

ISAIAH 60:1–3, 5–6 (NRSV)

Sometimes the world can seem like a gloomy place. In this passage, the author writes to a people who have spent long, dark years in exile, and casts a wonderful vision of the city of Jerusalem, where God will draw all people to himself and everything will be filled with hope, love, light and peace. Not only that, but this light-filled city will act as a magnet to draw in people from all over the world.

There's a wonderful picture of women and men, boys and girls, young and old, streaming in with gifts to offer to the praise and glory of God. This image of people from the Gentile nations coming to offer gifts for the worship of a king calls to mind the wise men, who came from afar to worship Jesus, the King, at his birth (Matthew 2:1–12). There's even mention of gold and frankincense included in their gift-bringing too.

This is a lovely passage to read and reflect on, with all its imagery of light and glory. The promise that 'your heart shall thrill and rejoice' is enough to lift the most weary eyes, hearts and spirits, even in the most challenging of circumstances. The joy that is promised in this passage is not the short-lived cheerfulness of a fleeting feel-good moment, but is grounded in the revelation of God himself among his people.

Having God shine his light on the inhabitants of the city is what brings the joy, and that joy is in turn given back in the praise of the Lord. Arise, shine!

EMMA INESON, BISHOP TO THE ARCHBISHOPS OF CANTERBURY AND YORK

Lent

IN THIS SECTION we journey through Lent and Holy Week. We begin by hearing the challenging cry of Isaiah: 'Here am I, send me.' Can you and I say the same? Valerie Eker suggests that 'for each of us there has to come a time when we reach the end of our own capabilities. We need to be anointed afresh by God's own Spirit and offer ourselves to be the vessels through which he acts.'

Maybe our daily prayer for this season could be 'Lord, anoint me afresh', as we enter into places of questioning, lament and loss. In such places we can find ourselves held by the honesty and hope of holiness as truth is revealed afresh. The truth of who we are, about the world of which we are part and of what both can be in the light of the one who is the way, the truth and the life.

Throughout these reflections – which include some truly inspiring stories – there is a profound sense of God quietly working his purposes out. Gareth Russell helpfully points out that 'the miracle is perhaps not so much in the answer [to prayer] but in the presence of the Almighty while we wait'.

Our journey ends at the tomb of Jesus. There Rachel Treweek points out that we know that on Easter morning we will 'celebrate his rising from the dead which can never be undone. Yet in the present as we live our joy, we also carry our fears and struggles, because the shalom of complete transformation, made possible by Christ's death and resurrection, is not yet fully here.' It is in that intertwined reality of joy and struggle that we make this journey.

ANDREW ROBERTS, HOLY HABITS PIONEER

Week 1
Into the wilderness

Ash Wednesday: A fresh anointing

'Woe to me!' I cried. 'I am ruined! For I am a man of unclean lips, and I live among a people of unclean lips, and my eyes have seen the King, the Lord Almighty.' Then one of the seraphim flew to me with a live coal in his hand, which he had taken with tongs from the altar. With it he touched my mouth and said, 'See, this has touched your lips; your guilt is taken away and your sin atoned for.' Then I heard the voice of the Lord saying, 'Whom shall I send? And who will go for us?' And I said, 'Here am I. Send me!'

ISAIAH 6:5–8 (NIV)

It is said that fish have no idea what water is. They are so fully immersed in its liquidity that they have nothing to compare it with. It is simply taken for granted as the norm of their existence.

So it was for Isaiah. Until he had his amazing vision of God, he judged himself and his neighbours only by the requirements of the law. By its light he had prophetic understanding of the many injustices they perpetrated, and he had spoken out against them vigorously.

Yet at the sight of God himself, enthroned and highly exalted, Isaiah was completely stricken. He realised with absolute certainty that he – who had so faithfully used his mouth to speak truth on God's behalf – was woefully impure and lived among a people who were also impure.

It was simultaneously a revelation of God's true nature, 'Holy, Holy, Holy', and of his own.

One might think that this would be the end of his work for God. How could he, knowing his own corruption, ever speak on behalf of God? Only if something of God's own holiness were to cleanse him, which is what happened when his mouth was touched by the live coal from the altar. With it he was pronounced by God to be cleansed all through.

Perhaps for each of us there has to come a time when we reach the end of our own capabilities. We need to be anointed afresh by God's own Spirit and offer ourselves to be the vessels through which he acts.

Ash Wednesday is the perfect time to begin denying ourselves and laying ourselves open to a new working of God within us. Then we can say, with the apostle Paul, 'It is no longer I who works, but Christ who works through me' (see Galatians 2:20).

VALERIE EKER, RETIRED TEACHER AND SPIRITUAL DIRECTOR

The legitimacy of lament

The hearts of the people cry out to the Lord. You walls of Daughter Zion, let your tears flow like a river day and night; give yourself no relief, your eyes no rest. Arise, cry out in the night, as the watches of the night begin; pour out your heart like water in the presence of the Lord. Lift up your hands to him for the lives of your children, who faint from hunger at every street corner.

LAMENTATIONS 2:18b–19 (NIV)

Our western culture has forgotten how to lament and grieve; we are too busy, we move too fast – not just physically but in every way. We are a move-on, the-show-must-go-on culture, restlessly seeking to alleviate our pain with possessions and comfort – restlessly, because these things never deliver. A long time ago, our firstborn son died in a cot death at nine-and-a-half weeks. Someone in that blur of a time spoke these words to me that I have not only never forgotten, but which were a lifeline: 'This will take you at least four years to recover from.' It was, and still is, a beautiful liberation. Much more recently, in October 2019, my beloved only sister was killed in a brutal car crash in South Africa. I am still deeply mourning and lamenting her loss… and it may be that you too are struggling with loss, whether a death or something else. All of us are living with losses great and small brought by Covid-19.

God himself laments through the mouths of the prophets: 'I weep with the weeping of Jazer… I drench you with my tears… my inner parts moan like a lyre' (Isaiah 16:9, 11, ESV); 'For these things I weep; my eyes flow with tears; for a comforter is far from me, one to revive my spirit; my children are desolate, for the enemy has prevailed' (Lamentations 1:16, ESV). The Bible offers us a language of lament in many places, but supremely in Job, the Psalms, Jeremiah and Lamentations.

Lamenting is lots of things – it's weeping, it's gut-wrenching sobs. It's acknowledging our feelings of anger, betrayal, confusion, distress and more. Confessing the mess of our feelings, our inner turmoil, to God, and to appropriate others, significantly impacts our mental health and well-being. So let's be a people who recover lament.

ANITA CLEVERLY, AUTHOR AND SPEAKER

Honest to God

O Lord, you know... that on your account I suffer insult. Your words were found, and I ate them, and your words became to me a joy and the delight of my heart; for I am called by your name, O Lord, God of hosts. I did not sit in the company of merrymakers, nor did I rejoice; under the weight of your hand I sat alone, for you had filled me with indignation. Why is my pain unceasing, my wound incurable, refusing to be healed? Truly, you are to me like a deceitful brook, like waters that fail.

JEREMIAH 15:15–18 (NRSV)

One of scripture's most outstanding qualities is its honesty, its warts-and-all character. The Bible tends not to feature glossy heroes and glamorous heroines who always get things right; rather, it introduces us to ordinary, fallible human beings whose openness to God is what makes them extraordinary. Jeremiah is one of scripture's ordinary people; as a young man he had questioned and reluctantly responded to God's unexpected call to him to tell the truth about the consequences of his community's unfaithfulness to the Lord.

For some 40 years Jeremiah struggled to work out his calling to pass on a difficult and unpopular message. His story is punctuated with outspoken laments against God as the stress of his work threatens to overwhelm him. Death threats (11:18–20) and the unnerving success of his opponents, especially of treacherous family members (12:1–6), are all woven into prayer – seven 'confessional' passages between chapters 11 and 20 that allow us to listen in on the prophet's inner life, his dialogue with God. The prayer of chapter 15 is perhaps the most poignant because it focuses on the heart of his calling and the agonising conflict this provokes in Jeremiah. God's warning message that he has transmitted faithfully, even joyfully (v. 16), seems not to be working; people are rejecting and scorning it. Jeremiah feels a failure, lonely and marginalised and is breathtakingly honest about his experience of being let down by God (v. 18).

I wonder how many of us would include prayer of this kind in the story of our relationship with God. What does prayer like this say about that relationship? Have we ever told God, with Jeremiah's openness, about our loneliness, anger, hurt and disappointment? Can we trust him to hear and understand? And will we wait and listen, as Jeremiah did, to God's response (vv. 19–21)?

PAULINE HOGGARTH, RETIRED BIBLE MINISTRIES COORDINATOR,
SCRIPTURE UNION INTERNATIONAL

A word bleeding through the darkness

'Why is light given to one in misery, and life to the bitter in soul, who long for death, but it does not come, and dig for it more than for hidden treasures; who rejoice exceedingly, and are glad when they find the grave? Why is light given to one who cannot see the way, whom God has fenced in? For my sighing comes like my bread, and my groanings are poured out like water. Truly the thing that I fear comes upon me, and what I dread befalls me. I am not at ease, nor am I quiet; I have no rest; but trouble comes.'

JOB 3:20–26 (NRSV)

In the western world we often live as though we deserve to not suffer, or, at least, as though suffering shouldn't happen to us. For many of us, therefore, Job's outcry above is hard to relate to.

Covid-19 knocked many of us in this regard, threatening our sense of security, our perceived freedoms, our physical and mental health, destroying both jobs and lives. It has been bleak! However, facing the daily threat of death, the oppression of forced restrictions, being crushed emotionally, losing livelihoods – these are already a part of life for so many people in the world. Moreover, that is the story we witness here in the Bible. If we struggle with today's passage, maybe that says just as much about us as it does about Job.

Throughout history, people have suffered in so many tragic or evil ways, but many of our churches fail to respond faithfully. We might evade issues altogether, so that our faith isn't 'rocked'. Or we may 'focus on the positives' and sing that praise chorus a few more times until we feel 'happy'. But that often compounds the pain of those who feel like Job, for whom suffering is a biblical reality.

Scripture witnesses to the God who is revealed not despite but through suffering, most fully and finally in Christ's own lament in Gethsemane and on Golgotha. If you are suffering today, I cannot make you feel happier, but I can point you towards Job's words, which enfold you into God's word of promise that you are intimately known, and held in God's love, which bleeds through the darkness even when we can't see. And those of us who feel fine, let us recognise that we are called to lift all things to God in prayer, rather than to try to explain stuff away like Job's friends did.

TIM JUDSON, MINISTER, HONITON FAMILY CHURCH, EAST DEVON

It's not all about you...

Then the Lord answered Job out of the whirlwind and said: 'Who is this that darkens counsel by words without knowledge? Dress for action like a man; I will question you, and you make it known to me. Where were you when I laid the foundations of the earth? Tell me, if you have understanding. Who determined its measurements – surely you know! Or who stretched the line upon it? On what were its bases sunk, or who laid its cornerstone, when the morning stars sang together and all the sons of God shouted for joy?'

JOB 38:1–7 (ESV)

Job has been – like Josef K. in Kafka's *The Trial* – accused (and punished) for dreadful but unspecified crimes by what seems an endlessly vindictive, hidden authority. He has cried out repeatedly for his 'day in court' when he can confront the one who is both his accuser and his judge and see himself vindicated. Now, finally, God shows up! Job might have hoped for an apology. Indeed, we readers, who know that his sufferings have been unmerited – the result of the apparently frivolous wager between the Lord and the 'Satan' in the book's prologue – might have thought that God would declare his servant 'not guilty' and, perhaps, explain what lay behind the dreadful trauma he has suffered.

So it is indeed surprising that, far from being abashed, or even repentant, the Lord comes out slugging! He rebukes Job for his presumption. 'Look at creation,' he cries. 'You have no idea of how it came into being! Who are you to take issue with me?' Much of the rest of the book's final chapters amplify this theme in poetry of astonishing power and beauty.

Really? How does that help a suffering Job and, indeed, ourselves, when, perhaps, we face crushing loss and, even worse, must witness the suffering of loved ones? Well, trembling, might we not dare to consider that, at just such times, we must lift our eyes from our own troubles, vast and painful as they may be, and set them in an even greater perspective, that of the Lord God's cosmic concerns? In the end, like Job, we shall discover that God's will is to restore us, but the path to that restoration lies through a recognition that while our horizon is limited, there is one who sees further, more clearly, more lovingly, than do we.

PETER HATTON, METHODIST MINISTER

Justice and mercy

**His way is in the whirlwind and the storm, and clouds are the dust of his feet...
Bashan and Carmel wither and the blossoms of Lebanon fade. The mountains
quake before him and the hills melt away. The earth trembles at his presence,
the world and all who live in it. Who can withstand his indignation? Who can
endure his fierce anger? His wrath is poured out like fire; the rocks are shattered
before him. The Lord is good, a refuge in times of trouble. He cares for those
who trust in him.**

NAHUM 1:3–7 (NIV, abridged)

When I was at senior school, we had a particular teacher who was renowned
for being a strict disciplinarian. He was an excellent teacher and was well
respected. We were teenagers and sometimes did things we should not do.
This of course made him angry, and he would let us know about it! He cared
enough about us to show us where we went wrong and would bring correction
and discipline to help us grow.

In today's culture of tolerance, we sometimes find it difficult to understand
a God who is intolerant of our sins, who cares enough to bring discipline to
cause a course correction. God is both kind and fierce. He is indeed slow to
anger (Psalm 103:8), which is a sign of his loving kindness, but he is also a
righteous judge (Psalm 75:7) and cannot let sin go unpunished. If he did, he
would not be a good God at all.

In the passage above, the prophet Nahum describes God's terrible wrath
and judgement of his enemies, but he balances this with the mercy and
protection he shows to those who trust in him.

Indeed, Jesus shows us both sides of God's character when he died on the
cross. Both justice and mercy meet at the cross of Christ – *his* death to pay for
our sin: a divine exchange where justice is done, yet mercy is given to those
who do not deserve it.

As we continue our journey through Lent, we may find ourselves facing
times of discipline. When this happens, do not lose heart. Instead, turn to
Jesus. We shall find our safety in Christ because he cares for those who
trust in him.

MATT McCHLERY, AUTHOR AND SONGWRITER

Comfort through the years

Do you not know? Have you not heard? The Lord is the everlasting God, the Creator of the ends of the earth. He will not grow tired or weary, and his understanding no one can fathom. He gives strength to the weary and increases the power of the weak. Even youths grow tired and weary, and young men stumble and fall; but those who hope in the Lord will renew their strength. They will soar on wings like eagles; they will run and not grow weary, they will walk and not be faint.

ISAIAH 40:28–31 (NIV)

I was introduced to these verses in 1993 at an Anglican Renewal Ministries event in Harrogate. I knew no one as I entered the conference centre. Outside my comfort zone – to what had I committed myself? – after a warm welcome, through laughter and tears, singing and dance, I found acceptance, forgiveness and the love of God.

Over the years these verses have comforted and sustained me. The writer of Isaiah begins this chapter with the words 'Comfort, comfort my people, says your God'. We have come to think of the word 'comfort' as associated with compassion, when we comfort a person in distress or who faces a difficult time, but the original meaning is 'to strengthen'. The passage speaks of God's longing to strengthen us, to encourage us, to walk alongside us, to run with us, be it a sprint or a marathon. The writer implores us to sense that longing with our eyes and to hear it with our ears. The promise is that we will receive God's love through the good times and the bad. He speaks through the quiet words of a neighbour or friend; he shows us through the actions of family or colleagues and the wonder of his creation.

God's ambition for each of us, young and old, is greater still. As a loving parent, God wants the best for his children. To those who hope – a very significant word, for without hope we are indeed lost – his promise is not only that our strength will be renewed but that 'we will soar on wings like eagles'.

Isaiah's words beckon us when tired and weary, to pause, to listen, to hear that still small voice.

And Jesus invites us to 'come unto me, all ye that labour and are heavy laden, and I will give you rest' (Matthew 11:28, KJV), to find the peace which passes all understanding and to renew our strength for life's journey.

PHILIP ARUNDEL, NORTH YORKSHIRE

Standing back to back

Two people are better off than one, for they can help each other succeed. If one person falls, the other can reach out and help. But someone who falls alone is in real trouble. Likewise, two people lying close together can keep each other warm. But how can one be warm alone? A person standing alone can be attacked and defeated, but two can stand back-to-back and conquer. Three are even better, for a triple-braided cord is not easily broken.

ECCLESIASTES 4:9–12 (NLT)

Which of us has not felt lonely at some point in our lives? A survey by the charity Campaign to End Loneliness concluded that in the UK over nine million people would say that they were always or often lonely. Feeling lonely does not always mean that you are physically or socially isolated from others, although for many during the Covid-19 lockdown this would have been their experience; this is a loneliness that passes as family and friends reunite.

For others there may be a deeper, emotional loneliness; a feeling that no one can truly understand what they are going through, possibly the loss of someone they loved dearly. Very sadly our six-year-old granddaughter, Amelia, unexpectedly died recently, which has left a deep sense of loss and loneliness within our family. They say time heals, which I am sure it does, but there will always be an empty seat around the dining table.

It is at times like these that we need the help, support and encouragement of others, rather than putting on a brave face and saying we are fine when we are not. Over the years I have learnt that asking for help is a sign not of weakness but of strength. I suspect when Solomon in his wisdom wrote, 'A person standing alone can be attacked and defeated, but two can stand back-to-back and conquer,' he was thinking of soldiers in the battlefield, but it can equally apply to us today. There are times we will probably all need someone to stand with us to help take on the challenges of life. Or it may be there is someone you know right now who you need to stand back to back with for their encouragement. Let us all do our part to overcome loneliness.

STEPHEN AND MANDY BRIARS, PUBLISHERS, *TOGETHER* MAGAZINE

Hope in a world of pain

After this I saw four angels standing at the four corners of the earth, holding back the four winds of the earth, that no wind might blow on earth or sea or against any tree. Then I saw another angel ascending from the rising of the sun, with the seal of the living God, and he called with a loud voice to the four angels who had been given power to harm earth and sea, saying, 'Do not harm the earth or the sea or the trees, until we have sealed the servants of our God on their foreheads.'

REVELATION 7:1–3 (ESV)

What in the world is God up to, when there is warfare, disease, hunger and death all around? That is the question raised when the lamb, slain yet standing, opens the seals on the scroll, the will of God for the world in Revelation 6, and permits (though does not himself summon) the four horsemen to ride forth. And in the interlude between the sixth and seventh seal, in Revelation 7, the answer is: he is raising up a holy people who will sing a song of hope in a world of suffering and despair. John describes this answer using language saturated with Old Testament imagery.

The image of the four horsemen comes from Zechariah 6:2–8, and, just as in Zechariah, these are now interpreted as four winds. John combines this with images from Ezekiel 9, where Jerusalem is under judgement and siege, but a faithful remnant are marked on their foreheads to protect them. But for John, it is not a city but the whole world which faces judgement, and those protected are not a remnant but the followers of the lamb – and they are not simply saved for themselves.

John hears the number being counted out – a census being taken of the Israel of God (compare Numbers 1:2), disciplined in worship and ready for spiritual warfare. Yet when he turns to see them, they are too many to count and come from 'every nation, tribe, people and language', a multicultural, ethnically diverse fulfilment of God's promise to Abraham, that through his offspring all nations will be blessed (Genesis 18:18). These have come through suffering ('tribulation', Revelation 7:14) yet are caught up with praise – beacons of hope in a world of pain. This, then, is our vocation: to suffer in and with the world, yet to point to the hope of the world to come.

IAN PAUL, THEOLOGIAN AND WRITER AT **psephizo.com**

And finally

People from the Negev will occupy the mountains of Esau, and people from the foothills will possess the land of the Philistines. They will occupy the fields of Ephraim and Samaria, and Benjamin will possess Gilead. This company of Israelite exiles who are in Canaan will possess the land as far as Zarephath; the exiles from Jerusalem who are in Sepharad will possess the towns of the Negev. Deliverers will go up on Mount Zion to govern the mountains of Esau. And the kingdom will be the Lord's.

OBADIAH 19–21 (NIV)

I'm not sure why, but when I was little, my mum would often say at the end of a film or TV programme, 'and they all lived happily ever after, except the squirrel'. I never did find out the significance of the squirrel, but the passing of the years has taught me that endings are not always 'happily ever after'.

In the first 18 verses of this feisty little book, Obadiah has pronounced blistering judgement on Edom for its treatment of God's people. They have stood idly by while enemies attacked, ridden in on their coat-tails to plunder Jerusalem, and now they must pay. Afterwards, though, in the last three verses of the book, it is a different story. It is like the swash of a wave back down across the shingle after it has deposited its full force on the beach.

What was wrong will be put right. What was lost will be restored. Those who were scattered to the wilderness will be gathered, and Mount Zion will be at the epicentre of God's kingdom plans again. To be exiled from the land of promise was a bitter pill, and to return to it once again would be a sweet blessing. The God who had seen the indignities suffered by his people would see them right in the end.

The Christian belief in God's prevailing goodness is much more robust than the wish to 'live happily ever after'. Rather, it is a belief, both tested and proved, that his way is always better and that his way will prevail. Sometimes the bitterest pill of suffering can be washed down by the sweet belief in his prevailing goodness. We may not see it today, or even tomorrow – but it will come, as surely as night follows day.

RICHARD LITTLEDALE, BAPTIST MINISTER, AUTHOR AND BROADCASTER

The shadow of the light

The Lord *is* my shepherd; I shall not want. He makes me to lie down in green pastures; He leads me beside the still waters. He restores my soul; He leads me in the paths of righteousness For His name's sake. Yea, though I walk through the valley of the shadow of death, I will fear no evil; For You *are* with me; Your rod and Your staff, they comfort me.

PSALM 23:1–4 (NKJV)

The word 'shadow', in verse 4 of this much-loved psalm, conjures up many memories.

We recall the shadow of a birch tree under which we sometimes sit to rest, relax and take in the view after a strenuous climb.

We think also of the shadow of a colossal steam engine at the end of a railway line in a station. The locomotive had left the carriages behind at the platform and was taking on water in preparation for the next stage of its journey.

We will never forget the cries of joy as we played with our children, and then our grandchildren, chasing their shadows. Once standing on their shadow, it was then their turn to run frantically to catch ours! Our family name for this game is 'shadow catch'.

When we read the phrase, 'though I walk through the valley of the shadow of death', we sometimes replace the word 'death' with 'difficulty'. The text then reads, 'though I walk through the valley of the shadow of difficulty'.

The valley in the psalmist's day was deep, and the sides extremely steep. It was a dangerous and dark place to walk through; a place where robbers were known to hide in waiting. Yet as we walk through this foreboding valley, there is also a shadow. What causes a shadow? Light.

So in our walk through any difficulty, the shadow reminds us of the constant light of the world, Jesus Christ, the Son of God. It is Jesus who creates the light that forms the shadow. Even though we may not always sense his presence, he remains as close to us as a shadow.

It is during our difficult times that we recall Jesus' promise in Matthew 28:20 (NLT): 'And be sure of this: I am with you always, even to the end of the age.'

TIM AND JEAN HOWLETT, AYLESBURY

Week 2
Wait for the Lord

Withdraw for a while

All the springs of the great deep burst through, and the sluices of heaven opened… One pair of all that was alive and had the breath of life boarded the ark with Noah, and those that went aboard were a male and female of all that was alive, as God had commanded him. Then Yahweh shut him in.

GENESIS 7:11b, 15–16 (NJB)

How often we can feel overwhelmed, flooded, by our difficulties! We can't see a way ahead or a way out. The problem might be intractable; the situation might have no solution. So what can we do when it's all too much? Well, we can build our ark: a place of shelter that can keep us afloat until the waters subside, as God assures us they surely will. We need to sit and wait it out until something new appears.

What I find so moving about this story is that God first advises us to build our ark, to fill it with everything that we need, all that is generative of life. And then, when all is ready, God closes the door on the ark. And it is this that moves me so much; that God himself shuts us in, safe, until it is time to go back out into the world.

All of us need our inner ark, and we do well to build it before the flood comes. Our inner world, to a large extent, creates our outer world: how I respond to life's challenges depends on how I interpret them. First of all, do I accept that I am related to something infinite? That I have been loved into existence? If I do, then I am already connected to a much bigger picture. My problems and my life are never meaningless. There is a purpose in whatever I am experiencing. 'God alone knows!' we might exclaim in exasperation, as our rational mind exhausts itself trying to work it out. Life is bigger and more mysterious than we can capture with our rational mind.

What the story of Noah shows us is that we cannot solve everything in a linear, rational way. Life is too complex and so much of it is a mystery. But we can trust in a benevolent divine. When times are harsh, we can withdraw for a while, sit it out, not fretting over solving something that is currently beyond us, and wait in hope until some solid ground appears again.

ANNE DONALD, ORGANISATION CONSULTANT, COACH AND VICE-PRESIDENT, BRF

Must we wait?

Out of the depths I cry to you, Lord; Lord, hear my voice. Let your ears be attentive to my cry for mercy. If you, Lord, kept a record of sins, Lord, who could stand? But with you there is forgiveness, so that we can, with reverence, serve you. I wait for the Lord, my whole being waits, and in his word I put my hope. I wait for the Lord more than watchmen wait for the morning, more than watchmen wait for the morning. Israel, put your hope in the Lord, for with the Lord is unfailing love and with him is full redemption. He himself will redeem Israel from all their sins.

PSALM 130 (NIV)

It seems there is a psalm for every situation. We may not be brilliant at writing worship songs, but who of us has not had moments like the psalmist here? Times of 'depths' in life are unavoidable. We all face difficult days when light seems to have vanished, the worries are overwhelming and the future is uncertain. For the psalmist, these desperate feelings are linked to an aware-ness of sin; he knows that without forgiveness, he could not even come near to God. But he does not hold back – he knows that God is all love and will hear his cry. He knows that God redeems and restores.

So he puts that knowledge into action. He does not try to fix it all himself or ignore God. With his 'whole being', he throws himself and his situation on God's mercy. He consciously and deliberately places his hope in God and his word. He chooses to look and wait for his Lord.

I don't know about you, but I find that this turning to God in wholehearted trust does not always come easy. I can easily drown in the troubles, find my eyes full of tears and struggle to look up for the dawn. Waiting is often hard. In the middle of tough times with no guaranteed outcomes, we just want the pain to stop and the reassurance to arrive.

And yet, our God is so kind and gracious. If we can follow the psalmist's example and watch for the sunrise; if we can bring our 'whole being', or as much we can manage; if we can grab our hope by the scruff of the neck and choose to place it in God; then we discover that he was waiting for us all along. We never wait alone.

DI ARCHER, CEO, TASTELIFEUK, AUTHOR AND SPEAKER

He's in the waiting

When his master heard the story his wife told him, saying, 'This is how your slave treated me,' he burned with anger. Joseph's master took him and put him in prison, the place where the king's prisoners were confined. But while Joseph was there in the prison, the Lord was with him; he showed him kindness and granted him favour in the eyes of the prison warden.

GENESIS 39:19–21 (NIV)

In the spring of 2008, my wife had a miscarriage. We had hoped to start a family and had just moved back from India, where we had been working, when we found out she was pregnant. We had been full of expectation, but one night when I was working in another part of the country, I received the call that my wife had lost the baby.

For the next ten years, doctors termed it 'unexplained infertility', and we tried all the possible options offered to us, but nothing seemed to bring a breakthrough. We waited. We cried. We prayed. We questioned. Then we waited some more. Ten years after the miscarriage and having been told we had a 1.4% chance, we welcomed our little daughter into the world.

Often when we hear testimonies in church or even when we read the stories of the heroes of the faith, our focus is on the miracle, the resolution, the answered prayer. But when Joseph was in the prison, he didn't foresee what was to come. He didn't know the resolution was in sight. He wouldn't have predicted he would soon become prime minister – in this moment, he was a prisoner. Lost. Forgotten. Outcast. And yet, it is in this moment that the verses we read say, 'the Lord was with him' and that he 'showed him kindness' and 'granted him favour'.

Too often we attribute the presence of God, the kindness of God and the favour of God to those whose story has seemingly resolved, those who have experienced their miracle. And not everyone experiences their miracle.

In my experience, and in these verses, the miracle is perhaps not so much in the answer but in the presence of the Almighty while we wait.

GARETH RUSSELL, MANAGING DIRECTOR, JERSEY ROAD PR

A new purpose

Follow God's example, therefore, as dearly loved children and live a life of love, just as Christ loved us and gave himself up for us as a fragrant offering and sacrifice to God... For you were once darkness, but now you are light in the Lord. Live as children of light (for the fruit of the light consists in all goodness, righteousness and truth) and find out what pleases the Lord.

EPHESIANS 5:1–2, 8–10 (NIV)

I once spoke at a secular conference for childless couples. Heartbroken over their infertility, many attendees despaired at their future. Having walked the childless path too, I tried to encourage them. 'You can have a meaningful identity without becoming parents,' I said. 'I believe you are fearfully and wonderfully made, and there's new purpose for you to find.'

A woman later approached me in tears. 'Thank you,' she said. 'I've felt worthless being childless and needed to hear that I'm fearfully and wonderfully made.' I asked the woman if she had a faith of any kind. 'I walked away from God years ago,' she said. 'But I need a relationship with him again.'

Times like this remind me how profound the gospel is. Some identities, like 'mother' and 'father', are hard for some to attain in this broken world. Others, like those based on a career, can be lost through unemployment. But through Jesus we can become God's 'dearly loved children' – an identity that can never be lost. And then we can 'live a life of love' – a purpose that transcends any parental or employment status.

Psalm 139 tells us that all human beings are fearfully and wonderfully made (Psalm 139:14), and in John's gospel those who follow Jesus become children of God: 'Yet to all who did receive him, to those who believed in his name, he gave the right to become children of God – children born not of natural descent, nor of human decision or a husband's will, but born of God' (John 1:12–13).

Once in despair, that woman left in hope – about to find an identity and a new purpose bigger than this world can give.

SHERIDAN VOYSEY, INTERNATIONAL SPEAKER, BROADCASTER, REGULAR PRESENTER OF BBC RADIO 2'S *PAUSE FOR THOUGHT* AND AUTHOR, **sheridanvoysey.com**

A place of prayer

We set sail from Troas and took a straight course to Samothrace, the following day to Neapolis, and from there to Philippi, which is a leading city of the district of Macedonia and a Roman colony. We remained in this city for some days. On the sabbath day we went outside the gate by the river, where we supposed there was a place of prayer; and we sat down and spoke to the women who had gathered there. A certain woman named Lydia, a worshipper of God, was listening to us; she was from the city of Thyatira and a dealer in purple cloth. The Lord opened her heart to listen eagerly to what was said by Paul.

ACTS 16:11–14 (NRSV)

When Paul arrives in Philippi, he discovers a group of women who meet beside a river in what was known as a 'place of prayer'. He shares with them about Jesus and subsequently at least one of them, Lydia, becomes a believer. From that small beginning a church is established in that city.

I love that phrase 'a place of prayer'. In the Celtic world places of prayer were often regarded as 'thin places', places where the vast distance between earth and heaven seemed to reduce; places where it seemed easier to encounter the presence of the divine. The site of the first Christian church in Ireland at Saul in County Down is regarded as such a place.

This has led me to ask: where in our lives do we find 'thin places'? Where do we find it easier to be aware of the presence of God? For some it may be in church, but it could also be a comfortable corner of your home. For others, like the women in Philippi, it may be in the outdoors, surrounded by the beauty of nature.

So today choose, if you can, to visit your place of prayer. Be still, try to set aside the distractions and concerns which will surely come. Perhaps light a candle, play a piece of music or read a verse from the Psalms, whatever helps you to be open to the Lord. Then invite him to draw near to you and, like Lydia, listen to the prompting of the Spirit speaking to your heart.

HENRY HULL, DEAN OF DOWN, CHURCH OF IRELAND, AND FORMER BRF STAFF MEMBER

Waiting, preparation and hope

'The voice of one crying in the wilderness: "Prepare the way of the Lord; Make His paths straight."' John came baptising in the wilderness and preaching a baptism of repentance... Then all the land of Judea... went out to him... And immediately, coming up from the water, [Jesus] saw the heavens parting and the Spirit descending upon Him like a dove. Then a voice came from heaven, 'You are My beloved Son, in whom I am well pleased.' Immediately the Spirit drove Him into the wilderness. And He was there in the wilderness forty days, tempted by Satan.

MARK 1:3–13 (NKJV, abridged)

The beginning of Mark's gospel presents a picture of immense hope at a time when the nation of Israel was facing many uncertainties under Roman occupation. The people had been waiting a long time for the coming of the Messiah, so when the voice of John cried out in the wilderness to prepare the way of the Lord, we can imagine their feelings of expectancy as they sensed that their waiting was finally coming to a conclusion. It's no wonder many went out into the wilderness to meet this man! But, with hopes raised, the hearts of people needed to be prepared and made straight for Christ's coming; John's baptism of repentance would have been fundamental in that preparation.

Jesus, too, needed time to prepare. Thus, after his baptism, and the endorsement of the Father as the Spirit descended upon him, Jesus was immediately 'driven' by the Spirit into the solitary place of the wilderness. It was there, while facing Satan's temptations, that Jesus prepared for what lay ahead. The fruit of that preparation, as he went about in the power of the Spirit to announce the good news of God's kingdom, is still very evident – bringing hope to many.

We too need times of waiting and preparation in order to bring Christ's message to a needy world. For me, that meant taking time out to learn Portuguese in order to serve as a missionary in Mozambique. It was not easy at first; I wanted to 'get going', until one day the language itself taught me a valuable lesson. The Portuguese verb 'to hope', *esperar*, also means 'to wait'.

It was then that I understood the valuable lesson from John – that waiting is intertwined with preparation, and both are intertwined with hope in Christ Jesus.

CHRISTOPHER HEMBOROUGH, MISSIONARY

God will hold me fast

But you, dear friends, by building yourselves up in your most holy faith and praying in the Holy Spirit, keep yourselves in God's love as you wait for the mercy of our Lord Jesus Christ to bring you to eternal life… To him who is able to keep you from stumbling and to present you before his glorious presence without fault and with great joy – to the only God our Saviour be glory, majesty, power and authority, through Jesus Christ our Lord, before all ages, now and forevermore! Amen.

JUDE 20–21, 24–25 (NIV)

Uncertainty has been the watchword of these last few years. Living through them has felt like being in a sci-fi movie, except that nothing was resolved in a few months. In my own life, the advent of Covid-19 coincided with retirement, and the new paths I thought would open up rapidly closed down. Restrictions were hard for everyone, but the suffering of those most deeply affected must not be forgotten as the world begins to recover.

In difficult days Jude here offers us a way to find strength and hope by trusting not in human resources but in God's strength and grace. Jude was writing to a Christian community holding on in the midst of a godless and turbulent society. It doesn't sound so different from our western world today.

So what advice can we draw from Jude for our living today? Jude bids his readers first of all to build 'yourselves up in your most holy faith' and pray 'in the Holy Spirit'. That might seem at first to depend on our own effort, but praying in the Holy Spirit changes the picture. By staying close to God first, we can draw strength from God's love and mercy at work in our lives. But when we are open also to the Holy Spirit, he can work from within to make us more like Jesus day by day.

In the end we don't do it on our own, for it is God who is able to keep us from falling. It is God who will bring us through. May we know that whatever comes, God alone can indeed hold and keep us, through 'this troublous life' and into eternity. And may he give us grace to seek him more and more each day as we 'wait for the mercy of our Lord Jesus Christ' to bring us to eternal life.

MERCIA FLANAGAN, RETIRED ANGLICAN PRIEST

Week 3
Preparation practices

Being present in the present

Everything on earth has its own time and its own season. There is a time for birth and death, planting and reaping, for killing and healing, destroying and building, for crying and laughing, weeping and dancing, for throwing stones and gathering stones, embracing and parting. There is a time for finding and losing, keeping and giving, for tearing and sewing, listening and speaking. There is also a time for love and hate, for war and peace.

ECCLESIASTES 3:1–8 (CEV)

If you read this passage very slowly, taking a long time, what do you notice? What word or phrase jumps out today? I wonder what you would add to or take from the 'time for everything' list.

Isn't time a funny thing? It seems to speed up when we want it to go slow and it drags on endlessly when we wish it would be faster. Events of the past can seem both moments ago and yet very distant simultaneously, while our emotions can be as raw and visceral as at the occurrence itself, yet tempered or changed by time passing.

Busyness and the perception of 'not having time' pervades our culture and lives. I recall unhappily the (numerous) times I frustratingly shouted at my small children to 'hurry up', often in tasks that they were incapable of hurrying in, such as putting shoes and coats on!

During that season of my life, a wise Christian friend suggested that I try to be more 'present in the present'. I must say it has been a transformative practice in my life of faith which has increased my awareness of God's presence and activity in myself, those around me and in the world. It has also enabled me to notice some of my blind spots, like realising the gap in expectation between a three-year-old and an adult perception of 'hurry'. I found that simply removing the phrase 'hurry up' helped my sanity and, strangely, our more timely arrival in a better frame of heart and mind.

Wondering how to start? How about rereading the Bible passage again, slowly, and see what you notice now?

Glory to the Father and to the Son and to the Holy Spirit; as it was in the beginning, is now and shall be forever. Amen

YVONNE MORRIS, DISCIPLESHIP ENABLER (CHILDREN, YOUTH AND FAMILIES), DIOCESE OF OXFORD

Praying in secret

'When you pray, you must not be like the hypocrites, because they love to stand and pray in the synagogues and at the street corners, so that people will see them... But when you pray, go into your room, shut the door and pray to your Father in secret... And when you pray, say, "Our Father in heaven, hallowed be your name, your kingdom come, your will be done, on earth as in heaven. Give us the bread we need today, and forgive us our debts, as we forgive our debtors. Don't bring us into trial, but rescue us from evil."'

MATTHEW 6:5–13 (my translation)

Do you notice the strange mismatch between the way in which Jesus presents the Lord's Prayer here and the way in which we usually pray it? Most of us – perhaps all of us – only ever say the Lord's Prayer within public worship, where we use it as a wonderful way of bringing ourselves back to basics. Whatever else we might be praying about, we can be confident that, when we say the Lord's Prayer together, *we are asking for the things that God most wants to give to us and to the world*: true worship, the presence of his kingdom, the doing of his will, the provision of our daily needs, the forgiveness of our sins, freedom from situations that really test us and victory over evil. It's great to ask for these things regularly, and together.

But here's the mismatch: Jesus gives us this prayer in the context of telling us how we should pray *on our own*, or 'in secret', as he puts it in verse 6. It is not presented as a model for public, shared prayer, but as something to hold before God in private.

Of course it's not *wrong* to pray it publicly. The issue Jesus is addressing is the *misuse* of the public space by the spiritual giants, who were all admired but whom Jesus roundly calls 'hypocrites': they were seeking others' admiration for their charitable giving and for their praying (vv. 2, 5). But Jesus wants us to enjoy being seen *by God*, not by others – and the best place for that is 'in secret', and the best words for that are simply the ones he taught us. They will both reveal and shape our hearts. So will you use the Lord's Prayer 'in secret'?

STEVE MOTYER, VISITING LECTURER, LONDON SCHOOL OF THEOLOGY

Open house, open heart

The elder, To my dear friend Gaius, whom I love in the truth... It gave me great joy when some believers came and testified about your faithfulness to the truth, telling how you continue to walk in it. I have no greater joy than to hear that my children are walking in the truth. Dear friend, you are faithful in what you are doing for the brothers and sisters, even though they are strangers to you... We ought therefore to show hospitality to such people so that we may work together for the truth.

3 JOHN 1, 3–5, 8 (NIV)

You can imagine the elder picking up his one remaining sheet of papyrus, wondering how to squeeze as much on to it as he possibly could. In his punchy letter, we see a glimpse of the early church at the end of the time of the apostles. It's a tense time, full of change, clashing characters and conflicting agendas. The old hands had to sort out with the new how the church could best be effective in this moment of transition.

How wonderful to read of the deeply appreciative personal love between the elder and Gaius. We can feel the warmth of their friendship; we can see that friendship in the truth of Christ is still more important to the church than any formal structure. I like to think of this lovely man Gaius as having a physical disability of some sort, which means he can't go off on adventures to share the gospel himself, but can and does make it possible for others, through the resources at his disposal: his home, his time, his meals, his money. Gaius opens his home to other Christians on their own journeys, whether he knows them or not: he embodies Christian hospitality and proves how powerful it is as a means of passing on the story of Jesus in actions and words.

Churches today can be hospitable in the tradition of Gaius. We can provide a warm welcome to old friends and new acquaintances, those at the beginning of a journey and those far down it. We can open our hearts and homes, provide what others need for the next step on their journey closer to Christ and send them out provided for, rested and blessed to be an active part of God's kingdom.

Jesus, open my life to others.

LUCY MOORE, MESSY CHURCH FOUNDER, BRF

Delight in the sabbath

'If you keep your feet from breaking the Sabbath and from doing as you please on my holy day, if you call the Sabbath a delight and the Lord's holy day honourable, and if you honour it by not going your own way and not doing as you please or speaking idle words, then you will find your joy in the Lord, and I will cause you to ride in triumph on the heights of the land and to feast on the inheritance of your father Jacob.' For the mouth of the Lord has spoken.

ISAIAH 58:13–14 (NIV)

I am old enough to remember when Sundays meant things actually stopped or closed for the day. Very few people attended work on that day; shops were shut; factories were quiet; and even public transport had different time-tables to the rest of the week, with fewer travel options. Regular neighbourly Sunday activities included going to Sunday school, washing and polishing the car, mowing the lawn, playing out with friends, taking the family out for a pleasant drive, visiting grandparents, enjoying a roast dinner, making a trifle for afternoon tea and watching *Sunday Night at the London Palladium* on TV.

Sundays were a delight. They were something to look forward to. There was a completely different pattern on a Sunday compared with the rest of the week. It was like the birthday of the week; fun, a day to smile. Nowadays we accept a more blended week, with shops open all hours and every day.

God loves us so much that he gives us guidance in our daily lives. He is our most dedicated and loving friend. He wants to hang out with us and listen to our stories. This is how real friendship looks. So, today, let's take time to plan the joy and delight of being with him, whenever we can schedule our own sabbath. Find time to talk to God, laugh with God, enjoy being in his presence.

God does not want us to become weary and burdened. He knows we need sabbath rest and restoration. The best path to this is to find space to love and honour him, and then he will uplift us by dedicating other days to us too. Delight in smiling together.

JANE LEADBETTER, MESSY CHURCH SUPPORT TEAM MEMBER
AND FORMER BRF STAFF MEMBER

Giving cheerfully

But this *I say*: He who sows sparingly will also reap sparingly, and he who sows bountifully will also reap bountifully. *So let* each one *give* as he purposes in his heart, not grudgingly or of necessity; for God loves a cheerful giver. And God *is* able to make all grace abound toward you, that you, always having all sufficiency in all *things*, may have an abundance for every good work. As it is written: 'He has dispersed abroad, He has given to the poor; His righteousness endures forever.' Now may He who supplies seed to the sower, and bread for food, supply and multiply the seed you have *sown* and increase the fruits of your righteousness, while *you are* enriched in everything for all liberality, which causes thanksgiving through us to God.

2 CORINTHIANS 9:6–11 (NKJV)

As a professional fundraiser, I spend a lot of time thinking about giving and receiving. What encourages people to choose to donate their money and time to BRF so that we have the funds and skills to continue growing our ministry? And how can I share stories and information about the difference those gifts make?

I never fail to be amazed by the generosity of our volunteers and supporters, and it's true that every penny really does make a difference.

My grandparents were very kind people, and I grew up often hearing the phrase, 'If you give it, you get it back.' They were correct about this; I have seen countless examples in my life and in the lives of those around me. The Bible teaches us a lot about giving, and these verses seem particularly relevant to me as I write this piece.

During this time of Lent, as I reflect upon giving, I give thanks to God for everything he gives to me, for those who give to BRF and for Jesus, who gave everything for us on the cross. Maybe today we should take a little extra time to thank God for all he gives to us and to pray for those cheerful givers who make such a difference to our own lives and those around them.

Thank you, Lord, for all you give to us.

JULIE MacNAUGHTON, HEAD OF FUNDRAISING, BRF

Give, and give life

And now, brothers and sisters, we want you to know about the grace that God has given the Macedonian churches. In the midst of a very severe trial, their overflowing joy and their extreme poverty welled up in rich generosity. For I testify that they gave as much as they were able, and even beyond their ability. Entirely on their own, they urgently pleaded with us for the privilege of sharing in this service to the Lord's people. And they exceeded our expectations: they gave themselves first of all to the Lord, and then by the will of God also to us.

2 CORINTHIANS 8:1–5 (NIV)

The two seas in Israel are quite a contrast. The Sea of Galilee is full of life; the Dead Sea contains no life at all. They are fed by the same river, the Jordan. The difference is that the Sea of Galilee receives water and gives it out. The Dead Sea receives but does not give out. To receive but not to give out is a kind of death. To live is to give.

My vocation, as a fundraiser, is to help people enter into the joy of giving and to persuade some senior charity staff that fundraising is not an extractive process or a necessary evil.

The Macedonian churches that Paul had planted in Thessalonica, Philippi and Berea had certainly discovered the joy of giving. They didn't have to be persuaded by a well-crafted fundraising brochure from Paul. They didn't need to have their arms twisted. They didn't have a clever JustGiving page telling them what the previous person had given. No, there was a rich well of generosity within them that wanted to give to the distressed Christians in Jerusalem. Their generosity surpassed Paul's expectations.

What motivated this generosity? Perhaps it was the clear understanding that God is generous – a generosity that flows through the scriptures, right from the extravagance of creation to Jesus' ultimate generosity: giving himself for them on the cross.

We are not to be coerced into giving, as Paul goes on to say in 2 Corinthians 9:7: 'for God loves a cheerful giver'. Let's allow our giving to flow out of the joy of knowing what Jesus has done for us, remembering the Sea of Galilee rather than the Dead Sea. Giving gives life, both to the giver and the receiver.

ANDREW BARTON, TRUSTEE, BRF, AND FREELANCE FUNDRAISING CONSULTANT

Aim for the top

I am now rejoicing in my sufferings for your sake, and in my flesh I am completing what is lacking in Christ's afflictions for the sake of his body, that is, the church. I became its servant according to God's commission... to make the word of God fully known, the mystery that has... now been revealed to his saints... which is Christ in you, the hope of glory. It is he whom we proclaim, warning everyone and teaching everyone in all wisdom, so that we may present everyone mature in Christ. For this I toil and struggle with all the energy that he powerfully inspires within me.

COLOSSIANS 1:24–29 (NRSV, abridged)

To climb the world's highest mountains doesn't just require strength, skill and experience, but also a willingness to endure suffering day after day in thin air at sub-zero temperatures. Paul has the same kind of determination. The world is saved through the suffering of Jesus, but living out his ways will also involve suffering and hardship. What's inspiring about Paul is the way he embraces that path not for what he will gain but for what he can do for others, by enabling them to find God's best for their lives. Few of us will have the influence Paul had, but each of us needs a sense of purpose in our life. Can you put into words what yours is?

Paul wants to see every person everywhere come to maturity in Christ. That involves two stages: coming to Jesus and becoming like Jesus. Mountaineers have a simple goal: to get to the top. To do that they have to work out a route, then climb it. To pursue maturity in Christ and to help others find it, we need the same clarity of purpose. One way to do that is to identify the different aspects of our lives – our relationship with prayer and the Bible, our work, rest, money and possessions, church, creation and the environment, other people, especially those who are different, justice and social responsibility – and then look at what Jesus said and did in each of these areas.

What one step could we take day by day which would make us more like Jesus in each part of our lives? It will take more than one day to work out what we need to do every day, but we already have the Spirit of Jesus to energise us. Why not get started today?

SIMON REED, CHURCH LEADER, SPEAKER AND AUTHOR

Week 4
Accepting forgiveness

But I don't do it!

I do not understand my own actions. For I do not do what I want, but I do the very thing I hate. Now if I do what I do not want, I agree that the law is good. But in fact it is no longer I that do it, but sin that dwells within me. For I know that nothing good dwells within me, that is, in my flesh. I can will what is right, but I cannot do it. For I do not do the good I want, but the evil I do not want is what I do. … Wretched man that I am! Who will rescue me from this body of death? Thanks be to God through Jesus Christ our Lord!

ROMANS 7:15–19, 24–25a (NRSV)

We all at different points in our lives look back and reflect on the choices we have made, the directions that could have been different and how we might go forward.

Paul knows such moments of reflection deeply. His conversion illustrates it – Christ's voice in the light asks him why he kicks 'against the goads' in Acts 26:14. Persecuting the Christians gave him power but went against the way he was being directed by God.

Being aware that I could be different gives little comfort. My desire to be a better person – more compassionate, closer to my ideals – only gets me so far. The muscly models on the posters in the gym offer little encouragement as I look at the feeble weights that I am lifting.

I do not think that most people, including the apostle Paul, are evil. Working in the NHS, I see countless good, compassionate acts, some thoughtlessness and inconsiderate behaviour and some serious failures of systems.

Our motives are often compromised; our actions have effects we cannot imagine. Who is the real me that God is calling me to be?

There is a long tradition of Christian reflection, examining oneself in the light of God's love. Walking alongside others is a key element in hospital chaplaincy, where I meet people in desperate circumstances or where they have time to reflect.

We aren't perfect. Our vision is limited, 'for now we see in a mirror, dimly' (1 Corinthians 13:12). But we can respond to the one who holds us with compassion.

HARRY SMART, SENIOR HOSPITAL CHAPLAIN, NORTH LINCOLNSHIRE

A new covenant

'This is the covenant that I will make with the people of Israel after that time,'
declares the Lord. 'I will put my law in their minds and write it on their hearts.
I will be their God, and they will be my people. No longer will they teach their
neighbour, or say to one another, "Know the Lord," because they will all know
me, from the least of them to the greatest,' declares the Lord. 'For I will forgive
their wickedness and will remember their sins no more.'

JEREMIAH 31:33–34 (NIV)

The name of Jeremiah is synonymous with gloom. And with good reason.
Jeremiah's prophecy – from a 40-year period around 600BC – is full of gloomy
warnings of impending disaster for the nation of Judah if the people continue
to oppress the poor and follow other gods. But his prophecy contains power,
beauty and humour. He was clearly not the unremitting misery which posterity
has declared him. His message conveyed hope as well as warning.

Jeremiah had no choice but to spell out graphically the consequences for
the nation of the course it was on. At the time, his warnings were unpopular
and largely ignored. In 586BC, the disaster which he foretold occurred. Nebuchadnezzar's army destroyed Jerusalem. Large numbers of citizens were
carted off to exile in Babylon.

However, there are glimmers of hope all the way through Jeremiah's
prophecy. There is a way back. Disaster is not inevitable. A different future
is possible.

In the end, the people rejected the way back they had been offered. Disaster
struck. But then Jeremiah looked far ahead. He came up with one of the
most remarkable Old Testament accounts of what – one day – Jesus would
accomplish. It dates from almost 600 years ahead of the events it foretells.
Not surprisingly, it is quoted repeatedly in the New Testament, for example
in Hebrews 10:16–17.

All of us have rejected God, just as the people Jeremiah was speaking to
did. But now, as Jeremiah foresaw, there is a new covenant that we can all
benefit from. God has put it in place through Jesus. It means that we can be set
free from the consequences of our own selfishness – which would otherwise
ensnare us permanently – and come to know God for ourselves.

STEPHEN TIMMS, LABOUR MP FOR EAST HAM

A close encounter

Soon another Feast came around and Jesus was back in Jerusalem. Near the Sheep Gate in Jerusalem there was a pool, in Hebrew called *Bethesda*, with five alcoves. Hundreds of sick people – blind, crippled, paralysed – were in these alcoves. One man had been an invalid there for thirty-eight years. When Jesus saw him stretched out by the pool and knew how long he had been there, he said, 'Do you want to get well?' The sick man said, 'Sir, when the water is stirred, I don't have anybody to put me in the pool. By the time I get there, somebody else is already in.' Jesus said, 'Get up, take your bedroll, start walking.' The man was healed on the spot.

JOHN 5:1–9a (MSG)

Our party, visiting Israel, had entered the old city of Jerusalem by the Sheep Gate and were on our way to the Pool of Bethesda. One gentleman came by my side and shared something with me that I have passed on to many over the years: Jesus would have been on his way to the temple, as it was the sabbath and a Feast Day. The temple was over to the left, but Jesus made a determined turn to the right to visit the pool, and there he had a close encounter with a man whose life was forever changed. We don't know the man's name, we don't know why he was chosen from among the many who would have been there at that time, but we do know that he bore witness to the fact that it was Jesus who had healed him.

There are many people in the Bible whose lives were changed by Jesus when they had an encounter with him. Some cried out to Jesus for him to meet their needs. We know of one man who was carried by his friends to Jesus in order that he could be healed. In this story, we read of Jesus going out of his way to meet with the man and touch his life. Jesus himself tells a story of a shepherd who left 99 of his 100 sheep in order to go looking for the one who was lost, and when he found it, he went home rejoicing.

Jesus hasn't changed. He still looks for those who need his touch, and if that is you today, then embrace a close encounter with him so that you can be a recipient of his love and care.

MARGARET DENNISON, CHURCH LEADER AND LOCAL PREACHER

God is ecstatic – about me!

The Lord, your God, is in your midst, a warrior who gives victory; he will rejoice over you with gladness, he will renew you in his love; he will exult over you with loud singing as on a day of festival. I will remove disaster from you, so that you will not bear reproach for it. I will deal with all your oppressors at that time. And I will save the lame and gather the outcast, and I will change their shame into praise and renown in all the earth. At that time I will bring you home, at the time when I gather you; for I will make you renowned and praised among all the peoples of the earth, when I restore your fortunes before your eyes, says the Lord.

ZEPHANIAH 3:17–20 (NRSV)

It is so easy to pick up a false image of God from popular culture – one that depicts him as some sort of grumpy, grudging killjoy for whom nothing is good enough. This not-very-interested, strict, schoolmaster image of a scowling face could not be further from the truth.

In a wonderful insight, Zephaniah puts paid to any idea that God is half-hearted about me or his people. He doesn't just put up with me grudgingly, grumbling about me as never-quite-good-enough.

No, God does not hold anything back about his delight about me – he sings loudly, shouts at the top of his voice, dances a jig, whoops with pleasure over each of his uniquely created people. It is almost unseemly – and would be quite out of place in some of our strait-laced modern-day gatherings.

We are reminded that Jesus, God become man, wasn't a party-pooper either. On the contrary he was in demand, incredibly popular – and got invited to all *those* parties – you know, the ones that sinners go to – much to the annoyance of the authorities. People wanted to be with him, to listen to his stories, to know and feel his touch on their lives. Our God is intensely passionate and involved.

He is still super-passionate about all of his creation, and that includes me and it includes you too: we are his crowning glory, made in his image. Doesn't that make you want to join in God's dance of joy? Whatever regrets or shame we carry, God's promise is to turn it into praise and renown in all the earth. Why not join the dance?

DAVID DORRICOTT, MANAGING DIRECTOR, AFD GROUP, ISLE OF MAN

Yes and amen

But as surely as God is faithful, our message to you is not 'Yes' and 'No'. For the Son of God, Jesus Christ, who was preached among you by us – by me, Silas and Timothy – was not 'Yes' and 'No', but in him it has always been 'Yes'. For no matter how many promises God has made, they are 'Yes' in Christ. And so through him the 'Amen' is spoken by us to the glory of God.

2 CORINTHIANS 1:18–20 (NIV)

Waiting is a hard concept for us to understand in our current world. We can access everything instantly and order things to be delivered next day. And yet there is also this conflicting rhetoric of lasting damage and impact. Your digital footprint can stay with you for years; a foolish video posted as a teen can be the reason you don't get a job in later life.

It can be hard for us to understand God and his promises to us. In a way, we want all of God's blessings as a follower of Christ right now! We throw our toys out of the pram when we don't see prayers being answered right away or in the way we expect, and we doubt his existence if he doesn't turn up in the allotted time slot we've given him. We are all too willing to decide that our experience of God, or lack of it, is once and for all, and that there is no way back to faith in him.

This Lent, I am reminded that God's promises *will* come to fruition – they are 'Yes' in Christ. His forgiveness of our sins is coming at Easter time, and yet it is already complete now. Christ is the perfect answer and antidote to our impatient world and the 'lasting damage' we think we've incurred, because he has already forgiven us and will continue to forgive us forever more. If we choose to say 'Amen' and accept that his promise is for us, then we can face this conflicting world with confidence. We can even contemplate who in our own lives needs the promise and certainty of our forgiveness, and what lasting impact that breath of fresh air would have on their lives.

RACHEL RIDLER, YOUTH, CHILDREN'S AND FAMILIES WORKER,
HATFIELD ST LAWRENCE CHURCH

Unity through humility

As a prisoner for the Lord, then, I urge you to live a life worthy of the calling you have received. Be completely humble and gentle; be patient, bearing with one another in love. Make every effort to keep the unity of the Spirit through the bond of peace. There is one body and one Spirit, just as you were called to one hope when you were called; one Lord, one faith, one baptism; one God and Father of all, who is over all and through all and in all. But to each one of us grace has been given as Christ apportioned it.

EPHESIANS 4:1–7 (NIV)

Have you watched a game of football between eight-year-olds? Each player chases the ball, sometimes tackling their own teammates for it. The best players run through tackles but forget to pass. The poor kid in goal picks the ball out of a net three times his height. That's okay; they're only eight. If they carry on in football, they will learn the value of passing, that working hard for each other helps the team to thrive and that tackling your own players leads to arguments!

In this passage, Paul is writing to the church in Ephesus and saying, in effect, in church and life you're acting like a bunch of eight-year-olds. He then offers some coaching advice.

In multiple contexts, workplace, families and church, the most critical aspect of a healthy environment is the 'team culture' that is set. Culture eats strategy for breakfast. Behaviours are best caught not thought. What we do and say should match.

These verses then speak of the type of cultures we are called to shape: either in a church context, where Paul encourages us to 'keep the unity of the Spirit through the bond of peace' or more widely in the works of service the church is called to fulfil. In both, we are called to set a different tone: to be willing to ask for forgiveness, to helpfully name issues to resolve, to put ourselves out when we see others struggling. It doesn't come naturally to move from being one of a team to one team. It takes effort to cultivate such humility, gentleness, patience and forbearance.

Fortunately, this isn't about relying on our own efforts alone. It's about passing on the grace we receive and receiving grace from others. Such grace is not limited. If we feel so, try shouting, 'Give it to me!'

NICK SHEPHERD, PROGRAMME DIRECTOR FOR SETTING GOD'S PEOPLE FREE, CHURCH OF ENGLAND

Give it all to God

Always be full of joy in the Lord. I say it again – rejoice! Let everyone see that you are considerate in all you do. Remember, the Lord is coming soon. Don't worry about anything; instead, pray about everything. Tell God what you need, and thank him for all he has done. Then you will experience God's peace, which exceeds anything we can understand. His peace will guard your hearts and minds as you live in Christ Jesus.

PHILIPPIANS 4:4–7 (NLT)

My daughter and I are currently enjoying reading the Mr Men and Little Miss stories by Roger Hargreaves. One of our favourite stories is about Mr Worry and his day out with Little Miss Naughty. Amazingly, Mr Worry manages to stop Little Miss Naughty from doing lots of naughty things, because he explains all his worries, things she had never even thought about, until the very end of the story when she trips him up and he falls over but… all the things he was worried might happen didn't, and she laughs and runs away.

Mr Worry worries about everything. I wonder how much you worry.

It's a natural thing to do, isn't it? When I am worried, I will go and talk to my mum, and her usual answer is, 'Stop worrying and give it to God!' This passage from Philippians explains why.

When we give our worries, our thoughts and our frustrations to God, he gives us peace. When we tell God about those things that keep us awake at night, the silly day-to-day things or even the bigger world issues that are out of our control – God will still give us peace. We need to be honest with God, tell him what we need and thank him for all we have.

God gives us peace! A peace that we just can't explain, a feeling that moves us to be calm even in the middle of chaos. God then stops more worries coming in, protecting our minds and our hearts from hurting more. How wonderful is our God!

What are you worrying about today? Give it to God. Receive his peace and move from being like Mr Worry to being more like Little Miss Naughty, or, even better, Little Miss Chatterbox, as you talk to God.

YVONNE CAMPBELL, GENERAL SECRETARY, CONGREGATIONAL FEDERATION

Week 5
The way of holiness

Walking in the way of holiness

And a highway will be there; it will be called the Way of Holiness; it will be for those who walk on that Way. The unclean will not journey on it; wicked fools will not go about on it. No lion will be there, nor any ravenous beast; they will not be found there. But only the redeemed will walk there, and those the Lord has rescued will return. They will enter Zion with singing; everlasting joy will crown their heads. Gladness and joy will overtake them, and sorrow and sighing will flee away.

ISAIAH 35:8–10 (NIV)

Walking is one of the most fundamental of human activities: getting around on two legs is something which essentially sets humans apart from other animals. A baby learning to walk achieves a significant milestone. When my baby sister was brought home from hospital, I asked my mother, 'Can it walk?' On being told 'not yet', ever the pragmatist, I asked: 'Then what's it got legs for?'

We have other ways of travelling now, but in Bible times, walking was for most people the only way to get around, so the image of walking occurs frequently in scripture. Most people – including Jesus – would walk thousands of miles in their lifetime. One of the amazing things about the incarnation is to realise that Jesus literally walked many miles in our shoes: he knows the challenges we face.

Walking in Jesus' time would have been arduous and dangerous – think of the story he told of the good Samaritan. However, the picture in this passage isn't of a twisting, indistinct path, with robbers lying in wait for unwary travellers, and confusing crossroads potentially leading to the wrong destination. Rather, what is described is more akin to a modern motorway; and only the redeemed, authorised by the King of kings, can travel this highway.

Of course, we know from personal experience that our journey isn't always smooth, and that the road we walk in this life is often difficult and challenging, both physically and spiritually. However, we also travel knowing that we are promised a safe and joyful arrival at our ultimate destination.

> When we walk with the Lord, and abide in his word, what a glory he sheds on our way. While we do His good will, He abides with us still, and with all who will trust and obey.
> John Henry Sammis (1846–1919)

MURDO MACDONALD, MOLECULAR BIOLOGIST

How will you run?

Therefore, since we are surrounded by such a great cloud of witnesses, let us throw off everything that hinders and the sin that so easily entangles. And let us run with perseverance the race marked out for us, fixing our eyes on Jesus, the pioneer and perfecter of faith.

HEBREWS 12:1–2a (NIV)

I love sport. Over the course of my life I have participated in or watched so much, and conversations with family or friends often find us discussing the latest football results, who will win this year's Wimbledon or the next F1 race. However, there is one sport I have never enjoyed: long-distance running. I remember, as a kid, hating the days I knew my PE lesson would involve a cross-country race.

Our passage today makes it clear that we are all called to be runners, and it's not a sprint: it's a long-distance race. The writer to the Hebrews wants his or her readers to have prepared themselves for the race, and the instructions leave us in no doubt: anything which might hold us back must be discarded. By way of a first response, let's ask God whether there are hindrances or sins which would slow us down in our running today.

Having prepared ourselves for the race, the writer wants to make sure that we run well, so that we won't grow weary or lose heart. The audience this letter was first written to was in danger of doing just this. They were going through hard times, facing persecution for their faith; some had been in prison, while others had lost property and social status. The writer's directive is simple: 'fix your eyes on Jesus'. Isn't it easy, in the busy and complex lives we lead, to lose sight of the one we are called to follow? So as a second response, let's take a moment to refocus on our Saviour and Lord, King Jesus: the one who has gone before us; the one who modelled how life was meant to be lived and the one who died for us and is now seated beside our Father in heaven.

So today, this week, how will you run? With these words ringing in our ears, will we run 'with perseverance the race marked out for us'? I might hate cross-country running, but I want to run well the race God has prepared for me. I want my life to count for him and for his kingdom.

STEVE CLIFFORD, CHRISTIAN LEADER, AUTHOR AND SPEAKER

Life is not fair

'When those hired about five o'clock came, each of them received the usual daily wage. Now when the first came, they thought they would receive more; but each of them also received the usual daily wage. And when they received it, they grumbled against the landowner, saying, "These last worked only one hour, and you have made them equal to us who have borne the burden of the day and the scorching heat."'

MATTHEW 20:9–12 (NRSV)

In this unfair world, it can be tempting to think only of ourselves. Look after number one. Every man for himself. In this story of Jesus, some workers have toiled for the whole day, while others are late to the party, yet everyone gets paid the same. How is that fair? Yet it is clear from Jesus' telling of the story, and the rest of Matthew 20, that this is how God, the very creator of life, works. The last shall be first, and the first shall be last.

In Jesus' time, if you were standing idle in the marketplace at five o' clock, it would not be because you were lazy, but rather because no one had decided to hire you, which would mean, in all probability, that your family would not eat that day. The employer in the story is clear: everyone, regardless of the amount of work they've done, will eat.

Jesus is equally clear in this conviction. When his disciples argue over who will sit at the right hand of God, Jesus tells them that whoever wishes to be great must first become a servant (vv. 20–28). When his followers try to silence two blind men who want his help, Jesus stops to grant their request for sight to be restored (vv. 29–34).

In coming to earth as a person, to live with us, teach us and, ultimately, to sacrifice himself for us, Jesus demonstrates the importance of service, not by merely showing it to us, but by truly being with us, putting the needs of the vulnerable before anyone else.

Thinking of ourselves, being jealous of others or passing judgement is not the answer. Only in serving everyone, especially the vulnerable, can we work for God's vision of peace, justice and hope to become a reality for all.

SIMON PETERS, WALKING THE WAY PROJECT MANAGER, UNITED REFORMED CHURCH

Godly messiness

Without oxen a stable stays clean, but you need a strong ox for a large harvest... The Lord now chose seventy-two other disciples and sent them ahead in pairs to all the towns and places he planned to visit. These were his instructions to them: 'The harvest is great, but the workers are few. So pray to the Lord who is in charge of the harvest; ask him to send more workers into his fields.'

PROVERBS 14:4; LUKE 10:1–2 (NLT)

Sometimes you feel immediately that a verse applies to you and speaks to you; sometimes the opposite is true. I don't mind admitting that I have never considered keeping oxen, so I consulted my trusty *NLT Life Application Study Bible* to see a bigger picture. To paraphrase:

> What's the point of a stable without animals? You can have a clean and tidy life free of people-problems if you shut out people – but then your life will have lost its purpose and be empty of meaning.

Aha! That made sense, and straightaway someone came to mind who would benefit from learning the lesson of this verse; someone who complains of being lonely but who is houseproud and has fixed routines – and when it comes down to it, doesn't actually want anything to interfere with a tidy life.

So I thought: I wonder if I should share this verse with that person? Then bam! It hit me – does God ever do that to you? I was so busy judging someone else and seeing how they could improve that I hadn't noticed how much this also applied to me.

No, tidiness isn't my thing (as anyone who has visited will testify). Instead I prioritise time in our garden where I thoroughly enjoy just pottering about by myself. God doesn't mind me enjoying our garden – he created it, after all – but he does want me to prioritise relationships and play my part in Christ's whole body. He also wants me to look for opportunities to share his good news with those who don't know him. I won't find that alone in my garden and without dealing with the messiness of human relationships. Do I want a big harvest? Yes, I do (Luke 10:2)! Do you? Perhaps we need to go out and risk getting some oxen.

ALISON DORRICOTT, COMPANY DIRECTOR, AFD GROUP, ISLE OF MAN

James on Twitter?

And the tongue is a fire. The tongue is placed among our members as a world of iniquity; it stains the whole body, sets on fire the cycle of nature, and is itself set on fire by hell... But no one can tame the tongue – a restless evil, full of deadly poison. With it we bless the Lord and Father, and with it we curse those who are made in the likeness of God. From the same mouth come blessing and cursing.

JAMES 3:6, 8–10a (NRSV)

James's caution on the use of careless speech is so relevant, even after 2,000 years. But what would he make of 21st-century social media? If the tongue alone can wound, what about the keyboard or the phone? Today's technology provides us with a megaphone. Cruel tweets can take on a life of their own – and are even harder than spoken words to retract. You can take a post down or apologise for it, but you can't control how many of your followers will already have picked it up and passed it on.

And yet from the same medium come both blessing and cursing. Social media, along with Zoom and WhatsApp, were a lifeline for many during lockdown, keeping them connected with each other and with worshipping communities. Prayers and comfort were spread, along with valuable information. So what might James say? How might he caution us?

He probably wouldn't tell us to avoid social media altogether. But he would urge us to be careful, prayerful and kind, to think before we press the send button. Perhaps, too, he would remind us of the words of the psalmist: 'Search me, O God, and know my heart; test me and know my thoughts' (Psalm 139:23). It is easy to hide our motives from ourselves, especially in justifying our speech – electronic or otherwise. It is easy to be hurtful or dishonest on social media without fear of retribution. But we are all accountable for our words and actions before God.

Not only must we think before we tweet, but we must also be prepared to accept the consequences of our words, in whatever form we utter them. While we should have the courage to speak out against evil, we should also be prepared to repent if we unexpectedly or unnecessarily cause hurt.

RICHENDA MILTON-DAWS, EDITOR, *TRANSFORMING MINISTRY*,
AND LICENSED LAY MINISTER, DIOCESE OF BRISTOL

The healing touch of holiness

There was a woman who had been suffering from haemorrhages for twelve years… She came up behind [Jesus] and touched the fringe of his clothes, and immediately her haemorrhage stopped. Then Jesus asked, 'Who touched me?' When all denied it, Peter said, 'Master, the crowds surround you and press in on you.' But Jesus said, 'Someone touched me; for I noticed that power had gone out from me.' When the woman saw that she could not remain hidden, she came trembling… she declared in the presence of all the people why she had touched him, and how she had been immediately healed. He said to her, 'Daughter, your faith has made you well; go in peace.'

LUKE 8:43–48 (NRSV, abridged)

Before and after Jesus walked this earth, holiness has often been understood to be a pure state of being that can only be maintained by remaining separate from things deemed to be unclean. Jesus smashed through this understanding. His incarnate holiness was not separate or aloof, paranoid about its own purity, but got involved, passionate about the well-being of others.

Jesus made a habit of welcoming and touching people who were easily labelled as unclean and who were shunned as a consequence. In this instance, he tore through the taboo of uncleanliness on the part of women bleeding, which has afflicted and ostracised far too many before and since. With no anxiety about his own state of (holy) being, Jesus welcomed the touch of the woman and added dignity and peace to the healing that he had gifted to her. Jesus' holiness made her whole again, restoring not just her physical health but also her place of equal value within the community.

In recent times we have rediscovered the importance of safe and appropriate touch in making us whole as human beings. One of the many curses of coronavirus was the way it denied us the opportunity to hug, to hold or to touch in ways that bestowed dignity, healing and peace. Some of us will have specific callings to healing ministries in the medical professions or prayer. Safe and appropriate touch is an important part of such ministries and one way in which a sense of holiness as well as healing can be conveyed.

A healing touch of holiness can be as simple as an unrushed handshake complemented by a warm smile and bright eyes that say, 'I care.' When it is safe to offer such touches, may we do so, especially to those who today feel shunned or ostracised.

ANDREW ROBERTS, HOLY HABITS PIONEER

Battling to the end

The Israelites said to Gideon, 'Rule over us... because you have saved us from the hand of Midian.' But Gideon told them, 'I will not rule over you, nor will my son rule over you. The Lord will rule over you.' And he said, 'I do have one request, that each of you give me an earring from your share of the plunder'... They answered, 'We'll be glad to give them... Gideon made the gold into an ephod, which he placed in Ophrah, his town. All Israel prostituted themselves by worshipping it there, and it became a snare to Gideon and his family.

JUDGES 8:22–27 (NIV, abridged)

Gideon, who started life as a timid mouse, became a mighty warrior. Having fought successfully against the Midianites, he wasn't allowed to enjoy his victory for long. Judges 8 tells us he had to continue to battle against criticism (vv. 1–3), exhaustion (v. 4), non-cooperation (vv. 5–9) and further hostility from the defeated kings and people of Sukkoth (vv. 10–21). What leader has not faced these enemies? But his greatest battle was still to come. It was the battle he faced with himself.

Heady with their success, Israel wanted to make Gideon and his heirs their king. He rebuffed them with the correct theological reply: 'The Lord [alone] will rule over you.' But everything he then did suggested that he didn't really believe this. He asked them to donate gold from their plentiful spoils so that he could make an ephod – an extravagant apron – out of it. It was more than a fashion statement. Ephods like this were worn by priests. It was a short step from the making of the garment to the worshipping of the garment, to it becoming an idol. Consequently, Israel, and Gideon himself, compromised their wholehearted devotion to God and fell into the trap of idolising a human-crafted object. They foolishly worshipped in a way that would lead them to national ruin again.

Gideon should have known better. Perhaps he thought he was beyond the simple obedience he had shown to God in earlier days. Perhaps pride, or self-pity, got the better of him. Whatever the reason, he teaches us that we never retire from the spiritual battlefield. The enemy may change, but opposition continues to the end. We can never afford to relax or give up in our fight against temptation. Don't fall at the last hurdle. Keep following God faithfully to the end.

DEREK TIDBALL, RETIRED PASTOR AND BIBLE COLLEGE LECTURER

Holy Week

Palm Sunday: A humble king

The next day the great crowd that had come to the festival heard that Jesus was coming to Jerusalem. So they took branches of palm trees and went out to meet him, shouting, 'Hosanna! Blessed is the one who comes in the name of the Lord – the King of Israel!' Jesus found a young donkey and sat on it; as it is written: 'Do not be afraid, daughter of Zion. Look, your king is coming, sitting on a donkey's colt!'

JOHN 12:12–15 (NRSV)

Can you remember a significant turning point in your life? A time when you have changed direction, or faced a time of suffering, joy or transformation? Perhaps there have been several. Today's passage tells us of a vital turning point in the life of Christ and in John's gospel. The raising of Lazarus (John 11) has seen the culmination of a ministry characterised by compassion, teaching and miracles. The pleading Mary and Martha saw Jesus weep with pity at their loss, as he gave Lazarus his breath once more.

But the miracle has provoked the wrath of the authorities, who begin to plot Jesus' death, a death anticipated by Mary in the costly anointing of Jesus' feet (John 12:1–8), and a fate towards which Jesus now rides as he enters Jerusalem. The scene is rich with symbolism: shouts of 'Hosanna!' herald a saviour monarch, and the palm branches welcome a national leader, for people who seek freedom from their Roman captors, and Jesus' riding on a donkey fulfils the prophecy of Zechariah 9:9. But the scene is also heavy with dramatic irony, for Jesus is not that kind of king; as we shall hear later in John's gospel, Christ's kingdom is 'not from this world' (John 18:36). This is the servant King, who rides towards his arrest, torture and death; a man of sorrows who becomes 'despised and rejected by others' (Isaiah 53:3). With humility Christ rides towards the agony and the tomb, out of which he will rise again, bringing freedom not just to a nation and a people in first-century Palestine, but to all humanity for all time. Freedom indeed.

Pray for courage as you face the troubles in your life today. Welcome the servant King, that he may set you free.

JONATHAN ARNOLD, DIRECTOR OF COMMUNITIES AND PARTNERSHIPS, DIOCESE OF CANTERBURY

Monday: Devotion declared

Six days before the Passover, Jesus came to Bethany, where Lazarus lived, whom Jesus had raised from the dead. Here a dinner was given in Jesus' honour. Martha served, while Lazarus was among those reclining at the table with him. Then Mary took about half a litre of pure nard, an expensive perfume; she poured it on Jesus' feet and wiped his feet with her hair. And the house was filled with the fragrance of the perfume.

JOHN 12:1-3 (NIV)

All of the gospels record a woman anointing Jesus, and three of them set the anointing during Passion Week. Matthew (26:6–13), Mark (14:3–9) and John (12:1–8) are closer to one another than Luke's version, set earlier in Jesus' ministry (Luke 7:36–50).

Jesus goes for a meal, perhaps in Bethany, perhaps at the home of Simon the Leper, which may well be the home of Mary, Martha and Lazarus. Mark and Matthew have the woman anoint Jesus' head, and John and Luke his feet. In all three a jar of ointment is poured over Jesus and in John and Luke the woman dries Jesus' feet with her hair.

A sensual moment of adoration of Jesus – but a moment which Jesus ties into his own death. The anointing of his body precedes his death and becomes a sign of the future tragedy. By expressing her devotion at this meal in the days running up to the crucifixion, the woman is able to show her devotion to the living Jesus rather than just to his corpse.

There is something in this which mirrors Thomas' questioning of the disciples in John 20 – I can't believe you unless I see him, unless I touch him, unless I put my hand in his side. A macabre intimacy with Jesus' wounds; an intimacy which Thomas shuns when he actually comes face to face with Jesus. Instead, Thomas declares his devotion through his words.

The woman's devotion to Jesus is sensual. It involves massaging oil into his feet, drying them with her hair. In Mark's version, Jesus declares that where the gospel is preached what she has done shall be retold – *in memory of her*. That phrase echoes through time itself. We remember the woman because of her sacrificial act of devotion, because she stepped out and did something the men around her didn't understand. We remember her because she showed her love.

How will we show our love to Jesus today?

PETER PHILLIPS, DIRECTOR, CENTRE FOR DIGITAL THEOLOGY, DURHAM UNIVERSITY

Tuesday: The way, the truth and the life

Let not your heart be troubled: ye believe in God, believe also in me. In my Father's house are many mansions: if it were not so, I would have told you. I go to prepare a place for you. And if I go and prepare a place for you, I will come again, and receive you unto myself; that where I am, there ye may be also. And whither I go ye know, and the way ye know. Thomas saith unto him, Lord, we know not whither thou goest; and how can we know the way? Jesus saith unto him, I am the way, the truth, and the life: no man cometh unto the Father, but by me.

JOHN 14:1–6 (KJV)

These verses are profound, and have long been part of my life for different reasons. I have two particular reflections. First, I read law at university and the whole passage was one of the lessons at evensong the day in 1969 before my Jurisprudence examination. Because these verses were used by some in the American Realists' school of Jurisprudence as part of the syllabus, I wrongly assumed that it was a sign that it would be in the examination the following day. Needless to say, it wasn't, and was a clear sign to me that God had more important things to worry about than my Jurisprudence examination.

Second, verse 6 is quite a challenge for Christians. I am not a theologian, but I do wonder about its meaning and its implications particularly for those who have a different faith. Does it really mean that eternal life is only available to followers of Jesus Christ or, more broadly, is eternal life available to all those who observe the principles set out by Lord Jesus whatever their faith? What I am sure of is that, to those of us who know Jesus, we must follow his example. To fail to do so is sinful.

I am not alone in finding this passage of scripture both comforting and profound. The whole passage, taken together with the rest of the gospels, encapsulates my view of what being a Christian means and what I hope is the heavenly reward for those whose faith is in Jesus Christ and who faithfully follow him.

MICHAEL WRIGHT, PROFESSOR EMERITUS, CANTERBURY CHRIST CHURCH UNIVERSITY

Wednesday: Cross-shaped love

Surely he has borne our infirmities and carried our diseases; yet we accounted him stricken, struck down by God, and afflicted. But he was wounded for our transgressions, crushed for our iniquities; upon him was the punishment that made us whole, and by his bruises we are healed. All we like sheep have gone astray; we have all turned to our own way, and the Lord has laid on him the iniquity of us all.

ISAIAH 53:4–6 (NRSV)

Some scenes demand a response from us; we cannot just sit there unmoved. For me it is sunsets. When the suns dips in the horizon and the clouds light up in various hues of gold, amber and red, and parts of the blue sky turn aquamarine and violet, I find myself transfixed. The glory of God just screams out of the scene and I stand there, awestruck. This is one of those scenes.

Like the early Christians, I cannot help but read these words in the light of Good Friday. Of all the New Testament authors who quote Isaiah 52:13—53:12, I am most drawn to 1 Peter: 'He himself bore our sins in his body on the cross, so that, free from sins, we might live for righteousness; by his wounds you have been healed' (1 Peter 2:24). Peter calls us to survey the scene and examine our lives. Christ suffered for us. He bore our sins so that we might be set free from their power over us, so that we might break from the past and live renewed lives of holiness, justice and love. Those hideous wounds inflicted on his body as the thorns pierced his skin, as the lead in the whip scourged his back, as the nails were hammered into his forearms and as he hung there dying, have brought healing into our lives.

So Peter calls us to focus on what Christ has done and on the example that he has set us. The glory of God screams out from the scene, revealing to us the shape of God's love – a cross. As we stand there awestruck, Peter calls us to show the same cross-shaped love, not least when we too suffer unjustly. 'Love so amazing, so divine, demands my soul, my life, my all' (Isaac Watts).

ANDY ANGEL, VICAR, AUTHOR AND TEACHER

Maundy Thursday: Lament in Gethsemane

My soul is bereft of peace; I have forgotten what happiness is; so I say, 'My endurance has perished; so has my hope from the Lord.' Remember my affliction and my wanderings, the wormwood and the gall! My soul continually remembers it and is bowed down within me. But this I call to mind, and therefore I have hope: The steadfast love of the Lord never ceases; his mercies never come to an end; they are new every morning; great is your faithfulness. 'The Lord is my portion,' says my soul, 'therefore I will hope in him.'

LAMENTATIONS 3:17–24 (ESV)

Lamentations has been called the wailing wall of the Bible – a poem of pain, a song of survivor's sorrow, a Gethsemane of the human soul. God is absent, silent, questioned, blamed. It is relentless, brutal, honest; bereft of peace or happiness. Through it, we reflect on the experience of those who survived the catastrophic destruction of Jerusalem – and on our own experiences of abandonment and anguish. No wonder we rush on to find God's compassion and faithfulness here – perhaps declared rather than believed or affirmed by personal experience. We are tempted to ditch the dirge and skip to the light of morning, the empty tomb, the resurrection we all know is coming in the hindsight of history.

Yet no glib answers nor a rushing too soon to encouraging verses can replace the process of lament when stumbling, shocked and displaced, through the rubble of our lives. To lament is to feel our full humanity and vulnerability as Jesus did; to weep, to feel abandoned, to see no end to suffering and no sense in it. To lament is to respond with utter honesty to our exiling experiences when we are far from ourselves and everything we thought we knew and believed to be true. Lament is not a place to dwell indefinitely, but neither must it be denied. It is necessary preparation for deep healing and homecoming.

Our voices echo that of Jesus in his own human Gethsemane. We cry out to God that things should be different. Lament exposes what we need for recovery. We move through our trauma, even while in it, and reach out for God's future and his faithfulness. We hope for new beginnings, renewal of faith and deeper discoveries. We place our hopes in the unceasing mercies of God, not always visible in our lament but always present and new.

RENITA BOYLE, STORYTELLER

Good Friday: The sky turned black

It was now about noon, and darkness came over the whole land until three in the afternoon, for the sun stopped shining. And the curtain of the temple was torn in two. Jesus called out with a loud voice, 'Father, into your hands I commit my spirit.' When he had said this, he breathed his last. The centurion, seeing what had happened, praised God and said, 'Surely this was a righteous man.'

LUKE 23:44–47 (NIV)

Teaching at a primary school for children with emotional and behavioural difficulties, the children became my heroes as I learned about their challenging lives. Teaching wasn't easy, but I and all the staff loved them, and helping them to find their way in the world was deeply rewarding.

I was given the task of leading the assemblies during Lent and excitedly took them on the Easter journey leading to Jesus' death and resurrection.

Daniel (not his real name) was a nine-year-old boy constantly being rejected by his mother, full of insecurities and anger; desperately in need of acceptance but fighting every inch of the way. One of Daniel's traits was that he rarely completed a piece of work, or if he did, he tore it up, because despite encouragement, he decided that anything he produced was never good enough.

Assemblies were not always the calmest of occasions as the children could kick off at any time. However, at my Good Friday assembly they all seemed really engaged. Miraculous!

On returning to school after the Easter holidays, Daniel presented me with a paper scroll. Unfurling it, a picture emerged: a picture he had drawn… a completed picture… a picture of Christ on the cross amid a black sky. I was thrilled.

As we talked, Daniel said that he kept thinking about people hurting Jesus when Jesus had done nothing wrong. He remembered that the sky went black and said that that was how he felt most of the time. I asked Daniel about the white in the top corner of the picture. That damaged little boy looked at me, gave a hesitant smile and said, 'But you said it didn't stay black and there was hope. I think Jesus knows how I feel, and I think he might even love me.'

JANINE GILLION, TEACHER AND AUTHOR

Holy Saturday: The in-between time

For God alone my soul waits in silence, for my hope is from him. He alone is my rock and my salvation, my fortress; I shall not be shaken. On God rests my deliverance and my honour; my mighty rock, my refuge is in God. Trust in him at all times, O people; pour out your heart before him; God is a refuge for us.

PSALM 62:5–8 (NRSV)

Holy Saturday is the in-between day of waiting. Yesterday, on Good Friday, we stood at the foot of the cross, yet tomorrow we will celebrate Christ's resurrection.

However, imagine those first disciples on the sabbath after Christ's crucifixion. Their hopes and dreams regarding the promised Messiah seemed to be crumbling within them and around them. Following Jesus' arrest, most of them had fled. Peter was living with his failure, whereas Judas had hung himself. That first 'in-between Saturday' seemed far from holy. It was a bleak day of waiting in despair and fear, not knowing what lay ahead.

Today, on Holy Saturday, Jesus Christ's followers know that Easter morning will bring songs of alleluia as we celebrate his rising from the dead, which can never be undone. Yet in the present as we live our joy, we also carry our fears and struggles, because the shalom of complete transformation, made possible by Christ's death and resurrection, is not yet fully here. One day, there will be no more tears, no more death, no more pain, and God's kingdom will be fully here on earth as in heaven, but for now we inhabit the in-between days, often reflecting a long Holy Saturday.

Psalm 62 is a Holy Saturday prayer that embodies this authentic discipleship. The writer was aware of life's batterings; and the injustice and delusions of the world seem prevalent. Yet God's love, hope and promises are unchanging.

As we pour out our hearts to God (v. 8) amid life's mess and all that resonates with crucifixion, we cling fast to the hope writ large in the empty tomb of Easter morning. In our yearnings, a still place of holy peace is possible as we wait and trust. God is our refuge and the source of our hope.

RACHEL TREWEEK, BISHOP OF GLOUCESTER

Easter

ASTER is a time when we recall God's story of salvation in the death of Jesus Christ on the cross and his resurrection. It was a major turning point in God's dealings with his people, when redemption became available to all. Jesus Christ became the bearer of our transgressions and our way back to God. The prophetic words found in Isaiah 53 are reminders of the depth of pain that Jesus suffered, so that we and others can experience new life and be reconciled with God.

In early Christian tradition, baptisms typically took place at Easter. They were preceded by intensive periods of teaching and instruction. Today, some Christians will use the period of Lent to study the Bible to recall the journey that took Jesus to the cross, and during Holy Week they will use vigils to prepare for their Easter celebrations. It is a reminder of the passion and suffering of Jesus before the glory of the resurrection.

The readings in this section affirm the key aspects of our faith and what it means to follow Jesus in everyday life. Each day we are living the promises of new life through the Spirit, with Jesus dwelling in us. It is a choice to follow Jesus, and Gavin Calver's reflection reminds us that there is a cost involved. God demonstrated his love for us on the cross when Jesus paid the ultimate price for our sins. It is God's incredible love, sacrifice and forgiveness that makes us an Easter people.

KAREN LAISTER, HEAD OF MARKETING, COMMUNICATIONS
AND STRATEGIC RELATIONSHIPS, BRF

He is risen, alleluia!

They found the stone rolled away from the tomb, but when they entered, they did not find the body of the Lord Jesus. While they were wondering about this, suddenly two men in clothes that gleamed like lightning stood beside them. In their fright the women bowed down with their faces to the ground, but the men said to them, 'Why do you look for the living among the dead? He is not here; he has risen! Remember how he told you, while he was still with you in Galilee: "The Son of Man must be delivered over to the hands of sinners, be crucified and on the third day be raised again."' Then they remembered his words.

LUKE 24:2–8 (NIV)

Around the world today, Christians will be proclaiming in church services, 'He is risen, alleluia!' During the previous few weeks, many of us will have embarked on a journey. A journey that takes us through the penitential season of Lent, the sombre days of Holy Week and the darkness of Good Friday. Our pilgrimage finally culminates in the celebration of the resurrection of Jesus Christ on Easter Sunday. We have remembered and recalled the story of salvation, sacrifice and hope; we have made a journey from darkness to light.

The women's natural instinct drew them to the place they could be close to Jesus, to express their grief and embody his suffering. When they discovered the tomb empty, a penetrating light rendered them fearful. The words of the two men, 'Why do you look for the living among the dead?', must have sounded odd to the women, as they struggled with their loss and the disappearance of Jesus' body. In their distress and disorientation, they are told to recall what Jesus had told them in Galilee – forewarning his followers about his suffering and resurrection. In other words, these events weren't unexpected.

Jesus had been destined to experience the cruelty of crucifixion. Death was not the end of the story, but instead it led to a jubilant new beginning. Like the women, we recall the story of our faith. We linger for a time in the darkness and remind ourselves of the suffering and sacrifice of Jesus Christ. Our sorrow is replaced with gratitude and joy, when we finally make it to Easter Day and proclaim, 'He is risen, alleluia!'

KAREN LAISTER, HEAD OF MARKETING, COMMUNICATIONS
AND STRATEGIC RELATIONSHIPS, BRF

The promise of new life

But you are not in the flesh; you are in the Spirit, since the Spirit of God dwells in you. Anyone who does not have the Spirit of Christ does not belong to him. But if Christ is in you, though the body is dead because of sin, the Spirit is life because of righteousness. If the Spirit of him who raised Jesus from the dead dwells in you, he who raised Christ from the dead will give life to your mortal bodies also through his Spirit that dwells in you.

ROMANS 8:9–11 (NRSV)

This verse appears within a chapter that begins with a great acclamation of liberation for those who have been freed from bondage to the law into new life in the Spirit, and it ends with one of Paul's most exuberant outpourings about how we are held within the love of God, from which nothing can ever separate us.

Throughout the chapter, Paul contrasts the old ways of thinking about God, ourselves and our struggles against sin with our true position in Christ, while recognising that, even if we trust in Christ, we will continue to suffer and wrestle with the tendency to forget our identity as children adopted into the family of God, completely known, accepted and loved.

But Paul stresses that if we have turned to Christ, our spiritual inheritance is secure. He then makes the electrifying claim that if we have God's Spirit within us, God will do for us what God has already done for Jesus – and raise us to new life.

Paul bases this conviction on the truth of the resurrection, which is so crucial for him because of his life-changing encounter with the risen Christ (see Acts 9). Since that encounter, Paul had also come to believe that we do not have to wait until death to inherit this new life; it is given to us now, by faith.

Paul staked everything on this belief. He had come to understand that if we are willing to let go of the old way of seeing ourselves, to die to ourselves, we will become increasingly filled with the new life of the risen Christ, so much so that elsewhere he could write of his own experience, 'I have been crucified with Christ; and it is no longer I who live, but it is Christ who lives in me' (Galatians 2:19–20).

CHRISTINA REES, WRITER AND COMMENTATOR

The cost of following the king

Then Jesus said to his disciples, 'Whoever wants to be my disciple must deny themselves and take up their cross and follow me. For whoever wants to save their life will lose it, but whoever loses their life for me will find it. What good will it be for someone to gain the whole world, yet forfeit their soul? Or what can anyone give in exchange for their soul?'

MATTHEW 16:24–26 (NIV)

This is not a nice, fluffy warm passage that we like to dwell on, and it's clear from the verses that precede it that Peter's ears didn't want to hear about the pathway of suffering that lay ahead for his Messiah (16:21–22). However, the call to follow Jesus, to really lay down our nets, is a call to abandon what we want for what he wants. This is such a costly passage for those of us raised in the wealthy west.

Did you know that comfort is not a biblical concept? Our understanding of comfort is not the same as 'Comfort, comfort my people, says your God' (Isaiah 40:1). The prophet is not talking about grabbing a nice drink, getting cosy on the sofa and making yourself feel better with a good movie! Biblical comfort is about knowing that God will take care of us in days to come, because he is with us. It's not that the Lord doesn't care about our needs – he most definitely does – but what we think we need might be a bit different to what he says will lead to life.

Jesus does not want us to have earthly, worldly, fleshly concerns, but to die to self and run after life that is only found in Jesus and his path to eternity. Our human life is short, but we will reign forever with our king. Perhaps a good question for us to ask is, 'Lord, is there anything you want me to leave behind, to fully follow you?' And then pray for the courage to let it go.

GAVIN CALVER, CEO, EVANGELICAL ALLIANCE

What is love?

I may be able to speak the languages of human beings and even of angels, but if I have no love, my speech is no more than a noisy gong or a clanging bell... Love is patient and kind; it is not jealous or conceited or proud; love is not ill-mannered or selfish or irritable; love does not keep a record of wrongs; love is not happy with evil, but is happy with the truth. Love never gives up; and its faith, hope and patience never fail. Love is eternal.

1 CORINTHIANS 13:1, 4–8a (GNT)

When my husband and I got married, we were given 1 Corinthians 13:1–13 as an illustrated calligraphy poster. They were words of encouragement to guide us in our new relationship together. Looking back, I wonder if we romanticised this passage. After 26 years of marriage, there have been times when my love has been patient and kind, but I have to confess there have been times when I have been selfish and irritable.

Our poster was given as friendly advice, a reminder for day-to-day living and an opportunity to say sorry when things went wrong. This passage is Paul's advice about relationships to a new church in Corinth, a trading port where people met from many countries and traditions, all bringing their influences to the culture and the people.

When Jesus was asked, 'What is the greatest commandment?' (Matthew 22:36–40), he talked about our love for God and our love for each other. As so often happens in the Bible, this was a complete sea-change. Jesus made it inescapably clear that it wasn't about doing something because the law said you should. It was about freely giving people attention, spotting that someone needs to be loved. God's love for us is beyond anything we can comprehend, as the parable of the lost son reminds us (Luke 15:11–32). God's love for humanity was in the ultimate sacrifice of his Son, Jesus, on a cross, to wipe away our sins and give everyone a new start in their relationship with him.

Our world needs us more than ever to demonstrate transformed relationships. If we follow Paul's advice, I wonder what difference it would make?

JULIE JEFFERIES, PARTNERSHIP AMBASSADOR, OPEN THE BOOK

Loving the world too much?

For I am already being poured out like a drink offering, and the time for my departure is near. I have fought the good fight, I have finished the race, I have kept the faith. Now there is in store for me the crown of righteousness, which the Lord, the righteous Judge, will award to me on that day – and not only to me, but also to all who have longed for his appearing. Do your best to come to me quickly, for Demas, because he loved this world, has deserted me and has gone to Thessalonica. Crescens has gone to Galatia, and Titus to Dalmatia. Only Luke is with me.

2 TIMOTHY 4:6–11a (NIV)

'Demas, because he loved this world, has deserted me' (v. 10). I clearly remember reading these words as a child and being confused. Demas loved the world, but aren't Christians meant to love the world? Didn't God love the world so much that he sent his Son? And yet I sensed the apostle Paul's disappointment. He's gutted that his friend has made a bad choice.

Demas had been a gospel worker with Paul while he'd been in prison in Rome. Now he's abandoned him because, as the New Living Translation puts it, 'Demas... loves the things of this life.' He'd chosen short-term pleasure. He'd chosen the present over the future. He'd chosen the material over the spiritual.

Reading this was the first time I questioned whether it is possible to love the world too much. If the world is all there is, then we miss out on being part of something far greater in Christ. There is a bigger view, and yet, even after all his work, Demas had missed it.

Sometimes, either from happy distraction or disillusionment, we can limit our vision to our situation and circumstance. But if we fix our eyes up and beyond to Christ, he can give us hope powerful enough to take us even through grief and deep enough to beat any quick thrill. As a child, I decided I didn't want to be like Demas. I saw a choice, and chose in that moment to follow Christ rather than love the world too much. We keep needing to choose!

LAURA TRENEER, EDITOR AND CONSULTANT

Living out our baptism

What shall we say, then? Shall we go on sinning, so that grace may increase? By no means! We are those who have died to sin; how can we live in it any longer? Or don't you know that all of us who were baptised into Christ Jesus were baptised into his death? We were therefore buried with him through baptism into death in order that, just as Christ was raised from the dead through the glory of the Father, we too may live a new life.

ROMANS 6:1–4 (NIV)

Baptism is something that Christians often disagree about: the age at which baptism can be done, the manner in which it should be done and what, if anything, baptism brings about in the person who is baptised.

But there is something that all Christians should be able to agree about baptism: how it should shape and direct the continuing lives of those who have been baptised. The basis of this is the way that baptism joins us to Jesus Christ in his death and resurrection. When Jesus died, the sin of the world was carried by him down to judgement. All of the most terrible things that we have ever done, as well as all of those seemingly lesser actions or non-actions that have still worked to spoil and deface God's good world, received the condemnation they deserved.

But Jesus didn't stay dead! On Easter Day, he rose again with all of that sin that he had carried – including ours – still wonderfully dead and gone.

If we have been joined to Jesus through baptism, then we are joined to him in this sinless state. This is a wonderful blessing. But it is also central to our Christian calling, because those who are baptised are called to reflect this status in the reality of our lives – to live a new life as people whose sin is dead and gone. This is tough. It's much easier to carry on sinning and simply rely on God's forgiveness. But this is to deny our baptism and the wonderful status given to us. Every time, on the other hand, that we resist sin and temptation, we are living out the new identity won for us by Jesus Christ and demonstrating our loyalty and gratitude to him.

STEPHEN KUHRT, VICAR, CHRIST CHURCH, NEW MALDEN

Life from death

The angel said to the women, 'Do not be afraid, for I know that you are looking for Jesus, who was crucified. He is not here; he has risen, just as he said. Come and see the place where he lay'… The women hurried away from the tomb, afraid yet filled with joy, and ran to tell his disciples. Suddenly Jesus met them. 'Greetings,' he said. They came to him, clasped his feet and worshipped him. Then Jesus said to them, 'Do not be afraid. Go and tell my brothers to go to Galilee; there they will see me.'

MATTHEW 28:5–6, 8–10 (NIV)

That first Good Friday, everything went dark and dead for Jesus' followers, especially their bright, living hope of a new era championed by their friend and teacher.

Jesus had explained before: 'Very truly I tell you, unless a grain of wheat falls to the ground and dies, it remains only a single seed. But if it dies, it produces many seeds' (John 12:24). Obviously, this had fallen on deaf ears.

Now, after a long, dead Saturday, Sunday morning had dawned. Jesus' tomb was empty, and there followed the totally transformative seeing, meeting, being with, speaking with and worshipping the alive-again Jesus.

I love that the Christian faith celebrates being alive, *really* alive. From the dead places of people's lives, new, eternal life can sprout and flourish because of Jesus. He is risen, alive, life-giving, active and always with us – *always*, even past death.

Jesus, I'm sorry, then, for the times I've made it seem as if the Christian faith is about the dead, the dull, the distant, the denying, the delusional and the desperate, rather than the real, the living and the indestructible.

I'm revived and given hope again with the emerging of Christ from the tomb, as imagined by Luigi Santucci in *Wrestling with Christ* (Collins, 1972):

I'm going out into the light, for this is the dawn of Easter. Joseph's garden is bright with dew beneath my feet. The eastern sky is tinged with blood. What currency blood is! It alone buys. I'm buying everyone. I'm buying sorrow and pain, blasphemy and perdition. On Calvary Hill I spat out the sponge dipped in vinegar, but now I'm swallowing Death so that it won't go on sprouting. It will be the final horror of my passion. And then music, music until the end of the world.

TERRY CLUTTERHAM, FORMER CULTURE AND INNOVATION DIRECTOR, SCRIPTURE UNION ENGLAND AND WALES

Pentecost

WHEN LOOKING for ways to describe the kingdom of God, Jesus often turned to the grain field and the vineyard as analogies. 'A farmer went out to sow his seed,' Jesus says at the start of one of his parables (Matthew 13:3, NIV). 'There was a landowner who planted a vineyard,' begins another (Matthew 21:33). Similarly, Paul, when asked about the resurrection body, uses the imagery of sowing and reaping to explain this mystery (1 Corinthians 15), describing the resurrection of Christ as 'the firstfruits of those who have fallen asleep' (v. 20).

It is fitting, then, that it is the day of Pentecost – a festival to celebrate the harvest – when the Holy Spirit comes upon the disciples gathered in the upper room. If 'the harvest is the end of the age' (Matthew 13:39), the events of Pentecost as described in Acts 2 are nothing short of the 'end of the age' breaking into the present. The resurrection life, of which Jesus is the firstfruits, was now being made available to 'everyone who calls on the name of the Lord' (Acts 2:21).

The readings in this section begin to unpack what this end-of-the-age life looks like. The Holy Spirit empowers us to do God's work in the world; grows in us the fruit of love and its accompanying virtues; transforms us into a new creation; enables us to overflow with thanksgiving and generosity; bears witness that we are children of God; and so much more. In short, the Holy Spirit is none other than God present within us.

This, Peter explains in his Pentecost sermon, is a fulfilment of what Joel prophesied. It is interesting that earlier in the same passage that Peter quotes, Joel's promise is of an abundant harvest: 'The threshing-floors will be filled with grain; the vats will overflow with new wine' (Joel 2:24). Perhaps it is no coincidence that the disciples at that first Pentecost were accused of being drunk.

DANIELE OCH, PRODUCTION MANAGER, BRF,
AND UK EDITOR, *THE UPPER ROOM*

Power from on high

When the day of Pentecost had come, they were all together in one place. And suddenly from heaven there came a sound like the rush of a violent wind, and it filled the entire house where they were sitting. Divided tongues, as of fire, appeared among them, and a tongue rested on each of them. All of them were filled with the Holy Spirit and began to speak in other languages, as the Spirit gave them ability... And at this sound the crowd gathered and was bewildered, because each one heard them speaking in the native language of each.

ACTS 2:1–4, 6 (NRSV)

Wind and fire have always mediated the presence of God. There was the wind from God that swept over the face of the waters before creation began; the burning-but-not-consumed bush out of which God spoke to Moses; the pillar of fire by night that led the Israelites out of Egypt; Mount Sinai wrapped in smoke when Moses received the ten commandments because the Lord had descended upon it in fire; Elijah, taken up into heaven in a whirlwind, in a chariot of fire.

Wind and fire hold great power. Often, and to the great sorrow of God, this power can be a destructive force, a hurricane that flattens a city or a forest fire that razes everything in its path. Flames fanned by wind are the most powerful of all. But fire also refines and purifies. It can forge strength out of weakness, wholeness out of brokenness. Raw metal can be worked into an object of beauty, worthless scrap wrought into something of value. Bellows help.

The disciples had been promised power from on high, and they got it: power to make disciples of all nations, to be Christ's witnesses to the ends of the earth, to feed his sheep. And that same power is still at work today, giving the Spirit-filled a burning passion to spread the gospel, setting the church on fire. The refreshing, renewing, empowering Spirit, who will work through our lives to bring Christ to the world; who will strengthen our faith and revive us with the breath of God's own life; who will fill our hearts and kindle in us the fire of God's astonishing love.

Because we need God's power to do God's work. Without it, we can do nothing.

TIM HEATON, PRIEST AND AUTHOR

The fruit of the Spirit

Live by the Spirit, I say, and do not gratify the desires of the flesh... The fruit of the Spirit is love, joy, peace, patience, kindness, generosity, faithfulness, gentleness and self-control. There is no law against such things. And those who belong to Christ Jesus have crucified the flesh with its passions and desires. If we live by the Spirit, let us also be guided by the Spirit. Let us not become conceited, competing against one another, envying one another.

GALATIANS 5:16, 22–26 (NRSV)

For some unknown reason, a couple living near us once tied lemons on to a tree in their garden. It was a distinctly odd thing to do, but it illustrated rather well the central message of this brilliant short passage in Galatians. Only a life fed by the Spirit can produce genuine fruit that will last. Behaviour that you 'tie on' to your life is like a lemon destined for the compost. You can't fake it.

Paul is still in dispute with those elements in the Galatian church that are disturbing its spiritual harmony. He has expressed his frustration throughout the letter ('You foolish Galatians!', 3:1), but now he turns to the final test of where truth lies, which is the quality of the lives the Spirit produces. Love, joy and peace are qualities relating to God; patience, kindness and generosity are qualities relating to others; and faithfulness, gentleness and self-control are qualities concerned with personal holiness. But all are the natural result of a life aligned with God through the indwelling of the Spirit.

Such growth may indeed be 'natural', but it doesn't happen without our determined cooperation. We can't sit back and say, 'The Spirit will do it all for me.' We have a daily task of aligning ourselves with the Spirit of Jesus (the one who fully displayed these nine qualities) in order to distance ourselves from the 'works of the flesh' (5:19) that so easily reassert themselves. We have consciously to intend not only to live by the Spirit but also to be guided by the Spirit, day to day. That's what makes our life of prayer so central.

We need to start each day with the prayer, 'Lord, please fill me with your Spirit today.' Then the fruit will grow.

JOHN PRITCHARD, BISHOP, WRITER AND SPEAKER

The transforming Spirit in community

Now the whole group of those who believed were of one heart and soul, and no one claimed private ownership of any possessions, but everything they owned was held in common. With great power the apostles gave their testimony to the resurrection of the Lord Jesus, and great grace was upon them all. There was not a needy person among them, for as many as owned lands or houses sold them and brought the proceeds of what was sold. They laid it at the apostles' feet, and it was distributed to each as any had need.

ACTS 4:32–35 (NRSV)

It is difficult to imagine a community like this, despite its appeal. Even in the happiest of families or the closest of friendship groups, the notion of being 'of one heart and soul' seems impossible. We tend to assume that we will have different desires, but hope at least that we will accept those differences and disagree gracefully. However, for this community which has received God's Spirit in a very profound way, transformation reaches them at the core. This unity brought about by the Spirit is not only felt inwardly; unity is demonstrated as the privileged lay down their wealth, sharing with those who lack.

This kind of passage can be challenging when we consider how far we are from this image. In the church, there is rarely unity about some of the matters that are dearest to our hearts and the most important for the world. We might imagine that if we were clearer or bolder, we could convince others of our perspective. We often assume that unity can occur on our terms. Yet here in Acts, we see that it is through the Holy Spirit that unity is brought about – a unity formed not around one human perspective over another, but around the ultimate intention of God for us all.

The Holy Spirit draws us into God's vision for humanity and the world, in which the flourishing of all creation (and particularly 'the least of these') is facilitated. Unity, as we see here, costs the privileged, who are led to even the scales for the disadvantaged; it is not those already marginalised who carry the burden. In our own lives and contexts, may we remain open to the Spirit whose presence creates a unity built with kindness, for the sake of the witness of the church in the world.

SELINA STONE, LECTURER IN THEOLOGY, ST MELLITUS COLLEGE

Time to be thankful

Count seven weeks from the time you begin to put the sickle to the standing corn. Then celebrate the Festival of Weeks to the Lord your God by giving a freewill offering in proportion to the blessings the Lord your God has given you. And rejoice before the Lord your God at the place he will choose as a dwelling for his Name – you, your sons and daughters, your male and female servants, the Levites in your towns, and the foreigners, the fatherless and the widows living among you. Remember that you were slaves in Egypt.

DEUTERONOMY 16:9–12a (NIV)

The Festival of Weeks ('Shavuot' in Hebrew) was one of the three key festivals for God's people, along with Tabernacles ('Sukkot') and Passover ('Pesach'). Its Greek name – 'Pentecost' – simply meant 'fifty', because it was held 50 days after the second day of Passover (corresponding to the seventh Sunday after Easter).

A celebration of God's yearly blessings, it marked the harvesting of the spring wheat (the last of the grain crops to ripen), and families would take their first fruits in a pilgrimage to Jerusalem, to offer them in thanksgiving and enjoy a meal together. According to Jewish tradition, the festival also marked God's giving of the law to Moses at Sinai, so it also had a sense of thankfulness for God's guidance as to how communities should live and work together.

When Christians think of Pentecost, it is almost always as 'the day the Holy Spirit came'. Keeping in mind its original context of 'harvest thanksgiving' is an important reminder that our faith has deep roots. Jesus' Jewishness was integral – not incidental – to his life and ministry. Similarly, the story of our faith begins in the Old Testament, which is often now referred to as the 'Hebrew Bible' to underline how we should avoid thinking of it as 'old' in the sense of 'antiquated' or 'redundant'.

That original sense of 'thanksgiving' also reminds us, in our Pentecost-related reflection, of how much blessing can flow from thankfulness. Rather than simply prioritising daily intercession, we could consider taking as much time to note God's good gifts to us – as individuals, as churches and as communities – and give thanks. Perhaps we, like the Jerusalem crowds in Acts 2, may then find God's Spirit unexpectedly released upon us.

NAOMI STARKEY, CLERIC AND PIONEER EVANGELIST, CHURCH IN WALES, FORMER BRF STAFF MEMBER AND FORMER EDITOR, *NEW DAYLIGHT*

Time to be generous

'From the day after the Sabbath, the day you brought the sheaf of the wave offering, count seven full weeks. Count fifty days up to the day after the seventh Sabbath, and then present an offering of new grain to the Lord... When you reap the harvest of your land, do not reap to the very edges of your field or gather the gleanings of your harvest. Leave them for the poor and for the foreigner residing among you. I am the Lord your God.'

LEVITICUS 23:15–16, 22 (NIV)

As we read in the previous reflection, Pentecost has its roots in the Old Testament Feast of Weeks. Like Deuteronomy 16 (and Numbers 28), Leviticus 23 presents a list of 'the appointed festivals of the Lord' (v. 1). In the middle of the Leviticus list, however, following the instructions for the Feast of Weeks, we find an additional stipulation. The Israelites are commanded not only to offer some of their harvest to the Lord, but also to leave some of their harvest 'for the poor and for the foreigner' (v. 22).

It seems at first that this command interrupts the flow of this chapter – why repeat an instruction about helping the poor, already given in 19:9–10, halfway through a list of 'sacred assemblies'? But, as we see so often in the Bible, the former fits hand-in-glove with the latter. At the heart of the worship of God lies a concern for our neighbour.

Thus, when Jesus is asked which is the greatest commandment, his response is clear: 'Love the Lord your God.' But he then adds another, which, he says, is 'like it': 'Love your neighbour as yourself' (Matthew 22:34–40).

The same thread runs through Pentecost, when the outpouring of the Holy Spirit results in the disciples not only praising God and preaching to thousands, but also selling their 'property and possessions to give to anyone who had need' (Acts 2:44–45).

The gift of the Spirit is often longed for to renew our worship, less so to redistribute our wealth. Perhaps the two belong closer together than we'd like to think.

DANIELE OCH, PRODUCTION MANAGER, BRF, AND UK EDITOR, *THE UPPER ROOM*

Experiencing Pentecost

On the last day of the festival, the great day, while Jesus was standing there, he cried out, 'Let anyone who is thirsty come to me, and let the one who believes in me drink. As the scripture has said, "Out of the believer's heart shall flow rivers of living water."' Now he said this about the Spirit, which believers in him were to receive; for as yet there was no Spirit, because Jesus was not yet glorified.

JOHN 7:37–39 (NRSV)

It was a draining season in my life that brought me to ask deep down for the Holy Spirit. Pentecost was a feast I celebrated. I accepted the Holy Spirit was in me as one of the baptised. My enthusiasm for God had diminished, though, and it showed in my incapacity to resist temptations besieging me. I knew what was right but could not do it. In my mind I pictured God, but my heart felt empty.

It was then I recognised my need for spiritual guidance and sought it. My guide saw through my predicament to an unrecognised thirst for God and encouraged me to keep faith in our Lord Jesus to provide. 'Let the one who believes in [Jesus] drink... Out of [their] heart shall flow rivers of living water.'

The Holy Spirit came, and still comes. A flow of joy, love and praise welling up from within burst out after a weight of sin and unbelief lifted from my heart, through repentance and putting fresh faith in God, to remake and empower me. Sometimes we think of the Spirit coming from above and outside of us, as in Acts 2:1–4. Other times God works by searching us out and empowering us from the inside, as in John 7:37–39. My experience of renewal was like a hidden spring emerging to flow once more on the surface of my life.

When life is draining, it can be a signal to search the scriptures and seek help from fellow believers. Through having our thirst for God identified, and encouragement to expect the release of the Holy Spirit, we enter afresh the flow of joy, love and praise that started at Pentecost and will never end.

JOHN TWISLETON, PRIEST, AUTHOR AND BROADCASTER

God's gloves

'I am sending you out like sheep among wolves. Therefore be as shrewd as snakes and as innocent as doves. Be on your guard; you will be handed over to the local councils and be flogged in the synagogues. On my account you will be brought before governors and kings as witnesses to them and to the Gentiles. But when they arrest you, do not worry about what to say or how to say it. At that time you will be given what to say, for it will not be you speaking, but the Spirit of your Father speaking through you.'

MATTHEW 10:16–20 (NIV)

When Jesus sent his twelve apostles off to preach and heal, he gave them very clear instructions, and warned them (and us) that following him never ensures an easy life! Yet he also promised that when we face difficult situations, the Holy Spirit will show us what to say.

As a young mum, living in a busy housing estate, I was so painfully shy that I never talked to my neighbours. One morning at the school gate, I overheard them talking about my next-door neighbour who had died in the night. 'How sad for his wife,' they agreed, 'never parted in 60 years and had no children.' I felt that the Lord wanted me to take her flowers and offer help, but I told him firmly I was so scared I wouldn't know what to say. I argued with him as I hoovered the house – until I noticed my gloves lying empty and limp by the door and sensed him say, 'An empty glove is useless, but it can do amazing things when it's filled by a skilful hand. Let me use you to help your neighbour.' So, rather unwillingly, I picked some daffodils and nervously knocked on her door. I can't remember what I said, but she must have felt comforted because we became such close friends the children called her their adopted Gran!

Those empty gloves helped me understand what it means to be filled with the Holy Spirit. When we are willing to be his gloves, he gives us the power to do and say things that would be completely impossible for us on our own.

So the next time we face a difficult conversation, interview or challenging question, we simply need to open ourselves to 'the Father's Spirit' and allow ourselves to be his gloves.

JENNIFER REES LARCOMBE, AUTHOR, SPEAKER AND DIRECTOR,
BEAUTY FROM ASHES TRUST

The day after the Day

'And afterwards, I will pour out my Spirit on all people. Your sons and daughters will prophesy, your old men will dream dreams, your young men will see visions. Even on my servants, both men and women, I will pour out my Spirit in those days. I will show wonders in the heavens and on the earth, blood and fire and billows of smoke. The sun will be turned to darkness and the moon to blood before the coming of the great and dreadful day of the Lord. And everyone who calls on the name of the Lord will be saved.'

JOEL 2:28–32a (NIV)

'Which came first? The chicken or the egg?' Or, given the many links, quotations and allusions that connect Joel and the other prophets of the Old Testament, was Joel being quoted… or was he quoting others?

Most likely, I think, Joel was a man soaked in scripture and his little book summarises many of the themes of the prophets. A natural disaster, namely a terrible plague of locusts, has led to the national disaster of famine. Like the prophets before him, Joel sees in this the hand of God and calls the people to repentance – but particularly, and powerfully, because what *has* come to pass is like what *will* come to pass later. What the nation has been through in Joel's day will be repeated more seriously on God's ultimate judgement day. This is 'the Day of the Lord', spoken of so frequently by the prophets.

However, Joel also collects their prophecies of hope and adds words that we still hold dear. 'Afterwards' becomes, in Peter's mouth at Pentecost, 'in the last days', making it clear that it will be the decisive and final intervention. Joel reminds us that God calls us to repentance because he longs to have mercy on us, restore us and bless us. Supremely, what he wants to do is fill his people with his presence. No more will the experience of God be confined to a few anointed leaders and prophets, instead 'all people' (v. 28) will directly know God and be used as his servants, understanding his purposes and speaking his truth (v. 29).

Yes, the 'day of the Lord' will be 'great and dreadful' (v. 31), but when we call on God's name in repentance, salvation is sure and life in the Spirit begins.

PAUL HARCOURT, NATIONAL LEADER, NEW WINE ENGLAND

The uncomfortable gift

'And as I began to speak, the Holy Spirit fell upon them just as it had upon us at the beginning. And I remembered the word of the Lord, how he had said, "John baptised with water, but you will be baptised with the Holy Spirit." If then God gave them the same gift that he gave us when we believed in the Lord Jesus Christ, who was I that I could hinder God?'

ACTS 11:15–17 (NRSV)

We learn from Peter that the gift of Pentecost, the permanent presence and dynamic filling by the Holy Spirit, is a stretching and uncomfortable gift.

Peter discovered that what happened to him and his companions on the day of Pentecost was unique only in one limited sense: Pentecost was the first time, the inaugural occasion that launched an era. And that era had just been extended to people of a different race and culture to the church as it had existed thus far: to Gentiles, whom Peter's Jewish heritage, until now, had taught him to avoid – let alone the extended household of an officer from the Roman occupiers!

But Peter went to them under the explicit direction of the Holy Spirit. He had begun to preach, and without so much as a 'by your leave', the same Spirit interrupted him ('as I began to speak') and filled his audience, as at Pentecost ('as it had upon us at the beginning'). Then he had to give an account of his action to his peers, who had not seen what he had seen, and had not yet understood what he now understood. It was not comfortable at all. But it was God.

His understanding of Jesus' words had been expanded. 'You will be baptised with the Holy Spirit' (Acts 1:5) was not just a promise to Jews. As Jesus had poured out the Spirit on the day of Pentecost (Acts 2:33), so he was doing it again, across historic barriers. He still does. Peter had been stretched, and his understanding expanded. So it will be for anyone who is open to being filled with the Holy Spirit. Being filled is never being finally full. When Jesus expands you, he creates room for more, for the sake of others. Pray for the uncomfortable gift!

GRAHAM CRAY, HONORARY ASSISTANT BISHOP, DIOCESE OF YORK

Sighs too deep for words

Likewise, the Spirit helps us in our weakness; for we do not know how to pray as we ought, but that very Spirit intercedes with sighs too deep for words.

ROMANS 8:26 (NRSV)

Sighs – or groans, as some translations put it – that are too deep to be expressed in words. There is something about this verse which has always tugged at me.

Our experience of God inevitably takes us beyond what our imaginations can grasp or find words for. If we say God is infinite, we are saying that there is always more to God than we can reach for. If we say God is eternal – not just endless but outside time – then God is beyond the limits of what we can describe in words.

There are times when we sense something deeper, something beyond, that we barely glimpse and cannot put into words. For many of us, the experience of bereavement is one such time. I know a beautiful cliff-top in Cornwall where there is a bench with a view straight out to sea: a memorial plaque on the bench has a poem to a lost loved one, full of longing to meet again 'where the sea meets the sky'. As I look out to sea, I can see what the poet sees: a transcendent reality, always receding beyond the reach of my understanding.

So often, those are moments of yearning. Paul understood this: hence the sighs – or groans – too deep for words. Why? Why is it that those moments when I am transported beyond words – by a piece of music, for example – are so often moments of melancholy, rather than of exhilaration?

Much of the time, we accumulate as though there were always a tomorrow; we spend as though there were no tomorrow. Until the day and the year come when we say – in the words of Ecclesiastes – that we have no pleasure in them. The day when we realise that there will someday be a tomorrow without us – and when we look back on the waste and the wrong in our lives and feel the loss.

Those times are often when it is least easy to pray. But those are the very times of weakness when, as Paul puts it, the Spirit of God is near us – in us, even – interceding with sighs too deep for words.

STEPHEN GREEN, MEMBER OF THE HOUSE OF LORDS

From simple stillness to shining greatness

We are not like Moses. He put a covering over his face so the Jews would not see that the bright light was passing away... Yes, to this day, there is a covering over their hearts whenever the Law of Moses is read. But whenever [anyone] turns to the Lord, the covering is taken away. The heart is free where the Spirit of the Lord is... All of us, with no covering on our faces, show the shining-greatness of the Lord as in a mirror. All the time we are being changed to look like Him, with more and more of His shining-greatness. This change is from the Lord Who is the Spirit.

2 CORINTHIANS 3:13–18 (NLV, abridged)

There is a deeply rooted tradition within our Christian heritage of what is known as 'illumination' and 'unification'. This teaching can mostly be found in the writings of those we commonly call the Christian mystics, but also in the Eastern Orthodox church. It is the process which is described above of us both reflecting the shining glory of the Divine (illumination) and also becoming one with God (unification).

Quite often, in the years that I spent as a church minister, from the pulpit I would entreat the hearers to stop trying to be 'good Christians', because if we do that we only set ourselves up to fail. We are not called to make ourselves better Christians, to transform ourselves; we are called to 'be transformed', as the apostle Paul told the church in Rome, and as he tells the church in Corinth in this passage. The Divine work in us will transform us, so instead of spending our energy on trying to be a good Christian, and failing, we should direct our efforts into simply allowing the Divine Spirit to work within us.

As we live our lives with unveiled hearts and minds, we create the inner environment for transformation by letting go of egoistic control. The Spirit works within us, and we simply begin to become more Christlike. We become that which we were striving to be.

But how do we begin to be in that place, ready to receive transformation? The overwhelming consensus from the mystics is through contemplation: the practice of stilling our inner being, creating the inner environment for the Divine to work on us, within us. It is as simple as sitting and being, simply creating a still quiet inner sense. Why not try it?

DAVID COLE (BROTHER CASSIAN), EXECUTIVE DIRECTOR, WAYMARK MINISTRIES, AND UK DEPUTY GUARDIAN, THE COMMUNITY OF AIDAN AND HILDA

Children of God

Heirs, as long as they are minors, are no better than slaves, though they are the owners of all the property; but they remain under guardians and trustees until the date set by the father. So with us; while we were minors, we were enslaved to the elemental spirits of the world. But when the fullness of time had come, God sent his Son, born of a woman, born under the law... so that we might receive adoption as children. And because you are children, God has sent the Spirit of his Son into our hearts, crying 'Abba! Father!' So you are no longer a slave but a child, and if a child then also an heir, through God.

GALATIANS 4:1–7 (NRSV, abridged)

Our deepest identity does not come from the roles we play, at work, at home or in church. Our deepest identity – who we truly are – is as *children* of God. John writes in his prologue 'to all who received [Jesus], who believed in his name, he gave the power to become *children* of God' (John 1:12). Paul asserts this, not only as a fact about those who believe but also as a matter of *experience* for the believer. So that we can experience this intimacy and closeness of relationship, God sends the Spirit of his Son into our hearts, crying, 'Abba! Father!'

Paul says the same thing in a different way in Romans: 'For all who are led by the Spirit of God are children of God... When we cry "Abba! Father!" it is that very Spirit bearing witness with our spirit that we are children of God' (Romans 8:14–16). It is the Holy Spirit who allows us to enter fully and freely into this close relationship with God.

If our relationship with God has become a bit dry or formal or 'adult', let us pray for the Holy Spirit to soften our hearts to help us to be who we really are with God, with all our joys and struggles, and to give God space to be who God is with us. Teresa of Ávila wrote that the most common reason for experiencing dryness in prayer is praying as if God were not present.

So let us pray with the faith of a child, trusting implicitly his presence with us and his love for us. Jesus said, 'Unless you change and become like children, you will never enter the kingdom of heaven' (Matthew 18:3).

JOHN STROYAN, BISHOP OF WARWICK

Fireworks of the Spirit

Dear brothers and sisters, you are dearly loved by God and we know that he has chosen you to be his very own. For our gospel came to you not merely in the form of words but in mighty power infused with the Holy Spirit and deep conviction... You received the word with the joy of the Holy Spirit, even though it resulted in tremendous trials and persecution.... The message of the Lord has sounded out from you not only in Greece, but its echo has been heard in every place where people are hearing about your strong faith.

1 THESSALONIANS 1:4–8 (TPT, abridged)

When God threw heaven open and the Holy Spirit burst on a handful of hiding, huddling believers at Pentecost, sparks were lit that have never stopped burning. Flames of religious devotion in Paul and Silas were fanned into Christ-centred mission. Their passion took them on many journeys to make Jesus known across the world.

So Paul and Silas arrived at Thessalonica, in northern Greece, and began to preach the good news of Jesus in the synagogue. Here, Paul recalls how despite the bruises of recent beatings in Philippi, the Holy Spirit's power ignited his words and weakness into a dynamic presentation of Jesus. The Spirit kindled the hopes of Jews and God-fearing Greeks into delight that what Paul proclaimed was absolutely true: Jesus was the long-awaited Christ who had to suffer and rise from the dead. The gospel beacon was lit and a little church was born. These believers had no illusions that the Christian life would be easy. Indeed, riots followed, but the Holy Spirit lavished on them a joy way beyond explanation. That eloquent testimony to the extraordinary power of God challenged and changed, strengthened and satisfied, and gave life; and hope spread like wildfire across the region.

Have you witnessed it? It may not involve fireballs and fanfares, but there is nothing more beautiful than observing the Pentecost fire reach across national borders. Migration and travel are key in the Spirit's strategy. In my mind's eye, I see the refugee who found a home in Christ. I recall the Chinese student for whom, after three years' Bible discussion, the penny finally dropped. I remember the atheist Japanese au pair articulating biblical insights which were simply God-given. The Spirit's power and conviction gets into their bones. Another torch in the darkness. God's fireworks burning bright across a shadowy world.

FIONA BARNARD, ESOL TUTOR AND INTERNATIONAL STUDENT CHAPLAIN

The comforter

Comfort, O comfort my people, says your God. Speak tenderly to Jerusalem, and cry to her that she has served her term, that her penalty is paid, that she has received from the Lord's hand double for all her sins. A voice cries out: 'In the wilderness prepare the way of the Lord, make straight in the desert a highway for our God. Every valley shall be lifted up, and every mountain and hill be made low; the uneven ground shall become level, and the rough places a plain. Then the glory of the Lord shall be revealed, and all people shall see it together, for the mouth of the Lord has spoken.'

ISAIAH 40:1–5 (NRSV)

The world needs the songs of Isaiah 40 now as much as at any time for many years. These songs were written to bring comfort at the end of the long exile of God's people in Babylon. The word 'comfort' means much more than empathy or consolation. 'Comfort' has two components in English: 'com' meaning 'with', and 'fort' from the Latin *fortis* meaning 'strength and courage'.

The songs of this prophet are intended for those who wait upon the Lord to renew their strength (see 40:31). That renewal comes through words of tenderness and forgiveness. It comes through the renewal of hope and of God's salvation. It comes in later chapters through the promise of new servant leadership marked by integrity and suffering.

The opening words of Isaiah 40 will be echoed in the gospels. This is the place where Mark begins his story of Jesus. According to John, the Spirit is given the title of Comforter (echoing the old Greek translation of this passage) as the Spirit is given to strengthen our hearts through faith (John 14:26). The Spirit comes to us with great gentleness yet with abundant life.

Many across the world are tired beyond measure, worn down by the multiple ongoing effects of the Covid-19 pandemic. Somehow, in this time, Christian disciples need themselves to receive God's comfort and strength and to offer this same comfort to a weary world. This is the season to learn to run and not be weary, to walk and not faint. This is the season to find our voice again as we are called, in our turn, to sing songs of hope to a lost generation: Comfort my people, says your God.

STEVEN CROFT, BISHOP OF OXFORD

Together
through the generations

Past and present

W E AS THE PEOPLE of God have always learned from our past. Again and again in the Old Testament, the Israelites were reminded of God's ways by looking to what had happened to the generations before them. They were urged to teach God's words to their children, 'talking about them when you are at home and when you are away, when you lie down and when you rise' (Deuteronomy 11:19), so that the nation wouldn't collectively forget what God had done for them. This is why the story of their rescue from slavery in Egypt is repeated so often in the Old Testament.

Equally, today, we tell stories of what has happened in the past to encourage and inspire. We read stories from the Bible, both the Old and New Testaments; we look to the saints and theologians of the past; we learn from those older than us in our families, churches and communities.

This section collects together the wisdom of Christians who have gone before us. There is a treasure trove in the archives of BRF's Bible reading notes, and this is just a small selection of what is available. Some of these writers are no longer with us, while others are still writing. All have something valuable to offer us in the present day.

As we delve into these words from the past, let's heed the words of the psalmist:

**We will tell to the coming generation
the glorious deeds of the Lord, and his might,
and the wonders that he has done.**
PSALM 78:4

RACHEL TRANTER, EDITORIAL MANAGER, BRF,
AND JOINT EDITOR, *GUIDELINES*

Rekindle the gift

Paul, an apostle of Christ Jesus by the will of God, for the sake of the promise of life that is in Christ Jesus, to Timothy, my beloved child: Grace, mercy, and peace from God the Father and Christ Jesus our Lord. I am grateful to God – whom I worship with a clear conscience, as my ancestors did – when I remember you constantly in my prayers night and day. Recalling your tears, I long to see you so that I may be filled with joy. I am reminded of your sincere faith, a faith that lived first in your grandmother Lois and your mother Eunice and now, I am sure, lives in you. For this reason I remind you to rekindle the gift of God that is within you through the laying on of my hands; for God did not give us a spirit of cowardice, but rather a spirit of power and of love and of self-discipline.

2 TIMOTHY 1:1–7 (NRSV)

As Paul begins this letter, he hands Timothy the first key to 'the promise of life' (v. 1): Timothy is to look to the past. Paul knew the power in having ancestors who have loved God (v. 3). Timothy could not claim the impeccable lineage of Paul (see Romans 11:1), but he had a believing grandmother and a believing mother. He had an inheritance. Never underestimate the influence of the faith of those who have gone before, and never stop praying for the generations to come.

Second, Paul reminds Timothy of his commissioning. I am always deeply moved by ordination services, in whichever tradition they take place. The word 'sacrament' is often applied to those occasions. In the words of Cranmer's Book of Common Prayer, a sacrament is 'an outward and visible sign of an inward and spiritual grace'. When Timothy was ordained and Paul laid his hands upon him (v. 6), something happened in the spiritual realm: God the Holy Spirit conferred upon him power and self-discipline (v. 7) – the very things he needed!

Look to your past today. Remember those who have prayed for you. Remember those times when you have been ordained, commissioned or simply prayed for, and rekindle the gift of God that was given to you on those occasions.

JENNIFER OLDROYD, AUTHOR AND EDITOR

Unconditional love

For I am convinced that neither death nor life, neither angels nor demons, neither the present nor the future, nor any powers, neither height nor depth, nor anything else in all creation, will be able to separate us from the love of God that is in Christ Jesus our Lord.

ROMANS 8:38–39 (NIV)

These are very grand, stirring words, aren't they? The promise they contain is exactly what most of us (me included) want to hear, but many years ago I felt sick every time I heard them because they sounded so hollow and meaningless to my ears. Why was that? Well, I was going through a difficult time, and confidence in God was part of those difficulties. Someone would read out a verse like the one quoted above, speak about the unchanging, never-ending love of God, then a little later quote some other verse that apparently indicated the ease and finality with which any one of us could separate ourselves from God. It used to drive me mad. Since then, I've met other Christians, especially those whose confidence is never high anyway, who are puzzled by the way in which this paradox is trotted out so readily by people who haven't really thought it through. For all those people (and for myself) here are a few humble(ish) observations.

God loves us without any condition whatsoever. Whatever we are or aren't – whatever we do or don't do, he will go on loving us just the same. Consider the story of the prodigal son. Could anything be more transparently clear than the passion with which this father regards the son who has left home? Let me spell it out.

Even as the prodigal was in the act of sleeping with prostitutes and pursuing whatever other activities he was engaged in, his father, knowing full well the sort of thing he was doing, was loving him and watching out for his return and planning the kind of celebration that would accompany that return. Do we honestly think that this consistency and depth of love and affection is going to be changed or reduced by lapses and mistakes made by the prodigal after he has returned home? Don't misunderstand me, I don't mean that we have a licence to sin. What I'm trying to convey is that this whole thing – this whole salvation/Jesus/crucifixion/resurrection/repentance/heaven *thing* is God's idea and initiative. He so loved the world…

ADRIAN PLASS, AUTHOR, STORYTELLER AND PERFORMER

True bread

Jesus then said to them, 'Truly, truly, I say to you, it was not Moses who gave you the bread from heaven; my Father gives you the true bread from heaven. For the bread of God is that which comes down from heaven, and gives life to the world.' They said to him, 'Lord, give us this bread always.' Jesus said to them, 'I am the bread of life; he who comes to me shall not hunger, and he who believes in me shall never thirst.'

JOHN 6:32–35 (RSV)

My favourite quotation is St Augustine's, 'Lord, you have made us for yourself, and our hearts are restless till they find their rest in you.' It's what Jesus is on about here. By calling himself the bread of life, he is claiming to be that which satisfies all our deepest longings, as food calms the pangs of hunger. To feed our souls on him is to be at last at peace.

And yet we may well wonder if it is true. Christians seem to have deep longings which their faith never makes up for. Loneliness, troubled marriages, anxiety for children, all these and more are part of our normal life. And not only does faith often seem a poor substitute, but we pity (and sometimes fear) those who rechannel all their frustrations into religion.

I don't think, though, that Jesus intended for us to be free of life's troubles. What he promises is something else – a sense that under the storms of life is a deep calm which can never be shaken, an awareness of the presence of God which allows us to see all our other experience as secondary.

Also, I don't believe that Jesus was offering a magical cure. It's not a matter of simply saying 'I believe' and waiting for the heavenly peace to descend. It's a matter of digesting the bread of life; of letting Christ become a part of us in every aspect of our life. Our whole Christian life is a process of feeding and nourishing ourselves in him – through worship, prayer, learning and meditation.

In our communion, this process is dramatically symbolised. As we digest the bread and wine, we pray that we will similarly be pervaded by the presence of God. And eventually we will. Jesus truly is the bread of life, but that bread is no quick junk-food snack. It is a leisurely banquet which takes all our life to assimilate; and then truly satisfies our every need.

MARCUS MAXWELL, AUTHOR, PRIEST AND FORMER TRUSTEE, BRF

A test of love

[Jesus said,] 'I give you a new commandment, that you love one another. Just as I have loved you, you also should love one another. By this everyone will know that you are my disciples, if you have love for one another.' Simon Peter said to him, 'Lord, where are you going?' Jesus answered, 'Where I am going, you cannot follow me now; but you will follow afterwards.' Peter said to him, 'Lord, why can I not follow you now? I will lay down my life for you.' Jesus answered, 'Will you lay down your life for me? Very truly, I tell you, before the cock crows, you will have denied me three times.'

JOHN 13:34–38 (NRSV)

The disciples are gathered in the upper room, and the atmosphere is sombre. Jesus is talking as though some great crisis lies just ahead, which will involve his leaving them and 'going away'. And although he speaks of a 'counsellor' or helper who will come to their aid, they are clearly worried and perplexed.

It is in this context that we must see both the 'new commandment' and the warning to Peter. They must learn to love each other, because only then would they be able to fulfil Jesus' mission for them in his absence. Their love for one another would unite them, and their unity would convince the world and bring it to faith in Jesus. It was true then, and it's true now, that the most attractive thing about the Christian Church is the love its members show to each other; and conversely that the most unattractive thing about the Church is when they don't.

The warning to Peter is stark. His profession of love – even to the point of death – is challenged. As it happened, he was prepared to die for Jesus. At least, he took a sword and was prepared to fight the soldiers who came to arrest him, which would probably have cost him his life (see 18:10). But he caved in before an apparently less serious threat, denying that he knew Jesus when challenged by a servant girl.

Sometimes we are better able to withstand the big tests than the little ones. Sometimes physical courage is easier than emotional or spiritual courage. The thing that Peter didn't know was himself. Unsurprisingly, Jesus knew Peter better than Peter did!

Lord, help me to love others, and to love you, with a love that doesn't boast or make huge claims, but flows from gratitude and trust. For Jesus' sake. Amen

DAVID WINTER, AUTHOR, BROADCASTER AND FORMER EDITOR, *NEW DAYLIGHT*

Our helper God

For I, the Lord your God, hold your right hand; it is I who say to you, 'Do not fear, I will help you.' Do not fear, you worm Jacob, you insect Israel! I will help you, says the Lord; your Redeemer is the Holy One of Israel. Now, I will make of you a threshing-sledge, sharp, new, and having teeth; you shall thresh the mountains and crush them, and you shall make the hills like chaff. You shall winnow them and the wind shall carry them away, and the tempest shall scatter them. Then you shall rejoice in the Lord; in the Holy One of Israel you shall glory.

ISAIAH 41:13–16 (NRSV)

If she really knows what God is like, Israel need never be afraid. God holds her with his right hand, and as he does so the power of the living God flows into her. God loves Israel, but he knows her for what she is – faithless and powerless, unless she responds to his love and receives his strength. She is as weak as a worm, and as insignificant as an insect (and that word could be 'louse').

Yet she was still created in the image and likeness of God, made to be indwelt by the living God and to live in relationship with him. Created to be a nation of priests and a holy nation. And if she (and if we) will allow it, the worm will be transformed into a threshing sledge. To thresh something is to separate the grain from the chaff – a picture of judgement.

Sometimes the mere presence of a holy person can make someone aware of their own sinfulness. It is as if the presence of light shines into the darkness and reveals someone's life as it really is.

Think about your own weaknesses. Imagine that God-in-Christ, who is Jesus, is holding your hand with his right hand. Believe that he can help you – and thank him that he will. Then remember the words of Jesus: 'I am the light of the world' (John 8:12, NRSV). 'You are the light of the world… let your light shine before others, so that they may see your good works and give glory to your Father in heaven' (Matthew 5:14–16).

SHELAGH BROWN, FORMERLY BRF STAFF MEMBER AND EDITOR, *NEW DAYLIGHT*

Jesus, our great and sympathetic priest

Since, then, we have a great high priest who has passed through the heavens, Jesus, the Son of God, let us hold fast to our confession. For we do not have a high priest who is unable to sympathize with our weaknesses, but we have one who in every respect has been tested as we are, yet without sin. Let us therefore approach the throne of grace with boldness, so that we may receive mercy and find grace to help in time of need.

HEBREWS 4:14–16 (NRSV)

We dive into the letter to the Hebrews at one of those comforting passages which the writer alternates with explanation and warning about falling away.

It's no wonder that those verses have been used in worship, to encourage us to turn towards God and focus on the welcome we will receive. In some traditional Holy Communion services, the first few words come around the middle of the service, just before we confess our sins. They remind us that we can approach God in the confidence of love that casts out fear. Jesus has been through it all – including being tempted by sin, just like us, so he knows from the inside what it's like (though, unlike us, he withstood the test). So we can be confident that Jesus understands. We don't have to be perpetually snivelling about our sins, nor pick at the scabs of our failures – we can look towards God. He will be merciful when we need it most.

This paints a picture of mature, balanced Christians who are grown up enough to have acknowledged their imperfections, but who have put their sins behind them. We can get beyond navel-gazing, turn to Christ and consider his wonderous mercy. He is the sympathetic judge who knows how tough life can get.

Why do we find it so difficult to reach this balance in our Christian lives? We wallow in our own, often unimportant, sin and sometimes spare a passing thought for how great God is, but we don't usually bring these two key elements together. This is odd, because they do belong with each other: God's goodness (which deserves a longer look) and our sins, which can be forgiven.

As far as the east is from the west, so far has he set our sins from us (Psalm 103:12, Common Worship Psalter).

RACHEL BOULDING, FORMERLY AUTHOR AND DEPUTY EDITOR, *CHURCH TIMES*

All-sufficient grace

Therefore, to keep me from being too elated, a thorn was given to me in the flesh, a messenger of Satan to torment me, to keep me from being too elated. Three times I appealed to the Lord about this, that it would leave me, but he said to me, 'My grace is sufficient for you, for power is made perfect in weakness.' So, I will boast all the more gladly of my weaknesses, so that the power of Christ may dwell in me. Therefore I am content with weaknesses, insults, hardships, persecutions, and calamities for the sake of Christ; for whenever I am weak, then I am strong.

2 CORINTHIANS 12:7–10 (NRSV)

Paul bares his heart, allowing us to feel his pain and weakness. He shares his deep sadness, the agony of what he terms his 'thorn in the flesh', a debilitating problem that he longed to be rid of, which he prayed he might be relieved of and yet which continued to afflict him.

Many suggestions have been put forward as to what this affliction was, but it seems to have been a severe physical problem. It may have been a form of epilepsy, migraine attacks, eye trouble or a combination of all these, together with raging fevers that left him exhausted. He knew the healing power of Christ, was used to bringing it to others, and yet he himself did not receive it – certainly not in the way he prayed and hoped for. He must have prayed many times for relief, but speaks of three particular times when he made his 'end of my tether' appeals for release.

The answer comes. It takes the form, not of release, but the assurance of the presence and strength of Christ in and through his affliction and weakness. No one could ever point at Paul and say, 'Well, it's alright for him. If he had to cope with what I have…' Paul was a living witness to the overwhelming power of Christ in and through all situations and conditions.

It is understandable and human to ask 'Why?' in the face of suffering, but, like Paul, we cannot demand an answer. We can only be content to accept and recognise that, in the topsy-turvy events of life, God is at work and shows his glory in and through us. As Paul did, we need to discover the contentment and joy that comes from realising that.

MARGARET CUNDIFF, FORMERLY PRIEST, WRITER, BROADCASTER AND CHAPLAIN

Taking Jesus seriously

When Jesus came down from the mountainside, large crowds followed him. A man with leprosy came and knelt before him and said, 'Lord, if you are willing, you can make me clean.' Jesus reached out his hand and touched the man. 'I am willing,' he said. 'Be clean!' Immediately he was cleansed of his leprosy.

MATTHEW 8:1–3 (NIV)

The authority of Jesus was amazing; he could speak a word and physical healing happened. So, if leprosy responded to his words immediately, how seriously do we take them? All too often we look at the promises of Jesus and file them under the 'too good to be true' heading.

One of Jesus' promises that challenges us can be found in John 10:10: 'I have come that they may have life, and have it to the full.' This verse appears quite a long way through a section that actually begins with the healing of a blind man at the beginning of John 9. Jesus healed the blind man, who was subsequently questioned by the Pharisees and thrown out of the synagogue. Jesus found him and spoke to him again, and then we discover the Pharisees rejoining the conversation. It is in this context, presumably with the man who had been healed standing by, that Jesus spoke the words promising fullness of life. How seriously do we take them?

This is one of the big challenges facing us as we ponder the healing stories of Jesus. Do we actually believe that it is his desire to heal us? Perhaps we are so used to seeing a lack of healing that it is his willingness to heal that we question. This is at the heart of Matthew's story about the man with leprosy. In fact, the leper's first words to Jesus are a question about his willingness to heal – and Jesus responds with an unequivocal 'I am willing.'

The willingness of Jesus to heal is an outworking of his mission to bring abundant life to the world. However, it is not just the world in general for which he is concerned, but for each of us personally.

If you are sick – whether physically, emotionally or in any other way – what do you believe God's will is for you?

JOHN RYELAND, DIRECTOR, THE CHRISTIAN HEALING MISSION

Trust in the Lord

My child, do not forget my teaching, but let your heart keep my commandments; for length of days and years of life and abundant welfare they will give you. Do not let loyalty and faithfulness forsake you; bind them round your neck, write them on the tablet of your heart. So you will find favour and good repute in the sight of God and of people. Trust in the Lord with all your heart, and do not rely on your own insight. In all your ways acknowledge him, and he will make straight your paths. Do not be wise in your own eyes; fear the Lord, and turn away from evil. It will be a healing for your flesh and a refreshment for your body.

PROVERBS 3:1–8 (NRSV)

There is a big difference between learning about wise sayings and truths and applying them to ourselves. We have to know inwardly that they are right for us, then we shall want them to be part of our make-up. The prophet Jeremiah foresaw the time when God would put his law in the people's minds and write it on their hearts (Jeremiah 31:33). Then, the people would want to accept the law for themselves and make it part of their everyday lives.

'Trust in the Lord with all your heart, and do not rely on your own insight.' This is another gem that has been handed down through the generations. Trust like this may not be in our hearts naturally – and we must cultivate it if we are to depend on God for understanding and guidance. It is a grace we may pray for, with confidence. Jesus urged his disciples to trust in God and trust also in him about what would happen to him after his death and, indeed, he urges us to do the same regarding our own passing (John 14:1–3).

We are simply not meant to know all the answers or to bear the whole weight of our burdens on our own. Acknowledging them before God and placing them in his hands can lift the heaviness from our hearts and bring a real sense of lightness and peace. Looking to God in everything means praying, however briefly, as we go along. We may never know beforehand which way our path may suddenly turn or even how we will react, but we can know for sure that God's wisdom is greater than our own.

CHRISTINE CHAPMAN, SOCIAL WORKER, COUNSELLOR AND AUTHOR

While we were yet sinners

But God proves his love for us in that while we still were sinners Christ died for us. Much more surely then, now that we have been justified by his blood, will we be saved through him from the wrath of God. For if while we were enemies, we were reconciled to God through the death of his Son, much more surely, having been reconciled, will we be saved by his life. But more than that, we even boast in God through our Lord Jesus Christ, through whom we have now received reconciliation.

ROMANS 5:8–11 (NRSV)

One of the dominant notes of evangelical revival in the eighteenth century was the sense of sheer wonder and amazement that God actually cares for each one of us! The great hymn of Charles Wesley reflects this:

> And can it be that I should gain
> An interest in the Saviour's blood?
> Died he for me who caused him pain,
> For me who him to death pursued?

The initiative is always with God. The cross shows us how much Jesus loves us and how far he was prepared to go to bring us wayward children home to the Father. It was while we were still in a state of enmity, hostility and rebellion as sinners that Christ gave his life for us.

Although Christ loves us just as we are, he loves us too much to leave us there. Through his death we are reconciled to God, loved, accepted and treated 'just as if we had never sinned'. This, though, is but the beginning of a process of transformation. We need to be saved by his life (v. 10); to be open to the moulding of the Holy Spirit, so that as we participate in the life of Christ we become more like him. After all, Jesus is not just our saviour, but also the Lord, who deserves trust, honour and obedience. This is the process of sanctification about which John Wesley said, 'If we are looking for anything other than perfect love, we are looking wide of the mark.' As our love for God deepens, it is reflected in our love for our fellow human beings. The more we are transformed by the love of God, the more we can share that love with others.

PETER GRAVES, METHODIST MINISTER AND CHAPLAIN

Jesus, the mystical vine

[Jesus said,] 'I am the true vine, and my Father is the vine-grower. He removes every branch in me that bears no fruit. Every branch that bears fruit he prunes to make it bear more fruit… Abide in me as I abide in you. Just as the branch cannot bear fruit by itself unless it abides in the vine, neither can you unless you abide in me. I am the vine, you are the branches. Those who abide in me and I in them bear much fruit, because apart from me you can do nothing.'

JOHN 15:1–5 (NRSV, abridged)

Here is an organic image which relates back to Israel's past as the vine of God (Isaiah 5:1–7; Psalm 80:8), and which Jesus uses to describe the relationship between himself and his disciples, for they are branches of the central vine.

Isaiah 5 speaks of degeneration and barrenness in the vine which was expected to bear fruit, and in contrast Jesus speak of himself as the 'true vine'. What Jesus is saying is that no establishment or religious legalism and regulations can communicate life: only vital, abiding fellowship with Jesus can do that. As the sap flows through the vine and into the branches, promoting sustenance and fruitfulness, so the Holy Spirit flows from the life-giving Jesus into the lives of those who live in his fellowship. 'Abiding' is the key word. The branch does not have to sweat and strive, as if it were independent of the parent vine. Jesus makes it clear: 'Apart from me you can do nothing.' All the branch has to do is to abide, allowing the sap to flow, and the natural outcome will be that in the course of time, fruit will appear.

Jesus desires the pattern of his life to be our example, allowing his mystical life to be manifested in our body, mind and spirit. This is brought about by fellowship around word and sacrament, and by developing a contemplative life of prayer that will be the mainspring of a compassionate life in the world. He goes on to speak of stages in fruit-bearing: fruit (v. 2), more fruit (v. 2) and much fruit (vv. 5, 8), and this is brought about by disciplined pruning. Elsewhere Jesus speaks of fruitfulness in terms of thirtyfold, sixtyfold and a hundredfold (Mark 4:8). Such disciplined pruning is carried out by the vinegrower. The Father cuts away all that is unproductive and unloving in our lives, so that our fruitfulness may bring joyful fulfilment to us, and glory to him.

BROTHER RAMON SSF, FORMERLY FRANCISCAN FRIAR AND AUTHOR

Christian behaviour

Humble yourselves, therefore, under God's mighty hand, that he may lift you up in due time. Cast all your anxiety on him because he cares for you. Be alert and of sober mind. Your enemy the devil prowls around like a roaring lion looking for someone to devour. Resist him, standing firm in the faith, because you know that the family of believers throughout the world is undergoing the same kind of sufferings. And the God of all grace, who called you to his eternal glory in Christ, after you have suffered a little while, will himself restore you and make you strong, firm and steadfast. To him be the power for ever and ever. Amen... Greet one another with a kiss of love. Peace to all of you who are in Christ.

1 PETER 5:6–11, 14 (NIV)

These verses deserve to be read over and over again for at least two reasons. They contain wise advice for every Christian and they communicate with power the care with which Peter prayed for and nurtured fellow Christians – particularly those in any kind of leadership role.

Peter was well aware that Christian leadership is both demanding and a privilege. The demands are not merely draining but also often give rise to feelings of anxiety. Wisely, he points out that God is bigger than the challenges that face leaders. What is more, no leader is called to do God's work in God's way without God's support. God cares for and equips every person he has called into ministry.

Peter was also well aware that Satan takes a special interest in Christian leaders. He therefore gives leaders three challenges: to stand firm in their faith, resist the enemy and recall that Christians worldwide face similar attacks.

Many Christians long to pray for the leaders of their church or fellowship, but fail to do so because they are unaware of their needs. One powerful way to overcome this problem is to pray a 'holding prayer' for such people. To do this, we simply come into the presence of God and imagine that we are holding the needs of our leaders in our hands. We raise those hands up to God – not necessarily saying anything, but recognising that God knows, understands and will not only hear our prayers but also act in the way that is best.

JOYCE HUGGETT, FORMERLY COUNSELLOR, SPIRITUAL DIRECTOR AND AUTHOR

Differences need not divide

How good and pleasant it is when God's people live together in unity! It is like precious oil poured on the head, running down on the beard, running down on Aaron's beard, down on the collar of his robe. It is as if the dew of Hermon were falling on Mount Zion. For there the Lord bestows his blessing, even life forevermore.

PSALM 133 (NIV)

The precious and expensive oil of priestly anointing was used without sparing. The dew of Mount Hermon saturates the ground. When people – families, fellowships, groups of friends – meet and share God's love there is a sense of his abundant provision. Differences do not divide, but add to the occasion. Unity comes as we rejoice in what he has done in our individual lives and for us as a body.

At times of national rejoicing, differences of politics, faith or economic standing fall away. A church building project is completed or we gather to pray for a group going off on a mission – and we are one in purpose, earlier differences forgotten. On special family occasions our attention is on those getting married or whose birthday it is or whose death we mourn, and past quarrels are of no consequence.

That, of course, is the ideal, but if we do not believe it can happen, we may be sure it will not. It is imperative that we learn to rejoice in difference, forgiving and being forgiven, and show the world that God does provide, pointing to him and not in accusation at each other.

I remember once asking a 17-year-old student what she was doing on Christmas Day. Perhaps I should have known better. Her mother regularly takes off and leaves her and her younger brother without food or money. She said she would probably be alone – 'I don't think my mother will be there.'

I spend Christmas each year with family and friends and I am reminded that those of us who have the opportunity of togetherness in Christ and of sharing his love must realise how blessed we are and cover our differences with love. It is 'there' in his will, which is Mount Zion, that he gives us his blessing which will overflow – like the oil – to those in need.

ANNE ROBERTS, FREELANCE WRITER, LOCAL PREACHER AND CHURCH ADMINISTRATOR

Trusting

Likewise the Spirit helps us in our weakness; for we do not know how to pray as we ought, but the Spirit himself intercedes for us with sighs too deep for words. And he who searches the hearts of men knows what is the mind of the Spirit, because the Spirit intercedes for the saints according to the will of God. We know that in everything God works for good with those who love him, who are called according to his purpose.

ROMANS 8:26–28 (RSV)

Often we spend a great deal of time outlining to God what is best for the world. Telling him how things are and how they should work and how we feel. As if he doesn't know already!

A glance at the psalms always reminds me that it's when we are in the depths of despair that our conversation with God becomes most real. (For examples, see Psalm 22 or Psalm 69.) Pain cannot be 'dressed up' in pious platitudes or quaint traditional phrases. When a person is hurting, all they feel is the hurt. 'Help!' says it all, when things are so bad that there is nothing left to be said. There is no greater tutor of prayer than pain, whether physical or emotional. It brings our agendas to a silent halt and enables us to open our hearts and lives to the mastery of God's spirit. But are our inarticulate stabs at communication with an almighty God who is in control all we have to rely upon? Paul highlights grounds for hope.

The Holy Spirit knows how to pray, even when we do not. Maybe we should spend less time wrestling with words and more time listening to him as the Spirit quietly and powerfully brings to the Saviour everything we would have said if only we had known how, 'with sighs too deep for words'. 'Trust' is being still and believing that God's agenda is moving towards the very best for us – regardless of the external evidence of our present circumstances. He will not refuse to enter into them with us, because he has plans for us; plans designed with one single motivation – unconditional love. Even standing still in trust is a movement forward in his will.

HILARY McDOWELL, FORMERLY DRAMATIST, WRITER AND BROADCASTER

The privilege of prayer

And this is the boldness we have in him, that if we ask anything according to his will, he hears us. And if we know that he hears us in whatever we ask, we know that we have obtained the requests made of him.

1 JOHN 5:14–15 (NRSV)

I wonder if we realise fully the tremendous privilege we have in prayer.

What a privilege, first of all, to be able to come before a holy, almighty, creator God, king of the universe, and have direct access into his presence through the blood of Christ, and call him 'Father'.

What a privilege to be able to adore him, praise him, worship him, thank him for who he is and for what he has done.

What a privilege to confess our sins to him, knowing that we can count on his mercy and forgiveness and cleansing.

What a privilege to be able to come before him with our needs, knowing that he is interested in them and will supply them and satisfy them 'according to his riches in glory in Christ Jesus' (Philippians 4:19), because he loves us and cares for us.

What a privilege, too, to bring before him the needs of others, to intercede on their behalf. What a privilege to be prayed for, to know that others are interceding for us.

What a privilege to be able to come at any time and know that God is listening and will hear our prayers.

What a privilege to come before him in silence and solitude and spend long moments in his presence in worship, praise, adoration, thanksgiving, confession, supplication and intercession, and just commune with him.

What a privilege to be able to come during the hustle and bustle, the noise and busyness of life and cry out to him in that secret place.

What a privilege to pray with others, to encourage them and be encouraged, knowing that the Lord has promised to be present with us, to hear and answer our prayers.

Let us avail ourselves of this great privilege!

BERYL ADAMSBAUM, WRITER, TEACHER, TRANSLATOR AND COUNSELLOR

Celebrating safety

**My heart, O God, is steadfast, my heart is steadfast; I will sing and make music…
I will praise you, Lord, among the nations; I will sing of you among the peoples.**

PSALM 57:7, 9 (NIV)

A psalm of praise and adoration, celebrating the immensity of God's power and glory. Written by David himself. Full of the sort of confidence you would expect from God's anointed.

What you just might not have noticed is the context of this song of praise. The Hebrew title is 'A psalm by David, after he fled from Saul in the cave'. These confident words follow David's desperate plea to God to hold him safe in the shadow of his wings until the raging storms have passed. Storms of jealousy which, having wreaked havoc with Saul's sanity, have crashed into David's path like a tornado, sweeping all familiar landmarks away and hurling him into the wilderness. Apparent disaster for this young man, destined to be king, who until recently had held so much power and attracted so much popular support. But for David, whose worst enemy was never Saul but rather his own passions and ambitions, it proved to be literally God-sent as it threw him back into the arms of the Father who had cared for him so intimately when he was a boy.

None of us would ever ask to be thrown into the wilderness, our reputation in shreds, our integrity tarnished and our popularity spent, but what this wonderful song of praise reminds us is that God's constant love 'reaches the heavens; his faithfulness touches the skies' (v. 10). If today you know that you too have been storm-driven into the wilds, don't hide away from God – run towards him. He is the only rock big enough and strong enough to shelter you.

Dear Lord, let us celebrate your goodness, your strength and your glory, however blown about our lives feel today. Amen

BRIDGET PLASS, AUTHOR AND SPEAKER

Grief turned to joy

[Jesus said] 'In a little while you will see me no more, and then after a little while you will see me. Very truly I tell you, you will weep and mourn while the world rejoices. You will grieve, but your grief will turn to joy.'

JOHN 16:19b–20 (NIV)

It is easy to imagine the fear and consternation that these words struck in the hearts of Jesus' followers. For two whole years, he had been at the centre of their lives, and they had probably come to trust him with everything.

Like all Jewish people, they had great hopes for the future when their triumphant Messiah would take up the reins of power. They had already seen Jesus heal the sick, walk on water and gather enormous enthusiastic crowds around him, but now suddenly he would be snatched away from them to be crucified – the most terrifying of all Roman executions. Every day he had led and guided them, but – now in his own words – he was going to a 'place where they could not follow', leaving them fearful for their own lives and full of unanswered questions.

For anyone who has ever lost a loved one, these words may ring horribly true. However strong our faith, there may well be moments when we are driven to wonder whether the promise of eternal life can really be true. Like the disciples hiding away behind closed doors, when loved ones have left us we too may feel lost, abandoned, even hopeless. Is it really possible that this terrible grief we are experiencing could ever be 'turned to joy'? Is the heaven we trust in a reality or just an impossible dream?

C.S. Lewis once said, 'Joy is the serious business of heaven.'

Heavenly Father, please help me to trust you with the promise that our grief will be turned to joy when we see you in heaven. And give us the eyes of faith to trust our loved ones to you, in the certain knowledge that we shall meet again in heaven.

ANN WARREN, FREELANCE WRITER, COUNSELLOR AND ARTIST

Deborah the prophetess

At that time Deborah, a prophetess, wife of Lappidoth, was judging Israel...
She sent and summoned Barak son of Abinoam... and said to him, 'The Lord,
the God of Israel, commands you, "Go, take position at Mount Tabor... I will
draw out Sisera... and I will give him into your hand."' Barak said to her, 'If you
will go with me, I will go'.

JUDGES 4:4–8 (NRSV, abridged)

Deborah appears without preamble in the pages of the Hebrew scriptures. She
is an unexpected presence, the fourth of Israel's judges and the only woman
to have filled that role.

When we meet her on this occasion, she is setting out the battle plan that
will ensure the defeat of Sisera, an enemy of her people who has 900 iron
chariots at his disposal. Barak does not question Deborah's leadership or
judgement. He asks her to accompany him on the mission, which he does
perhaps because he feels that this will increase his chances of survival. We are
given no privileged insight into Deborah's mind, but we get the impression of
a woman with considerable knowledge, wisdom and skill, who calmly faces
the task set before her and efficiently takes it in hand.

Deborah's leadership was exercised within the social constraints of her
time. As a woman, she could not appropriately hold court under her own
roof, so she sat 'under the palm of Deborah... and the Israelites came up to
her for judgement' (v. 5). She has been praised for her impressive gravitas as a
female leader in a male world and, conversely, criticised for a leadership style
that is stereotypically male. Female leaders of today are in good company!

Whether we are pioneers because of our gender, ethnicity, sexuality, age
or social background, being 'the first' carries considerable challenges. We are
swept up in other people's expectations and projections and have to face our
own insecurities. In all of this, may we, like Deborah, find ways in which we
can feel comfortable in our own skin.

You are called to be yourself, not someone else. Each of us reflects God
uniquely in the world. Remember this, as you learn to be more fully and more
comfortably the person God has created you to be.

ROSEMARY LAIN-PRIESTLEY, PRIEST AND AUTHOR

Do not settle for less

Terah was the father of Abram, Nahor, and Haran; and Haran was the father of Lot. Haran died before his father Terah in the land of his birth, in Ur of the Chaldeans… Terah took his son Abram and his grandson Lot son of Haran, and his daughter-in-law Sarai, his son Abram's wife, and they went out together from Ur of the Chaldeans to go into the land of Canaan; but when they came to Haran, they settled there. The days of Terah were two hundred and five years; and Terah died in Haran. Now the Lord said to Abram, 'Go from your country and your kindred and your father's house to the land that I will show you.'

GENESIS 11:27a–28; 11:31—12:1 (NRSV)

The calling of Abraham (as Abram became known) is one of the most famous Bible passages. If you start at Genesis 12, you gain the impression of a dramatic conversion – as if God called Abraham out of stability into a nomadic journey. Wind back a little, though, and you find that this is not quite the case; the search for the promised land had already begun.

Abraham's story belongs to a time of migrations in the Near East. He spent his early adulthood on the move, heading for Canaan, but, halfway there, he made a brief stop in Haran that somehow stretched on. God's call, some years later, was not out of the blue. The death of his father opened the way for reassessment. Abraham heard God's call and continued the journey he began in his youth.

Dramatic conversions are unusual. For most of us, the catalysing moments of calling lead us to fulfil what lies undiscovered at the centre of our being. Perhaps it is something that was cut off by circumstances – discouraging teachers, broken relationships, loss of confidence, finances, domestic responsibilities and more.

God does not usually call us in the opposite direction from where we were headed, but the call often pulls us out of what we've settled for, reignites our dreams and puts us back in touch with a sense of vocation that got buried along the way.

MAGGI DAWN, MUSICIAN, AUTHOR AND THEOLOGIAN

The good shepherd

'The one who enters by the gate is the shepherd of the sheep. The gatekeeper opens the gate for him, and the sheep hear his voice. He calls his own sheep by name and leads them out. When he has brought out all his own, he goes ahead of them, and the sheep follow him because they know his voice. They will not follow a stranger, but they will run from him because they do not know the voice of strangers… I am the good shepherd. The good shepherd lays down his life for the sheep. The hired hand, who is not the shepherd and does not own the sheep, sees the wolf coming and leaves the sheep and runs away – and the wolf snatches them and scatters them. The hired hand runs away because a hired hand does not care for the sheep. I am the good shepherd.'

JOHN 10:2–5, 11–14a (NRSV)

Flocks in Israel were not driven from behind, but led by their shepherds, each using a unique call. Each flock would learn to recognise the voice of its shepherd and his call. At night, all flocks were corralled together in the communal village sheepfold. One shepherd would stand watch to protect them from predators and thieves and the other shepherds would go to their homes. Any thief, of course, would avoid the gate where the watchman was located and enter by climbing over the wall. The following morning, the shepherds would return and, after being recognised by the night watchman, would enter the fold to call out their flock and lead them to fresh pasture.

Based on this farming scene, Jesus tells truths about himself. His is the authentic voice of God and his flock will recognise his voice. He is the true shepherd, rather than a hired hand who does not care for the welfare of the flock. It is a story of the familiarity between Jesus and his followers. It also speaks of God protecting his people. It was the shepherd's job to protect the flock, to put his own life on the line for the sheep's welfare.

Do we recognise the voice and appreciate the loving care of Jesus the true shepherd?

NICK READ, PRIEST, DIRECTOR, THE BRIGHTSPACE FOUNDATION, AND AGRICULTURAL CHAPLAIN, HEREFORD DIOCESE

Praise when life is tough?

I will bless the Lord at all times; his praise shall continually be in my mouth. I will glory in the Lord; let the afflicted hear and rejoice. Glorify the Lord with me: let us exalt his name together.

PSALM 34:1–3 (NRSV)

At any time, on any day, some people in the world will be finding life pleasant, peaceful and joyful, while others are suffering pain, anxiety or fear. When life is enjoyable for us, we may find it relatively easy to praise God, but what about when it is tough? Here the psalmist sets us the example of praising God at all times. All times will include those days or periods in our lives when things are really hard – times of disappointment, illness, loss or drudgery. Can we honestly praise God under such circumstances?

We don't usually doubt the rightness of praising God when life is pleasant for us, but at those very times there will be others somewhere for whom it is tough. Is it still right for us to praise God then, even though others are having a hard time? Yes, it must be, because the reason for our praise is that God is actually good and loving and worthy of praise.

So what about when we are the ones who are suffering? What is different then? Our circumstances and feelings have changed, but the character of God has not changed. If he was worthy of praise before, he is still worthy of praise now, even if we cannot understand what he is doing (or not doing!).

When life feels tough we can be honest, not pretending to have feelings of enjoyment or happiness that we do not have. Yet it is still possible, though not always easy, to continue to affirm and trust in the goodness of God, who will one day bring us out of our present difficulty and draw good out of it for us (see Romans 8:28).

Gracious Father, when we find life tough, we are sometimes tempted to doubt your love or your power. Please help us not only to hang on to you at those times, but also to praise you in all circumstances, through Jesus Christ, our Lord. Amen

MOLLY DOW, AUTHOR, TRAINER AND SPIRITUAL DIRECTOR

The Bible and families

ONE GREAT STORY ARC of the Bible is family. The family of the patriarchs become the people of God, and then the Hebrew nation. This is a family that can trace its origins through blood ties, to which those Old Testament lists bear witness. It is a family of faith in the one true God, who longs to dwell in the midst of this family, as symbolised by tabernacle and temple.

Jesus was born into this family, as the gospel genealogies make clear; and, through his death and resurrection, membership is now open to all. This greater family is also related by blood, but in a different way; everyone in this family is a spiritual blood relation, connected to God through Christ.

Belonging to God's family both embraces and transcends our 'nuclear' families. In both cases, however, the love that holds them together is of God, 'from whom every family in heaven and on earth derives its name' (Ephesians 3:15, NIV). In this big family, godparents, older friends, guardians and those who live on their own all have a role in helping everyone to come to fullness of life. This is the family promised to Abraham – 'more numerous than the stars in the sky' (see Genesis 15:5). This is the family that is commanded to pass on the story of salvation to the next generation. This is the family that connects old and young in mutual blessing. This is the family for whom Christ died.

In the Bible, family isn't a narrow concept. It's multidimensional, inclusive and God-shaped. In this family we have many grandparents, multiple parents, a multitude of siblings and countless other relatives. At the same time, we are all children in this family, called to love one another and bear the family likeness, which was God's plan from the very beginning.

MARTYN PAYNE, FREELANCE WRITER AND TRAINER
AND FORMER BRF STAFF MEMBER

Pass it on

I am reminded of your sincere faith, which first lived in your grandmother Lois and in your mother Eunice and, I am persuaded, now lives in you also. For this reason I remind you to fan into flame the gift of God, which is in you through the laying on of my hands.

2 TIMOTHY 1:5–6 (NIV)

When my goddaughter was about 14, her church was going through a rough patch. There were internal conflicts and no young people left of her age. I asked why she continued to attend, when there were other churches close by with thriving youth ministries. She looked me in the eye and said very firmly, 'Because Granny says it makes a difference that I'm here.' Her grandmother's wisdom meant that my goddaughter didn't just 'go' to church: she knew she belonged there. Being part of the community of faith made a difference to her – and she made a difference to them.

Family plays an important part in helping children and young people grow and flourish in their relationship with God through Jesus. Seeing the generations living out their faith, talking about their faith, modelling what it means to be a follower of Jesus (however imperfect that walk might be) makes its mark on younger generations. Paul recognises the impact of Lois and Eunice on Timothy, the young man he had befriended, mentored and seen grow as a leader. Timothy had been nurtured in faith by his family, and now he, still a young man, was nurturing others.

John Westerhoff, who wrote about and studied how faith grows, noted the importance of a sense of belonging, of being part of a community in which faith is lived out across the generations. Children and young people need the community of the church, which is wider than their kin family. I have no kin-children, but I have been blessed by being part of a wider faith family in which I am invited to play my part in befriending and nurturing younger generations, who in turn teach and challenge me in my faith.

Your presence in the community of faith makes a difference to children and young people like my goddaughter. The challenge to us as adults is how we might allow them to make a difference to us.

MARY HAWES, NATIONAL CHILDREN AND YOUTH ADVISER, CHURCH OF ENGLAND, AND ASSISTANT PRIEST, ST MARY WITH ST ALBAN, TEDDINGTON

God-talk in the home

These are the commands, decrees and laws the Lord your God directed me to teach you to observe in the land that you are crossing the Jordan to possess, so that you, your children and their children after them may fear the Lord your God as long as you live by keeping all his decrees and commands that I give you, and so that you may enjoy long life... These commandments that I give you today are to be on your hearts. Impress them on your children. Talk about them when you sit at home and when you walk along the road, when you lie down and when you get up.

DEUTERONOMY 6:1–2, 6–7 (NIV)

Here's Moses, the great leader, speaking God's words to the people of Israel before they enter the promised land. Moses is very old and knows that he won't be going with them. So now is the time to teach them God's commandments. 'This is how you are to live in the land that God has given you,' he says. 'Not just you,' he adds, 'but all the generations to come.'

Our short extract from Deuteronomy doesn't look at what Moses' hearers are supposed to do and not do. Instead, it focuses on the 'how' – how are the people to relate to God's decrees and laws? We learn from Moses that they are to internalise God's commandments, so that they become second nature. They must immerse themselves in God's word. They should talk about his laws and teach them to their children.

How should we, in our very different context, respond to this teaching? Could God be saying to us that our homes must be places where God's words are ever-present in the everyday of family life – on the school run, at mealtimes, in the bath, in the supermarket queue?

If you have children or grandchildren, you might wonder whether the word 'impress' could seem a little heavy-handed for this generation. But it does convey the urgency and importance of making our homes places where God-talk is natural and frequent. Research tells us that time spent at home is much more influential on children than time spent at church, however good the teaching on Sundays might be. BRF's Parenting for Faith resources are a great place to look for encouragement and support!

BILL LATTIMER, BRF SUPPORTER

Letting go, trusting God

If the Lord doesn't build the house, the builders are working for nothing. If the Lord doesn't guard the city, the guards are watching for nothing. It is no use for you to get up early and stay up late, working for a living. The Lord gives sleep to those he loves. Children are a gift from the Lord; babies are a reward. Children who are born to a young man are like arrows in the hand of a warrior.

PSALM 127:1–4 (NCV)

Have you ever lain awake, tossing and turning, worrying about your family or your work? It's easy to feel overwhelmed and, for many of us, our response is to work harder and try harder – to rely on ourselves more. This psalm is a beautiful reminder that we don't need to. In fact, we shouldn't. We need to learn to lay those things down and stop trying to do it in our own strength.

God sees the big picture in a way that we never can. If we trust and rely on him, we can be free from that cycle of endless worry and hard work. It's not easy, but as we learn to step back, pause and ask God what to focus our time and attention on, he will guide us.

So what's stopping us? Often the challenge is laying down our 'right' to do it our way – our sense of independence and self-sufficiency. Today, let's start with a small prayer – 'Lord, I want to trust you and rely on you, not on myself. Show me how.'

Raising children can feel like a demanding and thankless task. But again, God sees the big picture. They are to be treasured, nurtured and enjoyed. He knows how powerful and important they are, both now and in the future, and wants to remind us of that. He sees their true value and worth, which can be easy for us to miss when we're buried in the daily tasks of caring for them. But nothing that we do for them is wasted. It's all part of preparing them for the adventure of life and getting to meet and know God along the way. If you have children in your life, let's thank God for them and trust him with them today.

ANNA HAWKEN, PARENTING FOR FAITH NATIONAL COORDINATOR, BRF

Commitment to family and relatives

Honour widows who are really widows. If a widow has children or grand-children, they should first learn their religious duty to their own family and make some repayment to their parents; for this is pleasing in God's sight... Give these commands as well, so that they may be above reproach. And whoever does not provide for relatives, and especially for family members, has denied the faith and is worse than an unbeliever.

1 TIMOTHY 5:3–4, 7–8 (NRSV)

These emphatic words, written in the first of two pastoral letters by Paul to his loyal follower Timothy, offered practical encouragement as Timothy took on the challenge of managing the growing church in Ephesus by demonstrating a model Christian life. In the absence of state care, benefits or pensions, Paul recognised that family was key to the well-being of the vulnerable.

Over 140 years ago, Mary Sumner founded the Mothers' Union. Her radical plan called on women from all walks of life to support one another and to recognise parenthood as one of the most important tasks. This organisation now works around the world to provide Christian care for families, seeking to address injustices that affect women and families. In Britain, the Children Act of 1989 championed the rights of children, and subsequent safeguarding legislation provides protection for vulnerable children and adults where care fails.

Many problems within the early church persist today. A steep rise in domestic abuse within families during the coronavirus pandemic has brought into sharp focus and reminds us of the stresses and strains on family life.

Paul also set out detailed guidelines for the care of widows. At the United Nations Commission on the Status of Women, I was shocked to hear first-hand stories of discrimination against widows in many cultures and countries today. The loss of a partner is devastating enough, but in addition to this many can be denied their inheritance, lose their home, be stigmatised and cut off from family support, forced into prostitution or extreme poverty. Such injustices need to be aired and addressed.

We need to love and care for our relatives, especially our own families, and to constantly pray that God will be with them in every part of their lives.

ROSEMARY KEMPSELL, FORMER WORLDWIDE PRESIDENT, MOTHERS' UNION

Missing women

[The daughters of Zelophehad said,] 'Our father died in the wilderness. He was not among Korah's followers, who banded together against the Lord, but he died for his own sin and left no sons. Why should our father's name disappear from his clan because he had no son? Give us property among our father's relatives.' So Moses brought their case before the Lord, and the Lord said to him, 'What Zelophehad's daughters are saying is right. You must certainly give them property as an inheritance among their father's relatives and give their father's inheritance to them. Say to the Israelites, "If a man dies and leaves no son, give his inheritance to his daughter."'

NUMBERS 27:3–8 (NIV)

In 2017, I decided that for a full year I would speed read the Bible and only stop to read in detail the passages which dealt with women. It was a year of revelation. Hitherto, like many of my generation, I had been brought up with the impression that women in the Bible were either chaste maidens or moral reprobates. It had never dawned on me that women might have been faithful advocates for God's justice.

But such are the women in this story. Zelophehad died leaving no sons – but five daughters. According to the law, they could not inherit their father's property on account of being female. The law required that in the absence of sons, a dead man's property be transferred to his brothers, which would have made these five girls dependent on their uncles. They petitioned Moses regarding this injustice, and Moses took it to the Lord in prayer, resulting in the perhaps unexpected answer from God: change the law.

As well as the daughters of Zelophehad, there are tens of other women in the Hebrew scriptures whose stories are largely untold, perhaps because in the case of Abigail, Rizpah, Esther, Hagar, Shiphrah and Puah (to name but a few), their faith in God and their witness to God's justice stand in stark contrast to the presumptuousness and arrogance of men. Indeed, when it comes to the gospels, I find it hard to think of one example of Jesus being in mixed company where the women do not give the men a showing-up.

Is that the reason why so many women's stories have been absent in Christian teaching? I suggest from experience that unless we acknowledge this imbalance, we may have a limited understanding of God's grace and our own vocation.

JOHN L. BELL, MEMBER, IONA COMMUNITY

All together

Children, obey your parents in the Lord, for this is right. 'Honour your father and mother'– which is the first commandment with a promise – 'so that it may go well with you and that you may enjoy long life on the earth.' Fathers, do not exasperate your children; instead, bring them up in the training and instruction of the Lord. Slaves, obey your earthly masters with respect and fear, and with sincerity of heart, just as you would obey Christ. Obey them not only to win their favour when their eye is on you, but as slaves of Christ, doing the will of God from your heart... And masters, treat your slaves in the same way. Do not threaten them, since you know that he who is both their Master and yours is in heaven, and there is no favouritism with him.

EPHESIANS 6:1–6, 9 (NIV)

These verses come into a broader conversation Paul is having about living holy and right lives. He addresses all individuals and then narrows in on specific groups: wives and husbands, children and parents, slaves and masters.

What strikes me so strongly is that he speaks directly to these groups. The book of Ephesians originally was a letter from Paul to his friends in small churches all around Ephesus. He expected these letters to be read personally and out loud in groups. He anticipated that people would share them from little house church to little house church.

So when he addresses women and men, children and slaves, it is because he expected them to be in the room. In a society that separated women from men and gave no rights to children or slaves, Paul expected that all these people would be in a room together – learning together, listening together, praying together and caring for each other.

I am struck by how often our children are separated from the adults, in their own children's groups, doing their own activities. While age-specific teaching has its strengths, I think it also can become a great weakness. There is something special about hearing the word of God together. There is something profound about hearing God's truth from each other and worshipping alongside each other. Paul expected that the children would be in the room. Do we?

RACHEL TURNER, PARENTING FOR FAITH PIONEER, BRF

Everyday giants of the faith

By faith Abraham, when called to go to a place he would later receive as his inheritance, obeyed and went, even though he did not know where he was going. By faith he made his home in the promised land like a stranger in a foreign country; he lived in tents, as did Isaac and Jacob, who were heirs with him of the same promise... And so from this one man, and he as good as dead, came descendants as numerous as the stars in the sky and as countless as the sand on the seashore.

HEBREWS 11:8–9, 12 (NIV)

How we long for our lives to achieve great things for God! We'd love to know that, in some small way, we managed to make a difference for God's kingdom. Maybe you have dreams of things you'd like to achieve for God. Maybe you feel the tug of a call on your life or you see a need you want to fill.

In Hebrews 11, the writer is encouraging his readers to look at the giants of the faith. Whatever life threw at them, they persisted, holding on to their faith and achieving what God had for them to do.

And isn't that what we want? It's easy to feel that we're not good enough or courageous enough, or to find that life just gets in the way. The pull of work, the responsibilities of caring, the busyness of family or simply our own frailties can sap our time and our energy, leaving us feeling like we've failed God.

But it's easy to read Hebrews 11 and miss the real story. 'Look at Abraham,' this passage seems to say. 'Look at Abraham and his model family. What an achievement for God! From them came the whole family of God that we are part of today.' A little dig into scripture, however, tells a different story. Abraham and his family were thoroughly dysfunctional. Genesis contains a tale of mistresses, lies, jealousy, quarrels, betrayal, abandonment, favouritism... but within all this, faith.

Faith is designed to work in and through real life. It's not about getting life sorted and then doing what God has planned for us. It's about muddling through, our eyes fixed on Jesus, and doing what we can. It works, because that's how God designed it to work. Your ordinary, messy, less-than-perfect life is exactly what God can work with to make a difference in the world.

BECKY SEDGWICK, PARENTING FOR FAITH LOCAL COORDINATOR, BRF

A heart in the right place

'Surely the day is coming; it will burn like a furnace. All the arrogant and every evildoer will be stubble, and that day that is coming will set them on fire,' says the Lord Almighty. 'Not a root or a branch will be left to them. But for you who revere my name, the sun of righteousness will rise with healing in its rays... See, I will send the prophet Elijah to you before that great and dreadful day of the Lord comes. He will turn the hearts of the parents to their children, and the hearts of the children to their parents; or else I will come and strike the land with total destruction.'

MALACHI 4:1–2, 5–6 (NIV)

This passage sounds threatening, yet at its core lies a beautiful sentiment – the hearts of parents and their children turning to one another. A turning heart conjures up images of a relationship strengthening and love deepening, and so it is clear that how parents and children get along with each other is important to God. But what does a turning heart look like?

If we think of a turning heart in the context of a romantic relationship, it manifests itself by wanting to spend time with the object of our affection. We think about the person often. We are interested in that person's life and want to listen to them talk about themselves. We also want to tell them things about ourselves. We want to please them and make them happy. And we want them to know how special they are.

Parents may do the same kind of things for their children. There are no guarantees, but if we think about our children, spend time with them, talk and listen to them, encourage them and accept them, there is a greater chance that their hearts will remain (or become) turned to us too. These things are often easier to do at the start of a relationship, when the children are young, but they can become harder to maintain as the years roll by. A heart turned towards someone can quickly turn away again. A turned heart is not a one-off change in emotion. Rather, it is a continual battle of the will.

So it is good each day to consciously take these steps to ensure our hearts remain in the right place – in other words, turned to those we love.

MARK CHESTER, PARENTING MANAGER, CARE FOR THE FAMILY

Playing in the streets

A message came to me from the Lord who rules over all... 'I will live among my people in Jerusalem. Then Jerusalem will be called the Faithful City. And my mountain will be called the Holy Mountain... Once again old men and women will sit in the streets of Jerusalem. All of them will be using canes because they are old. The city streets will be filled with boys and girls. They will be playing there... All of that might seem hard to believe to the people living then. But it will not be too hard for me.'

ZECHARIAH 8:1–6 (NIRV, abridged)

What do you think heaven is like? What do you think the kingdom of God should look like on earth? Near the end of the Old Testament, the prophet Zechariah was given a glimpse of an answer to those questions. He was speaking to the Jewish exiles who had returned from Babylon and who were now back in their own land, in the rebuilt city of Jerusalem. It was, however, a shadow of its former glory, so God promises them a better future for the end times. And that vision of heaven on earth is an intergenerational one, where the youngest and the oldest are together, sitting and playing safely with God in their midst.

This is what holiness looks like; this is how a faith-filled community can be recognised. In God's kingdom, the old are not marginalised because they are economically unproductive, nor are the young patronised for their playfulness; instead, they are both comfortably present with each other in the New Jerusalem.

We are in the end times, since the death and resurrection of Jesus. This vision is for us to work out right now, so that our churches become signs of the presence of God's kingdom. However, where churches have siloed off the generations for teaching and worship, this vision is in danger of being lost. Those who are older are best encouraged to be open to new things by the stimulating presence of children, whose curiosity is endless. And those who are younger are best helped to discover wisdom through the reassuring presence and experience of the elderly.

I wonder how your church community is actively pursuing this vision of heaven on earth. I wonder how these marks of the kingdom can be realised between the generations in our time.

MARTYN PAYNE, FREELANCE WRITER AND TRAINER AND FORMER BRF STAFF MEMBER

Setting the lonely in families

Sing to God, sing in praise of his name, extol him who rides on the clouds; rejoice before him – his name is the Lord. A father to the fatherless, a defender of widows, is God in his holy dwelling. God sets the lonely in families, he leads out the prisoners with singing; but the rebellious live in a sun-scorched land. When you, God, went out before your people, when you marched through the wilderness, the earth shook, the heavens poured down rain, before God, the One of Sinai, before God, the God of Israel. You gave abundant showers, O God; you refreshed your weary inheritance. Your people settled in it, and from your bounty, God, you provided for the poor.

PSALM 68:4–10 (NIV)

Families come in all sorts of shapes and sizes. The Bible honours families with no children and many children, blended and multigenerational families, single people who care for children and young people who care for older relatives. In this passage, God talks about how those without families can find one.

God loves everyone on the planet. But he often makes special mention of the fatherless and the widow. This is not because God thinks they are more valuable, but because they are more vulnerable. In the ancient world, a child growing up without the care and protection of a father often faced extreme difficulties. Some translations call them orphans. Similarly widows in a patri-archal society were often unable to earn money or protect themselves.

Widows and orphans might have been overlooked by the system, the authorities and by most other people in the community, but God is not too important to step up to help them. He will defend them. He will call families to embrace them as one of their own. There is nothing more godly than to look out for the needs of the vulnerable. This is underlined in James 1:27: 'Religion that God our Father accepts as pure and faultless is this: to look after orphans and widows in their distress.'

I wonder if God wants to set a lonely person in your family? Perhaps you could welcome a child that needs fostering or adoption, or an older person who needs care and protection, into your home.

KRISH KANDIAH, CONSULTANT, AUTHOR AND SPEAKER

Where is your treasure?

'Seek the Kingdom of God above all else, and he will give you everything you need… Sell your possessions and give to those in need. This will store up treasure for you in heaven! And the purses of heaven never get old or develop holes. Your treasure will be safe; no thief can steal it and no moth can destroy it. Wherever your treasure is, there the desires of your heart will also be.'

LUKE 12:31, 33–34 (NLT)

Families have endured intense new pressures throughout the course of the pandemic. Alongside health concerns, many have faced the agonising choice of putting a meal on the table or keeping a child warm and well dressed. How would these words of Jesus be received by them, when worrying about food and clothes is a very present experience?

Digging a little deeper, Jesus' words have so much to say here. It's not just about our own circumstances; our eyes are to be drawn to others, beyond our four walls, into neighbourhoods and communities. Seek God's kingdom, Jesus says, 'For where your treasure is, there your heart will also be.' If we cast our thoughts around the places we live, what needs are discovered? Do we respond by hoping God will simply take care of it or by noticing a call to action for ourselves?

Few of us missed the footballer Marcus Rashford's action taken in the face of child hunger and poverty, spurred on by the knowledge from his own experience that by not acting he'd be doing his community and the families he knew an injustice. He knew the need first-hand, powerfully using his status to influence and bring about profound change for those struggling in the face of so much hardship.

Life is indeed about more than clothes and food for ourselves. It's about ensuring our neighbour has those things too. It's about using what is within our own grasp and pocket to find ways to support families so that they have a sense of well-being and contentment. It's about joining in with campaigns and adding our voice to calls for change.

Let's play our part in God's kingdom, so that everyone, including the very youngest, no longer has to worry if they'll have enough to eat at the end of the day.

GAIL ADCOCK, AUTHOR AND CHILDREN, YOUTH AND FAMILY TEAM OFFICER,
THE METHODIST CHURCH

Grace, glory and epiphany

So do not be ashamed of the testimony about our Lord or of me his prisoner. Rather, join with me in suffering for the gospel, by the power of God. He has saved us and called us to a holy life – not because of anything we have done but because of his own purpose and grace. This grace was given us in Christ Jesus before the beginning of time, but it has now been revealed through the appearing of our Saviour, Christ Jesus, who has destroyed death and has brought life and immortality to light through the gospel.

2 TIMOTHY 1:8–10 (NIV)

Stuck in prison, and probably with a death sentence hanging over him, Paul could easily have lost heart. But 2 Timothy, possibly the final letter that he wrote, is in so many ways forward-looking. For himself, Paul looks forward to finishing the race. He expects to continue suffering for the sake of the gospel and then to receive the crown of righteousness prepared for him by the Lord himself – not because of anything he has done or merited but as an act of huge divine generosity. For Timothy, he looks primarily to the future and to the role he needs to play in leading God's church, and to remaining steadfast despite the pressures that will come.

But in looking to the future, Paul also looks to the past and to the bedrock of faith in Timothy's family that spanned three generations (Timothy himself, his mother Eunice and his grandmother Lois), a faith built on Jesus' appearing – his epiphany in his birth, life, death and resurrection. It's at that point that we can feel we have much in common with Timothy. Like him we have not met with Jesus in his earthly life, but the life that he lived here on earth is foundational for the Christian faith. As has often been said, 'Christianity is Christ', and everything flows from that.

In our own generation families remain a vital place for handing on our faith. But, as with Timothy, every person needs to make that faith their own. It is through this that they, too, come to share in the grace given in Christ Jesus before the beginning of time – the grace to savour like a cool drink on a dry and dusty day – as Paul did in his prison 20 centuries ago.

COLIN FLETCHER, BISHOP AND CHAIR OF TRUSTEES, BRF

Living a chosen life

Therefore, as God's chosen people, holy and dearly loved, clothe your-selves with compassion, kindness, humility, gentleness and patience. Bear with each other and forgive one another if any of you has a grievance against someone. Forgive as the Lord forgave you. And over all these virtues put on love, which binds them all together in perfect unity. Let the peace of Christ rule in your hearts, since as members of one body you were called to peace. And be thankful.

COLOSSIANS 3:12–15 (NIV)

Can you remember being given a key piece of advice that has helped you in life? Here Paul shares some important life guidance for us as individuals, families, friends and as members of our wider community.

First, he speaks words that affirm and encourage us. We are to recognise that we are chosen, holy and dearly loved. Maybe we know and feel that to be true, or maybe for some reason we find it hard to grasp sometimes. During the course of our lives, we can take knocks and feel disappointed or frustrated with ourselves, but we are chosen and loved unconditionally.

Paul then goes on to outline some key principles for daily life. The values he shares are key to our engagement with others, and are sometimes inter-connected. Compassion may be seen in an act of kindness; humility can be present with patience when encouraging someone to achieve something that we could do more quickly ourselves. It potentially becomes more challeng-ing as we are called to bear with one another, testing our patience further, to accept other people's quirks, to forgive when we are hurting and then to cover all of this with love. It can take time to do these things, and we all need help from others walking alongside, but in pursuing this we can grow in our own faith.

Verse 15 brings this message together as we seek to live in peace with everyone as 'members of one body'. It takes us beyond our family and friends to a wider community. In valuing all people, we gain a deeper relationship with one another and with God. So, these verses, while few, teach us much that can enhance our daily lives and bring honour to God.

JANE BUTCHER, VOLUNTEER ADVOCATE LEAD, BRF

Nothing to prove

What, then, shall we say in response to these things? If God is for us, who can be against us? He who did not spare his own Son, but gave him up for us all – how will he not also, along with him, graciously give us all things? Who will bring any charge against those whom God has chosen? It is God who justifies. Who then is the one who condemns? No one.

ROMANS 8:31–34a (NIV)

I have sometimes asked audiences, 'What is the greatest gift a parent can give a child?' All over the world people give the same answer: 'Love.' They are right, but there is another gift, and if this gift is not given first, a child will never believe they are loved. It is the gift of *acceptance*. In one of my school reports, my form teacher wrote, 'He is making no use of what little ability he has.' I have sometimes been afraid that God is like my form teacher:

Prayer: Weak. Robert tries hard to pray, but often he just doesn't know what to say and lets his mind wander.

Personal witnessing: Poor. Robert's attempts to turn bus-stop conversations around to the second coming are embarrassing.

Theological knowledge: Patchy. He still can't really explain the problem of suffering.

But God isn't like that. He isn't itching to write 'Could do better' over my life.

In these verses, the apostle Paul says that God is *for* me: he is on my side. Sometimes I wake too early, when it's still dark, and a voice whispers in my ear: 'If people really knew you, they wouldn't come to hear you speak or buy your books. You're a bit of a hypocrite, Rob. You don't pray enough, read the Bible enough...'

But then, so often, I hear a voice in my other ear: 'I know you. I know you better than you know yourself. I'm not as impressed with the books and speaking events as you appear to be, but I still love you. Nothing you do can make me love you more; nothing you do can make me love you less.'

I am not only loved; I am accepted. In a world that judges us by how we look, what we achieve or what we own, here is somebody who loves me – *anyway*. With him, there is nothing to prove: God is for me.

ROB PARSONS, FOUNDER AND CHAIRMAN, CARE FOR THE FAMILY

The Bible and old age

T HE BELIEF that our later years can be a time of flourishing runs like a golden thread through these reflections. That flourishing may not be physical, but it is real and true. As Catriona Foster writes: 'I love the fact that no matter what outward wasting away there may be, there can still be daily, unseen renewal.'

Carl Knightly takes up the theme: 'Whatever our age, as we serve the Lord, we will bear fruit and remain fresh.'

Another of our writers, Erica Roberts, has founded a charity, Caraway, based on the same conviction. In Isaiah 28, the caraway seed is harvested not by a threshing wheel or a cart, but by hand, with sticks – showing that beautiful herbs which add spice to life can be harvested by anyone at any season of life, even if they're frail and vulnerable.

Human flourishing is a key interest of one of the country's leading thinkers on ageing, James Woodward, Principal of Sarum College. Interviewing James for BRF's *Bible Reflections for Older People*, I asked what 'flourishing' means to him. 'It's about feeling that one's life has been, at least in part, worthwhile,' he said. 'My value doesn't depend on my mental powers… or being able to run about as I might once have done. There is instead a cherishing of the soul and the spirit and the heart… a rejoicing in the world around you, and the feeling that you've done as much as you can to leave the world a little better a place.'

ELEY McAINSH, PRESS AND MEDIA OFFICER, BRF,
AND EDITOR, *BIBLE REFLECTIONS FOR OLDER PEOPLE*

Hearing God's word

Eli, whose eyesight had begun to grow dim… was lying down in his room… Samuel was lying down in the temple of the Lord… Then the Lord called 'Samuel! Samuel!' and he said, 'Here I am!' and ran to Eli… He said 'I did not call; lie down again'… The Lord called again, 'Samuel!' Samuel got up and went to Eli… Now Samuel did not yet know the Lord, and the word of the Lord had not yet been revealed to him. The Lord called Samuel again a third time… Then Eli perceived that the Lord was calling the boy.

1 SAMUEL 3:2–8 (NRSV, abridged)

Eli, who was 'priest of the Lord' at the temple in Shiloh, had been a significant and influential figure. Shiloh was the central Israelite shrine where the ark of the covenant was kept, and Eli was its guardian. But he was growing old and losing his grip. Not only was he half-blind in a physical sense, but his moral authority and spiritual awareness were also waning, as his two sons, Hophni and Phinehas, behaved in ways which seriously undermined both their and his reputations as priests.

Yet in this vivid story, God uses the elderly Eli to advise and guide a young, inexperienced Samuel. Without Eli, Samuel would not have realised that God was speaking to him – and the whole future course of his life and ministry might have been different. How reassuring for those of us who are getting on a bit! Even when we're feeling rather useless and spiritually sidelined, God can still take the experience we have acquired over the years and deploy it so that others can hear his word to them – and in particular, his call on their lives.

But there's a challenge in this passage too. In the first place, Samuel has to listen to Eli in order to discover what is going on. Listening properly to Eli goes before listening in such a way that he can hear God. By the same token, Eli has to listen to Samuel so as to 'perceive' that 'the Lord was calling the boy'. Then, later in the story, Eli has to listen again to the message Samuel has received from God. It wasn't a message Eli wanted to hear; but just as Samuel heard the Lord, so too did his mentor. Young and old together, they needed each other: as, today, do we.

JAMES NEWCOME, BISHOP OF CARLISLE

Outrageous old age

Noah, a man of the soil, was the first to plant a vineyard. He drank some of the wine and became drunk, and he lay uncovered in his tent. And Ham, the father of Canaan, saw the nakedness of his father, and told his two brothers outside. Then Shem and Japheth took a garment, laid it on both their shoulders, and walked backwards and covered the nakedness of their father; their faces were turned away, and they did not see their father's nakedness... After the flood Noah lived for three hundred and fifty years. All the days of Noah were nine hundred and fifty years; and he died.

GENESIS 9:20–23, 28–29 (NRSV)

As part of my curacy training, I spent a day at an open prison. Predictably many things opened my eyes, but the real surprise was that there were sufficient incarcerated OAPs for them to have a separate common room; many of the younger prisoners worked as carers for older inmates. I realised that my unconscious bias was to imagine older people in the sanitised images used in equity release and high-end care home advertisements.

The passage in Genesis, which recounts the 650-year-old Noah getting so drunk that he lies naked in his tent (a significant act of impurity), reminds us that older people face the same challenges as everyone else and can fail as spectacularly. The tendency of society to portray older people as sitting in high armchairs with a benign smile, or as Harold Steptoe-like disarming rogues, only serves to diminish them and the challenges they face.

To be properly present with older people, we need to accept that they grieve, face temptation, are understandably irritated or are simply tired out. They may not want to be 'marvellous for their age' but rather one of God's children with all the challenges and blessings that brings.

Some seek to break out of the box in which society would most conveniently like to park them by wearing purple or being deliberately outrageous, but that can get exhausting even for extroverts. So let us be open-hearted and love older people as they are, walking with them through the thistled and nettled paths of their lives, so that they can reach their destination at peace.

BRIAN DUNLOP, CHAIR OF TRUSTEES, CHELTENHAM AND BISHOP'S CLEEVE
ANNA CHAPLAINCY FOR OLDER PEOPLE

313

Seeing the unseen

Therefore we do not lose heart. Though outwardly we are wasting away, yet inwardly we are being renewed day by day. For our light and momentary troubles are achieving for us an eternal glory that far outweighs them all. So we fix our eyes not on what is seen, but on what is unseen, since what is seen is temporary, but what is unseen is eternal.

2 CORINTHIANS 4:16–18 (NIV)

If you look into the distance with reading glasses, the view is blurred. You can see close-up things clearly, but you cannot focus on the bigger picture.

Perhaps that's a bit like our tendency to focus only on what's going on for us in the here and now. And for many of us as we get older, that focus is often on physical aches and pains. Perhaps you experience first-hand the truth of Paul's statement, 'outwardly we are wasting away'? Often our own view, and that of society and the media, is that increasing age has a downward trajectory.

Today's passage reverses the view that 'it's all downhill from now on'. Something is happening within us that is moving in the opposite direction. We are reminded here that there is a whole other realm – a bigger picture – another story.

Somehow, in the weakness and struggles of the human condition, God is transforming us on the inside, growing an inner glory. This is a spiritual thing that is happening in the unseen realm, and it is great news even for people who are living with extreme physical or mental frailty. I love the thought that no matter what outward wasting away there may be, there can still be daily, unseen renewal.

We can choose to focus only on our present physical life and circumstances, or we can look beyond to things unseen and eternal. Take a moment to sense the wonder of this. Paul wanted his readers to be greatly encouraged and full to the brim with hope by the thought of something so much greater than the physical here and now, something 'beyond all measure... a vast and transcendent glory and blessedness never to cease!' (v. 17, AMPC). This is not just for the future – it's happening inside you now!

CATRIONA FOSTER, PASTOR FOR OLDER PEOPLE, ST JOHN'S CHURCH, HARBORNE

Your place in his story

Boaz took Ruth and she became his wife… and she gave birth to a son. The women said to Naomi: 'Praise be to the Lord, who this day has not left you without a guardian-redeemer… He will renew your life and sustain you in your old age. For your daughter-in-law, who loves you… has given him birth.' Then Naomi took the child in her arms and cared for him. The women living there said, 'Naomi has a son!' And they named him Obed. He was the father of Jesse, the father of David.

RUTH 4:13–17 (NIV, abridged)

Old age might seem a bleak prospect. Nothing to look forward to, no one to care for – or, to care for you – and not much money. Yet in God's story we find reminders of his faithful care, surprising provision and renewed life – even for those of us who are older.

Life hadn't been easy for Naomi. Escaping famine, she and her family had left Bethlehem as refugees. After her husband and two adult sons died, Naomi decided to return home. To her surprise, her foreign daughter-in-law, Ruth, wanted to go with her (1:14). Somehow Naomi's faithful living through the years had made an impression: 'Your God [will be] my God' (1:16). It turns out that both Naomi and Ruth have a very special place in God's story.

In those times, family and marriage were essential for a woman's economic survival. The 'guardian-redeemer' system provided for this (see Ruth 3—4). The nearest relative was expected to marry and care for a widow. So Boaz marries Ruth (even though she was only the foreign daughter-in-law) – and Naomi is provided for in her old age.

More than this, she becomes the carer and joyful step-grandmother of Ruth's baby. A miracle of God's provision has happened! This once-destitute older woman has a 'son', and a home in Bethlehem (1:19). Unknown to her, this baby would be special for the whole world – the grandfather of King David, the ancestor of the Messiah, Jesus (Matthew 1:5–6, 16). Without Naomi's faithfulness and trust, we wouldn't be reading this particular nativity story today.

Who knows what God has planned for our lives? Meanwhile, we too – whatever our circumstances – can trust his provision and purposes, even into our old age (v. 15). We also have a place in his story. Praise God for his blessings through your life!

'**TRICIA WILLIAMS,** AUTHOR, WRITER AND EDITOR OF BIBLE AND FAITH RESOURCES

Choose life

I call heaven and earth to record this day against you, that I have set before you life and death, blessing and cursing: therefore choose life, that both thou and thy seed may live: That thou mayest love the Lord thy God, and that thou mayest obey his voice, and that thou mayest cleave unto him: for he is thy life, and the length of thy days: that thou mayest dwell in the land which the Lord sware unto thy fathers, to Abraham, to Isaac, and to Jacob, to give them.

DEUTERONOMY 30:19–20 (KJV)

Although far from simple, we do well to be honest with ourselves: we are all prone to illusions or, worse, delusions. As we grow older, we discover that the nature of faith is such that it wavers: there are 'dry periods'; we take paths that turn out to be blind alleys; and we can easily lose our way. Despite the best of intentions, it is all too easy to be seduced away from daily observances, from acts that may be right as well as difficult, and from the path that God has chosen for us.

Of course, we know that it is human to compromise: we must be reasonable and not obsessed, we tell ourselves. After all, 'life is complex', and 'everything is relative'. But if we are not careful, soon we are in danger of being consumed by our own pride, of believing sin to be 'simple shortcomings', or worse, our 'lovable little idiosyncrasies'.

We all need some help with this. Here in Deuteronomy, the scalpel of scripture, while acknowledging our humanity, cuts all our potentially deadly complexities away, while the surgical retractor shows us instead a simple, stark, clear message: 'It's one thing or the other: life or death.' Cutting away the nonsense frees us for the growth vital to life: we have free will, we must exercise it and we must *choose*. Scripture here succinctly reminds us of our lineage and of the blessings of God's love, contrasting them with the inevitable 'cursings' we must sadly face in the darkness of everyday life. It emphasises whose we are, where we came from, our place in God's family and what our priorities should be: simply, to love God and to obey his voice.

DONALD MOWAT, RETIRED PSYCHIATRIST

Lifelong purpose and protection

Deliver me, my God, from the hand of the wicked, from the grasp of those who are evil and cruel. For you have been my hope, Sovereign Lord, my confidence since my youth. From birth I have relied on you; you brought me forth from my mother's womb. I will ever praise you... Since my youth, God, you have taught me, and to this day I declare your marvellous deeds. Even when I am old and grey, do not forsake me, my God, till I declare your power to the next generation, your mighty acts to all who are to come.

PSALM 71:4–6, 17–18 (NIV)

I expect that we can all think of individuals who have played a key role in our lives over the years: men and women who have not only passed on their wisdom and their stories of faith but have also prayed faithfully for us. Our inherent value before God throughout our lifetime is woven beautifully throughout this psalm, as David reflects on God's faithfulness to him, even now in his later years.

Psalm 71 reminds us that life is a journey, from cradle to grave, a journey in which we create relationships, gain experience, forge memories and seek wisdom. Travelling through these different seasons, we gain new perspectives and insights of God's faithfulness to us. Despite the obvious despair of the psalmist, he returns with confidence to his own lifelong experience of God's goodness.

As he reflects on his youth, I wonder if David was recalling those days as a shepherd out on the hills, when God not only protected him from physical danger but equipped him for what lay ahead: courage for the task, confidence in his skills and a commitment to serve a faithful God. Even as the psalmist struggles, we hear his passionate cry to share his story of faith and redemption with the next generation.

In my role as chaplain for older people, there is no greater privilege than sitting alongside an older person, hearing their story and being blessed by the spiritual wisdom gained from the long memory of God's faithfulness. In our society, where youth is revered, the older generation can so easily be forgotten and undervalued, and yet this psalm reminds us of the potential God sees in us throughout our lives. Whatever our age, I wonder how we, too, can commit to pray for and share our faith story with the next generation.

ERICA ROBERTS, ANNA CHAPLAIN FOR OLDER PEOPLE, SOUTHAMPTON

Feeble hands and weak knees

Strengthen the feeble hands, steady the knees that give way; say to those with fearful hearts, 'Be strong, do not fear; your God will come, he will come with vengeance; with divine retribution he will come to save you.' Then will the eyes of the blind be opened and the ears of the deaf unstopped. Then will the lame leap like a deer, and the mute tongue shout for joy. Water will gush forth in the wilderness and streams in the desert.

ISAIAH 35:3–6 (NIV)

'Strengthen my feeble hands, steady these knees that give way' is my go-to arrow prayer that I regularly pray when I need reassuring that even if the situation or task ahead seems impossible to me, God is in control and will enable and strengthen me to get through it.

Set within the beautiful poetry of Isaiah, the passage my prayer is based upon takes us into a wilderness of desolation and despair, amid which God sends his restorative promise to the Babylonian exiles, who are hundreds of miles away from their homeland. They are losing hope and vision, and cannot see beyond their present situation. But God can, and he reminds them of his transforming power which will strengthen them and get them through to a better place. God doesn't magically eliminate their wilderness; he enables them to journey through it.

Sometimes it may seem as if we are living in a wilderness, a place bereft of hope. Maybe this is as a result of loneliness, ageing, loss, illness, stress, financial burden, physical or spiritual exhaustion... there are endless reasons that can take us to a place where we feel lost and unable to cope. But we are not alone, for there is no wilderness in God's presence. There is hope and promise, strength and peace, and a sure knowledge that he will be victorious over all things.

We cannot break the powers which bind us by ourselves, but through Jesus God's promise is made complete. The chains that bind us are broken and we are set free. There is no mountain too high to climb, no valley too deep to overcome and no wilderness too desolate to get through. Jesus is our light in the darkness (Luke 11:33–36) and the way through whom we are more than conquerors (Romans 8:35–37).

KATIE NORMAN, METHODIST LOCAL PREACHER AND FOUNDER, MESSY VINTAGE

Hope against hope

Who against hope believed in hope, that he might become the father of many nations, according to that which was spoken, So shall thy seed be. And being not weak in faith, he considered not his own body now dead, when he was about an hundred years old, neither yet the deadness of Sarah's womb: He staggered not at the promise of God through unbelief; but was strong in faith, giving glory to God; And being fully persuaded that, what he had promised, he was able also to perform. And therefore it was imputed to him for righteousness. Now it was not written for his sake alone, that it was imputed to him; But for us also, to whom it shall be imputed, if we believe on him that raised up Jesus our Lord from the dead.

ROMANS 4:18–24 (KJV)

Our modern, digitised, instant-access media, our materialism, rationalism and post-war western social trends represent massive changes in a short time period. In the first world at least, we are becoming ever more technologically oriented, ever pressured to 'achieve'. Biomedical and surgical advances easily persuade us that ageing rationally equates with failure, loss and ultimately death, particularly of our sensory faculties and cognitive competence. Perhaps even a generation ago, it was clearer that older age was a time to embody hope and virtue, to master the emotions and to apply hard-won wisdom acquired through lived experience.

Post-war social restructuring, particularly in the west, has made 'family' and 'church' more fluid concepts; it can be harder for us to see our direct familial connection with Abraham. Nonetheless, our beloved forebear, however old he may have been, still shows us the way and still embodies hope against hope for us. No matter what his rational mind might have told this centenarian, he was having nothing to do with failure or death. His promise from God, carried with great and lively faith, persuaded him against all odds that he would deliver, as ancestor of a great nation.

It was not a matter of status, worldly recognition or achievement for him, but simply of God's will and God's love. Great faith undoubtedly demands and embraces both emotional and rational elements; we can, and should, connect and integrate them in ourselves.

HARRIET MOWAT, MANAGING DIRECTOR, MOWAT RESEARCH LTD

Age is no barrier

Let no one despise your youth, but set the believers an example in speech and conduct, in love, in faith, in purity. Until I arrive, give attention to the public reading of scripture, to exhorting, to teaching. Do not neglect the gift that is in you, which was given to you through prophecy with the laying on of hands by the council of elders. Put these things into practice, devote yourself to them, so that all may see your progress. Pay close attention to yourself and to your teaching; continue in these things, for in doing this you will save both yourself and your hearers.

1 TIMOTHY 4:12–16 (NRSV)

Timothy was Paul's 'loyal child in the faith' (1 Timothy 1:2). Paul entrusted to him the care and nurture of early Christian congregations, but his credentials were questioned by those he sought to lead. What were their grounds for undermining his leadership? Simply that he was too young to hold a position of authority. We are all guilty of unconscious bias when it comes to age. We can look at a young person and think, 'What do you know when you have experienced so little of life?' Equally, when we see someone who is old and frail, we can discount their perspective, believing that their best years are behind them.

The Bible challenges assumptions about people that are based solely on age. Young Timothy was God's chosen leader of the early church. St Benedict also valued what younger people brought, suggesting in his Rule of Life that when the brothers are summoned for counsel, 'The Lord often reveals what is better to the younger' (ch. 3). Jesus was unhappy when the disciples discouraged children from coming to him. He rebuked them, saying, 'It is to such as these that the kingdom of heaven belongs' (Matthew 19:14).

Timothy was encouraged to challenge those who despised his youth and denied the gift God had given him; he was to demonstrate his right to hold a position of authority by the way he spoke and behaved and through his teaching from the scripture. We can expect God to call us to serve him, regardless of our age. And we can see him at work in others, no matter how young or old.

JULIA BURTON-JONES, ANNA CHAPLAINCY CHURCH LEAD, BRF

Flourishing and fruitfulness

The righteous will flourish like a palm tree, they will grow like a cedar of Lebanon; planted in the house of the Lord, they will flourish in the courts of our God. They will still bear fruit in old age, they will stay fresh and green, proclaiming, 'The Lord is upright; he is my Rock, and there is no wickedness in him.'

PSALM 92:12–15 (NIV)

Have you ever reflected on what it means to flourish, and what that might mean for you? And whether you are 'useful'? Because this Bible passage is a wonderful encouragement. As 'righteous' people (believers made right with God, through Jesus), God promises us that we will flourish and be fruitful, and that doesn't stop at any age!

So, what of flourishing? We who love the Lord are planted in the house of the Lord, and we will *flourish* in the courts of our God. A successful plant puts down roots in soil and takes goodness from the soil to enable it to grow, even into a huge cedar tree. We may not feel strong in human terms or feel like we are flourishing, but as we spend time with our Lord in prayer and as we read the Bible, we will grow, flourish and bear fruit. Because we will more and more find joy in God's immeasurable, never-ending love for us, and when things are difficult in life, our eternal hope becomes even more precious.

This Bible passage tells of God's plans for us all the days of our lives, including in our later years, where we will 'still bear fruit'. Society will often tell us that our usefulness reduces with age, but not in God's eyes! Indeed, older believers often have more life experience in both blessing and suffering, and so bear witness to the preciousness of knowing Jesus.

Whatever our age, may we be encouraged, knowing that God has plans for us, for the whole of our lives, as we continue to follow him. Whatever our age, as we serve the Lord, we will bear fruit and remain fresh, so let us think about how we can use the gifts God has given us and be thankful.

CARL KNIGHTLY, DIRECTOR OF CHURCH NETWORKS, LONDON CITY MISSION, AND FORMER CEO, FAITH IN LATER LIFE

The small offering

As Jesus looked up, he saw the rich putting their gifts into the temple treasury. He also saw a poor widow put in two very small copper coins. 'Truly I tell you,' he said, 'this poor widow has put in more than all the others. All these people gave their gifts out of their wealth; but she out of her poverty put in all she had to live on.'

LUKE 21:1–4 (NIV)

Imagine the scene in the temple courtyard. People are gathering to deposit their money into a box for freewill offerings. It is busy and the disciples are impressed by the spectacle. Jesus, however, is not taken in by the fine clothes and signs of importance shown by the teachers of the law. He lets his eyes slip over them and when he looks up, he sees a poor widow. Perhaps others have hardly noticed her. But Jesus sees her. He does not glance and look away; he sees her for the person she is and understands what it has cost her to give her two very small coins. He sees the willing worship and sacrifice that her gift represents. She has given all that she has to live on, trusting God for her future.

Many older people, often widows, living in their homes and in care homes, perhaps unnoticed by the busy passing world, have little money of their own to offer. However, for those whose privilege it is to minister with them, we give witness to what they freely give without expectation or reward. They often share all they have – rich stories of their lives, faith stories, wholehearted worship, their trust, their own selves – all shared with us in Jesus' presence.

These shared experiences may seem a small offering to others, but praise God, he sees and uses small things. Remember what Jesus could do with five loaves and two fishes (John 6), or what faith the size of a mustard seed can produce (Matthew 17:20). God has chosen those who are poor in the eyes of the world to be rich in faith and to inherit the kingdom he promised to those who love him (James 2:5). For those ministering with older people, it is an amazing blessing.

SALLY REES, ANNA CHAPLAINCY LEAD FOR WALES

Meeting the thief

Listen to this secret truth: we shall not all die, but when the last trumpet sounds, we shall all be changed in an instant, as quickly as the blinking of an eye… The dead will be raised, never to die again… So when this takes place, and the mortal has been changed into the immortal, then the scripture will come true: 'Death is destroyed; victory is complete!'

1 CORINTHIANS 15:51–54 (GNT, abridged)

When you get to my age, you begin to think about what comes next. And the Bible really does tell us a great deal about that if we look. I love this passage where Paul tells us we will be changed 'in the blinking of an eye'. That means that, when my clock stops ticking, I will be there in my new, resurrection body in an instant, just as Jesus said to the dying thief, 'Today you will be in Paradise with me' (Luke 23:43).

Did you notice that Jesus didn't say 'in heaven'? I think we get the idea of 'going to heaven' from the medieval monks, because the Bible tells us nothing like that. I like to say that believers will go to be with Jesus. The question I ask myself then is, 'Where will Jesus be when my time comes?' The answer has to be, in Paradise. But the Bible doesn't tell us where that is… or does it?

In the beginning, God separated light from darkness, and he named the light Day and the darkness Night. So God actually created time for us to live in! When my clock ceases to tick, I shall pass into eternity where there is no time. In eternity, God, in the person of Jesus, is already back here on planet earth for the second time as he promised. We, who are alive now, are still waiting for that to happen, but Jesus and that thief are there already! Here is where I take a guess, but I feel it is the right one. When Jesus comes again, 'according to the scriptures', he will fulfil all the Old Testament prophecies of the 'peaceful kingdom' and 'Paradise' will be here on earth. I'm hoping to meet that thief here.

Most of us question what happens when we die. Here, in the Bible, is the answer. Good news that is worth sharing!

PAUL GRAVELLE, SELF-SUPPORTING PRIEST, NEW ZEALAND

A song of trust and confidence

The Lord is my shepherd, I lack nothing. He makes me lie down in green pastures, he leads me beside quiet waters, he refreshes my soul. He guides me along the right paths for his name's sake. Even though I walk through the darkest valley, I will fear no evil, for you are with me; your rod and your staff, they comfort me. You prepare a table before me in the presence of my enemies. You anoint my head with oil; my cup overflows. Surely your goodness and love will follow me all the days of my life, and I will dwell in the house of the Lord forever.

PSALM 23 (NIV)

This well-known psalm is often chosen at funerals; it's a wonderful affirmation of God's presence, protection and provision throughout life.

But it is also a song for every day, and I regularly include Psalm 23 when I lead worship. The poetry and rhythm of the six verses easily become familiar, and the lovely people with whom I worship at Messy Vintage sessions know it off by heart. It's also good to sing and there are some wonderful musical versions.

It feels to me a bit like a creed – a statement of truth, of what I believe – but also a song of trust and confidence in God, my shepherd and my king.

If we listen to the shepherd's voice, as sheep do, he will provide for all our needs, body and soul. He will lead us along the right ways, paths of blessing, because that is his nature. As part of our faithful following, the path may well take us into the woods, up mountains and through dark valleys – times of difficulty, sadness, suffering and despair. God doesn't promise to take us out of these places, nor does he leave us to walk them alone; in all of it, he is a constant presence, though we may not always be aware of him.

Along the way, we will be chased by enemies and we may question whether goodness and mercy are following us too. The word 'follow' can be translated better as 'pursue' or 'chase after'. So goodness and mercy will chase us, our whole life long, until we find ourselves at the banqueting table in God's house, where we take our place, with others, in God's kingdom.

JILL PHIPPS, LAY MINISTER, DIOCESE OF PORTSMOUTH

Proclaiming the kingdom of God

As they were going along the road, someone said to him, 'I will follow you wherever you go.' And Jesus said to him, 'Foxes have holes, and birds of the air have nests; but the Son of Man has nowhere to lay his head.' To another he said, 'Follow me.' But he said, 'Lord, first let me go and bury my father.' But Jesus said to him, 'Let the dead bury their own dead; but as for you, go and proclaim the kingdom of God.' Another said, 'I will follow you, Lord; but let me first say farewell to those at my home.' Jesus said to him, 'No one who puts a hand to the plough and looks back is fit for the kingdom of God.'

LUKE 9:57–62 (NRSV)

One of my early memories is the brown booklet lying on top of my mother's Bible which she faithfully read daily. Then, the package of BRF notes, which arrived at regular intervals in the post, from a Mrs Hance in Sidcup, which included notes for my brother and me. The importance of my mother's daily Bible reading inspired me and was a vital milestone in my faith journey. Various BRF resources have encouraged me, and 70 years later, *Guidelines* lies on top of my own Bible to aid my daily feast of God's word!

During my life I have been blessed to have been taught and inspired by Christians who have faithfully introduced me to Jesus and mentored my discipleship, which has brought me immeasurable joy in knowing him. So I have always been concerned to pass on the good news of Jesus to the next generation; to 'proclaim the kingdom of God', as Jesus commands in this passage. Hence, I have appreciated BRF's resources for schools, to use, to support prayerfully and, where possible, financially down the years. The Bible verse which has spurred me on throughout my life is the words of Jesus in Luke 9: 'No one who puts a hand to the plough and looks back is fit for service in the kingdom of God' (v. 62).

So, as BRF celebrates its 100th birthday, I shall be among those praising God for its important part in my life, as many others will be doing with me.

ANGELA COOKE, EAST SUSSEX

How should we live?

Tell

'To proclaim the good news of the kingdom.'

I T'S A PROBLEM.

Faced with the prospect of talking about our faith, evangelists light up and nearly everyone else senses an uneasy feeling of guilt. It's worse because we know it's easy to talk with warmth and even wisdom about some other things: sport, holidays, favourite recipes, music or art. Yet not every topic is universally welcomed. Model railway enthusiasts or bus number collectors know that the nerd image lurks. Behind all this, English culture has some e-words it hates: it dislikes earnestness, is suspicious of enthusiasm and disapproves of evangelism.

So how to navigate this terrain?

The 14 contributions that follow explore this. As I read through them all, I wondered if a theme emerges, as people reflect on scripture and their own stories. Put simply, it's this: small things actually count – or, put another way, 'they are telling'.

The writers note what is carried by small hinges, the power in seeds, the significance of a letter, the treasure in a clay jar, doing our normal jobs well, the gift of a pot of homemade jam. Honesty also heaves a sigh of relief that we are given second chances and may not know the significance of our contributions.

In all these ways, little things can be signs of a life that provokes helpful questions in others. Living a Christ-centred everyday life may be far more 'telling' than we thought. Read on and ask God which image of a 'little thing' may fit your story.

GEORGE LINGS, CONSULTANT, COMPANION OF NORTHUMBRIA
COMMUNITY AND VICE-PRESIDENT, BRF

Seize the day!

Devote yourselves to prayer, being watchful and thankful. And pray for us, too, that God may open a door for our message, so that we may proclaim the mystery of Christ, for which I am in chains. Pray that I may proclaim it clearly, as I should. Be wise in the way you act towards outsiders; make the most of every opportunity. Let your conversation be always full of grace, seasoned with salt, so that you may know how to answer everyone.

COLOSSIANS 4:2–6 (NIV)

If you visit the Roman Baths in the city of Bath, Somerset, you can see artefacts which show that there were Christians among those who came from Rome in the first century. Is it a coincidence that one of the first-century church's most powerful preachers had been imprisoned in Rome?

Big doors swing on small hinges. A short conversation can have a life-changing impact. How did the door to the gospel open across Europe? Paul was asking God for opportunities to pass on the good news of the gospel. Could it be that what he said to his jailers was passed on by Roman soldiers and their servants as the Roman empire spread?

We can learn so much from Paul, the prisoner. Even in prison, he was always looking for opportunities to tell people about Christ. Even though he was a gifted evangelist, he asked for prayer that he would speak clearly. He relied on God, not his own abilities. He was also careful to act and speak graciously and to think about how to speak in ways that meant people wanted to listen.

We can't predict what might happen when we start a conversation. We can pray that God will open doors and give us the right words to say. It could lead to salvation. Doors only open as we push them and walk through them.

It can be easy to ignore open doors. Ask God to make you aware of opportunities and to give you the courage to speak up. Some personalities find this easier than others – but the challenge is for everyone.

Let's follow Paul's example and pray, asking God to open our eyes, ears and hearts to the open doors he gives us regularly to tell people sensitively and appropriately about Jesus.

ROY CROWNE, PRESIDENT, HOPE TOGETHER

Jesus is Lord

If you confess that Jesus is Lord and believe that God raised him from death, you will be saved... We do not live for ourselves only, and we do not die for ourselves only. If we live, it is for the Lord that we live, and if we die, it is for the Lord that we die. So whether we live or die, we belong to the Lord. For Christ died and rose to life in order to be the Lord of the living and of the dead.

ROMANS 10:9; 14:7–9 (GNT)

'Jesus is Lord' sums up the essence of the Christian life. It was with these words on their lips that the first Christians were baptised and later with these words on their lips that many were martyred for their faith. I was vividly reminded of this truth when at the age of 13 I was baptised a stone's throw away from the River Limmat in Zurich, where hundreds of Anabaptists had been drowned for their faith. Afterwards I was given a certificate on which was the scripture text: 'If we live, it is for the Lord that we live, and if we die, it is for the Lord that we die. So whether we live or die, we belong to the Lord.'

Christians are people who have surrendered their lives to Jesus and so seek to live for him. Precisely how we make Jesus Lord of our lives will vary according to our circumstances. In principle, it means that in every area of our lives we are accountable to him. At work, for instance, Jesus is our ultimate 'boss' and so there is no place for half-heartedness; and similarly Jesus has a claim on the way we use our leisure hours. All that we have and are is held 'in trust' and so we are called to live life responsibly. This affects how we bring up our children and how we treat others; how we spend our money and how we use our homes; how we care for the environment and how we live life together.

Thank God, along with the challenge, that there is also security. For whatever happens, 'we belong to him'. There is nothing in life or death which can separate us from his love and care (Romans 8:38–39).

PAUL BEASLEY-MURRAY, AUTHOR, SPEAKER AND MINISTRY CONSULTANT

Seeds of hope

'As the heavens are higher than the earth, so are my ways higher than your ways and my thoughts than your thoughts. As the rain and the snow come down from heaven, and do not return to it without watering the earth and making it bud and flourish, so that it yields seed for the sower and bread for the eater, so is my word that goes out from my mouth: it will not return to me empty, but will accomplish what I desire and achieve the purpose for which I sent it.'

ISAIAH 55:9–11 (NIV)

I had just got a new research-based job with Church Army. It did feel like responding to a call, but I felt I hadn't much clue how to do it. Nor could I see the sort of role this played in the wider church or know what effect this research might have.

I don't remember how I ended up reading Isaiah 55, but it was a lightbulb moment in which God gave me a biblical image to live by. In ways that remain unfathomable, God has created processes and cycles of fruitfulness in the biological and in the spiritual world. What is fruitful produces seeds. I realised that part of our task was to spot and name what in God's church and kingdom was being fruitful. We first visited to understand what others were doing. Then we wrote up and published their stories; if you like, we were gathering and packaging seeds.

Yet it was the next stage in this process that was most diagnostic. Our task was not to make things happen, such as sowing those seeds elsewhere by ourselves. No, it was more modest, risky and uncertain – all we were to do was make seeds available to other sowers. We had no control whether those seeds would be used at all, or sown wisely. We had to trust that God's seeds would not return to him empty and they would achieve the purposes for which he sent them.

I don't know what you are called to do and be. I encourage you to ask God and follow his calling. Don't fret that it may seem small; seeds have extraordinary power. Don't fuss unduly about the outcome. You can be content to seem powerless, even weak, yet make a great difference.

GEORGE LINGS, CONSULTANT, COMPANION OF NORTHUMBRIA COMMUNITY
AND VICE-PRESIDENT, BRF

The bestseller Christian

Are we starting to commend ourselves again? Or do we need, like some [false teachers], letters of recommendation to you or from you? [No!] You are our letter [of recommendation], written in our hearts, recognised and read by everyone. You show that you are a letter from Christ, delivered by us, written not with ink but with the Spirit of the living God, not on tablets of stone but on tablets of human hearts. Such is the confidence *and* steadfast reliance *and* absolute trust that we have through Christ toward God.

2 CORINTHIANS 3:1–4 (AMP)

If we're going to be a book, let's be worthy of the Booker Prize – a recommended leading literary novel. If we're going to be a letter, let's be a true love letter.

A lifestyle that demonstrates and speaks of obedience and faithfulness to the word of God really does have page-turner potential: a Christian walk that reaches out and loves when it feels hard, gives sacrificially when it feels scary to do so and forgives when you'd rather hold a grudge. It's page-turner stuff, to stand in the midst of chaos, when everyone around you is reading you, observing your life and compelled to find out what's going to happen next. Will you sink or swim?

Paul reminds the Corinthian converts that they are living letters. Practically speaking, the only Bible that some people will ever read is us. Our lifestyle is the only communication that has the ability to introduce them to a Saviour who can transform their lives.

Have you ever considered that you're a living communication? Let's ensure a wrong attitude doesn't hinder the redeeming message we carry. Consistency in behaviour and being the same person in all aspects of our lives is key.

Essentially, our lifestyle must reflect the love letter that you read over and over again and the book that you can't put down. Let's become more attractive to the people around us – to the point that our compassion and holiness is so evident that they have to ask: What is it about you? And you say: Well, I know a man who can turn your life around. Let me tell you my good news…

ESTHER KUKU, WIFE, MOTHER AND COMMUNICATIONS PROFESSIONAL

Treasure in clay jars

Therefore, since it is by God's mercy that we are engaged in this ministry, we do not lose heart… For it is the God who said, 'Let light shine out of darkness,' who has shone in our hearts to give the light of the knowledge of the glory of God in the face of Jesus Christ. But we have this treasure in clay jars, so that it may be made clear that this extraordinary power belongs to God and does not come from us.

2 CORINTHIANS 4:1, 6–7 (NRSV)

Paul's second letter to the Corinthians could be subtitled 'A portrait of myself as a clay jar'. We are given vivid descriptions of beatings, riots, hunger, stonings and shipwrecks. We are introduced to Paul's punishing workload and the daily pressure of his 'concern for all the churches' (11:28). 'His letters are weighty and forceful,' say his opponents, 'but in person he is unimpressive and his speaking amounts to nothing' (see 10:10). This hardly seems like a mighty apostle we're reading about here, let alone the brash, self-righteous Pharisee of his youth. This is a picture of a man emerging from a period of extreme stress, perhaps even a nervous breakdown.

But this fragile clay oil lamp still has a flame burning within it. This battered old container is full of the richest of battle spoils. For the same God who proclaimed, 'Let there be light!' at the dawn of creation has proclaimed, 'Let there be light!' once more in the heart of this extraordinary man – more specifically, the 'light of the knowledge of the glory of God in the face of Jesus Christ'.

We're reminded here, perhaps, of Jesus' parable of the man finding treasure, who in his joy sold everything he had to buy the field where he'd found it (Matthew 13:44). Paul was that man, truly sold out for the gospel – except that it's not that *he* had found the treasure, but rather that the treasure had found *him*, in the shape of that glorious encounter with the risen Christ.

And what an encouragement to us, who are all too aware of our own struggles and frailties: that the glory is focused on the message we proclaim, and not on the strengths and abilities of we who proclaim it.

ANDREW WATSON, BISHOP OF GUILDFORD

One greater than John

[John the Baptist] confessed freely, 'I am not the Messiah.' They asked him, 'Then who are you? Are you Elijah?' He said, 'I am not.' 'Are you the Prophet?' He answered, 'No.' Finally they said, 'Who are you? Give us an answer to take back to those who sent us. What do you say about yourself?' John replied in the words of Isaiah the prophet, 'I am the voice of one calling in the wilderness, "Make straight the way for the Lord."'

JOHN 1:20–23 (NIV)

It began in Luke 1, with Zechariah the priest and his wife Elizabeth. They are old and childless. Then the angel Gabriel visits. Zechariah is in the middle of his priestly duties, but God will gladly mess up our act of worship when he wants to announce a miracle. Nine months later, John is born.

Then nothing for three decades. At this point, there have been no words of scripture for 400 years. There have been no prophetic voices. Darkness dominates. And then, in God's time, on to history's stage he strides: John. This man is not the light; he is called to point to the light. God has saved his best preacher for the darkest time.

'I am not the prophet and I'm not Elijah. I am the voice of one crying in the wilderness.' But later, after John is dead, a similar conversation takes place. Jesus asks John's disciples about John. And when they cannot answer, Jesus tells them that John was the prophet who was to come, the one who came in the spirit of Elijah.

Oh! That's awkward. A contradiction in scripture. John says he wasn't; Jesus says he was. Yet we can reconcile this quite easily. Are you ready? Don't miss this: the most significant man ever to be born of a woman (Jesus' words), the one who came in the spirit of Elijah, the Prophet… didn't know it! He has no idea of his significance. There was no false humility on the part of John. He simply didn't know. And yet he did it anyway. He stood and he spoke and he proclaimed truth and he baptised. He did what he was called to do and didn't recognise his worth, his value, his significance.

I meet people all the time – you may be one of them – who have so much worth, are so valuable, so significant. Yet it is likely that you don't even know it. Don't worry. You're in good company.

MARK GRIFFITHS, DEAN FOR DISCIPLESHIP, ST PADARN'S INSTITUTE, CHURCH IN WALES

Second chance Jonah, first chance Nineveh

The word of the Lord came to Jonah a second time, saying, 'Get up, go to Nineveh, that great city, and proclaim to it the message that I tell you.' So Jonah set out and went to Nineveh, according to the word of the Lord. Now Nineveh was an exceedingly large city, a three days' walk across. Jonah began to go into the city, going a day's walk. And he cried out, 'Forty days more, and Nineveh shall be overthrown!' And the people of Nineveh believed God; they proclaimed a fast, and everyone, great and small, put on sackcloth.

JONAH 3:1–5 (NRSV)

Jonah has tried running away from God, but now God calls him again. The first time he had run away from Nineveh, but now he obeys and sets out for the city. God gives him a second chance. Fear and failure are not the end of this story. God does not send for an upgrade; God offers Jonah a second chance and he takes it.

And what a city Nineveh was! It was the capital of the superpower of the times, the Assyrian empire. The area of the whole greater city was over 100 acres. Everything in the city proclaimed, 'We Assyrians rule.' They conquered through military might and terror. Into the centre of power and authority God sent one unremarkable person. A reluctant prophet, a lone voice proclaiming that Nineveh was in danger of being overthrown! A crazy message. The greatest power resided here; why would they ever listen to Jonah? But they did!

That's the whole point of Jonah. Jonah is getting a second chance so that Nineveh can have a first chance to experience the compassion of God. I wonder where you might be scared of talking about your faith today. Where are the places and who are the people with whom you would rather keep quiet? Or where, if you try to say something, you feel it will not go well? It might be very close to home. But God wants you to speak, not to test you but simply because he loves the people you are speaking to and wants them to know his love and compassion. He can use you today in the most unexpected places, if you will trust him. He gives us second chances to give others a chance to meet this loving God.

DAVE MALE, DIRECTOR OF EVANGELISM AND DISCIPLESHIP, CHURCH OF ENGLAND

Good work

For by grace you have been saved through faith. And this is not your own doing; it is the gift of God, not a result of works, so that no one may boast. For we are his workmanship, created in Christ Jesus for good works, which God prepared beforehand, that we should walk in them.

EPHESIANS 2:8–10 (ESV)

The apostle Paul clearly knew a thing or two about work. He was a scholar, activist, church planter, preacher, writer, and tentmaker (Acts 18:3). He was a self-starter, had a great work ethic (2 Thessalonians 3:8) and overcame tremendous discouragement.

In Ephesians we get a glimpse of Paul's theology of work. We are, he writes, God's 'workmanship'. Inevitably, we're taken back to the beginning of our story and God's work of creation. He makes humans in his image (what's that if not work?), blesses them and commands them to 'be fruitful'. We've been 'created in Christ Jesus', writes Paul, for an important purpose: to do good works, which God has prepared for us to do.

Paul is sometimes thought of as being opposed to works. Doesn't he write that it's by grace we are saved, not works? Well, yes, he does (v. 8), but what Paul is opposed to is the idea that salvation can be earned (it's a gift), not the idea that living out our salvation takes effort. Grace is not opposed to effort; it's opposed to earning.

Paul's invitation to his readers, and by extension to us, is to be co-workers with God in the everyday, Monday to Saturday too, not just Sunday. How can we do this? If we produce goods or services, we can ensure that what we produce really is 'good' and 'of service'. And, whether in paid employment or not, we can daily practise what we at LICC call the 6Ms: We can *model* godly character, *make* good work, *minister* grace and love, *mould* culture, be a *mouthpiece* for truth and justice, and be a *messenger* of the gospel – speaking about Jesus with those around us.

In doing all this, we will be fulfilling our human calling and revealing what salvation actually looks like.

PAUL WOOLLEY, CEO, THE LONDON INSTITUTE FOR CONTEMPORARY CHRISTIANITY

Pause before posting

My dear brothers and sisters, take note of this: everyone should be quick to listen, slow to speak and slow to become angry, because human anger does not produce the righteousness that God desires... Do not merely listen to the word, and so deceive yourselves. Do what it says. Anyone who listens to the word but does not do what it says is like someone who looks at his face in a mirror and, after looking at himself, goes away and immediately forgets what he looks like.

JAMES 1:19–20, 22–24 (NIV)

Most of us will be familiar with the notion that God calls us to be 'slow to anger'. But how does this relate to our increasingly digital lives? We are asked to take our everyday life and place it before God (Romans 12:2), and social media is now embedded in our everyday – sometimes for better, sometimes for worse. Unfortunately, we see increasingly negative interactions online, where quick reactions are expected and when nuance can be hard to express.

In today's verses we are asked to be 'quick to listen', 'slow to speak' and 'slow to become angry', the very opposite of what many default to online. With declining numbers actively churchgoing, our social media interactions may be the only 'face of God' that some people will ever see. Christian debates online, unfortunately, can be some of the most graceless, leading to concerns about non-Christians observing such negative dialogue.

Others are troubled about any push for 'false unity': disagreement can offer opportunities to work through differences in a constructive way (online and offline). James encourages us to be 'quick to listen'. When we take time to listen closely and are not racing to give easy immediate responses nor driven by a determination to get our 'right' answer across, there is a better chance of understanding the intention behind what has been said (or posted).

In being 'quick to listen', we therefore have more opportunities to be 'slow to speak' and think about how we put the fruit of the Spirit (Galatians 5:22–23), including patience and self-control, into action. Online, as elsewhere, our interactions are with other human beings, uniquely created by God, each with different strengths and vulnerabilities. As James 1:22–23 says, don't just listen to the word, but act upon it, including taking steps to be 'slow to anger'.

BEX LEWIS, FORMERLY SENIOR LECTURER IN DIGITAL MARKETING,
MANCHESTER METROPOLITAN UNIVERSITY

The Lord has spoken

On this mountain the Lord of hosts will make for all peoples a feast of rich food, a feast of well-matured wines, of rich food filled with marrow, of well-matured wines strained clear. And he will destroy on this mountain the shroud that is cast over all peoples, the sheet that is spread over all nations; he will swallow up death forever. Then the Lord God will wipe away the tears from all faces, and the disgrace of his people he will take away from all the earth, for the Lord has spoken. It will be said on that day, Lo, this is our God; we have waited for him, so that he might save us. This is the Lord for whom we have waited; let us be glad and rejoice in his salvation.

ISAIAH 25:6–9 (NRSV)

These words come at the climax of the first part of Isaiah's prophecy. The house of Judah – to whom they were written – was a small nation, surrounded on all sides by military and political threats. In the face of forces that often seemed beyond their control, Judah's insecurities and frailties had been exposed. The people had looked for political and military security in human solutions, rather than setting their hope on the living God and what he had promised.

These words are in fact the last lines of a song. It starts in the first person – perhaps with Isaiah himself taking the lead vocal: 'O Lord, you are *my* God' (v. 1). But at the end it swells into a chorus of praise: 'Lo, this is *our* God' (vv. 9–10). And in between is a vast multisensory picture of what God will bring about in the last days: it's a feast of colours, aromas and tastes (vv. 6–8). It is on this promise, says Isaiah, that we should be focusing our hope.

For so many of us, these last months have been a time of risk and insecurity. Maybe – like Judah – you too have been tempted to look away from God and to trust in other things. Here is an invitation for us to rejoin a bigger song: to refocus on God's promise once more and to live with the hope of heaven in our lives and on our tongues, so that the chorus can be ours: 'Let us be glad and rejoice in his salvation.'

PAUL WESTON, TUTOR AND SENIOR LECTURER IN MISSION STUDIES, RIDLEY HALL, CAMBRIDGE

Rekindling the flames

When the day of Pentecost came, they were all together in one place. Suddenly a sound like the blowing of a violent wind came from heaven and filled the whole house where they were sitting. They saw what seemed to be tongues of fire that separated and came to rest on each of them. All of them were filled with the Holy Spirit and began to speak in other tongues as the Spirit enabled them.

ACTS 2:1–4 (NIV)

Jesus had returned to heaven. Like a champion climbing the podium, he'd completed the task, and there had been a time to celebrate his victory. But now he'd gone and his disciples felt scared and alone. Jesus, the Son of God – speaking words of truth, showing his power, giving comfort and hope – was no longer with them and there was a big hole in their lives. The more they considered Jesus' words, 'Go into all the world and make disciples,' the more impossible this task must have seemed, leaving them feeling deflated and now having just to wait, but unsure of what they were waiting for.

During the time of Covid-19, many longed for normal life again. Many of us feel alone and deflated, and maybe our passion for Jesus and the gospel is only smouldering.

But then, as the disciples were together in one place, the Holy Spirit came, breathing his Spirit into them and rekindling the flames of passion. These deflated disciples were filled with his Holy Spirit, and were transformed, restored, renewed, reborn and ready to share the gospel with everybody, everywhere, going in the knowledge that Jesus would always be with them through his Spirit, as he had promised.

Have you ever tried balloon modelling? You start with a deflated balloon but then add your breath, bringing the balloon to life before shaping it into something special. This is like what God wants to do with us. He breathes his Spirit into us and then shapes our lives into something special.

Holy Spirit, help us to remember that YOU are with us as we go through this dark valley. Please fill us, rekindle our passion, restore and renew us as you did with the disciples on the day of Pentecost.

JOHN HARDWICK, COUNTIES EVANGELIST, CHRISTIAN CHILDREN'S PRESENTER
AND WRITER

Be prepared

In your hearts revere Christ as Lord. Always be prepared to give an answer to everyone who asks you to give the reason for the hope that you have. But do this with gentleness and respect, keeping a clear conscience, so that those who speak maliciously against your good behaviour in Christ may be ashamed of their slander. For it is better, if it is God's will, to suffer for doing good than for doing evil.

1 PETER 3:15–17 (NIV)

The church was packed for Katie's funeral. When the vicar asked, 'Raise your hand if Katie ever gave you a jar of homemade jam,' most people raised a hand. 'And who was prayed for by Katie?' Again, nearly everyone had been prayed for by this much-loved 85-year-old.

Katie radiated the love of Jesus, and she was always ready to give a reason for the hope she had. The mourner I sat next to at her funeral had never been to church before, but had visited Katie's home and knew about the hope Jesus gives.

Hope is one of the hallmarks of the Christian faith. Because of Jesus' death and resurrection, we have hope for now and for the future, whatever life throws at us.

Peter challenges us to keep our lives centred on Jesus, to live lives that provoke questions and to be ready to answer those who ask us about our faith. Our words and actions together point people to Jesus. Often we don't know the outcome when we sow seeds of truth and hope into other people's lives.

The most encouraging times I've had are when people have contacted me after several years to say that a letter or conversation has led them to explore faith for themselves: one of the students on the same course as me at university; a fellow trainee journalist in my first newspaper job; a lodger who lived with us for a year when my husband and I were first married.

Because we know the difference Jesus makes to life, we want others to know him too. Let's be people who have thought through the reasons for the hope we have; people who are known for doing good; people who are ready to speak up – and always with gentleness and respect.

CATHERINE BUTCHER, AUTHOR, JOURNALIST AND COMMUNICATIONS DIRECTOR, HOPE TOGETHER

The power of multiplication

[Jesus said,] 'Other seed fell into good soil and brought forth grain, growing up and increasing and yielding thirty and sixty and a hundredfold.'

MARK 4:8 (NRSV)

A hundredfold increase is almost impossible. Scholars tell us that the average yield would have been 7.1 times what was sown, so a thirtyfold harvest would have been remarkable, sixtyfold unheard of, and a hundredfold the stuff of dream and legend. And that is the point – when it comes to the word of God, we are not dealing with anything normal, but with something otherworldly, supernatural and beyond anything that could happen through even the most successful of natural processes.

The apostle Paul uses the language of the natural world when he talks about planting churches: 'I planted, Apollos watered, but God gave the growth' (1 Corinthians 3:6). That same kingdom power is at work in church planting today. We play our part, but the growth is something only God can give.

I have seen this time and again in my work with church planting. Over ten years in the East End of London, we saw five churches renewed and restarted. The Sunday attendance of these churches rose from 72 to over 700, a tenfold increase (*Love, Sweat and Tears: Church planting in East London*, Tim Thorlby, Centre for Theology & Community, 2016). Not a hundredfold, but not a bad start! This story is one of many repeating all around the country. I think of Harbour Church (**harbourchurchportsmouth.org**) in Portsmouth, planted by Alex Wood in September 2016. Since opening their doors, Alex writes, 'We've seen God do amazing things.' They have grown from 15 to 500 people coming each Sunday. They have launched five ministries to the city of Portsmouth. They run a city-centre coffee shop. They have become one church in three locations, and they are about to be involved in renewing two more. God has given the growth.

So let's grasp hold of Jesus' words afresh. Believe in the power of the Word of God! Pray for multiplication in different parts of your life – planting seeds of faith in your conversations with neighbours and colleagues. Invite God to multiply his presence in and through you. Let's get behind the starting of new Christian communities and churches, praying for these to grow and multiply across our land. And let's play our part, and be astonished at the growth God can bring. Who knows – it may even be a hundred times what we sow!

RIC THORPE, BISHOP OF ISLINGTON

Face to face with Jesus

When it was noon, darkness came over the whole land... Jesus cried out with a loud voice, 'Eloi, Eloi, lema sabachthani?' which means, 'My God, my God, why have you forsaken me?'... Then Jesus gave a loud cry and breathed his last. And the curtain of the temple was torn in two, from top to bottom. Now when the centurion, who stood facing him, saw that in this way he breathed his last, he said, 'Truly this man was God's Son!'

MARK 15:33–39 (NRSV, abridged)

This raw account of one man's death is perhaps where Christian faith begins. The whole account is worth reading, inhabiting and pondering. Yet the centurion's confession is pivotal. A man's life is given up (v. 37), the fabric of the universe is torn in two (v. 38) and a Roman soldier is the first to see that this is indeed God's Son.

In this moment Jesus displays, for all to see, the likeness of God: he is God's Son. He does so in the way he dies, revealing a God with us, even through sin and death, suffering with and for us.

This is the moment Jesus 'saves us', and Mark describes this cosmic shift as the barrier between us and a holy God is ripped apart. Mel Gibson in his film *The Passion of the Christ* portrays something similar as a tear forms in the Father's eye and falls to the ground with earth-shattering force.

Watching Jesus carefully is a Roman centurion, one of those directly responsible for Jesus' death. Perhaps as he looks Jesus in the eye, the centurion knows himself loved and forgiven. A wonderful confession spills unformed from his mouth.

And Mark invites all of us to a similar face-to-face moment, to our own confession. Once made personal, everything changes for us here too. We receive him, believe in his name and find the power to become children of God. To return here is to dwell awhile where our faith began, face to face with the one who saved us.

> **I stand amazed in the presence of Jesus the Nazarene**
> **and wonder how he could love me a sinner, condemned, unclean.**
> **How marvellous! How wonderful! And my song shall ever be:**
> **How marvellous! How wonderful! Is my Saviour's love for me!**
> Charles H. Gabriel (1856–1932)

JOLYON TRICKEY, MANAGER, RESOURCE-ARM'S ALONGSIDE SCHEME
(PRAYERFUL COMPANIONS FOR CHURCH LEADERS)

Teach

'To teach, baptise and nurture new believers.'

J UST BEFORE lockdown I was given a television. So began a new adventure – at the age of 72! While others complained about repeated programmes, I enjoyed watching *Antiques Roadshow* for the first time, fascinated by the variety of 'treasures' people brought. I soon realised that some did not know what they held in their hands, others did not know how to use their treasures and others had no idea what the monetary value might be.

As we think about teaching, these reflections help us to know what it is we are giving to others – as we tell them 'the old, old story, of Jesus and his love', sharing with them the riches of God's grace as we gossip the gospel in everyday life, by speaking of what we know. Like Philip, we can answer the questions of those who ask, 'About whom, may I ask you, does the prophet say this?' (Acts 8:34, NRSV). What is this Christian 'thing' I have discovered? I need to know the facts. Recently I was asked to recommend a book for a young person wanting to know more about the gospels – the authors and when they wrote. This is important for those who are exploring faith.

But of course, they will also want to know how it works. Here, our words do not teach as powerfully as our lives. So some reflections focus here – on how the first disciples learned to be like Jesus because they journeyed with him and saw how he was, what he did and how he depended on his heavenly Father for everything. We are reminded that Christian friends can be influential in our growth in grace, because they show us how to love, live and take up our cross daily (Luke 9:23).

Once we understand the gospel and how it works for us, in us and through us, we begin to appreciate its value. A 'concert of praise' begins in our hearts, spreads to our lips and flows out from our lives. Then we will teach – spontaneously, continually and gladly.

CHRISTINA BAXTER, FORMER PRINCIPAL, ST JOHN'S NOTTINGHAM, AND VICE-CHAIR OF TRUSTEES, BRF

From generation to generation

O my people... I will teach you hidden lessons from our past... stories our ancestors handed down to us. We will not hide these truths from our children; we will tell the next generation about the glorious deeds of the Lord... He commanded our ancestors to teach them to their children, so the next generation might know them – even children not yet born... So each generation should set its hope anew on God, not forgetting his glorious miracles... Then they will not be like their ancestors... refusing to give their hearts to God.

PSALM 78:1–8 (NLT, abridged)

My grandfather came down to London from Liverpool to work as a civil servant. The first Sunday he went to church, where a beautiful young woman in the choir caught his eye. In due course, they married. Their first child was born in 1922. The story of their romance has passed down the generations. More significantly, their love of the stories of the 'glorious deeds of the Lord' has been passed down, to the fifth generation.

Psalm 78, the second longest psalm, leads worshippers through five centuries of Israel's history, from Moses to David. Throughout these years God's people frequently turned away from him, yet God, with his inexhaustible patience and commitment, never deserted them.

These stories must not be hidden but told truthfully – the good and the bad. Setting them to music in this psalm meant they would be sung again and again, and not forgotten. Each generation could discover God for themselves. Then he would become the source of their hope. They would 'give their hearts to God' and refuse to follow the rebellious example of their ancestors.

We are the product of past generations of our family and more broadly of our society. Somewhere on our timeline, someone taught us the stories of Jesus. BRF has been doing this for 100 years. God now commands our generation to tell those younger than us about his faithfulness, centuries after the psalmist's story. Many from younger generations cannot forget the stories of Jesus because they have never even heard his name. They have had no opportunity to put their trust in him.

How can I most effectively communicate the story of God's salvation in all its fullness, and tell others why it matters to me? Who will be in my audience?

RO WILLOUGHBY, WRITER AND LAY MINISTER

Saturated in his words

Fix these words of mine in your hearts and minds; tie them as symbols on your hands and bind them on your foreheads. Teach them to your children, talking about them when you sit at home and when you walk along the road, when you lie down and when you get up. Write them on the door-frames of your houses and on your gates, so that your days and the days of your children may be many in the land the Lord swore to give your ancestors, as many as the days that the heavens are above the earth.

DEUTERONOMY 11:18–21 (NIV)

'I can't do that!' my eight-year-old huffed as we grappled with the nine times tables one rainy afternoon. Lacking inspiration, I pondered throwing in the towel and was about to suggest doing some baking when brilliance hit. We spent the rest of the afternoon creating nine times tables posters and putting them up all around the house. By the time my child had carefully drawn the posters, he had up to 5x9 down. By the end of the week, after looking at these posters, especially the strategically placed one in the bathroom, the whole family could recite the nine times table.

These verses from Deuteronomy urge us to be creative with how we share God's words with those around us. We learn that it's as easy as talking about them when taking a walk or being inventive by writing them on doorframes or tying them to our foreheads… well, maybe that's taking it too far for today's culture! But we can print out words from scripture and pin them up in our homes. Or listen to an audio version of the Bible on a daily walk or commute. Or even grab a 'colour the Bible' colouring book. We do this so that when we have those days when we say, 'I can't pray', 'It's too hard to love my neighbour today' or 'Where is God in my pain?', we have God's words of life at our fingertips, ready to give us hope and remind us of his promises.

The added bonus of being saturated in his word is that when the family gathers, no matter what shape your family takes, you're equipped to be able to share God's words with each other, and the news of God's love, grace and mercy gets passed on to the next generation.

RHIANNE O'ROURKE, ORDINAND AND PARENTING FOR FAITH SPEAKER

The servant teacher

The Lord God has given me the tongue of a teacher, that I may know how to sustain the weary with a word. Morning by morning he wakens – wakens my ear to listen as those who are taught. The Lord God has opened my ear, and I was not rebellious, I did not turn backwards. I gave my back to those who struck me, and my cheeks to those who pulled out the beard... The Lord God helps me; therefore I have not been disgraced; therefore I have set my face like flint, and I know that I shall not be put to shame.

ISAIAH 50:4–7 (NRSV, abridged)

In a series of juxtapositions, Isaiah shows the massive gulf between the people of Israel and the Lord's obedient servant: whereas there is 'no one' who listens or obeys God (v. 2), the servant listens to what God is saying (v. 4); whereas Israel is unconvinced about the Lord's love and power (v. 2), the servant is confident of the Lord's help and nearness (vv. 7–9); whereas Israel suffers for its sin and rebellion (v. 1), the servant suffers because of his obedience (vv. 5–6).

So the servant stands apart from his people at every point: here is the prophetic role in its purest form – the teacher who faithfully brings the word of the Lord to the people, even when they are unresponsive and rebellious. And Jesus, the true servant of the Lord, clearly had the three characteristics mentioned here, during his ministry: *a listening ear* (v. 4), often rising early to pray, *an instructed tongue* (v. 4), speaking only what the Father had taught him to say, and *a face like flint* (v. 7), setting his face steadfastly to Jerusalem, knowing terrible suffering awaited him there.

These are also the key requirements for any of us who have a teaching ministry in worship services, in small groups, in children's or youth work, in mission initiatives, in schools or in families:

A listening ear: waking early to pray, to seek God's face, to read his word and to listen out for his voice.

An instructed tongue: speaking the word of the Lord into particular situations and different contexts, knowing how to sustain the weary and encourage the faint-hearted.

A face like flint: courage to speak what God has given us, to take the consequences and to endure the cost – for the love of Jesus and the world he loves.

WILL DONALDSON, DIRECTOR OF NEW CONGREGATIONS, DIOCESE OF OXFORD

From small beginnings

Later that same day Jesus left the house and sat beside the lake. A large crowd soon gathered around him, so he got into a boat. Then he sat there and taught as the people stood on the shore. He told many stories in the form of parables... Here is another illustration Jesus used: 'The Kingdom of Heaven is like a mustard seed planted in a field. It is the smallest of all seeds, but it becomes the largest of garden plants; it grows into a tree, and birds come and make nests in its branches.'

MATTHEW 13:1–3a, 31–32 (NLT)

As a member of the Barnabas in Schools team, I often shared this parable with many children. I started by placing a tiny mustard seed in front of me, and then as I told the story I created a tree and added small birds, miniature nests and little eggs. Excitement grew as the eggs hatched and more birds arrived. As we looked at the tree filled with birds, we wondered together about why Jesus told this story. The children thought about what small action they could do to bring the kingdom of God into their class or school.

I find it encouraging that one small idea can grow and extend the kingdom of God. In the summer, a member of my Bible study group was struck by an article in BRF's *Bible Reflections for Older People* about a project knitting angels to bless a community. She knitted an angel and shared the idea with the group. Others in the group who are keen knitters joined in. Another person created some reflective prayer ideas to go with the angels, while another sourced some treats to go with the angels. By Christmas, what had started with one person knitting an angel resulted in over 200 people in our community receiving a bag of blessings, taking God's love into many homes.

I wonder if you have a tiny idea niggling in your head that might bring the kingdom of God to someone else.

JANE WHITTINGTON, SCHOOLS OFFICER, DIOCESE OF GUILDFORD, AND TRUSTEE, BRF

Showing the way

Show me your ways, Lord, teach me your paths. Guide me in your truth and teach me, for you are God my Saviour, and my hope is in you all day long. Remember, Lord, your great mercy and love, for they are from of old... Good and upright is the Lord; therefore he instructs sinners in his ways. He guides the humble in what is right and teaches them his way. All the ways of the Lord are loving and faithful towards those who keep the demands of his covenant.

PSALM 25:4–6, 8–10 (NIV)

I remember with deep affection the faithful women who taught me in Sunday school. I think they kindled in me a passion to teach. Along with my Crusader (now Urban Saints) leaders, these women showed me the way to follow God through their teaching, their modelling, their encouragement.

What they were doing was what we read about God doing with David in this psalm. When we read the story of David in the Bible, we see that he got himself into a few scrapes that definitely needed forgiveness. But what we see in this psalm is David talking to a God whom he sees as compassionate, merciful, full of loving-kindnesses (the word is plural in Hebrew). It is that God whom David is asking to show him the way and teach him the paths. A helpful image for me is an early photograph of me being held up by my arms and supported in my early, faltering steps. The image of God as a loving family member whom I can trust, in whom I can put my hope and who will guide me in the right way is immensely comforting, even now.

Life is not always easy, as Maya Angelou comments: 'We delight in the beauty of the butterfly but rarely admit the changes it has gone through to achieve that beauty.' These changes can involve facing up to when we have done wrong or drifted from the way, waiting, trusting God's timing and processes and ensuring we remain humble and teachable.

What opportunities do we have to teach and nurture others in the things of God that have been taught to us? How might we show someone the way that we have found to be life-giving? Even a simple conversation or the sharing of a story can help someone else along their path.

SALLY NASH, AUTHOR, THEOLOGICAL EDUCATOR AND MENTOR

Like a little child

People were bringing little children to Jesus for him to place his hands on them, but the disciples rebuked them. When Jesus saw this, he was indignant. He said to them, 'Let the little children come to me, and do not hinder them, for the kingdom of God belongs to such as these. Truly I tell you, anyone who will not receive the kingdom of God like a little child will never enter it.' And he took the children in his arms, placed his hands on them and blessed them.

MARK 10:13–16 (NIV)

In these verses, Jesus says we must be like little children to receive the kingdom of God. He is angry with his disciples when they try to prevent parents from bringing their children for a blessing. He lets his disciples know that children are to be valued. This passage echoes a theme found throughout the gospels: Jesus always seeks out and welcomes those regarded as unimportant at the time – the excluded, the marginalised, the sick, women and children.

Two phrases stand out: 'Let the children come to me' and 'Receive the kingdom of God like a little child.'

Jesus welcomes the children to come to him for a blessing. How do we welcome children into the faith? Jesus made time for the children. Making time to listen to children as they seek to understand their spiritual journey is essential, yet so often neglected. When do we set aside time to listen to and talk with children about the kingdom of God?

The key challenge of this passage is that if we do not receive the kingdom of God like a little child, we will never enter it. What does it mean to be like a child? One answer is to trust and freely accept the gift of the kingdom of God, as children willingly accept gifts. Little children are also full of curiosity and wonder, stopping on a walk to look at a raindrop on a leaf or the grass growing up in the pavement cracks. When do we wonder about the kingdom of God?

We need to make time to stop, reflect and wonder about creation like a little child and to be curious about the kingdom of God. What does it mean for me to receive the kingdom of God like a child?

ANN CASSON, SENIOR RESEARCH FELLOW, NATIONAL INSTITUTE FOR CHRISTIAN EDUCATION RESEARCH, CANTERBURY CHRIST CHURCH UNIVERSITY

Embracing our inner child

'O Jerusalem, Jerusalem, the city that kills the prophets and stones those who are sent to it! How often would I have gathered your children together as a hen gathers her brood under her wings, and you were not willing!'

LUKE 13:34 (ESV)

That little boy playing beneath the pew during Sunday worship may not have looked like he was taking in very much. But he was. The people who taught him to sing, 'Wide, wide as the ocean, high as the heavens above, deep, deep as the deepest sea, is my Saviour's love,' somehow touched his heart.

I know it is true. I was that little boy. Even when I shouted out the wrong answer, when clearly the right one was 'Jesus', these good people loved me into the kingdom.

So why were these early years so significant in my faith development? In his book *Mindsight*, Dr Daniel Siegel shows how 'neuroscientists have found that the right hemisphere [of the brain] is the more developed and more active during the first years of life... Our right hemisphere gives us a more direct sense of the whole body, our waves and tides of emotion, and the pictures of lived experience that make up our autobiographical memory. The right brain is the seat of our emotional and social selves,' explains Siegel.

As Dallas Willard often said, 'Everyone gets a spiritual formation; the question is whether it is any good.'

Grasping the importance of this helps to explain why some scriptures have such resonance with us, such as Jesus's lament over Jerusalem. Jesus recognised the value of early childhood (Luke 18:16) and he used stories and metaphors that tapped into right-brain thinking. From the contemporary perspective of neurological development, and in the best traditions of spiritual formation, reaching back into our most formative years could help us become more like Jesus.

Why has 'The Lord is my shepherd' become our undisputed favourite psalm? Is it in part because it speaks directly to our right brain, our early years, the need for reassurance, intimacy and comfort? 'He makes me lie down... he leads me... he restores me... he comforts me... he prepares a table for me... he anoints me... he gives goodness and mercy... he dwells with me.' Sit with these words and meditate on them and we will come close to the heart of God and also to the heart of our own inner child.

JAMES CATFORD, CHAIR, SPCK AND RENOVARÉ US

Local place and sacred space

[Joshua said,] 'Pass on before the ark of the Lord your God into the middle of the Jordan, and each of you take up a stone on his shoulder, one for each of the tribes of the Israelites, so that this may be a sign among you. When your children ask in time to come, "What do those stones mean to you?" then you shall tell them that the waters of the Jordan were cut off in front of the ark of the covenant of the Lord. When it crossed over the Jordan, the waters of the Jordan were cut off. So these stones shall be to the Israelites a memorial forever.'

JOSHUA 4:5b–7 (NRSV)

The built environment is a wonderful stimulus for curiosity. Children do ask, and children will continue to ask, 'What do these stones mean?' Within England and Wales today, the landscape remains rich in cathedrals, churches and chapels. These can be a clear reminder of a Christian heritage and of a faith imagined to last for ever. Seeing these cathedrals, churches and chapels, children do ask, and children will continue to ask, 'What do these stones mean?'

In some places these stones provide their own answer, as the new name 'Evan's Antiques' overlays the stone engraved 'Bethel Chapel', or as the village church is carefully fenced off behind the warning 'Danger. Keep out. Falling Masonry'. In some places these stones intrigue, but keep the secret to themselves. The door is locked and there is no signage. The church may still be in use, or it may not. Either way these stones have been given no voice.

In other places these stones welcome the curiosity, allow the curious to enter into the sacred space and gladly give access to their narrative. Here within the sacred space, the font speaks of Christian baptism, the lectern speaks of Christian scriptures, the pulpit speaks of Christian proclamation and teaching, and the altar speaks of the eucharistic feast. Here within the sacred space, the Christian narrative is proclaimed in the architecture, in the artwork, in the stained-glass windows and in the skilfully crafted signage written as a guide for the curious visitor.

Children do ask, and children will continue to ask, 'What do those stones mean?' It would be unfortunate, indeed, if we were to overlook the power of these buildings to fulfil the evangelistic purposes for which they were constructed.

LESLIE J. FRANCIS, PROFESSOR OF RELIGIONS AND PSYCHOLOGY, UNIVERSITY OF WARWICK, AND CANON THEOLOGIAN, LIVERPOOL CATHEDRAL

Growing in wisdom

After three days [Mary and Joseph] found [Jesus] in the temple, sitting among the teachers, listening to them and asking them questions. And all who heard him were amazed at his understanding and his answers... And he said to them, 'Why were you looking for me? Did you not know that I must be in my Father's house?'... And he went down with them and came to Nazareth and was submissive to them. And his mother treasured up all these things in her heart. And Jesus increased in wisdom and in stature and in favour with God and man.

LUKE 2:46–52 (ESV, abridged)

There are very few references in the gospel accounts to the childhood of Jesus, but this episode brings it to life with vivid reality. Initially we feel it from the perspective of his parents (for which parent has not known the stomach-wrenching moment when they fear their child is lost?), but then comes the dawning realisation that this is no ordinary boy but one with a unique role to play in salvation history.

Jesus' first recorded words tell us that he is special, as he claims a relationship with God which is deeper and more personal than anything that had been known or described before. His mother Mary does not fully understand, but treasures these things in her heart, as she has already glimpsed that there is an extraordinary future ahead. But how will Jesus prepare for such a future?

Sitting, learning and asking questions is the start of that journey, for the Bible is clear about the importance of teaching and passionate about wisdom-seeking. And that should be our horizon for wise education: a delight in wisdom and a passionate pursuit of it.

Wisdom is not a word that is much used in contemporary discussions of education, but it is essential for knowing how to live well in the sight of God and people (Proverbs 3:4). Jesus as a child 'grew in wisdom'. Teaching and developing wisdom must be central to any good education and at the heart of what it means to nurture our children in the faith – that they too might grow in wisdom and stature, to know what it is to live life in all the fullness which Jesus brings.

NIGEL GENDERS, CHIEF EDUCATION OFFICER, CHURCH OF ENGLAND

The gift of humiliation

Peter replied, 'Man, I don't know what you're talking about!' Just as he was speaking, the cock crowed. The Lord turned and looked straight at Peter. Then Peter remembered the word the Lord had spoken to him: 'Before the cock crows today, you will disown me three times.' And he went outside and wept bitterly.

LUKE 22:60–62 (NIV)

One of the extraordinary things about the gospels is their incredible honesty. It is one of the marks of their authenticity that these stories of Jesus and the early disciples give us a deeply human picture of the origins of the Christian faith. This is one such passage, which would have been read by people in the early church for whom Peter may well have been something of an elevated, heroic figure. And yet here he is, the founder of the Jesus movement, disowning Jesus on the eve of his crucifixion.

This is also a story that is recorded in each and every gospel. Clearly none of the gospel writers felt it should be airbrushed out to save Peter's reputation or memory. Instead, its raw presence tells us something crucial about the very nature of the Christian faith: that it is precisely through weakness and humiliation that salvation comes to us. It is precisely when all our pretence at strength and self-confidence are revealed as useless, in the face of our fundamental need for God and his forgiveness and grace, that we are most ready to receive it.

What is the turning point for Peter in his journey with Jesus and towards his ministry as 'the rock' on which Jesus built his church? Perhaps it was his declaration of faith (Matthew 16:16). Perhaps his anointing at Pentecost and his first public speech as leader of this new movement (Acts 2:14–40). But I think it was here, at rock bottom, when, alone and broken, he weeps and knows he does not have it in himself to be all that Jesus calls him to be. He must put all of his faith and trust in Jesus himself.

No one likes to be humiliated. But on the other hand, Peter's story suggests that we should not waste a good humiliation. It is in the experiences of our weakness and vulnerability that we are invited again and again to place our faith in the forgiveness and grace of God. Humiliation is a gift that no one wants, but when it comes it can be a very rich gift indeed.

PAUL BRADBURY, AUTHOR AND PIONEER MINISTER

Loving one another

And now, dear lady, I am not writing you a new command but one we have had from the beginning. I ask that we love one another. And this is love: that we walk in obedience to his commands. As you have heard from the beginning, his command is that you walk in love… If anyone comes to you and does not bring this teaching, do not take them into your house or welcome them.

2 JOHN 5–6, 10 (NIV)

For one of the shortest books in the Bible, 2 John packs a lot in. First, who is the mysterious 'dear lady' at the start? Most scholars agree this is probably an affectionate reference to the church, in much the same way as the analogies of 'bride' or 'wife' are used elsewhere in scripture to depict Jesus' followers en masse.

Then, who are these deceivers who bring teaching that isn't welcome? And why is the writer advising extreme caution in extending hospitality to strangers when other passages in the Bible recommend it wholeheartedly?

It is hard to imagine what it was like in the early years of the Christian church. Its growth depended on missionaries travelling great distances to share the good news. With no booking.com, homes were the only option for overnight accommodation. But the central teaching of the church was still being worked out; Jesus as both human and divine was not yet agreed doctrine. Here John advises Jesus' followers to show love but also use discretion in potentially hosting anyone promoting alternative theories of who Jesus was.

The detail here is instructive. The pictorial language of 'walking' reminds us that obedience and love are active, not passive. It is not only about internal beliefs and feelings; obedience and love are about how we live out our daily lives in practical ways.

As a family of three, owning a mid-terrace home with no spare room or garage, hospitality is a challenge I circle back to regularly. Would anyone be blessed by an overnight stay on a pull-out mattress surrounded by box files and sound equipment? Maybe not, but inviting someone into my home for a coffee is a way I can be active in my love for others. Hardly remarkable, but – as verse 5 states – this is nothing new; this teaching has been with us from the beginning.

CLAIRE DALPRA, SENIOR REVIEWER (RESEARCH AND TRAINING), CHURCH ARMY

A concert of praise

I will exalt you, my God the King; I will praise your name forever and ever. Every day I will praise you and extol your name forever and ever. Great is the Lord and most worthy of praise; his greatness no one can fathom. One generation commends your works to another; they tell of your mighty acts. They speak of the glorious splendour of your majesty – and I will meditate on your wonderful works. They tell of the power of your awesome works – and I will proclaim your great deeds. They celebrate your abundant goodness and joyfully sing of your righteousness. The Lord is gracious and compassionate, slow to anger and rich in love.

PSALM 145:1–8 (NIV)

Is praising God something you find easy, and do you do it regularly? Often, praising God comes easiest when things are going well in life and we are conscious of his goodness and grace. But what about the rest of the time? Maybe praise doesn't flow so easily then.

This is the last of the psalms attributed to David. Praise for God overflows from him; it bubbles out of him. In the first two verses of the psalm he praises God and then says why in verse 3 – because of God's greatness. In verses 4–7, generations join in the praise. Why? 'Because the Lord is gracious and compassionate, slow to anger and rich in love' (v. 8, quoting Exodus 34:6).

What can David teach us about living life for God? We don't know exactly when David wrote this psalm, but his focus on the character and attributes of God indicates he is not bound in his praise by the circumstances of his own life. He is looking up to see God, not looking down at his own situation. When we consider some of the aspects of David's life, we are reassured that his praise is neither naïve nor unrealistic. This is praise for God born out of experience of him in the nitty-gritty of life.

One of the sure ways we can nurture others in their faith is to show where our focus is fixed on a day-to-day basis. 'One generation commends your works to another' is how we are encouraged and strengthened. Who overhears your concert of praise?

I am no poet, but I do want my praise of the living God to flow out of me naturally, so that God is honoured and others encouraged to know him better.

ELAINE DUNCAN, CEO, SCOTTISH BIBLE SOCIETY

Be the gift

As for us, brothers and sisters, when, for a short time, we were made orphans by being separated from you – in person, not in heart – we longed with great eagerness to see you face to face. For we wanted to come to you – certainly I, Paul, wanted to again and again – but Satan blocked our way. For what is our hope or joy or crown of boasting before our Lord Jesus at his coming? Is it not you?

1 THESSALONIANS 2:17–19 (NRSV)

Archbishop Desmond Tutu told the story of a wise teacher who stood before his daughter, sensing unexplored potential, eyes blazing with love, holding his arms out, as though to enfold her life with his words, 'This is God's gift to you. Make it your gift to the world.' She changed from a liberal arts degree at Harvard University to pursue electrical engineering.

We each have our own set of gifts. We have mentors who have inspired us and taught us things in life, perhaps helping us to find our own giftings. Our relationships are a fundamental part of our human experience – even if, at times, the circumstances require us to think a little differently about how to nurture them. Paul longed to be with the Thessalonians again, teaching them and sharing in their lives, and even though he was not able to be with them in person, he made a plan to nurture their spiritual journey and encourage them.

The alternative technology that he had available at the time was a letter that he sent with one of his teammates (no postal service as we know it). Paul encouraged the Thessalonians: he was proud of the way they conducted their lives, in spite of their suffering. The people whom he had nurtured gave him hope and joy. The relationship worked both ways.

What is God's gift to you? Think about how this can become a gift to the world through the people that God has given you to nurture (even if it is only a few). Invest time in those relationships and leave a legacy. Then celebrate, with them and others, the hope and joy that you see as a result of your love.

JEAN PIENAAR, MOTHER AND MESSY CHURCH COORDINATOR, SOUTH AFRICA

Linger, listen, echo

For who has stood in the council of the Lord so as to see and hear his word? Who has given heed to his word so as to proclaim it?… Is not my word like fire, says the Lord, and like a hammer that breaks a rock in pieces?

JEREMIAH 23:18, 29 (NRSV)

As a lifelong teacher of the Bible and theology, these words pose a double challenge to me and to all who would help others understand the gospel of Jesus Christ.

First, I need to ask if I have lingered long enough 'in the council of the Lord' listening to him, so I can be sure that what I speak is, as far as is humanly possible, true to his purposes. This is why we at BRF do everything we can to help people read the Bible every day so it becomes like their life blood – a very part of them. But Jeremiah finds that he is commissioned to reprove others who are not listening to God; he is 'to pluck up and to pull down, to destroy and to overthrow' as well as 'to build and to plant' (1:10). All teachers know that correction is an important part of helping others to learn, though no one finds that easy when we are helping our fellow believers. But God's word is not only encouragement (for which we thank him) but also a call to repentance so that we can become more like Jesus. Then his word can be like a fire or a hammer – both effecting change.

Once when I was teaching on Ephesians in Sabah, Malaysia, at the end of the class a married man came to me in tears. The Lord had shown him that he was far from treating his wife as Jesus loves his church (Ephesians 5:25). My words were quietly spoken, but the Lord's word was like a fire in his heart. We should not be surprised when reading scripture produces tears, repentance, change – in those whom we are teaching, but, please God, also in us.

CHRISTINA BAXTER, FORMER PRINCIPAL, ST JOHN'S NOTTINGHAM, AND VICE-CHAIR OF TRUSTEES, BRF

Tend

'To respond to human need by loving service.'

WHEN JESUS was asked which was the greatest commandment in the law, he replied: '"Love the Lord your God with all your heart and with all your soul and with all your mind." This is the first and greatest commandment. And the second is like it: "Love your neighbour as yourself"' (Matthew 22:37–39, NIV).

Love for God and love for others go hand in hand. We see this throughout the Bible's narrative. In the Old Testament, the Israelites were not only given strict rules about how to worship God, but also about how they treated the foreigner, the poor and the needy among them. And in the New Testament, the early church was encouraged to care for one another and to express their faith not only in words, but also in deeds.

In the readings that follow, we reflect on this truth and explore how this works in practice. We will learn how God often meets us in our need through the loving kindness of others; how Jesus set the standard for loving service and how we can be channels of his love for others, often through simple, practical actions.

John Wesley wrote: 'Do all the good you can, by all the means you can, in all the ways you can, in all the places you can, at all the times you can, to all the people you can, as long as ever you can.' Let that thought inspire us as we consider the challenge of following Jesus' example of loving service.

JACKIE HARRIS, EDITOR, *DAY BY DAY WITH GOD*

The palm of his hand

'Shout for joy, you heavens; rejoice, you earth; burst into song, you mountains! For the Lord comforts his people and will have compassion on his afflicted ones. But Zion said, "The Lord has forsaken me, the Lord has forgotten me." Can a mother forget the baby at her breast and have no compassion on the child she has borne? Though she may forget, I will not forget you! See, I have engraved you on the palms of my hands.'

ISAIAH 49:13–16a (NIV, abridged)

Over my 34 years of presenting BBC Television's *Songs of Praise*, there are so many moments that stay in my mind.

One is an image I can still picture clearly from an interview I recorded with a lady several months after she'd been through terrible depression, following a sequence of bruising experiences. She talked about how she'd felt she was falling down a dark pit with nothing to cling on to – even prayer, because no one seemed to be listening. She finally came to the conclusion that there could be no God, because he couldn't be so heartless as to desert her when she was at rock bottom. But then, months later, with the benefit of hindsight, she realised she'd been too hurt at the time to recognise that God *was* there all along, especially at the darkest times. His love was in the plates of hot food delivered by her neighbour when she felt too low to cook for herself; in the 'How are you?' phone calls from worried friends, who then read between the lines, and arrived with a listening ear and a caring arm around her shoulders.

And that was when she held out her hands towards me. 'I couldn't see this at the time,' she said. 'But I know this was me, cupped in God's loving hands.'

I know that feeling. This verse from Isaiah – 'I will not forget you! See, I have engraved you on the palms of my hands' (v. 16) – always makes me feel just as that lady did: safe and supported by the hands that made me, and the God who knows me, warts and all. He knows my strengths and weaknesses, and how they work together in the unique set of qualities, abilities and opportunities that he created as 'me' – a one-off model, battered by life, but dearly loved by God.

PAM RHODES, BROADCASTER AND AUTHOR

This is how much I love you...

It was just before the Passover Feast. Jesus knew that the time had come for him to leave this world and go to the Father. Having loved his own who were in the world, he loved them to the end.

JOHN 13:1 (NIV)

Guess How Much I Love You is a famous children's book by Sam McBratney and Anita Jeram. In it, Little Nutbrown Hare and Big Nutbrown Hare each try to convince the other that they love them the most. Finally, as he snuggles into his bed, Little says he loves Big right up to the moon, and Big whispers that he loves Little right up to the moon – and back.

In our gospel passage, Jesus had up to this point been very active and upfront. He travelled around, interacted with people, preached and performed miracles. There was love in all these activities. But from this point 'he loved them to the end'. So what happened next? He washed the disciples' feet: he served instead of being served. He ate a meal with his disciples and said to Judas, 'What you are about to do, do quickly' (v. 27). He knew what was going to happen and did nothing about it – except to let it happen. He did not resist all that followed: being denied and forsaken by his friends, followed by his arrest, trial and crucifixion.

In these ways, Jesus was showing the full extent of his love. He was saying to his disciples, as he is now saying to us and to the whole world: 'This is how much I love you.' All that he did and said was included in that 'this'. But so, too, painfully and sacrificially, was all that he voluntarily exposed himself to, all the undeserved punishment that was heaped on him.

And what did that stupendous humbling and suffering achieve? The salvation of the world. The death of 'the just for the unjust, that he might bring us to God' (1 Peter 3:18, KJV). And also, finally, resurrection.

C.S. Lewis said, 'To love at all is to be vulnerable.' If your love is making you vulnerable, causing you anguish, you are in good company. Does this give you the courage and inspiration to keep praying and trusting that something deep and wonderful will come out of your painful and costly loving?

JEAN WATSON, WRITER AND SPIRITUAL ACCOMPANIST

Washing dirty feet

The evening meal was in progress, and the devil had already prompted Judas, the son of Simon Iscariot, to betray Jesus. Jesus knew that the Father had put all things under his power, and that he had come from God and was returning to God; so he got up from the meal, took off his outer clothing, and wrapped a towel round his waist. After that, he poured water into a basin and began to wash his disciples' feet, drying them with the towel that was wrapped round him.

JOHN 13:2–5 (NIV)

I watched a TV programme where a celebrity followed a Salvation Army officer on her daily round. He observed as, on her knees, she carefully and very cheerfully washed the filthy sore-covered feet of a homeless man.

We watch in our imagination God Almighty on his knees, an improvised apron around his waist, washing the dirty, road-weary feet of his disciples. See from his viewpoint one particular pair of feet. He holds them gently and, if he looks up, he gazes into the eyes of Judas. Jesus knows what this friend of his is about to do; he knows the contempt Judas has for him and the total rejection of his love. And Jesus bends to his task, washes, wipes each foot, places it carefully down.

His task completed, Jesus straightens up and says, 'I have set you an example that you should do as I have done for you' (v. 15). Is he calling his disciples to foot-washing? Not literally for most of us (though for some he does). Jesus explains his instruction: 'Love one another. As I have loved you, so you must love one another' (v. 34).

We would not understand the full import of that command if he had washed only the feet of his true friends. *He washed Judas' feet.* Now we know that Jesus' love is *unconditional*. And he calls us to that level of love.

Our loving service in Jesus' name is not just for friends and family; it's for the unlovely, the undeserving, the ones who don't love us. Some are called to 'frontline' service, in direct contact with the most needy. Others are called to loving, active and sacrificial support of those who are doing the 'down and dirty' work. All of us are called – to receive and to offer unconditional love.

JILL RATTLE, FORMER EDITOR, *DAY BY DAY WITH GOD*

God our loving Father

When Israel was a child, I loved him, and out of Egypt I called my son… It was I who taught Ephraim to walk, taking them by the arms; but they did not realise it was I who healed them. I led them with cords of human kindness, with ties of love. To them I was like one who lifts a little child to the cheek, and I bent down to feed them.

HOSEA 11:1, 3–4 (NIV)

These words portray God to be like a devoted father and mother. He helps the child step by step, lifting him when he stumbles, kissing him better. She patiently guides him through his day, with that strong maternal heart tie that's been there from before he was born. This beloved infant contentedly nuzzles their faces and receives choice food from their hands.

But the previous verses describe God's deep anguish. He'd rescued Ephraim (another name for Israel) from Egypt's bondage, working miracles, bestowing blessings and defeating enemies to bring them to the promised land. But instead of thanksgiving and praise and accepting his laws of life and love, they rejected him to worship cruel pagan gods.

It's sometimes hard to believe in God's unfailing love, knowing that we often go astray, get lost and feel failures. So let's replay in our imagination this 'video clip' of verses 3 and 4 and meditate on his unconditional, passionate, tender care. We'll never deserve or earn it; our only hope is to trust Jesus, who has redeemed, forgiven and accepted us into his family.

God's longing for Ephraim resonates with parents whose children have gone away, harbouring resentment, embracing bad lifestyles. Perhaps that's you or someone you know – desperate for the son or daughter 'in a far country' to come home. The Father patiently watches with us to welcome them back, so let's never give up on these wanderers. And he's promised always to be there for you and me too.

CELIA BOWRING, PRAYER COORDINATOR AND EXECUTIVE EDITOR, CARE

Double standards vs indiscriminate love

My brothers and sisters, believers in our glorious Lord Jesus Christ must not show favouritism. Suppose a man comes into your meeting wearing a gold ring and fine clothes, and a poor man in filthy old clothes also comes in. If you show special attention to the man wearing fine clothes and say, 'Here's a good seat for you,' but say to the poor man, 'You stand there' or 'Sit on the floor by my feet,' have you not discriminated among yourselves and become judges with evil thoughts? Listen, my dear brothers and sisters: has not God chosen those who are poor in the eyes of the world to be rich in faith and to inherit the kingdom he promised those who love him?

JAMES 2:1–5 (NIV)

Ever felt like you were being treated unfairly? Perhaps it was a childhood dispute where you felt a sibling was preferred or a work situation where you were overlooked or undervalued. Undoubtedly, we can all name a time where we felt the sharp sting of injustice.

Perhaps harder to name, and certainly more difficult to admit, are the times when *we* have given preferential treatment based on a person's appearance or some other perceived value – on the street, at home or at work.

In this passage, James strongly condemns this kind of favouritism existing in the church community. He is pointing out the utter incompatibility of faith in Jesus Christ and favouritism towards the rich at the expense of the poor.

This is still true today. Like it or not, we live in a world where the rich can get what they want – whether in the form of protection from violence or access to healthcare – and the poor just have to put up with it.

But James is clear: this is not the way of God's kingdom. The church should not operate like that; it should reflect God's indiscriminate love in the way it behaves – to rich and poor, strong and weak, lovely and unlovely alike. All human status pales into insignificance next to 'our glorious Lord Jesus Christ'.

The commands to love your neighbour as yourself and to not show favouritism are difficult to hear, and even harder to put into practice. They are also potentially world changing. Central to New Testament teaching, they remain central for Christ's followers today.

ALIANORE SMITH, CHURCH PARTNERSHIPS MANAGER, INTERNATIONAL JUSTICE MISSION

Be transformed

Do not be conformed to this world but be transformed by the renewal of your mind, that you may prove what is the will of God, what is good and acceptable and perfect... Let love be genuine; hate what is evil, hold fast to what is good; love one another with brotherly affection; outdo one another in showing honour. Never flag in zeal, be aglow with the Spirit, serve the Lord. Rejoice in your hope, be patient in tribulation, be constant in prayer. Contribute to the needs of the saints, practise hospitality... Rejoice with those who rejoice, weep with those who weep.

ROMANS 12:2, 9–13, 15 (RSV)

What do you most hope for in your friends and with those whom you meet, and where might you look for an answer?

Well, in some things, the *Book of Common Prayer* has all the best lines! The words used in the marriage service speak volumes: the couple promise 'to love and to cherish, for better for worse, for richer for poorer, in sickness and in health'. Elsewhere they vow to 'honour' each other. *Common Worship* adds still more: 'All that I am I give to you.' All these words are unconditional.

Many of these sentiments are there in our passage today. Love one another with mutual affection; outdo one another in showing honour; let love be genuine. All this runs far more deeply than mere sentimentality, for all is rooted in God: 'be aglow with the Spirit... Rejoice in your hope... be constant in prayer' (vv. 11–12) – some translations say 'pray without ceasing'. All this stems from the first words we read: 'Be transformed by the renewal of your mind, that you may prove what is the will of God' (v. 2).

'Be transformed' are the watchwords. It's hardly surprising, then, that some of the best answers to that first question are in the marriage service, for any lifelong relationship is unavoidably transformative. You cannot live with another person and not be changed. If that's true on the human level, then how much more must it be with God.

It is, of course, exactly what we see in Jesus. So close is his relationship with the Father that, in Gethsemane, Jesus calls God *Abba*, that is, 'Daddy'. We're back to that word 'unconditional' – just as Jesus gave of himself. *That's* what we hope for from others and, indeed, just what they should expect of us.

STEPHEN PLATTEN, BISHOP, WRITER AND VICE-PRESIDENT, BRF

What should we do next?

As [Jesus was] going into a village, ten men who had leprosy met him. They stood at a distance and called out, 'Jesus, Master, have pity on us!' When he saw them, he said, 'Go, show yourselves to the priests.' And as they went, they were cleansed. One of them, when he saw he was healed, came back... He threw himself at Jesus' feet and thanked him – and he was a Samaritan. Jesus asked, 'Were not all ten cleansed? Where are the other nine? Has no one returned to give praise to God except this foreigner?' Then he said to him, 'Rise and go; your faith has made you well.'

LUKE 17:12–19 (NIV, abridged)

Each community is unique and has its own specific range of needs. That means when it comes to the local church responding, it can be difficult to decide what to do first. Often, the challenge of answering the needs of the community can lead to paralysis, because we do not want to make the wrong choice. Even with prayerful consideration, it can feel overwhelming. As more churches become engaged in their communities, there is a risk of local churches simply copying whatever seems to be popular and on trend. Jesus does not invite us to do what is fashionable, but to genuinely serve.

In this passage, we see that Jesus identifies a deep social need, or a felt need. He identified a genuine need in the community of lepers. He recognised that their hope for healing was their single most important need and he answered it. That is why I call this a 'felt' need: we must be able to discern the greatest need by 'feeling' it as well as seeing it.

Genuine church-led community engagement starts with a profound understanding of the community. Begin by gaining an appreciation of the greatest felt needs and also the resources that exist among the community. There are a variety of ways that your church can find out what the deepest needs and resources of your community are. It is always beneficial to examine the local government strategic plan because they will have already invested significantly in understanding the community's social needs and assets. Beyond that there are informal approaches of listening to people in the community: listen to what parents are saying at the school gates, what medical staff are saying in surgeries and hospitals and what people talk about down the pub or sports centre.

What should we do next?

MATT BIRD, GLOBAL SPEAKER AND CEO, CINNAMON NETWORK INTERNATIONAL

Every little helps

When Jesus looked up and saw a great crowd coming towards him, he said to Philip, 'Where shall we buy bread for these people to eat?' He asked this only to test him, for he already had in mind what he was going to do. Philip answered him, 'It would take more than half a year's wages to buy enough bread for each one to have a bite!' Another of his disciples, Andrew, Simon Peter's brother, spoke up, 'Here is a boy with five small barley loaves and two small fish, but how far will they go among so many?' Jesus said, 'Make the people sit down.' There was plenty of grass in that place, and they sat down (about five thousand men were there). Jesus then took the loaves, gave thanks, and distributed to those who were seated as much as they wanted. He did the same with the fish.

JOHN 6:5–11 (NIV)

It's easy to look at ourselves, our skills and possessions, and feel we have nothing worthwhile to give to help the people around us. Maybe we've been influenced by others' attitudes to our potential offering and convinced ourselves of the truth of their observations. Maybe we feel overwhelmed by the size of a need and see our contribution as a drop in the ocean, making so little difference that there's no point in the gesture.

But here it seems that the young boy based his decision to offer his picnic for a communal lunch neither on the attitude of the disciples nor on the size of the crowd. Rather, he believed that somehow it would make a difference, despite the challenge of feeding so many. We're not told whether his action came from naivety or an active faith in Jesus' miraculous power. Either way, his selflessness led to the satisfying of physical hunger in the moment and became a shining example of how Jesus uses our little to provide for whatever need is pressing.

And so, as we consider what we have to offer in any given situation, we have a choice to make. Do we base our decision on the size of the challenge or the attitude of others, or do we accept that our role is to be willing to give of ourselves and trust God to do the rest? It may sound simplistic, but a childlike faith is what is valued and accepted by God.

We can also take heart that the boy didn't lose out by his selfless action – his hunger was still met by his own lunch and he may even have ended up eating more than the original amount. When we offer our resources to God, we'll never lose out.

BEV JULLIEN, CEO, MOTHERS' UNION

Meeting the need

While Jesus was having dinner at Matthew's house, many tax collectors and sinners came and ate with him and his disciples. When the Pharisees saw this, they asked his disciples, 'Why does your teacher eat with tax collectors and sinners?' On hearing this, Jesus said, 'It is not the healthy who need a doctor, but those who are ill. But go and learn what this means: "I desire mercy, not sacrifice." For I have not come to call the righteous, but sinners.'

MATTHEW 9:10–13 (NIV)

I was once invited to be part of a small church community in an 'area of deprivation'. People were proud and welcoming, brutally honest and passionate about their community, but they were also financially and educationally poor. A key part of this community was the community meal, offered each week by a different member. This particular week, a long table was laid out before the people. It was laden with bowls and plates containing a range of different items: grated cheese, bowls of salad, homemade avocado guacamole, tortilla wraps and steaming platters of frying meats and vegetables.

That week almost everyone left hungry. Although the meal was lovingly and sacrificially prepared and laid out, the people present had never been taught how to make and fold fajitas. Nor the simple rule that it was okay to make a mess. It remains a stark reminder for me that church folk can often invest much when it comes to hospitality – and yet for those people who have not ever experienced an abundant feast, even a simple gesture can be overwhelming.

Jesus spent his time with messy and messed-up people. Some did not know the 'rules'. Some just couldn't keep the rules. Others, like Matthew, knew, broke and rewrote the rules to their own advantage. Jesus is seen, time and time again, eating with those who others would steer clear of.

Food is either an equaliser or a source of division. Jesus made sure that he ate with the undesirables, shared feasts with his friends and broke bread with the broken. In so doing, he made sure that even the most messy and messed-up of people were seen, often named (as we see here with Matthew), and their needs met.

The overwhelming truth is that around a table with Jesus, no one leaves hungry.

JOANNE COX-DARLING, METHODIST MINISTER, MOTHER AND WRITER

Gifts to be shared

Above all, love each other deeply, because love covers over a multitude of sins. Offer hospitality to one another without grumbling. Each of you should use whatever gift you have received to serve others, as faithful stewards of God's grace in its various forms. If anyone speaks, they should do so as one who speaks the very words of God. If anyone serves, they should do so with the strength God provides, so that in all things God may be praised through Jesus Christ. To him be the glory and the power forever and ever. Amen.

1 PETER 4:8–11 (NIV)

'Whatever gift you have received…' (v. 10). What do you think of when you read this verse? God's gifts come in many shapes and sizes. The Bible lists some of them, but it is far from exhaustive. Think of some of the things you enjoy or excel at: gardening or sewing, perhaps, or languages, driving or sports. Might we see these things as gifts we have received that can be used in loving service?

When I was editing *Woman Alive*, we talked to many women who were using their skills and interests for good. Some were fundraisers for causes close to their hearts, others discovered the things they enjoyed doing enabled them to build community, empower others or reach out to those in need.

We heard about women knitting hats for seamen, driving people to hospital appointments, training assistance dogs, baking cakes for struggling families, teaching English and supporting immigrant families, creating community gardens, listening to children reading in school, providing lunches and company for those who are lonely or homeless and many more.

Like the young boy who gave his loaves and fishes to Jesus, we just need to be willing to share what we have. To bring our talents and interests – or simply our availability – into the loving presence of God to see what he can make of them.

I think many of us have a tendency to compare ourselves with others and then downgrade ourselves, but God distributes his gifts to everyone, 'just as he determines' (1 Corinthians 12:11). We all have a place and purpose in his kingdom. Let's recognise the good things that God has given us and encourage one another to see how we can use them to be a blessing to others.

JACKIE HARRIS, EDITOR OF *DAY BY DAY WITH GOD*

Mad, bad and dangerous to know

When [Jesus] had stepped out of the boat, immediately a man out of the tombs with an unclean spirit met him. He lived among the tombs; and no one could restrain him... When he saw Jesus from a distance, he ran and bowed down before him; and he shouted at the top of his voice, 'What have you to do with me, Jesus, Son of the Most High God? I adjure you by God, do not torment me'... Then people came to see what it was that had happened. They... saw the demoniac sitting there, clothed and in his right mind.

MARK 5:2–15 (NRSV, abridged)

Watch out, Jesus: there's no time for a risk assessment. The man from the Gerasenes was so used to being badly treated by others that when he sees Jesus, he's frightened: 'Do not torment me.' Yet he reached out to Jesus – even though he was afraid of doing so.

Afterwards, he's described as being 'in his right mind'. Many have speculated that he was mentally ill. He may well have been: verse 5 refers to self-harm. Stigma about mental illness has always existed. Perhaps that's why he was ostracised and, even when healed, was still afraid and wanted to go with Jesus in the boat (v. 18).

In an article for *Preach* magazine, Jo Swinney wrote, 'Depression, anxiety and mental anguish are not signs you are a bad Christian.' Feeling anxious or depressed at certain times is perfectly normal. But it's right to be concerned when those feelings affect our ability to function. When work, sleep, family life and other everyday matters are increasingly difficult, help needs to be sought. But, paradoxically (although not unusually), the act, or even the very thought, of seeking help may feel frightening at first, as it did for the man from the Gerasenes. We may be scared of 'what will come out' or worried about 'what's wrong' and concerned about what others will think.

'To be healed is much more than being cured,' writes Graham Reeves in *Two Other Men* (Instant Apostle, 2017). 'To be healed is to be accepting of one's situation, to be in harmony and peace with oneself, with others and with God. To be healed is to be reconciled with one's past and with one's future.'

Today, spend some time thinking about your mental well-being.

RICHARD FROST, AUTHOR AND BLOGGER

Instructions for living?

Live in peace with each other… encourage the disheartened, help the weak, be patient with everyone. Make sure that nobody pays back wrong for wrong, but always strive to do what is good for each other and for everyone else. Rejoice always, pray continually, give thanks in all circumstances; for this is God's will for you in Christ Jesus… May God himself, the God of peace, sanctify you through and through… The one who calls you is faithful, and he will do it.

1 THESSALONIANS 5:13–24 (NIV, abridged)

On the surface, this passage appears to be a handy guide for how to live as a good Christian. The Bible is complex, so when you reach sections like this that seem almost to bullet point how we should live, it can be tempting to breathe a sigh of relief and think, 'Phew, at last, a summary of what I need to do.'

On one level, it is that. Most, if not all, of us would agree that we should try to live in peace with one another, help the weak, be patient and so on. The key word, though, is that we *try*. Have you met a Christian yet who is able to live this way without ever slipping up? No. Because it's not possible. We must *try* to live this way, but ultimately we will all fall short.

As we read on, we see that this is not a list of instructions for us to follow on our own but a reminder that we do all of this with God. We are asked to 'Rejoice always, pray continually, give thanks in all circumstances; for this is God's will for you' (vv. 16–18). We must try to do the things listed, but the most important thing is to share it with God. To rejoice even when things go wrong, to pray about everything and to give thanks to God, no matter whether life is going well or not. Because the purpose of this passage, as with all the Bible, is to draw us closer to Jesus and our Father God. Through our successes and our failures we journey forward with him.

We must do all we can to live in a Christlike way, but in the end it is God, the God of peace, who will 'sanctify you through and through', because he 'is faithful, and he will do it'.

SARA SHEERIN, HEAD OF PEOPLE AND CULTURE, BRF

A humble entry

As they were untying the colt, its owners asked them, 'Why are you untying the colt?' They said, 'The Lord needs it.' Then they brought it to Jesus; and after throwing their cloaks on the colt, they set Jesus on it. As he rode along, people kept spreading their cloaks on the road... The whole multitude of the disciples began to praise God joyfully with a loud voice for all the deeds of power that they had seen, saying, 'Blessed is the king who comes in the name of the Lord! Peace in heaven, and glory in the highest heaven!'

LUKE 19:33–38 (NRSV, abridged)

At this point in Jesus' life, he is widely known for the miracles he performed and for his wise preaching. If social media had existed in his day, Jesus would have been a mega influencer. When celebrities visit towns and cities, how do they travel? More often than not, in order to live up to their followers' expectations of them, they arrive in luxurious, expensively engineered cars, chauffeur-driven to prove to the world their important status. The car door having been opened for them, they arrive at their destination fresh and as well-groomed and unflustered as when they started their journey.

Jesus, however, chose to arrive in Jerusalem, the most important city in Israel, on an untamed colt. Not for him a horse and chariot like the kings and armies used and, indeed, which his fame would have merited. What's more, 'they set Jesus on it' – imagine how ungainly that must have looked! How slowly the colt would have plodded, and how completely accessible he would have been to everyone.

Jesus travelled in total humility. But despite his humble mode of transport, as he entered the city, his followers celebrated his arrival by throwing their cloaks on the ground in front of him. Their abundant, joyous faith in Jesus didn't need fancy, physical trappings to prove to them that he was 'the king who comes in the name of the Lord!'

As we live out our Christian life, do we conduct ourselves with humility and grace, just as our Lord Jesus Christ did? Or do we feel we need additional physical forms of recognition to prove to the outside world that we are worthy, credible and good?

ELAINE LAMBIE, MESSY CHURCH SUPPORT TEAM MEMBER

Bubbling over with joy

Grace be unto you, and peace, from God our Father, and from the Lord Jesus Christ. I thank my God upon every remembrance of you, Always in every prayer of mine for you all making request with joy, For your fellowship in the gospel from the first day until now; Being confident of this very thing, that he which hath begun a good work in you will perform it until the day of Jesus Christ.

PHILIPPIANS 1:2–6 (KJV)

The letter from the apostle Paul to the Christians living in Philippi does not perhaps receive the attention of his other letters. This is strange, because the letter is an absolute gem. Philippi was an important town in eastern Macedonia and the church there can be traced back to Paul's second missionary journey, when he had a vision of a man begging him to come to Macedonia (Acts 16:9).

It is typical of Paul that he gives thanks right at the beginning of his letter, and this is surely an important lesson for us. Does giving thanks have priority in our prayers? We remember to pray for our family, our friends, our church, the sick and the poor, but do we always remember to give thanks for everything we have received in life? I often don't. I read somewhere that to be born in the western world hits the jackpot; you are fortunate to be in the richest 1% of humanity.

Next, Paul emphasises the importance of prayer, and what an example he sets. First, he tells the Philippians that they are constantly in his prayers. Then he writes: 'And this I pray that your love may abound yet more and more in knowledge and in all judgement. That ye may approve things that are excellent; that ye may be sincere and without offence till the day of Christ' (vv. 9–10).

Paul's letter bubbles over with joy, and yet he writes from prison in Rome. With no knowledge of what the future may hold for him, he thinks only of his fellow Christians. Revd Phil Moon writes of a church where the members had to learn Philippians by heart and recite it to the congregation. This is certainly not a bad idea!

NEIL SKIDMORE, STAFFORDSHIRE

Transform

'To seek to transform unjust structures of society, to challenge violence of every kind and to pursue peace and reconciliation.'

W E ARE LIVING IN A TIME when many of us are intensely aware that we inhabit a broken world. At every turn, we seem to be confronted with injustice, inequality, violence and corruption. In a time like this, the words of the Bible come to us with new power and authority. They bring fresh hope and a clear message of how we should now be living.

Around 2,700 years ago, the prophet Micah famously asked, 'What does the Lord require of you but to do justice, and to love kindness, and to walk humbly with your God?' (Micah 6:8, NRSV). These extraordinary words echo through the Bible and find their greatest expression and their fulfilment in the life and teachings of Jesus.

Jesus proclaimed the good news of the kingdom of God, and he demonstrated by his actions what this means. He always found time for the marginalised, the left behind and the forgotten ones. He healed the sick and set the captives free. He confronted the powers and authorities wherever they placed heavy burdens on the shoulders of the poor. This is what it means to do justice and to love kindness.

All of Jesus' actions flowed out of his relationship with his Father. He arose early in the morning to go to a place apart, in order that throughout each day he would be enabled to walk in humble obedience to the loving purposes of the Father. A heart of love and compassion is formed by daily intimacy with the God of love. This is what we see in Jesus, and this is how we become instruments of God's peace and justice in a broken world.

IAN COWLEY, AUTHOR AND SPEAKER

Kingdom come

After John was put in prison, Jesus went into Galilee, proclaiming the good news of God. 'The time has come,' he said. 'The kingdom of God has come near. Repent and believe the good news!' As Jesus walked beside the Sea of Galilee, he saw Simon and his brother Andrew casting a net into the lake, for they were fishermen. 'Come, follow me,' Jesus said, 'and I will send you out to fish for people.' At once they left their nets and followed him.

MARK 1:14–18 (NIV)

'The kingdom of God has come near.' I wonder what this statement means to you.

We often misunderstand Jesus' words and, by so doing, miss the awe and wonder of what is actually being announced. The phrase 'has come near' is a Jewish idiom that signifies a present reality. So Jesus was saying: 'The kingdom of God has come! Therefore, there are changes to be made to live in the totality of that truth.' From the context, both here and elsewhere, it is clear that the kingdom had arrived in the person of the Messiah, Jesus.

Jesus' ministry will unfold in the gospels as one which both declares and demonstrates the kingdom. If we look at the encounters that follow on from our reading, we see the kingdom in evidence as Jesus recruits his first kingdom-broadcasters and as he delivers demonised people and heals those with various diseases. Throughout the gospels, we read about God's kingdom of grace, justice and peace which restores, heals, and sets people free.

Of course, while the kingdom came in and through the Messiah King – we could even say that Jesus is the human face of the kingdom – the fullness of the kingdom is yet to come. For the biblical authors, sometimes they write about God's power at work in the midst of people right then; while at other times they write about the future and the world to come. We could say, 'The kingdom is already here… and yet there is even more to come!'

What difference does it make to you to know that you are part of God's kingdom right now?

Even as we wait for Jesus to return, our king extends an invitation to us to follow him and display his love and his power to everyone.

PHILIP GRASHAM, COLLEGE LECTURER AND TUTOR

You shall also love the stranger

The Lord your God is God of gods and Lord of lords, the great God, mighty and awesome, who is not partial and takes no bribe, who executes justice for the orphan and the widow, and who loves the strangers, providing them with food and clothing. You shall also love the stranger, for you were strangers in the land of Egypt.

DEUTERONOMY 10:17–19 (NRSV)

I came to the UK, aged eleven, with my parents in 1964, and felt very much an outsider, a stranger and alone. I have worked all my life for justice, overcoming exclusion and discrimination.

The Bible contains the command to 'love your neighbour as yourself'. Jesus based his parable of the good Samaritan on these words (Luke 10:29–37).

Yet this commandment is stated only once in Hebrew scriptures (Leviticus 19:18). Around 40 times, though, the Hebrew scriptures hold up the challenge to also 'love the stranger'. There is no other ethical requirement repeated so often. And Jesus' good Samaritan reveals exemplary values in a stranger.

A neighbour is someone who is a bit like yourself. A stranger is someone very different, and not the first person you might reach out to.

Hebrew prophets linked the stranger to the orphan and the widow. These were people who had no means to live independently and were most excluded in society. God 'executes justice' for them. Who are the people in this situation today? Children separated from families? Older people without support? People displaced by war and extreme weather, seeking sanctuary elsewhere?

God calls everyone to 'love the stranger', with a hunger for justice. My passion for justice for 'the stranger' created the City of Sanctuary vision and network, embracing people of diverse backgrounds and building cultures of welcome, hospitality and safety. It strives for the integration of all people, especially those whose lives are most in danger: victims of human trafficking, refugees and asylum seekers. A modest contribution alongside others.

We all know what it is like to be excluded and marginalised, a 'stranger' in our own homes, congregations, communities and companies, in our own 'land of Egypt' among associates. Do we not sometimes discern the stranger we are to ourselves? Love this stranger also.

INDERJIT BHOGAL, THEOLOGIAN AND MINISTER

Inside out

'Woe to you, scribes and Pharisees, hypocrites! For you tithe mint, dill, and cummin, and have neglected the weightier matters of the law: justice and mercy and faith. It is these you ought to have practised without neglecting the others. You blind guides! You strain out a gnat but swallow a camel! Woe to you, scribes and Pharisees, hypocrites! For you clean the outside of the cup and of the plate, but inside they are full of greed and self-indulgence.'

MATTHEW 23:23–25 (NRSV)

Gentle Jesus, meek and mild? Hardly. He could be challenging, even abrasive. If the gospel is good news to the poor, it may be bad news to the rich. And frequently his harshest words are for the most religious.

We are used to thinking of the Pharisees as the bad guys, who resisted Jesus and plotted to get him killed. But in their day they were respected as the purest of the pure, keeping every last requirement of the law. But maybe purity isn't the main focus of the life Jesus called us to. We talk a lot about God offering us forgiveness through the cross, but we often appear to be terrified of falling into the least sin.

Jesus broke the letter of the purity laws repeatedly: touching a haemorrhaging woman who was ritually impure, touching the dead, healing on the sabbath. Where the Pharisees feared they could be made impure by external things, Jesus seemed to believe not in contagious contamination but in contagious goodness; the Spirit who was in him could make the unclean clean, the unholy holy.

What would happen in our churches and world if we focused on justice and mercy to those on the fringes of society, instead of on our own doctrinal correctness? In 2 Corinthians, Paul tells his hearers that 'God… has made us competent to be ministers of a new covenant, not of letter but of spirit; for the letter kills, but the Spirit gives life' (2 Corinthians 3:5–6).

We must take care that our discipleship consists not of following a new set of 'Christian rules', which can make us judgemental and unkind, but of tuning in to the Spirit of Jesus within and among us, who makes us people of compassion and generosity.

VERONICA ZUNDEL, WRITER AND COLUMNIST

Let justice roll down

I hate, I despise your festivals, and I take no delight in your solemn assemblies. Even though you offer me your burnt-offerings and grain-offerings, I will not accept them; and the offerings of well-being of your fatted animals I will not look upon. Take away from me the noise of your songs; I will not listen to the melody of your harps. But let justice roll down like waters, and righteousness like an ever-flowing stream.

AMOS 5:21–24 (NRSV)

These words are among the most terrifying in the Bible. Imagine if the Lord were to denounce the worship of our churches in the same way: 'I hate your gatherings; I do not accept the gifts you offer me; take away from me the noise (not the sound, but the noise!) of your worship songs and choral anthems; I will not listen to the music of your organs or guitars.'

The prophet Amos was preaching to the northern kingdom of Israel, in about 760BC. It was a time of economic prosperity, but in which the richest in society were neglecting, and even oppressing, the poor. Yet the people of God could see no problem, and Amos was the mouthpiece for the Lord's terrible condemnation of Israel's complacency.

In the final verse, the Lord spells out what he wants from his people: to restore justice and righteousness (or fairness and honesty), so that the poorest in society are properly protected and provided for. The Lord calls for justice 'to roll down' and not just trickle down; and for righteousness to be ever-flowing, not intermittent or seasonal.

A sure sign of the greatness of any society is the way that it cares for its most vulnerable members. But that is also a key test for every Christian. In the way I use my time and money (the very things I want to offer to God in my worship), how am I helping to protect and provide for the most needy? Because if I am not part of the solution, then I am part of the problem. And if I am part of the problem, then my prayers and praises are not just unacceptable to God, but repugnant to him.

PETE WILCOX, BISHOP OF SHEFFIELD

Audacious faith

I am sending him – who is my very heart – back to you. I would have liked to keep him with me so that he could take your place in helping me while I am in chains for the gospel. But I did not want to do anything without your consent, so that any favour you do would not seem forced but would be voluntary. Perhaps the reason he was separated from you for a little while was that you might have him back forever – no longer as a slave, but better than a slave, as a dear brother.

PHILEMON 12–16a (NIV)

This audacious letter, brimming with love, grace and challenge, must have been shocking to Philemon. The Roman world depended on the work of thousands of slaves. Paul asks Philemon to consider manumitting Onesimus, part of his estate work force, a runaway slave and possibly a thief. Now born into the family of God, to Paul Onesimus is a son. He asks Philemon to sacrifice the work of a slave, but he himself is sacrificing his 'very heart'.

'Welcome him as you would welcome me,' Paul writes. Slave and free: all one in Christ Jesus. Let go of all resentment and pride. Change your heart. Act as the forgiving father in Jesus' parable of the prodigal son, he seems to urge.

Ouch. It is never easy to forgive, especially when the offence has resulted in financial loss and personal betrayal. Is there someone who has let me down, who God is calling me to forgive?

The worship of many gods formed part of the social fabric in Colossae. Philemon is commended for actively sharing his faith in this challenging environment. Freeing Onesimus, Paul suggests, will demonstrate his faith further and deepen his own spiritual understanding.

As a prisoner of Christ, Paul aligns himself with someone else deprived of freedom. In asking for his manumission, he is pushing back against the culture of slavery.

This challenges me to pray and to act – to end the evil of slavery in our day, knowing that as I do so, Jesus is lifted up and can draw others to himself, extending the kingdom in the world and in my heart.

The letter concludes with a statement revealing the strength of Paul's faith – trusting that as Philemon prays for his release, God will respond favourably: 'Make up a bed for me.' How can I express audacious faith today?

MICHELE D. MORRISON, WRITER

A people of justice

This is what the Lord says: 'Go down to the palace of the king of Judah and proclaim this message there: "Hear the word of the Lord to you, king of Judah, you who sit on David's throne – you, your officials and your people who come through these gates. This is what the Lord says: do what is just and right. Rescue from the hand of the oppressor the one who has been robbed. Do no wrong or violence to the foreigner, the fatherless or the widow, and do not shed innocent blood in this place."'

JEREMIAH 22:1–3 (NIV)

The world seems to be full of injustice. Everywhere you look, it is easy to find injustice and inequality on a global scale, but also unfairness closer to home. On any given day, our newspapers are filled with stories that reflect a world where people live with daily oppression.

Some are oppressed because of their race or gender; others are shunned because of their physical disabilities. Some do not have enough food to feed their families, while others are piling up mountains of food waste. A small number of nations own most of the world's wealth, while other countries face crippling debt burdens.

It is easy to despair. What a comfort to know that this is not how God intended things to be.

We are reminded in this passage from Jeremiah that God is clear about wanting us to be people who do what is right, who stand for all that is true and good and just. In a world of oppression, we are asked to rescue the oppressed. We are called by God to be people of peace, who look out for those who face oppression and injustice – the foreigners, the orphans, the widows, those who are marginalised and forgotten. What a wonderful reminder of who the people of God are supposed to be, no matter what we see around us.

In the face of injustice, may we remember that we are people who seek to do what is just and reflect a loving God, who is the source of all justice.

CHINE McDONALD, WRITER, BROADCASTER AND HEAD OF PUBLIC ENGAGEMENT, CHRISTIAN AID

Deliverance belongs to the Lord

O Lord, how many are my foes! Many are rising against me; many are saying to me, 'There is no help for you in God.' But you, O Lord, are a shield around me, my glory, and the one who lifts up my head. I cry aloud to the Lord, and he answers me from his holy hill... Deliverance belongs to the Lord; may your blessing be on your people!

PSALM 3:1–4, 8 (NRSV)

Psalm 3 is described as 'a Psalm of David, when he fled from his son Absalom'. This was perhaps the darkest moment in David's life. Absalom was David's dearly loved son and a born leader: charismatic, handsome and strong. But Absalom turned against his father and decided to lead a rebellion and seize the throne for himself. This is civil war, and in this psalm David is crying out to God to help him as he, the king, has been driven into the wilderness.

There is so much that we can draw from this story and this psalm. First, it is about suffering. The reality is that when we confront evil, when we fight for truth and justice, we will face opposition. Opting for a peaceful life by avoidance and denial, as David had previously done, does not solve anything. Sooner or later we will have to face reality.

This psalm is about pain, about trouble and treachery and times of testing. At his darkest and most desperate moment, David knows that the Lord alone can deliver him. David never gives up on his relationship with God. Even when things are really bad, David cries out, 'You, O Lord, are a shield around me.'

It is also about truthfulness and humility. 'Deliverance belongs to the Lord,' says David. I am not in control. Suffering can teach us humility and make us more fully human. This is what happened to David. Through his suffering he came to a new truthfulness and reality in his relationship with God, and in his love for his son Absalom.

And finally, it is about hope – ever more important in times of testing. Where does our hope lie? Our hope is in the Lord our God. In 1 Peter 1:3 we read, '[God] has given us new birth into a living hope through the resurrection of Jesus Christ from the dead.' David knows, even in his time of greatest testing, where his strength and hope come from: 'Deliverance belongs to the Lord; may your blessing be on your people!'

IAN COWLEY, AUTHOR AND SPEAKER

Are we content?

There is great gain in godliness combined with contentment; for we brought nothing into the world, so that we can take nothing out of it; but if we have food and clothing, we will be content with these. But those who want to be rich fall into temptation and are trapped by many senseless and harmful desires that plunge people into ruin and destruction. For the love of money is a root of all kinds of evil... Shun all this; pursue righteousness, godliness, faith, love, endurance, gentleness.

1 TIMOTHY 6:6–11 (NRSV, abridged)

Take a moment to be thankful for something. It is good to be content with what we have. Many people don't have enough for the basics of life, while others have much more than they need.

According to Oxfam, the world's richest 26 people own as much as the poorest 50%. Are we content with this growing inequality?

The desire to be rich harms not just the person who is trapped by the love of money. Others are harmed too. Today, as in Paul's time, the pursuit of riches is often at the expense of the poor. The story repeats itself in every generation. During the Covid-19 pandemic, the wealth of some millionaire business owners soared, while hundreds of thousands lost their jobs or were forced into unsafe working conditions.

Our lives are linked to our neighbours around the world: a T-shirt from Bangladesh, a banana from Ecuador. Where businesses put profit ahead of everything, the people making our clothes or growing our food may be unable to sufficiently feed and clothe their families. Low, unfair wages do not enable people to live fully and be content. When we seek to consume more and more without thinking of who or what is harmed by that desire, we trap ourselves and fail to love our neighbours.

As Christians, we are called to tell a different story about money, to be content and to recognise that everything comes from God for the good of all. What a different world we could shape if we pursued righteousness, godliness and love with our financial decisions and encouraged businesses to do the same.

Buying Fairtrade products, supporting ethical businesses, investing our pensions in building a fairer, more sustainable world – these are all ways we can pursue righteousness with money. What will you do?

ROSIE VENNER, MONEY MAKES CHANGE PROGRAMME MANAGER, ECCR

The secret of contentment

I am not saying this because I am in need, for I have learned to be content whatever the circumstances. I know what it is to be in need, and I know what it is to have plenty. I have learned the secret of being content in any and every situation, whether well fed or hungry, whether living in plenty or in want.

PHILIPPIANS 4:11–12 (NIV)

'I wish I were' and 'if only' are probably the two most destructive phrases any of us can think or utter. Unfortunately for all of us, Christians included, discontentment can insidiously creep in, throwing seeds of dissatisfaction into every area of our lives. If only I were... slimmer, richer, wiser, more popular, talented, confident – the list goes on and on.

And dissatisfaction often comes along with its cousin – comparison. A *Times* columnist wrote that her New Year's resolution was not to buy any more glossy women's magazines or scroll through Instagram. Peering into others' portrayals of their wonderful lives, careers, beautiful homes and talented children always left her disheartened and suddenly unhappy with her own lot in life.

So, how do we rid ourselves of dissatisfaction and comparison? We know that Jesus says, 'Come to me... and I will give you rest' (Matthew 11:28), but how does that actually work out? Paul gives us a big clue while writing his letter to the Philippians from prison.

In all his different circumstances, Paul has learned to be content. The key word here is 'learned'. Contentment doesn't come easily to us, nor did it to Paul. We need to actively pursue contentment, first by placing God at the centre stage of our lives, in all circumstances, and second by giving thanks. When we express heartfelt thanks, we begin to notice a feeling of gratitude. Along with gratitude comes contentment: 'Give thanks in all circumstances; for this is God's will for you in Christ Jesus' (1 Thessalonians 5:18).

At different times I have kept a gratitude journal for a month: jotting down at least three things every day, giving thanks. And it is amazing the difference it's made: rather than thinking about what I don't have, my thoughts and musings fill up with blessings and thanks rather than longings and regrets. When I focus on God and give thanks and praise to him, life is put back into perspective and God responds with his love and peace. Contentment is a gift from God and, like Paul, we can choose to receive it or not.

DEBBIE WRIGHT, MUM TO FOUR DAUGHTERS AND HEAD OF CREATIVE SERVICES, STEWARDSHIP

In control

But the fruit of the Spirit is love, joy, peace, forbearance, kindness, goodness, faithfulness, gentleness and self-control. Against such things there is no law. Those who belong to Christ Jesus have crucified the flesh with its passions and desires. Since we live by the Spirit, let us keep in step with the Spirit. Let us not become conceited, provoking and envying each other.

GALATIANS 5:22–26 (NIV)

Relationships are tough. No matter how much we love or respect someone, living with them, working with them or raising them will bring some of the hardest challenges of our lives. Often, those challenges are around control and how we relate to people with a will of their own.

Good control is self-control. Control, in itself, isn't one of the gifts of the Spirit. The gift of the Spirit is *self*-control, not *other*-control. The more you follow Jesus and allow his Spirit to fill you, the less you worry about controlling others and the more you gain control of yourself.

The desire for control is one of the greatest flaws of humankind; since the fall we have had a desire for power over people, to be somehow better or more powerful. It's one of the greatest deceits and, frankly, conceits that we fall for. We want to be like God and, just like Adam and Eve, we go about it in the wrong way.

We wish we could control events around us, even though a year like 2020 showed us more than any other year that we have even less control than we thought.

We wish we could control the people around us. We tell ourselves that it's for their own good, that if they would just do things the way we think they should they'd be more successful, more likeable, more like us.

We need to rewire our brain, lessen the scope of our control and embrace the reality that we can only, and should only, control ourselves. We were made in the image of a God who, ultimately, gave himself up on the cross for the sake of us all. It might feel challenging to relinquish power, but there's beauty in sacrificial love, in giving up our power. It's liberating, and if we truly embrace it, it will transform our relationships.

BEKAH LEGG, DIRECTOR, RESTORED

Child among them

Jesus and his disciples came to a house in Capernaum. There he asked them, 'What were you arguing about on the road?' But they kept quiet. On the way, they had argued about which one of them was the most important person. Jesus sat down and called for the twelve disciples to come to him. Then he said, 'Anyone who wants to be first must be the very last. They must be the servant of everyone.' Jesus took a little child and had the child stand among them. Then he took the child in his arms. He said to them, 'Anyone who welcomes one of these little children in my name welcomes me. And anyone who welcomes me also welcomes the one who sent me.'

MARK 9:33–37 (NIRV)

When a child is among a group of adults, they can be ignored or they can shape the whole situation. Jesus draws this child in to help the adults think entirely differently about their debate regarding greatness and importance. Imagine how the child feels, being held lovingly in the arms of Jesus. Some nervousness looking around the disciples, perhaps? Yet assured by Jesus' welcome. Just how special a moment this must have been, remembered for the rest of his, or her, life. Valued, loved, involved: this is how children should feel among Jesus' people all the time; yet so often, tragically, the opposite is true.

Yet this story is not primarily about the child. It is about what happens to the way adults view the world when a child is placed at the heart of things. It does something for our theology of the cross (which is what Jesus had been talking about before this happens). It does something for our theology of humanity; of the shape of being God's people; of being disciples. Too often we undertake all of this from an adult perspective only. When we do so, we miss significant insights into the true nature of God's rule and reign.

We need to place children among us because they are valuable and loved by God. We need also to do it to make sure that we keep Jesus' perspective even in what we describe in our adult way as 'the deepest theology'.

PAUL BUTLER, BISHOP OF DURHAM

Requirements for today

'With what shall I come before the Lord, and bow myself before God on high? Shall I come before him with burnt-offerings, with calves a year old? Will the Lord be pleased with thousands of rams, with tens of thousands of rivers of oil? Shall I give my firstborn for my transgression, the fruit of my body for the sin of my soul?' He has told you, O mortal, what is good; and what does the Lord require of you but to do justice, and to love kindness, and to walk humbly with your God?

MICAH 6:6–8 (NRSV)

What is God wanting of me today, and how can I best express myself to God in the way I decide to live today?

The prophet Micah has this debate with himself and wonders what he could offer to please God. He lists traditional sacrificial offerings, escalating the numbers, and even going to a personal extreme in his thinking. Would this be enough for God today? But then he is reminded that God has already revealed what the key requirements of the day are. Not more death, but life – to do justice, to love kindness, to walk humbly with God.

We often forget that the Christian life is about repeating 'what is good' and making it into a life habit. God has told us what the requirements of the day are – we just need to keep repeating them, seeking justice for others and remembering daily to act fairly in our own lives; offering loving, merciful, kind acts towards others each day; keeping our lives in perspective by living today in humility before God in the world.

We are small parts of God's much bigger heart for his world and its peoples – but every day we each can do something good and kind for the poor, the disadvantaged, the forgotten, for our neighbours, our workmates, our families. Every day we can put our lives into perspective and tread gently and with humility in God's world. However small, we repeat 'what is good'.

How could I practically do justice, embrace loving kindness, and better recognise my need to walk the earth in humility today? Maybe as we pray, God will direct us to a simple act today – one which embraces something that needs to develop further inside ourselves, and then externalise to others in the wider world. And tomorrow? Repeat.

IAN WHITE, SENIOR TUTOR, CLIFF COLLEGE

Being a child of God

For those who are led by the Spirit of God are the children of God. The Spirit you received does not make you slaves, so that you live in fear again; rather, the Spirit you received brought about your adoption to sonship... Now if we are children, then we are heirs – heirs of God and co-heirs with Christ, if indeed we share in his sufferings in order that we may also share in his glory.

ROMANS 8:14–15a, 17 (NIV)

In this wonderful chapter, Paul is describing what it means to live life in the Spirit. Here he brings awareness to the fact that it is the Spirit – Jesus' gift to us – that convinces us that we are children of God.

Being a child of God means that we share in the life and inheritance of Jesus Christ. We share in his relationship with his Father; we share in his sufferings in this world; and we share in the glorious inheritance of the riches of heaven given to us through him. Paul explains that this means our lives can now be free from fear, because we have the deep security of knowing that we are children of God. We no longer need to fear God, one another, suffering or the future because, as he goes on to say at the end of the chapter, nothing, but nothing, can separate us from the love of God in Jesus Christ.

We all suffer from fears, some rational and some irrational, but imagine a life without fear! This would make us bold for Christ, bold to fight for what is right, bold to preach the gospel, bold to be more truthful and bold to be more loving. It would mean making the most of every opportunity because we wouldn't be held back by our fears. We cannot do this on our own or in our own strength. These are all gifts of the Spirit that are freely given by God to all his children, so that we might live life in all its fullness.

Today let's pray that we know more of God's love in our hearts by his Spirit, so that we might understand what it means to live in the security of being a child of God. Then imagine what that might mean for seeking the freedom of others who have been enslaved by oppressive forces and need to be set free. Ask God to show you what life without fear could mean, for you and for those around you.

LUCY PEPPIATT, PRINCIPAL, WESTMINSTER THEOLOGICAL CENTRE

Transforming unity

'My prayer is not for them alone. I pray also for those who will believe in me through their message, that all of them may be one, Father, just as you are in me and I am in you. May they also be in us so that the world may believe that you have sent me. I have given them the glory that you gave me, that they may be one as we are one – I in them and you in me – so that they may be brought to complete unity. Then the world will know that you sent me and have loved them even as you have loved me.'

JOHN 17:20–23 (NIV)

This passage is most quoted in relation to the task of Christian unity where our Lord prays 'that they may all be one', praying for the world and that the world may know that Jesus and the Father are one.

Just as Jesus prays that the world may know that he and the Father are one, he also prays that the world may come to know Jesus 'so that the world may believe'. These words are crucial in terms of understanding the links between the unity of the church and the mission of the church. Disunity and mission can never go together. In order to witness effectively, we are entreated to be one, as Jesus and the Father are one. Disunity should be understood in this context as being unfaithful to the mission and call that Jesus made. And the focus of the unity is for the body of Christ, the church, but it must also include the world.

The word 'ecumenical' has its roots in the Greek word *oikomene*. This trans-lates as 'the whole creation' or 'the whole created order'. To be ecumenical is therefore to be caught up in the prayer of Jesus when he prays for the whole creation to be made one, so that the world might believe. The unity that our Lord is praying for has profound implications for the way in which we treat each other, but also the way we are involved in healing God's creation. We are bound up in the life and work of God revealed through his Son Jesus Christ. Our personal and work relationships, along with our lives as consumers – all are part of this prayer that Jesus offers to his Father for the oneness of the body of Christ and for his creation.

BOB FYFFE, GENERAL SECRETARY, CHURCHES TOGETHER IN BRITAIN AND IRELAND

Treasure

'To strive to safeguard the integrity of creation and sustain and renew the life of the earth.'

FOR MOST OF THIS BOOK we have considered the relationships between humanity and God, and between humans themselves. In this section, 'Treasure', we will turn our attention to the created order and to our wonderful planet, Earth. Our contributors have all taken different approaches to this topic, but some common themes emerge: the goodness of creation; environmental degradation; and our hope for the future.

'And God saw that it was good' (Genesis 1:10, NIV). Think of spring flowers, eagles' wings and cells dividing. All are part of God's amazing intricately designed world; not just God's handiwork, but his finger-work, as Peter Harris highlights in his reflection.

'The whole creation has been groaning' (Romans 8:22). Sadly, we are now all too aware of the environmental problems that beset our planet, and humanity bears responsibility for these. Climate change, biodiversity loss and plastic pollution are but the three that make our news most often. All of these issues are driven by human greed, overconsumption and sin.

'Work it and take care of it' (Genesis 2:15): this is often thought of as the first commandment to humanity, and is the basis for concepts like stewardship and creation care. If we are honest, though, we have been doing a pretty terrible job so far. But as several of our authors point out, there is a lot we can do practically to improve matters. And ultimately, we have the hope that God will redeem and renew creation – 'a new heaven and a new earth' (Revelation 21:1).

MARTIN AND MARGOT HODSON, OPERATIONS DIRECTOR
AND DIRECTOR OF THEOLOGY AND EDUCATION,
THE JOHN RAY INITIATIVE

Wisdom's call

'The Lord brought me forth as the first of his works, before his deeds of old... before the mountains were settled in place, before the hills, I was given birth, before he made the world or its fields or any of the dust of the earth. I was there when he set the heavens in place, when he marked out the horizon on the face of the deep... Then I was constantly at his side. I was filled with delight day after day, rejoicing always in his presence, rejoicing in his whole world and delighting in mankind.'

PROVERBS 8:22, 25–28, 30–31 (NIV)

Today's passage is the centrepiece of the book of Proverbs, setting up the woman Wisdom – God's wisdom vividly personified – as an authoritative teacher for anyone who will listen. She is fundamental to the universe, observing or helping with God's acts of creation. She knows the supreme skill with which God created: the order, structure and pattern he put in place.

Wisdom's dignity and authority in being the 'first of [God's] works' is balanced by her playful enjoyment of creation. She is, in turn, able to help us make sense of the created world. One of the most powerful tools we can use to explore and understand creation is science. We need wisdom to guide our exploration and to help us interpret and apply our discoveries. Most of us are not working scientists, but we can learn from science's discoveries. Any knowledge that we gain, in the context of our Christian faith, can inform the way we live.

The presence of wisdom in creation reminds us that not only can we learn from what we see around us, but we must also handle created things wisely. For example, seeing the wonder, abundance and value of creation in and of itself can inform and motivate the way we 'work it and take care of it' (Genesis 2:15).

Proverbs tells us that when we find Wisdom, learning from everything she has to teach us – through creation as well as other means – and put it into practice, we share her joy. Ultimately God's wisdom is revealed in his Son, 'the image of the invisible God, the firstborn over all creation' (Colossians 1:15). In Jesus we see God's wisdom in action, demonstrating a way of life that we can try to emulate with his help, finding both challenge and joy in the process.

RUTH M. BANCEWICZ, CHURCH ENGAGEMENT DIRECTOR,
THE FARADAY INSTITUTE FOR SCIENCE AND RELIGION, CAMBRIDGE

The work of God's fingers

Lord, our Lord, how majestic is your name in all the earth! You have set your glory in the heavens… When I consider your heavens, the work of your fingers, the moon and the stars, which you have set in place, what is mankind that you are mindful of them, human beings that you care for them?… You made them rulers over the works of your hands; you put everything under their feet: all flocks and herds, and the animals of the wild, the birds in the sky, and the fish in the sea, all that swim the paths of the seas.

PSALM 8:1, 3–4, 6–8 (NIV)

This wonderful psalm sings to us of God's glory seen in creation and tells us that all its wonderful diversity is before our eyes for us to study and to care for. It is clear from David's list that this doesn't mean we should simply look after domestic animals which are useful to us, but all that we can see in 'the wild… the sky… the sea' (vv. 7–8).

These recent times of global pandemic have been a call to 'consider' creation in an entirely new way. They have revealed much brokenness in the systems that we have put in place as we have attempted to master the world. But they have also opened up completely new opportunities to change our ways now that we can see how destructive they are, and to live regeneratively rather than depleting creation.

These remarkable lines tell us that even the planets and stars that we see in the sky are not merely God's handiwork, they are his finger-work. The word in verse 3 is quite precise and by its rarity very surprising – it signifies that in creation we can discover the delicacy and intention of God's loving and personal craft. As we do so, we understand better our own creator, who sets us also in place within his astonishing world.

As we witness the rapid degradation of creation in our times and as we see the social and community distress that it engenders, we urgently need to listen to the call of this psalm. As we read its lines, we can reconsider ourselves before our loving creator God, we can watch and listen to his groaning creation and we can seek its blessing in our work and worship.

PETER HARRIS, PRESIDENT EMERITUS, A ROCHA INTERNATIONAL

God's creatures

He makes springs pour water into the ravines; it flows between the mountains. They give water to all the beasts of the field; the wild donkeys quench their thirst. The birds of the sky nest by the waters; they sing among the branches. He waters the mountains from his upper chambers… He makes grass grow for the cattle, and plants for people to cultivate… The lions roar for their prey and seek their food from God…. How many are your works, Lord! In wisdom you made them all; the earth is full of your creatures.

PSALM 104:10–24 (NIV, abridged)

We might think of 'biology' and 'creation' as referring to two completely different ideas, but the Bible sees them woven together. In this theological poetry, all the creatures of the Earth are God's creatures. All they eat and drink, just as all we ourselves eat and drink, comes ultimately from God.

And here there is no hint of a God who starts the universe off with a Big Bang, then withdraws to let the world care for itself. No, here is a God who is upholding and sustaining all biological diversity in all its richness at every moment. This is sometimes referred to as God's 'immanence' in creation. Here we have an involved God, who makes the plants grow and who supplies the food for lions. The earth is full of God's creatures and the immense beauty and complexity of living things act as a constant reminder of God's wisdom in creation.

So what biologists are doing in their research is to understand how God's wonderful world of biological diversity functions. Everything is connected. Everything that lives depends on everything else, and this elegant interconnectedness is brilliantly described in the poetry of Psalm 104. The scope of biological diversity and complexity is so vast that thousands of biologists around the world still struggle to understand how it all works.

'How many are your works, Lord!' Sadly, those works are considerably less in number since we as humanity caused the extinction of so many. Diversity loss due to human environmental abuse is tragic, because this entails the loss of God's creatures. Because all the creatures of the world are God's creatures, this is a vivid reminder for us that we are to care for the world of biological diversity as God intended.

DENIS ALEXANDER, EMERITUS DIRECTOR, THE FARADAY INSTITUTE
FOR SCIENCE AND RELIGION, CAMBRIDGE

The imperative of creation care

[Christ] is the image of the invisible God, the firstborn of all creation; for in him all things in heaven and on earth were created, things visible and invisible, whether thrones or dominions or rulers or powers – all things have been created through him and for him. He himself is before all things, and in him all things hold together. He is the head of the body, the church; he is the beginning, the firstborn from the dead, so that he might come to have first place in everything. For in him all the fullness of God was pleased to dwell, and through him God was pleased to reconcile to himself all things, whether on earth or in heaven, by making peace through the blood of his cross.

COLOSSIANS 1:15–20 (NRSV)

Since the days of the early church, Christians have enjoyed singing together. This may be one of those early hymns, woven into the text, to offer praise to God and teach us his ways. The focus is on 'all things'. Everything is in view, as far as the eye can see and beyond: flora, fauna, geology, wind and ocean currents, distant stars and farthest galaxies are wrapped in Christ. The prepositions used – in, through, for, before, together, to – all give emphasis to this web of connection. Everything is connected in Christ and through Christ to all dimensions of creation.

He is the 'firstborn', affirming not only this connection, but also his preeminence over it all. He is also the 'firstborn of the dead', which connects him across time and space, including everything that is now extinct. God's purpose in Christ is to heal and bring to wholeness not only humanity but the entire created order. He died that not only humans but all created things might be reconciled to their creator God.

The gospels are full of stories of the growth of seeds, the choking of thistles, the beauty of lilies and the fruitfulness of trees. Jesus noticed, and so must we. We have the privilege and responsibility to care for the earth and to tread gently on it. Any damage to creation is a scar on the face of Christ. The invitation is laid before us to live more simply and humbly, so that others, especially the poorest, and the rest of creation may survive and thrive. Responding to the climate and biodiversity emergencies we face is not an optional extra in God's mission for his church; it is imperative to it.

GRAHAM USHER, BISHOP OF NORWICH AND FORMER TRUSTEE, BRF

Everything? Seriously? For God? Really?

And whatever you do, whether in word or deed, do it all in the name of the Lord Jesus, giving thanks to God the Father through him... Slaves, obey your earthly masters in everything; and do it, not only when their eye is on you and to curry their favour, but with sincerity of heart and reverence for the Lord. Whatever you do, work at it with all your heart, as working for the Lord, not for human masters, since you know that you will receive an inheritance from the Lord as a reward. It is the Lord Christ you are serving.

COLOSSIANS 3:17, 22–24 (NIV)

This is a revolutionary passage. It was revolutionary in the first century, and it is revolutionary today. We may not think that God cares about all the little things we do every day – the dishes, the drains, the deals – but these verses shatter that illusion. 'Whatever you do', Paul writes, first to the whole group (v. 17), then directly to the slaves (v. 22). His point? That all work – from the glorious to the unglorious and thankless – is seen and valued by God: from the home to the hospital, the factory to the field, the corporate office to the church.

This is vital to grasp, because if we don't believe that our daily tasks matter to God, then we're just wasting a big chunk of our lives. But we aren't. In fact, when we do whatever we do for God, it's so significant that there is a heavenly reward for it (v. 24).

But why are our ordinary tasks so significant? Because the truths of this passage are built on the truths of Colossians 1:15–20. Christ is the creator of 'all things' and everything we do has an impact on the creation he made, and on people created in his image. So of course he cares. In fact, he cares so much about *all things* that he shed his blood on the cross that he might bring peace, that is wholeness, to *all things*. So now we, his chosen people, are sent to participate with him in that redeeming, reconciling, renewing work. In Christ, all our 'whatevers' can contribute to making our bit of the world as much like he yearns for it to be before he returns to complete it. And that's surely a job worth doing.

This day, may you know the Lord's joy and presence and help in whatever you do.

MARK GREENE, MISSION CHAMPION, THE LONDON INSTITUTE FOR CONTEMPORARY CHRISTIANITY

Treasuring creation

'Don't hoard treasure down here where it gets eaten by moths and corroded by rust or – worse! – stolen by burglars. Stockpile treasure in heaven... Look at the birds, free and unfettered, not tied down to a job description, careless in the care of God. And you count far more to him than birds... All this time and money wasted on fashion – do you think it makes that much difference? Instead of looking at the fashions, walk out into the fields and look at the wild-flowers... Steep your life in God-reality, God-initiative, God-provisions. Don't worry about missing out.'

MATTHEW 6:19–20, 26, 28, 33 (MSG)

Jesus teaches us to not hoard possessions on earth and that we don't need to have the latest fashionable clothes. We need to hear this message now more than ever.

Hoarding more than we need is, quite literally, costing the earth. Most of the energy used in producing goods comes from burning fossil fuels. Greenhouse gases are released, contributing to climate change. When new fashions arrive and people throw away their older (but still usable) possessions, landfill sites fill up, and further greenhouse gases are released as items decompose. Plastic leads to pollution, causing health issues and killing animals that eat it. Greed is destroying the earth, and Revelation 11:18 states that those who destroy the earth will be destroyed.

So, how should we live? Jesus talks about storing treasure in heaven and seeking first God's kingdom – 'Steep your life in God-reality, God-initiative' (v. 33).

A big part of kingdom living is respecting and caring for the earth that he carefully and lovingly created. Jesus said, 'Look at the birds' (v. 26); 'Look at the wildflowers' (v. 28). Take some time to study the natural world this week and to consider how you can care for creation, because God cares about creation (Psalm 50:10–11). The poorest people tend to suffer most from the effects of climate change, such as floods and drought. Therefore, choosing not to accumulate unnecessary possessions is an act of justice and love for our neighbours. That is one way to seek God's kingdom, to 'steep your life in God-reality'.

DEBBIE HAWKER, PSYCHOLOGIST AND AUTHOR

Restoring Eden

'You have defiled the land with your prostitution and wickedness. Therefore the showers have been withheld, and no spring rains have fallen... I will take away their harvest,' declares the Lord. 'There will be no grapes on the vine. There will be no figs on the tree, and their leaves will wither. What I have given them will be taken from them... The whole land will be laid waste because there is no one who cares.'

JEREMIAH 3:2–3; 8:13; 12:11 (NIV, abridged)

Prophets such as Jeremiah liken humans' management of nature to that of a whore. In recent centuries big business, abetted by consumers, including many Christians, have made money god and raped the earth. Mass extinction threatens, yet still we pursue endless economic growth at nature's expense. The tragedy is that climate campaigners who look for a spirituality to undergird their efforts assume that Christianity has nothing to offer.

Yet creation comes from the heart of Christ (John 1:3), who wants us to adopt it as a sacrament and steward it well. The visible things God has created speak to us of the invisible qualities of God (Romans 1:20). God spoke to Moses through a bush, to Jeremiah through an almond tree, to astrologers through a star. God nods and beckons to us through every stone and stream. Urban dwellers heard the sounds of creation for the first time when Covid-19 shut down excessive noise. Jesus commands us to let God teach us through wild flowers and birds (Matthew 6:26–30). Followers of Jesus make listening to God in creation a regular spiritual practice.

From beginning to end, the Bible also calls us to be good stewards of creation. The second creation story asserts that God placed humans on the earth to tend it (Genesis 2:15). Many of Jesus' parables liken our relation to Earth to those who tend vineyards or farms. The gospels spell out that creation has such communion with its creator that when he was crucified the sun eclipsed and there was an earthquake. In the immortal words of 'The Dream of the Rood', 'All creation wept.'

So Christians need to rise up, to shop and travel in carbon- and animal-friendly ways, to bless nature and to ask Jesus, the second Adam, to show us how to restore communion with creation, our Eden.

RAY SIMPSON, AUTHOR AND FOUNDING GUARDIAN, THE COMMUNITY OF AIDAN AND HILDA

Keeping watch

I heard and my heart pounded, my lips quivered at the sound; decay crept into my bones, and my legs trembled. Yet I will wait patiently for the day of calamity to come on the nation invading us. Though the fig-tree does not bud and there are no grapes on the vines, though the olive crop fails and the fields produce no food, though there are no sheep in the sheepfold and no cattle in the stalls, yet I will rejoice in the Lord, I will be joyful in God my Saviour. The Sovereign Lord is my strength; he makes my feet like the feet of a deer, he enables me to tread on the heights.

HABAKKUK 3:16–19 (NIV)

When I was a child, my bedroom looked out across the Somerset Levels towards Glastonbury and the Mendip Hills. I could sit at the window and watch stormy weather moving across the wide landscape long before it reached us. Habakkuk spent a lot of time watching. He stationed himself on the ramparts of Jerusalem to observe the invading armies. For years, the people and leaders of his nation had ignored God's commands and had made unwise alliances, despite warnings from prophets like Habakkuk. Now the fields lay desolate as everyone took shelter in the city under siege. The future did not look good.

Today we face an environmental crisis of a size not known by any previous generation. Scientists have been warning governments for decades, but world leaders have only recently begun to take serious notice. Like Habakkuk, scientists keep watch of their measures of climate change, biodiversity loss, ocean acidification and many other problems. They see calamity advancing upon humanity and warn of a difficult future.

Habakkuk trusts in God's promise of future restoration, but he needs something to sustain him through the difficult times. He remembers God's mercy and trusts in his sovereignty over all creation. We too can gain strength by trusting in God's love for creation and for us. The future will not be easy, but God will give us perseverance to walk the pathway through these difficulties and play our part to establish a gentler and more sustainable world.

MARGOT R. HODSON, VICAR AND DIRECTOR OF THEOLOGY AND EDUCATION, THE JOHN RAY INITIATIVE

Choosing good trees

'Enter through the narrow gate. For wide is the gate and broad is the road that leads to destruction, and many enter through it. But small is the gate and narrow the road that leads to life, and only a few find it... Do people pick grapes from thorn-bushes, or figs from thistles? Likewise, every good tree bears good fruit, but a bad tree bears bad fruit. A good tree cannot bear bad fruit, and a bad tree cannot bear good fruit.'

MATTHEW 7:13–14, 16b–18 (NIV)

Walking under a bright, pale blue, cloudless winter sky, my eyes were drawn to a barren tree, stripped of its leaves by autumn storms and winter frosts, yet still majestic, silhouetted against the sky. Amazingly, the same patterns crop up in nature time and time again. The pattern of the branches is like that of the airways of our lungs. Trees are truly the lungs of the earth, controlling the level of carbon dioxide in the atmosphere, sustaining ours and the vast range of life that God declared to be very good.

We aren't always good at recognising good from bad trees, though. We cut down many of the world's natural forests that support a diverse range of life beneath their shady canopy. We replace them with bad trees that quickly suck the goodness out of the soil, limiting the fruitfulness of the living world.

When it comes to caring for creation, we have not always followed a narrow path that keeps in step with God's command to Adam to 'till and keep' the fruitful garden of Eden. We have carved a wide one, destructive of God's earth and the life that shares it with us. And we feel the consequences of global warming: forest fires, floods, coastlines washed away. Jesus' words seem to be coming true before our very eyes: 'Everyone who hears these words of mine and does not put them into practice is like a foolish man who built his house on sand. The rain came down, the streams rose, and the winds blew and beat against that house, and it fell with a great crash' (vv. 26–27).

Yet Jesus' words also bring hope. Changing our lives – how we travel, what we eat, how we use energy, protecting good trees – means that we build on firmer foundations. It is possible to walk the narrow path that leads to life as we listen to his word and do 'the will of my Father who is in heaven' (v. 21) for the earth, its peoples and its creatures.

DAVID GREGORY, CONVENOR, BAPTIST UNION ENVIRONMENT NETWORK AND CHAIR, THE JOHN RAY INITIATIVE

Treasure trashed?

Worship the Lord in the splendour of his holiness. Tremble before him, all the earth! The world is firmly established; it cannot be moved. Let the heavens rejoice, let the earth be glad; let them say among the nations, 'The Lord reigns!' Let the sea resound, and all that is in it; let the fields be jubilant, and everything in them! Let the trees of the forest sing, let them sing for joy before the Lord, for he comes to judge the earth. Give thanks to the Lord, for he is good; his love endures forever.

1 CHRONICLES 16:29b–34 (NIV)

I've come to value the natural world more than ever. During Covid-19 lockdowns, 'permitted exercise outdoors' meant very locally. I've loved watching the seasons develop on my daily round of our village's common. I've noticed how the plants and birds change – details like the colours of tree trunks or the way water flows. I've noticed many more people of all ages out enjoying it too. We're told that this 'mindfulness' in the outdoors enhances our sense of well-being. There's comfort in seeing nature continuing when so much else in our lives has ceased or is uncertain. You and I have added joy in that we know the one who made nature, and it sings his praises to us, if we listen.

But frightening forecasts of the end of life on earth fill the media. We humans have gone very wrong. Through our greedy use of resources, our massive pollution and fatal poisonings, we keep pushing our planet further towards global warming and mass extinctions. Scripture tells us that, ultimately, God will come to judge and put right all the damage caused by human sinfulness. He'll make 'a new heaven and a new earth' (Revelation 21:1). Meanwhile, he has charged us to worship him and look after this one.

Lockdown pauses have challenged me to ask God: what adjustments can I make to holidays, cars, food miles, gardening, consumption… And how can I pray, and campaign, for a greater, wider effect? Faced with such big and frightening questions, where to start – and end? Perhaps with 'Give thanks to the Lord, for he is good' (v. 34). Whatever else happens, his love and saving grace really will 'endure forever'.

CHRIS LEONARD, WRITER AND CREATIVE WRITING FACILITATOR

Checking our attitude

For ever since the world was created, people have seen the earth and the sky. Through everything God made, they can clearly see his invisible qualities – his eternal power and divine nature. So they have no excuse for not knowing God.

ROMANS 1:20 (NLT)

In this passage the apostle Paul is 'having a go' at non-believers. But as believers, it's easy for us to overlook the wider implications of what he is saying for us, too. Paul argues that every single one of us need only observe the amazing natural world around us to see the evidence of a powerful and perfect creator God – just as priceless jewels in a haul of treasure reflect the master jewellers who designed and fashioned them. And that begs questions of *our own* attitude towards God's treasure in creation. Do we ignore it? Or, worse, abuse it? Or do we love it but not acknowledge it as a gift from God and pointer towards him?

One side-effect of the Covid-19 pandemic has been to emphasise how important regular access to nature is for each of us – as well as how this is so much easier for some than for others. Yet we know that humans are despoiling nature and disrupting the climate at an alarming rate. This is a good moment to consider how we, as Christians, respond to the treasure of his creation.

We are called to love it as he does. Let me suggest three practical manifestations of 'loving nature'. First, we are to *enjoy it* as a gift from God, and regularly thank and praise him for it. Second, we are to *nurture it*: to do what we can at home, in our garden or in our local community to create space for nature. Third, when it is threatened, we can *protect it*: using our voices to ask our local, national and UK government to reject plans that destroy nature and to work to restore it instead.

In the quiet, think about an aspect of nature which thrills or amazes you, and thank God for the treasure of his creation. Then ask him to show you the next step he wants you to take to better care for it as a believer.

ANDY ATKINS, CEO, A ROCHA UK

Eager longing

For the creation waits with eager longing for the revealing of the children of God; for the creation was subjected to futility, not of its own will but by the will of the one who subjected it, in hope that the creation itself will be set free from its bondage to decay and will obtain the freedom of the glory of the children of God. We know that the whole creation has been groaning in labour pains until now; and not only the creation, but we ourselves, who have the first fruits of the Spirit, groan inwardly while we wait for adoption, the redemption of our bodies.

ROMANS 8:19–23 (NRSV)

These words from Paul are set in the midst of his remarkable eighth chapter of Romans. It is a chapter that begins with the great cry of 'no condemnation' and ends with the triumphant declaration that there is nothing that can separate us from God's love. The focus is on the freedom and security of the children of God. And it is clear that this story of redemption is not just a spiritual reality, because there are references to our earthly bodies and to creation. Paul's vision of redemption is not just individual, it is social. And it is not just social, it also includes creation. In Paul's vision of God's kingdom, humans and creation are intimately bound up. The health of one affects the other.

Paul is inviting his readers to become aware that creation has a voice. Specifically, it has a voice that is currently groaning. Perhaps one of the reasons why creation is eager to see God's Spirit-inspired children is because they are the ones who can do this listening. They are best placed to engage so deeply with it that they actually hear its longings. Creation, says Paul, is yearning to be set free from the power of decay. It also carries a conviction that these labour pains will produce new life.

God's children can hear this yearning, not least because we are fellow-yearners, crying out for the coming of the kingdom of God. We are in this together. There are all kinds of motivations that can drive us to take better care of this world into which God has placed us. Perhaps one of the most effective is to invite the Spirit of God to draw us into a deeper listening to the longings of creation.

MICHAEL MITTON, WRITER, SPEAKER AND CANON EMERITUS, DERBY CATHEDRAL

Striving to safeguard

And the Lord God planted a garden in Eden, in the east; and there he put the man whom he had formed. Out of the ground the Lord God made to grow every tree that is pleasant to the sight and good for food, the tree of life also in the midst of the garden, and the tree of the knowledge of good and evil... The Lord God took the man and put him in the garden of Eden to till it and keep it.

GENESIS 2:8–9, 15 (NRSV)

Here is the narrative of a first meeting. Two of God's beloved creations are introduced. Adam encounters Eden. Eden meets Adam. The man is placed in the garden with a sense of generous concern and gracious purpose. The garden is 'planted'; the person is 'formed'. The language speaks of God's care and intent.

The creator's love for the man was evident in the splendour of the environment chosen for him. It was a place of aesthetic beauty ('pleasant to the sight') and packed with bountiful provision ('good for food'). What was also abundantly clear was the intent that humankind would be good for the garden.

It has been pointed out that gardening requires lots of water – most of it in the form of sweat! In introducing humankind to the garden, God also unveiled our vocation: without a hint of negative connotation, the creator provided work. The name, Eden, comes from the Hebrew word meaning 'delight', and work was intended to be integral to human enjoyment of that delight. Only later, following people's rebellion, did work become frustrating – and even then it remained an important part of the calling of every person (3:17–19).

In recent decades, our minds have been challenged and refocused by a growing awareness of climate change, mass extinctions and other signs of environmental crisis. Christians have recognised afresh that the call to care for creation is central to God's purposes. We are invited to participate in God's mission to redeem all of creation. Churches around the world have adopted the 'Five Marks of Mission' and, in that summary of the holy task entrusted to us, we are reminded of our sacred duty 'to strive to safeguard the integrity of creation, and sustain and renew the life of the earth'.

STEVE AISTHORPE, RESEARCHER, AUTHOR AND COACH

Doing a new thing

See, I am doing a new thing! Now it springs up; do you not perceive it? I am making a way in the wilderness and streams in the wasteland. The wild animals honour me, the jackals and the owls, because I provide water in the wilderness and streams in the wasteland, to give drink to my people, my chosen, the people I formed for myself that they may proclaim my praise.

ISAIAH 43:19–21 (NIV)

God is always doing new things! This passage alludes to the time the Israelites spent in the wilderness before they entered the promised land and to their release from the present captivity in Babylon, but it also has hints of a time in the future when all creation will be reconciled and restored.

The word translated as 'wilderness' is *midbar* in Hebrew, while 'wasteland' is *yeshimon*. *Midbar* is usually taken to mean semi-arid pasture land where it is possible to carry out a nomadic lifestyle, tending flocks of domesticated animals, particularly sheep and goats. However, *yeshimon* represents a very arid desert. So bringing water to the wilderness and streams to the wasteland would be very much a new thing. It is difficult to be certain what the species of wild animals were; some translations have ostriches instead of owls and dragons replacing jackals! But whatever these animals were, they honoured God. It seems that they joined with humans in praising God for the sudden increased availability of water in the wilderness and wasteland and for the transformation of their circumstances. We also see creation praising God in Isaiah 55:12: 'The trees of the field will clap their hands.' This kind of idea is surely indicative of the future God has in store for creation, and we have a role to play in that.

In the last few years, God has been doing a 'new thing' with his church. Churches are finally catching a vision for environmental stewardship and creation care. Witness the phenomenal growth of the Eco Church scheme in England and Wales, the huge increase in requests for speakers in this area, and the Church of England resolution to reach net zero carbon emissions by 2030. Is it time for you and your church to join this movement?

MARTIN J. HODSON, ENVIRONMENTAL SCIENTIST AND OPERATIONS DIRECTOR, THE JOHN RAY INITIATIVE

Closing reflection: Hope and a future

This is what the Lord says: 'When seventy years are completed for Babylon, I will come to you and fulfil my good promise to bring you back to this place. For I know the plans I have for you,' declares the Lord, 'plans to prosper you and not to harm you, plans to give you hope and a future. Then you will call on me and come and pray to me, and I will listen to you. You will seek me and find me when you seek me with all your heart.'

JEREMIAH 29:10–13 (NIV)

Jeremiah's words, written to Jews who had been exiled to Babylon after the fall of Jerusalem, have always had a special resonance for me. The Jewish people had been living under the domination of the Egyptian and Babylonian empires and then had been forced to leave and settle in a foreign land. These words were for people experiencing suffering and hardship. God doesn't offer instant relief from their difficulties but promises, in the midst of their situation, that he has a plan for them, one that will give them hope and a future.

Nearly 35 years ago, I thought my own plans for the future were all mapped out. I was approaching the end of university, when suddenly everything seemed to fall apart. I was admitted to hospital for tests, but the doctors couldn't find anything medically wrong with me. The experience knocked me badly and destroyed my confidence. As I was recuperating at the home of friends, facing what seemed to be a very uncertain future, with so much having been stripped away, I read these words from Jeremiah. Even now, all these years later, I remember that moment so clearly. It was as if God spoke directly to me. The sense of reassurance, comfort and hope I received that day was very powerful. There have been many ups and downs along the way since then, and I have returned to these verses many times.

Whatever circumstances or challenges we may be facing today, we can put our trust and our hope in our loving God, confident that as we pray to him, he will listen, and as we seek him with all our heart, we will find him.

RICHARD FISHER, CEO, BRF

List of contributors

Names in **bold** are section editors.

Bola Adamolekun
Ian Adams
Beryl Adamsbaum
Gail Adcock
Steve Aisthorpe
Denis Alexander
Pat Alexander
Hilary Allen
Andy Angel
Di Archer
Jonathan Arnold
Philip Arundel
Angela Ashwin
Andy Atkins
Imogen Ball
Ruth M. Bancewicz
Fiona Barnard
Chris Barnett
Elizabeth Waldron Barnett
Andrew Barton
Christina Baxter
Paul Beasley-Murray
Carl Beech
John L. Bell
Inderjit Bhogal
Anthony Billington
Matt Bird
Amanda Bloor
Alistair Booth
Amy Boucher Pye
Rachel Boulding
Celia Bowring
Renita Boyle
Paul Bradbury
Mark Bradford

Steve Brady
Wendy Bray
Stephen and Mandy Briars
Shelagh Brown
Kate Bruce
Stuart Buchanan
Andy Buckler
Julia Burton-Jones
Ruth Bushyager
Catherine Butcher
Jane Butcher
Paul Butler
Rosie Button
Victoria Byrne
Lyndall Bywater
Gavin Calver
Yvonne Campbell
Ann Casson
James Catford
Christine Chapman
Alan Charter
Lisa Cherrett
Christopher Chessun
Mark Chester
Keith Civval
Anthony Clarke
Anita Cleverly
Charlie Cleverly
Steve Clifford
Terry Clutterham
David Cole
(Brother Cassian)
Joanna Collicutt
Gavin Collins
Angela Cooke

Anthony Cotterill
Stephen Cottrell
Ian Cowley
Paul Cox
Joanne Cox-Darling
Graham Cray
Steven Croft
Roy Crowne
Margaret Cundiff
Claire Dalpra
Claire Daniel
Maggi Dawn
Margaret Dean
Margaret Dennison
David Dewey
Andrew Dixon
Beth Dodd
Anne Donald
Will Donaldson
Alison Dorricott
David Dorricott
Molly Dow
Mags Duggan
Elaine Duncan
Brian Dunlop
Keith Dunnett
Carolyn Edwards
Roberta J. Egli
Valerie Eker
Jay Elliott
Rosalee Velloso Ewell
Jonathan Fillis
Stephen Finamore
Richard Fisher
Mercia Flanagan

Colin Fletcher
Faith Ford
Catriona Foster
Leslie J. Francis
Richard Frost
Bob Fyffe
Hannah Fytche
Nigel Genders
Gordon Giles
Janine Gillion
Rob Gillion
Lynn Goslin
Rachel Gotobed
Philip Grasham
Paul Gravelle
Peter Graves
Rosemary Green
Stephen Green
Mark Greene
David Gregory
Andy Griffiths
Mark Griffiths
Wendy Grisham
Trish Hahn
Isabelle Hamley
Cally Hammond
Helen Hancock
Paul Handley
Paul Harcourt
John Hardwick
Rob Hare
Jackie Harris
Paddy Harris
Peter Harris
Lydia Harrison
Ellie Hart
Hilary Hartley
Bob Hartman
Peter Hatton
Mary Hawes
Anna Hawken
Debbie Hawker
Sarah Hayes

Clare Hayns
Tim Heaton
Christopher Hemborough
Ali Herbert
Christopher Herbert
Ashley Hibbard
Susan Hibbins
Jamie Hill
Terry Hinks
Liz Hoare
Sally Hobson
Margot R. Hodson
Martin J. Hodson
Pauline Hoggarth
Rodney Holder
Dave Hopwood
Tony Horsfall
Tim and Jean Howlett
Chris Hudson
Joyce Huggett
Trystan Owain Hughes
Henry Hull
Deborah Humphries
Emma Ineson
Sheila Jacobs
Julie Jefferies
Lakshmi Jeffreys
Andy John
Tim Judson
Helen Julian CSF
Bev Jullien
Krish Kandiah
Rosemary Kempsell
Liz Kent
Paul Kerensa
Charlie Kerr
David Kerrigan
Carl Knightly
Stephen Kuhrt
Esther Kuku
Rosemary Lain-Priestley
Helen Laird
Karen Laister

Elaine Lambie
Bill Lattimer
James Lawrence
Tim Lea
Jane Leadbetter
Bekah Legg
Chris Leonard
Anne Le Tissier
Ann Lewin
Bex Lewis
Pam Lewis
Pauline Lewis
Karin Ling
Tim Ling
George Lings
Richard Littledale
Peter Lloyd
Alison Lo
Geoff Lowson
Murdo Macdonald
Ed Mackenzie
Julie MacNaughton
Dave Male
Phil Maltby
David Mason
Colin Matthews
Marcus Maxwell
Becky May
Andrew D. Mayes
Bob Mayo
Eley McAinsh
Matt McChlery
Chine McDonald
Hilary McDowell
Sarah Meyrick
Richenda Milton-Daws
Michael Mitton
Lucy Moore
Yvonne Morris
Michele D. Morrison
Barbara Mosse
Steve Motyer
Ross Moughtin

Donald Mowat
Harriet Mowat
Claire Musters
Iain Nash
Sally Nash
James Newcome
Katie Norman
Daniele Och
Clare O'Driscoll
Jennifer Oldroyd
Rhianne O'Rourke
Debbie Orriss
Michael Parsons
Rob Parsons
Ian Paul
Martyn Payne
Helen Paynter
Lindsay Pelloquin
Emma Pennington
Lucy Peppiatt
Ann Persson
Simon Peters
Peter Phillips
Jill Phipps
Jean Pienaar
Adrian Plass
Bridget Plass
Christine Platt
Stephen Platten
Sharon Prior
John Pritchard
Sharon Pritchard
John Proctor
Brother Ramon SSF
Stephen Rand
Carolyne Kaddu Rasmussen
Jill Rattle
Linda Rayner
Nick Read
Simon Reed
Gavin Reid
Christina Rees
Sally Rees
Jennifer Rees Larcombe

Pam Rhodes
Rachel Ridler
Walter Riggans
Andrew Roberts
Anne Roberts
Erica Roberts
Amy Scott Robinson
David Runcorn
Elizabeth Rundle
Tia Runion
Gareth Russell
Mark Russell
John Ryeland
Dawn Savidge
Becky Sedgwick
Tony Sharp
Mark Sheard
Sara Sheerin
Nick Shepherd
Hazel Sherman
Margaret Silf
Ray Simpson
Andrea Skevington
Neil Skidmore
Stephen Skuce
Harry Smart
Alianore Smith
Martyn Snow
David Spriggs
Naomi Starkey
Simon Stocks
Selina Stone
Fiona Stratta
John Stroyan
Paul Swann
Jo Swinney
Hannah Tarring
Carmel Thomason
Ric Thorpe
Debbie Thrower
Miriam Thurlow
Derek Tidball
Angela Tilby
Stephen Timms

Graham Tomlin
Rachel Tranter
Laura Treneer
Rachel Treweek
Jolyon Trickey
Michael Turnbull
Rachel Turner
John Twisleton
Graham Usher
Rosie Venner
Helen Vincent
Sheridan Voysey
David Walker
Sheila Walker
Jane Walters
Steve Walton
Henry Wansbrough
Olivia Warburton
Rosie Ward
Ann Warren
Andrew Watson
Jean Watson
Rebecca S. Watson
Justin Welby
Sally Welch
John Went
Paul Weston
Ian White
Jane Whittington
George Wieland
Pete Wilcox
Michael Wilkinson
David Williams
Helen Williams
Paul Williams
'Tricia Williams
Ro Willoughby
Russell Winfield
David Winter
Paul Woolley
Debbie Wright
Michael Wright
Nigel Wright
Veronica Zundel

List of Bible translations

Scripture quotations marked with the following acronyms are taken from the version shown. Where no acronym is given, the quotation is taken from the same version as the headline reference.

AMP: The Amplified® Bible, Copyright © 2015 by The Lockman Foundation. Used by permission. **Lockman.org**

AMPC: The Amplified® Bible, Copyright © 1954, 1958, 1962, 1964, 1965, 1987 by The Lockman Foundation. Used by permission. **Lockman.org**

CEB: Copyright © 2011 by Common English Bible.

CEV: The Contemporary English Version. New Testament © American Bible Society 1991, 1992, 1995. Old Testament © American Bible Society 1995. Anglicisations © British & Foreign Bible Society 1996. Used by permission.

ERV: The Easy-to-Read Version, copyright © 2006 by Bible League International.

ESV: The Holy Bible, English Standard Version, published by HarperCollins Publishers, © 2001 Crossway Bibles, a division of Good News Publishers. Used by permission. All rights reserved.

GNT: The Good News Bible published by The Bible Societies/ HarperCollins Publishers Ltd, UK © American Bible Society 1966, 1971, 1976, 1992, used with permission.

GW: God's Word Translation, copyright © 1995, 2003, 2013, 2014, 2019, 2020 by God's Word to the Nations Mission Society. All rights reserved.

JBP: The New Testament in Modern English by J.B. Phillips copyright © 1960, 1972 J.B. Phillips. Administered by The Archbishops' Council of the Church of England. Used by permission.

KJV: The Authorised Version of the Bible (The King James Bible), the rights in which are vested in the Crown, are reproduced by permission of the Crown's Patentee, Cambridge University Press.

MSG: *The Message*, copyright © 1993, 1994, 1995, 1996, 2000, 2001, 2002 by Eugene H. Peterson. Used by permission of NavPress. All rights reserved. Represented by Tyndale House Publishers, Inc.

Index of Bible references

New Testament

Friends of BRF

I never fail to be amazed by the generosity of our supporters.

BRF is a remarkable charity, but we can only do what we do with the help of our faithful supporters: volunteers, people who pray for us and spread the word about our work, and people who support us financially, both individuals who give donations and legacies, and charitable trusts.

Many of our supporters have become 'Friends of BRF', choosing to make a regular monthly gift to help ensure that our work can be sustained and developed in the coming years. Every single donation, whether occasional or regular, small or large, makes a huge difference and I, along with all my colleagues here at BRF, thank God for each one.

For information on the various ways in which you can support BRF, please visit **brf.org.uk/give**, contact a member of the fundraising team by email at **giving@brf.org.uk** or call **01235 462305** to speak to one of us direct.

With heartfelt thanks

Julie

Julie MacNaughton,
Head of Fundraising MCIOF(Dip)

Registered with
FUNDRAISING
REGULATOR

Daily inspiration

Bible reading notes to sustain, comfort, inform and challenge

If you have enjoyed these daily reflections, you might like to continue your journey through the Bible with the help of our popular Bible reading notes. There are five series to choose from, each with a different style and focus, but all designed to encourage daily Bible reading, reflection and prayer. There's almost certainly one that's perfect for you.

New Daylight

Our most popular series, *New Daylight*, is for everyone on their daily walk with God. Enjoy getting to know the writers, from well-loved regulars to exciting new voices. *New Daylight* has everything you need in one pocket-sized volume, including full Bible reading, reflection and prayer. There's also a large-format deluxe edition.

Day by Day with God

This series is specifically written for women, to help readers root their lives ever more firmly in the Bible. All the contributors are women and write from a woman's perspective. Whatever your current situation in life, you will be inspired and encouraged by these notes.

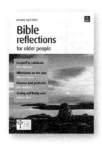

Bible Reflections for Older People

These notes grew out of our Anna Chaplaincy ministry and are written by older people, for older people. Each issue contains 40 undated reflections, written to bring comfort and encouragement, and a magazine section containing interviews, features, poems and a welcome letter from Anna Chaplaincy founder and pioneer, Debbie Thrower.

For more information on all our Bible reading notes, go to
brfonline.org.uk/our-notes

The Upper Room

'Where the world meets to pray' is a lovely description of *The Upper Room*. Uniquely, the readers of this series are also the writers, with contributions gathered from around the world. It has a worldwide readership of some three million, with over 70 different editions in 40 languages, and BRF is privileged to publish the UK edition.

Guidelines

Guidelines is our most serious and theological series and is popular amongst ministers, leaders and students. Each issue offers four months of in-depth Bible study written by leading scholars. Contributors are drawn from around the world, as well as the UK, and represent a stimulating and thought-provoking breadth of Christian tradition.

Bible reading apps

For readers on the move, we have iOS and Android app editions of *Guidelines*, *New Daylight* and *Day by Day with God*.

Reader feedback

'I want to express my – daily! – thanks for such inspirational writers and content… As I have several friends who also take part, I know my thanks are on behalf of many people who have found the notes a source of strength and support during challenging times.'

'My wife and I have been taking the BRF notes for many years now, and use them when we say the morning Office as part of our daily reading. We get so much out of them, and hope to continue to do so for many years to come.'

'These Bible study notes were such a support during lockdown when our church was shut and all I could get was a weekly service on television or radio. Thank you so much for all the work you and the writers do.'

For more information on all our Bible reading notes, go to
brfonline.org.uk/our-notes